Praise for *The End of Alchemy*

"Mervyn King may well have written the most important book to come out of the financial crisis. Agree or disagree, King's visionary ideas deserve the attention of everyone from economics students to heads of state." —Lawrence H. Summers

"If his book gets the attention it deserves, it might just save the world. . . . [King] thinks we need to change the relationship between our banks and our society, and fast. Most of us would be better off if we took his advice."
—Michael Lewis, *Bloomberg View*

"I have read umpteen books about the financial crisis of 2007–8 and its lessons. This is the cleverest one, brimming over with new ideas. While other 'lords of finance' publish memoirs, King has produced a brilliant analysis not only of what went wrong in the global financial system, but also of what went wrong in economics itself." —Niall Ferguson

"A remarkable account of the economic forces behind [the global financial crisis]." —Martin Wolf, *Financial Times*

"Mervyn King asks, 'Why has almost every industrialized country found it difficult to overcome the stagnation that followed the financial crisis in 2007–8, and why did money and banking, the alchemists of a market economy, turn into its Achilles heel?' He addresses these questions, and much more. For those endeavoring to understand the greatest financial crisis of our time and the future of finance, this highly provocative book is a must-read." —Alan Greenspan

"Refreshingly frank. . . . King has produced a worthy book."
—*Economist*

"Offers both a deeply examined critique of economics as usual and practical, controversial ideas on policy. It's a rare achievement."
—Clive Crook, *Bloomberg View*

"A sophisticated and highly approachable study of how modern finance has lost its way. Few individuals are more qualified than Lord Mervyn King to imagine the banking of the future. His book should be required reading."   —Henry Kissinger

"Drawing on years of scholarly study of banking history and his real world experience in fighting financial panic, Mervyn King has set out a new framework for monetary and financial reform. Seemingly simple in concept, it challenges prevailing banking and market practice. *The End of Alchemy* demands debate and a well-reasoned response."   —Paul A. Volcker

"An outstandingly lucid account of postwar economic policy-making and the dilemmas we now face. . . . It is rare to encounter a book on economics quite as intellectually exhilarating as *The End of Alchemy*—a dazzling performance indeed."
— John Plender, *Financial Times*

"Mervyn King has written a very important book. Certainly the best to have been written by any senior policymaker in place during the 2007–8 financial crisis, its explanations of finance and economics are excellent. . . . He writes throughout with a crisp and thoughtful grace and, as a text on banking and finance theory, the book is therefore able to illuminate complex topics with verve."   —Edward Price,
Interdisciplinary Journal of Economics and Business Law

THE END OF ALCHEMY

Money, Banking, and the Future
of the Global Economy

MERVYN KING

W. W. Norton & Company
Independent Publishers Since 1923
New York · London

For information about permission to reproduce selections from
this book, write to Permissions, W. W. Norton & Company, Inc.,
500 Fifth Avenue, New York, NY 10110

For information about special discounts for bulk purchases, please
contact W. W. Norton Special Sales at specialsales@wwnorton.com
or 800-233-4830

Manufacturing by Berryville Graphics
Production manager: Beth Steidle

Library of Congress Cataloging-in-Publication Data

Names: King, Mervyn A., author.
Title: The end of alchemy : money, banking and the future of the
global economy / Mervyn King.
Description: First edition. | New York : W. W. Norton & Company, [2016] |
Includes bibliographical references and index.
Identifiers: LCCN 2015048306 | ISBN 9780393247022 (hardcover)
Subjects: LCSH: Capitalism. | International finance. | International
banking. | Financial institutions. | Financial crises.
Classification: LCC HB501 .K46888 2016 | DDC 330.12/2—dc23
LC record available at http://lccn.loc.gov/2015048306

ISBN 978-0-393-35357-0 pbk.

W. W. Norton & Company, Inc.,
500 Fifth Avenue, New York, N.Y. 10110
www.wwnorton.com

W. W. Norton & Company Ltd.,
15 Carlisle Street, London W1D 3BS

1 2 3 4 5 6 7 8 9 0

FOR

Otto, Alexander, Livia and Sofie

CONTENTS

The endless cycle of idea and action,
Endless invention, endless experiment,
Brings knowledge of motion, but not of stillness;
Knowledge of speech, but not of silence;
Where is the wisdom we have lost in knowledge?
Where is the knowledge we have lost in information?

T.S. Eliot, *The Rock*, 1934

ACKNOWLEDGEMENTS

My biggest debt of gratitude is to the team with which I worked in the Bank of England for twenty-two years. When I arrived in the Bank in 1991 to become its Chief Economist, I soon realised how lucky I was. I was surrounded by a group of extraordinarily bright young economists who worked together as a team. Over the years, the Bank has managed to recruit exceptionally congenial as well as talented people. Without such committed staff, none of the achievements of the past twenty years – during which the Bank of England has changed from an institution operating in the shadows and behind the scenes to an independent central bank wielding enormous power – would have been possible. From my arrival on 1 March 1991, I was totally absorbed in a turbulent, yet ultimately constructive period for economic policy in the United Kingdom. Most of that period was spent in the magnificent Herbert Baker building, which fronts Threadneedle Street, with many weekends spent in international meetings in a range of windowless rooms from Basel to New York and Frankfurt to Washington. On the day of my departure on 30 June 2013, which coincided with the annual 'Governor's Day' party for Bank staff and their families at the Roehampton sports ground, I knew that I was leaving one family to return to my own. The warmth of our send-off was reciprocated.

All of my colleagues over the years deserve thanks for making my job much easier than it would otherwise have been. They include everyone on the staff of the Bank, as well as the members of the Monetary Policy Committee from 1997 to 2013, the Financial Policy Committee from 2011 to 2013, and the Board of the Prudential Regulation Authority in 2013. Because the Bank is a team, it would be invidious to pick out names, with the exception of one group. As I explain in the Introduction, this is not a memoir. Indeed, the recollections of the crisis that would be of most interest and importance are not those of the principals but of their private secretaries. Through their conversations with opposite numbers in government, at home and abroad, and the private sector, and with a wide range of people inside their own institution, their memoirs would be much more revealing, and dare I say it objective, than those of their bosses. I shall forever be indebted to my private secretaries and economic assistants during my time at the Bank: Alex Brazier, Alex Bowen, Mark Cornelius, Spencer Dale, Phil Evans, Neal Hatch, Andrew Hauser, James Proudman, Chris Salmon, Tim Taylor, Roland Wales, Jan de Vlieghe and Iain de Weymarn. As they move up the ladder in their respective careers, I shall watch with pride and friendship.

I am still asked how I coped with the stress of life at the Bank of England during the crisis. My reply – then and now – is that stress comes when you lose your job and have the responsibility of a family to support, not when you have a job with the wonderful dedicated and loyal support over many years from my office team including Aishah Aslam, Nikki Bennett, Ian Buggins, Carol Elliott, Alexandra Ellis, Sue Hartnett, Michelle Hersom, Lucy Letts, Michelle Major, Jo Merritt, Nicole Morey, Verina Oxley, Frances Pearce, Vicky Purkiss, Lisa Samwell and Jane Webster. Since leaving the Bank I have been indebted to my personal assistants, Rachel Lawrence in England and Gail Thomas in New York, for replacing that support team.

I am very grateful to both the Stern School of Business and the Law School at New York University for allowing me to join the community of faculty and students, and to participate in the broader intellectual life in that most extraordinary city. It could not have been a better adjustment path to integrate back into 'civilian' life. Robert S. Pirie encouraged and helped to facilitate my spending time in New York. He was a great friend until his sad death in early 2015. He is missed by so many. I am also grateful to the London School of Economics for allowing me to return to a place with happy memories and a most stimulating intellectual atmosphere.

Over the years I have learned an enormous amount from conversations with colleagues in academia and the policy world, many of whom straddled both. They are too numerous to mention, but among those with whom I spoke frequently are Alan Budd, my opposite number in the UK Treasury and then a fellow member of the Monetary Policy Committee; Martin Feldstein, my tutor at Harvard and with his wife Kate friends for over forty years; Stanley Fischer, who as Governor of the Bank of Israel and long-time friend was someone in whom it was possible to confide and discuss; Charles Goodhart, who was co-director with me of the LSE Financial Markets Group for several years and whose knowledge and judgement of central banking is legendary; Otmar Issing, who was the intellectual leader of the European Central Bank during its first critical years; Larry Summers, whose intellectual brilliance and imagination in policy analysis are unmatched; and John Vickers, who followed me as Chief Economist at the Bank of England and under whose chairmanship the Independent Commission on Banking produced a most effective report on the reform of banking in the UK. There are many others, and

I can only apologise for not including their names. I have also benefited greatly from conversations over many years with Bernard Connolly, one of the most perceptive writers on the global economy in recent years; Nick Stern, whose friendship both personal and intellectual over many years afforded great support; Adair Turner, who while Chairman of the UK Financial Services Authority worked with me during the crisis and whose ability to produce at speed incisive and innovative reports and books never ceases to amaze me; and not least Martin Wolf, whose books and columns for the *Financial Times* add up to one of the most important commentaries on our world.

Among those who provided detailed comments on earlier drafts of the manuscript are Alan Budd, Marvin Goodfriend, Otmar Issing, Bethany McLean, Geoffrey Miller, Ed Smith, and graduate students from the Stern School of Business and the Law School at New York University. I also benefited from visits to the University of Chicago, Princeton University, Stanford University and seminars with students at the London School of Economics. Invaluable research assistance was provided by David Low, Diego Daruich and Daniel Katz.

I am indebted to my literary agent, Andrew Wylie, whose encouragement and support were crucial to the completion of this enterprise. And I was fortunate to work with publishers who patiently and ceaselessly helped me to think carefully about the ideas in this book and how to explain them. At Little, Brown in the UK, my thanks go to Tim Whiting, Iain Hunt and Emily Burns, and at Norton in the US, to Drake McFeely, Jeff Shreve and Rachel Salzman.

This book is dedicated to my four grandchildren because it is their generation who will have to develop new ways of thinking about macroeconomics and to redesign our system of money and banking if another global financial crisis is to be prevented. Without my wife Barbara this book would have been neither started nor completed. Barbara speaks many languages and seems to find the right word when writing in each of them. She was and is my severest critic and strongest supporter – before, after and especially during the crisis.

PREFACE TO THE PAPERBACK EDITION

The End of Alchemy was, and is, written for the general reader and presumes no training in economics. Yet I hoped that economists too would find some of the ideas interesting. Since its original publication in the spring of 2016, I have been gratified by the response of both groups. The financial crisis occurred nearly a decade ago, and yet events have conspired to make those ideas still more relevant – slow growth of the world economy, the move to negative interest rates by a number of important central banks, growing tensions within the euro area, and renewed concern about the health of our banking system. Many of the continuing problems in the world economy relate directly to the four concepts that run right through the book: disequilibrium, radical uncertainty, the prisoner's dilemma and trust. The existence of radical uncertainty (the unknowable unknowns) means that people will inevitably make economic decisions which, with the benefit of hindsight, appear to be mistakes. Such mistakes can be large, and when they are, as I believe happened before the financial crisis of 2007–9, lead to a position of serious disequilibrium in the economy. Once in that position, neither businesses, households, banks nor even governments, can find a way out of the disequilibrium on their own – the prisoner's dilemma. Implicit cooperation with other players is the only way to return to a path of prosperity. But without trust among the players such a path may be difficult to find. Much of the period since the financial crisis bears out that view.

Economists and financial market participants have an exaggerated view of their ability to foresee the future. Take one example. Back in 1993, at the onset of the period of fifteen years that became known as the Great Stability (or Great Moderation), ten-year government bond yields in Germany and the United States were between 6 per cent and 7 per cent, and in the United Kingdom almost 8 per cent. This means that markets expected short-term interest rates in 2016 to be roughly in the same ballpark. How wrong can you be! Official short-term interest rates in most industrialised countries are today close to zero, or even negative, and ten-year bond yields at the time of writing are zero in Germany, around 1 per cent in the United Kingdom, and 1¾ per cent in the United States. The difference between the expectation then and today's reality must be one of, if not the, largest errors ever made in forecasts of interest rates. It reflects two large and unpredictable events that have transformed the situation out of all recognition: first, the adoption by many countries around the world of a commitment to stability as enshrined in central bank independence and an explicit inflation target; and, second, the dramatic events and consequences of the financial crisis of 2007–9.

The difference between earlier expectations and outturns reflects not stupidity but the impossibility of knowing in advance the scale and nature of the changes that would take place in the world economy and the way that, rightly or wrongly, policy would respond. Booms and slumps in our economies occur when prices fail to coordinate decisions to spend and to save. Radical uncertainty explains why this is a permanent feature of market economies. When we cannot imagine what the future may bring, we cannot create markets today for unspecified goods and services in the future. Sometimes investments are made for which there is no future demand and sometimes businesses fail to invest even when there is a demand for their output in future. The inability of markets in these instances to play their usual role of bringing supply and demand into balance is not so much a failure of markets as a logical consequence of radical uncertainty. Businesses and households are investing and saving for an unknowable future, and the markets in which their individual decisions might be coordinated simply do not exist. Any attempt to explain booms and slumps as the side effect of market frictions that prevent prices adjusting speedily misses the essence of those large swings in economic activity. Coping with radical uncertainty is the human condition.

Economists like to think that their approach to the subject is similar to that of scientists – observation of the world followed by the drawing of inferences that are encapsulated in theories. The experience of the financial crisis should lead us to question the theories that had been taken for granted beforehand. The proposition that new ideas are needed to guide us in the future was one that gained widespread acceptance after the Great Depression in the 1930s. That shattering experience ushered in a wave of intellectual turmoil, both economic and political. Economic policy in the post-war period was based on the new ideas generated by this intellectual ferment. Yet the recent financial crisis has provoked rather little by way of an intellectual or political revolution. Economists and politicians seem content to make modest changes and use the same models that found favour before the crisis. Most people from outside the closed policy world of government and the academy have reacted to this response with a certain degree of incredulity. Only economists could believe that negative interest rates are the solution to the problem of restoring economic growth and only bankers could believe that our system of money and banking is fundamentally sound.

A growing number of people mistrust the conventional wisdom, and with justification. As the book argues, the crisis was a failure of a system and the ideas that it represented. It is time to have the self-confidence and courage to question existing ideas.

Trust in government is at a low ebb across the democratic industrialised world, nowhere more clearly illustrated than in the 2016 referendum vote by the United Kingdom to leave the European Union ('Brexit') and the election of President Trump in the United States. Both events took the governing class by surprise. The inability of an elite to understand the concerns and fears of ordinary working people, so evident in the United Kingdom and the United States, as well as in the rest of Europe, stems in part from the failure to recognise that the economic ideas embraced as conventional wisdom by the profession and the political class have proved ineffective in creating rising living standards for many and in steering the world economy back to health after the financial crisis. In particular, the belief among central banks that just a little more monetary stimulus will see us home and dry has become harder and harder to maintain as a sustained recovery has proved elusive, and disillusion with a strategy of continual monetary easing among savers and members of the public has grown.

Since the initial publication of *The End of Alchemy*, three developments have reinforced its main arguments. First, economic recovery in much of the industrialised world has faltered, and central banks in a number of countries have been driven to increasingly desperate measures, such as negative interest rates. While most people look on in horror, the economics profession cheers from the sidelines and works hard to find ways to make it possible to impose even more negative interest rates.

Second, despite the deluge of regulation introduced since the financial crisis, there are real doubts about whether our banking system is now really safe. The banking system, bailed out and recapitalised in 2008–9, remains fragile, especially in Europe and China. At regular intervals, financial markets still exhibit concern over the health of banks. Even in the United States and the United Kingdom, banks are vulnerable to contagion from shocks to banks elsewhere. Third, the referendum on membership of the European Union held in Britain in June 2016 showed the contempt in which so-called economic experts were held by many members of the public. The conventional wisdom of the economic and political elite was rejected. Before condemning the public, it might be sensible to re-examine the conventional wisdom.

The Limits to Monetary Policy

For some eight years now, central banks around the world have been trying to generate an economic recovery. Despite their efforts, a sustainable recovery remains elusive. It is time to recognise the limits to monetary policy. Central banks can no longer provide further support to the economy because further monetary stimulus cannot bring about the permanent change in the pattern of spending that is needed. Today, the biggest threat to the future and independence of central banks comes from the danger of promising too much.

All this is far removed from the heady days of October 2008 when, in Washington DC, the G7 central bank governors and finance ministers promised to 'restore confidence in the financial system'. None of us at that meeting imagined that eight years later the extraordinary monetary and fiscal measures taken to stimulate the economy would not only still be in place, but that interest rates in many parts of the world would actually be negative and the need for monetary support would be even greater than at the height of the crisis.

In essence, the role of a central bank is extremely simple: to ensure that the right amount of money is created in both good times and bad times. This role is considered monetary policy in good times, and financial policy in bad times – the provision of liquidity to banks when there is a loss of confidence in the financial system. So why are central banks struggling to achieve their objectives today? In large part, their problem is that some of the ideas underpinning both monetary and financial policy have proved irrelevant to current problems.

After the experience of high and variable inflation in the 1970s and 1980s, governments in many countries handed responsibility for setting interest rates to independent central banks, which focused on the objective of price stability. For almost two decades this policy of inflation targeting proved highly successful. But it led to a confusion of stability with sustainability. The continuing fall in long-term real interest rates should have been a warning sign. Imbalances between spending and saving, both within and between major economies, meant that when the banking crisis hit in 2008, a monetary policy response was necessary but not sufficient to ensure a sustainable economic recovery. A collapse of confidence in 2008 created a large but temporary downward shock to spending. Expansionary monetary and fiscal policy was a sensible response to the shock. But that shock had ended by the close of 2009. Unfortunately, the underlying problems of a further and permanent downward revision to spending plans, to which monetary stimulus was not appropriate, remained.

The conceptual framework used by central banks was, and remains, flawed. Much damage has been done by the inappropriate application of economic 'models' to real problems. Imagine that you called a plumber to deal with a problem in your kitchen. You would expect a professional plumber to arrive carrying a box of tools from which he would select the appropriate instrument once he had diagnosed the problem. Suppose, however, that he arrived with a single tool, confident that whatever was wrong could be resolved by the use of his only instrument. Too many economists have run away with the idea that one model is all that is needed to guide policy.

Today's problem is that monetary economists have misdiagnosed the disease. They persist in believing that the reason for continuing slow growth, despite zero interest rates, is a temporary, albeit severe, negative shock to demand (a 'headwind'). Under that assumption, a sufficiently low – and, if necessary, negative – interest rate would persuade people to bring consumption spending forward from the future until the economy recovered. Low interest rates would be maintained until the headwind abated of its own accord, at which point the stimulus could be removed and the economy would return to growth along its steady path. The only impediment to returning to that path is the inability of central banks to make interest rates sufficiently negative to boost demand adequately. That is why so many economists mistakenly believe that the zero lower bound to interest rates is the biggest impediment today to economic recovery. To make it possible to implement negative interest rates, some economists have proposed abolishing cash or taxing bank deposits.

But it is dangerous to recommend such radical measures until you are sure of the correct diagnosis. As I describe in Chapter 8, our economy today is facing not a temporary headwind but a permanent fall in spending by households and businesses as they have come to realise that their spending before the crisis was on an unsustainable path. Only a new source of demand, such as exports, can fill the gap. Trying to fill the gap by cutting interest rates works for a while by encouraging businesses and households to bring spending forward. But by the same token it weakens future spending, which in turn reduces the incentive to invest. As time passes, further reductions in interest rates are necessary to maintain spending. In other words, only a path of continually falling interest rates can keep the economy close to full employment. Clearly, that cannot go on forever, and it has now run its course.

What is also missing from the conventional economic analysis is the possibility that the introduction of significantly negative interest rates may make households much more uncertain and less confident about the approach to economic policy that will be followed by central banks and governments in the future. If they abolish cash, what will they do next? Such uncertainty may lead households to save rather than spend more. A good illustration of this possibility occurred in January 2016 when the Bank of Japan announced a policy of negative interest rates to which the response of consumers and financial markets was . . . well, negative.

Fiscal policy may appear to be an attractive alternative to further monetary stimulus at this juncture. And there is no doubt that there are infrastructure projects in the public sector that would be easy to justify at even normal interest rates. But fiscal policy is no panacea, since it too brings spending forward at the expense of future demand when the higher public debt thereby incurred must be serviced through the collection of higher taxes. It is an appropriate response, as in 2008, to a temporary fall in spending but an inappropriate response to the long-run challenge of rebalancing the pattern of spending. Most advanced economies are not facing a temporary weakness of aggregate demand but are in a serious disequilibrium.

I fear that central banks are now caught in a trap of their own making. Continually falling interest rates have pushed asset prices up to levels that are sustainable only through expectations of further falls in interest rates or other forms of monetary policy stimulus. Rate increases might push the economy into a downturn and a collapse of asset prices. But rate cuts, or merely a continuation of present levels, risk a larger collapse of asset prices at a later date. The fact that central banks have continued to promise a recovery that is always around the corner, and been willing to adopt what seem to many people extreme policies with dangerous side effects, is undermining confidence in the ability of central banks to achieve that recovery. There are indeed limits to monetary policy.

Reforming Our Banks

The alchemy of money and banking is still with us. After almost a decade of reforms and new regulations, and protestations by central bankers and regulators that the banking system is now incomparably safer than before the crisis, it is troubling that the Italian banking system has again come under scrutiny and is clearly in need of recapitalisation, that Deutsche Bank has been so fragile with European bank share prices falling in 2016, and that such well-respected economists as former US Treasury Secretary Larry Summers have concluded that financial markets regard the banking sector today as no safer than before the crisis.

I have been heartened by the interest shown in my proposal (in Chapter 7) that central banks should act as a "pawnbroker for all seasons" (PFAS). Under the proposal the fear of bank runs that proved so devastating in 2008 could be banished. For many years, central banks had assumed that in a crisis they would act as the 'lender of last resort' described by Walter Bagehot in his classic study of the Bank of England in the nineteenth century, *Lombard Street*. But by 2008 the banking system had changed out of all recognition since Bagehot's day, when it was possible to respond to a crisis without any advance preparation. In those days, banks had a sufficiently large quantity of liquid government securities on their books to make it easy for the Bank of England quickly to assess the security against which it would lend cash for the full value of the collateral. But in 2008, banks brought very different collateral to their central bank, which then had to lend against illiquid loans to prevent a collapse of the system. To protect the interests of taxpayers, central banks lent only a proportion of the value of the assets provided as security. In effect, central banks were acting as pawnbrokers.

In future, I believe banks should be required to bring collateral to their central bank well in advance of a crisis so that they can obtain a cash credit line that can be called upon in times of crisis. Banks would be asked to position collateral with a value greater than the credit line to which they would then be entitled (there would be a 'haircut' on the collateral). The haircuts would act as an insurance premium paid in good times so the banks could draw on their cash credit line in bad times. If the credit line were sufficient to cover all deposits that could flee the bank quickly then this idea of the central bank as a PFAS would eliminate any concern about bank runs. Just as motorists are compelled to take out third-party car insurance to protect other road-users, so banks should be made to take out a certain amount of liquidity insurance in normal times so that they can access central bank provision of their liquidity needs in times of crisis.

There is much work to be done on the practical implementation of PFAS, and I am sure others can improve on the scheme. Professor Charles Goodhart (of the London School of Economics), for example, has suggested that bank assets in the form of overdrafts and committed lines of credit are too important a function of banking to ignore. They mean that the level of bank lending is sometimes determined by customers and is not under the immediate control of the bank (within the limits of the aggregate of committed facilities). Goodhart suggests that banks be given time to meet the PFAS rule when such facilities are activated by customers. Other improvements to the scheme could, I am sure, be made. But the important issue is the principle of mandatory ex-ante insurance provided by pre-positioned collateral to meet the claims of creditors who run.

The PFAS rule is not a pipe dream. Some central banks have already moved in that direction. For example, the Bank of England has for some time encouraged banks to pre-position collateral. As at end-February 2016, banks had pre-positioned over 240 loan portfolios with an aggregate nominal value of £410 billion. After applying the Bank's valuation and haircuts, the total drawable value was around £288 billion. Together with reserves at the Bank of around £400 billion, the effective liquid assets of the banking system were around £700 billion, about one-third of effective liquid liabilities. At the end of July, US banks had pre-positioned collateral with the Federal Reserve sufficient to produce a total lendable value of just under $1 trillion. There is a natural path from today's 'extraordinary' measures to a permanent solution to liquidity runs.

The main point of PFAS is that by putting in place an ex-ante insurance scheme, we can be no worse off than we are today, in which crises are managed simply by throwing a lot of money at the problem. Even if the haircuts are difficult to calculate, under PFAS we would be better off than if we respond to a crisis only by using overwhelming force once the crisis has broken out. If bank 'bailouts' were seen not as crisis interventions to save institutions in trouble, but as the payout from an insurance policy into which banks had been contributing regularly in normal times, then perhaps much of the understandable anger that accompanied the rescues of 2008 would have been tempered. It is all very well to throw the kitchen sink at the problem in the middle of a crisis, but it is vital to think deeply about the incentives facing banks between crises.

Lessons from the UK Referendum

The dangers of embracing a complacent conventional wisdom were revealed by the UK referendum on membership of the European Union in June 2016. *The End of Alchemy* does not discuss Brexit. Nor did I take any public stance on the issue either during or after the referendum, in deference to my successor at the Bank who had an extraordinarily difficult task as it was in navigating the line between staying out of political controversy and being transparent about his views of the likely evolution of the economy. I was grateful not to have to confront that challenge. After the result of the referendum was announced, and Britain's decision to leave the European Union had been made by a popular vote, I was surprised by the avalanche of apoplectic comment to the effect that people must have been fooled by lies and prejudice to vote for such an appalling outcome. *How could this have happened?* was the refrain. A similar reaction followed the election of President Trump in November 2016.

Part of the explanation is a growing gap between the economic and political elite, on the one hand, and a large numbers of ordinary working people, on the other. That gap reflects more than simply the unequal distribution of the spoils of growing prosperity that have resulted from globalisation. It reflects a lack of trust in the honesty of the arguments presented to the public. Of particular concern was the role of 'economic experts' in the referendum campaign. Economists can play a particularly important role in framing the arguments of a debate. From personal experience I believe that there was a demand for this by the British public. But instead the public was subjected to a propaganda war the like of which I cannot recall before in Britain, with both sides calling each other, and with some justification, liars. Nor was the press much better. Even those newspapers that like to think of themselves as more authoritative and informed than their tabloid cousins allowed, indeed encouraged, their editorial stance to infect their reporting of the campaign. No doubt their own commercial interests played a part. And during the campaign the role of economists was distorted into providing spurious quantification of the costs and benefits of Brexit. We cannot really know what these will be. But the claim by the Government that families would be £4,300 worse off in the event of Brexit was not an objective presentation of the facts, and was regarded by many people as scaremongering. There were similar distortions in the case put by the other side, but the damage to its credibility was greater for the Government.

The argument of the Government that Brexit would not only lead to a serious recession but would also necessitate the introduction of an emergency budget to raise taxes and cut public spending was seen by most people as wholly implausible, as so it proved. Even more bizarre was the view of some members of the Opposition who, having for several years criticised the Chancellor for raising taxes and cutting public spending during a period when the British economy was actually growing, now embraced austerity when confronted by the prospect of a recession. I do not want to suggest that these people are economically illiterate. Rather, the proposition reflected a decision to conduct a propaganda war borne out of panic when confronted by the possibility of a Leave vote. The nature of the campaign brought to mind the famous words of Edmund Burke after the Terror of the French Revolution reached its peak: 'The age of chivalry is gone. That of sophisters, economists, and calculators has succeeded; and the glory of Europe is extinguished forever'. The campaign was definitely in need of a referee to brandish a couple of red cards early on in the game to calm things down. In the event, they were shown in the tunnel after the game.

What was singularly absent from the campaign was a focus on the future of Europe. Europe faces two existential challenges. First, the failure to create a sustainable economic basis for the single currency, the euro. Second, the scale of mass migration, whether refugees or economic migrants, across the borders of the European Union. The first threatens to undermine the monetary union, and the second to undermine the commitment to the free movement of people within Europe, a laudable objective in earlier times but one that is almost impossible to sustain when confronted by an influx of millions trying to enter Europe.

Neither challenge has much to do with Brexit. Whatever the implications of such a decision for Britain itself, UK membership in the European Union is not an existential issue for Europe. The objective of the United Kingdom should be to promote sufficient self-confidence and realism among our European neighbours to help them understand that a forced political union will make the Continent less, not more, stable. Germany sacrificed its most successful achievement of a new and democratic post-war society – the Deutschmark – in the belief that binding itself into Europe through a monetary union would remove fears of an excessively powerful German state. The result has been the opposite. Germany is more powerful economically and politically today than in 1999, when monetary union began, and antagonism towards Germany in countries such as Greece and Italy is today greater than at any point since the end of the Second World War.

It is probable that the members of the euro area will try to press on with the creation of a fiscal and political union and to hold the Schengen area (a group of EU countries with no border controls between them) together. As things stand, the long march towards political union desired by the political elite governing the European Union is not likely to reach a democratic destination. Those who decry nationalism should realise that the attempt by an elite to impose political union on unwilling electorates is today the main driving force of the extreme nationalist sentiments that they abhor. Whatever our grandchildren and their descendants decide to do in Europe, it must be based on a democratically legitimate process if it is to avoid recreating the very divisions that the architects of post-war Europe so rightly strove to avoid.

In such circumstances, the inner core of the European Union would be a grouping with which the United Kingdom would have little in common. It is not clear why it would wish to be a member of such a club. Why would you want to be a member of a tennis club if you do not play tennis and indeed actively dislike the game, simply in order to play a game of bridge once a month? So it is hardly surprising that Britain has questioned its role in the European Union. It might well be said that Britain is not leaving the European Union; rather the European Union has left Britain. The move to monetary union transformed the nature of the European Union.

Not just in Britain, but around the industrialised world, the divide between the political class and a large number of disillusioned and disaffected voters threatens trust. At times it seems that the governing class has lost faith in the people and that the people have lost faith in the Government. And the two sides seem incapable of understanding each other. The financial crisis of the industrialised world, and the failure to enact more radical change, has redounded throughout such countries, as we see today in the United States. During 2016 and 2017 the leadership of many of the largest countries in the world either has, as in Britain and the United States, or will, as in Europe, change. To bridge the gap between leaders and voters will require political imagination, an understanding of the failures of the conventional wisdom, and a willingness to embrace new ideas. I hope readers will find some of those ideas in *The End of Alchemy* and be inspired to contribute their own thoughts to a public debate.

INTRODUCTION

'It was the best of times, it was the worst of times, it was
the age of wisdom, it was the age of foolishness, it was
the epoch of belief, it was the epoch of incredulity ... '

Charles Dickens, *A Tale of Two Cities*

The past twenty years in the modern world were indeed
the best of times and the worst of times. It was a tale of
two epochs – in the first growth and stability, followed in the
second by the worst banking crisis the industrialised world
has ever witnessed. Within the space of little more than a
year, between August 2007 and October 2008, what had been
viewed as the age of wisdom was now seen as the age of foolishness, and belief turned into incredulity. The largest banks in
the biggest financial centres in the advanced world failed, trig-
gering a worldwide collapse of confidence and bringing about
the deepest recession since the 1930s.

How did this happen? Was it a failure of individuals, institutions or ideas? The events of 2007–8 have spawned an
outpouring of articles and books, as well as plays and films,
about the crisis. If the economy had grown after the crisis at

the same rate as the number of books written about it, then we would have been back at full employment some while ago. Most such accounts – like the media coverage and the public debate at the time – focus on the symptoms and not the underlying causes. After all, those events, vivid though they remain in the memories of both participants and spectators, comprised only the latest in a long series of financial crises since our present system of money and banking became the cornerstone of modern capitalism after the Industrial Revolution in the eighteenth century. The growth of indebtedness, the failure of banks, the recession that followed, were all signs of much deeper problems in our financial and economic system. Unless we go back to the underlying causes we will never understand what happened and will be unable to prevent a repetition and help our economies truly recover. This book looks at the big questions raised by the depressing regularity of crises in our system of money and banking. Why do they occur? Why are they so costly in terms of lost jobs and production? And what can we do to prevent them? It also examines new ideas that suggest answers.

In the spring of 2011, I was in Beijing to meet a senior Chinese central banker. Over dinner in the Diaoyutai State Guesthouse, where we had earlier played tennis, we talked about the lessons from history for the challenges we faced, the most important of which was how to resuscitate the world economy after the collapse of the western banking system in 2008. Bearing in mind the apocryphal answer of Premier Chou Enlai to the question of what significance one should attach to the French Revolution (it was 'too soon to tell'), I asked my Chinese colleague what importance he now attached to the Industrial Revolution in Britain in the second half of the eighteenth century. He thought hard. Then he replied: 'We in China have learned a great deal from the West about how competition and a market economy support industrialisation and create higher living standards. We want to emulate that.' Then came the sting in the tail, as he continued: 'But I don't think you've quite got the hang of money and banking yet.'[1] His remark was the inspiration for this book.

Since the crisis, many have been tempted to play the game of deciding who was to blame for such a disastrous outcome. But blaming individuals is counterproductive – it leads you to think that if just a few, or indeed many, of those people were punished then we would never experience a crisis again. If only it were that simple. A generation of the brightest and best were lured into banking, and especially into trading, by the promise of immense financial rewards and by the intellectual challenge of the work that created such rich returns. They were badly misled. The crisis was a failure of a system, and the ideas that underpinned it, not of individual policy-makers or bankers, incompetent and greedy though some of them undoubtedly were. There was a general misunderstanding of how the world economy worked. Given the size and political influence of the banking sector, is it too late to put the genie back in the bottle? No – it is never too late to ask the right questions, and in this book I try to do so.

If we don't blame the actors, then why not the playwright? Economists have been cast by many as the villain. An abstract and increasingly mathematical discipline, economics is seen as having failed to predict the crisis. This is rather like blaming science for the occasional occurrence of a natural disaster. Yet we would blame scientists if incorrect theories made disasters more likely or created a perception that they could never occur, and one of the arguments of this book is that economics has encouraged ways of thinking that made crises more probable. Economists have brought the problem upon themselves by pretending that they can forecast. No one can easily predict an unknowable future, and economists are no exception. Despite the criticism, modern economics provides a distinctive and useful way of thinking about the world. But no subject can stand still, and economics must change, perhaps quite radically, as a result of the searing experience of the crisis. A theory adequate for today requires us to think for ourselves, standing on the shoulders of giants of the past, not kneeling in front of them.

Economies that are capable of sending men to the moon and producing goods and services of extraordinary complexity and innovation seem to struggle with the more mundane challenge of handling money and banking. The frequency, and certainly severity, of crises has, if anything, increased rather than decreased over time. In the heat of the crisis in October 2008, nation states took over responsibility for all the obligations and debts of the global banking system. In terms of its balance sheet, the banking system had been virtually nationalised but without collective control over its operations. That government rescue cannot conveniently be forgotten. When push came to shove, the very sector that had espoused the merits of market discipline was allowed to carry on only by dint of taxpayer support. The creditworthiness of the state was put on the line, and in some cases, such as Iceland and Ireland, lost. God may have created the universe, but we mortals created paper money and risky banks. They are man-made institutions, important sources of innovation, prosperity and material progress, but also of greed, corruption and crises. For better or worse, they materially affect human welfare.

For much of modern history, and for good reason, money and banking have been seen as the magical elements that liberated us from a stagnant feudal system and permitted the emergence of dynamic markets capable of making the long-term investments necessary to support a growing economy.

The idea that paper money could replace intrinsically valuable gold and precious metals, and that banks could take secure short-term deposits and transform them into long-term risky investments, came into its own with the Industrial Revolution in the eighteenth century. It was both revolutionary and immensely seductive. It was in fact financial alchemy – the creation of extraordinary financial powers that defy reality and common sense. Pursuit of this monetary elixir has brought a series of economic disasters – from hyperinflations to banking collapses. Why have money and banking, the alchemists of a market economy, turned into its Achilles heel?

The purpose of this book is to answer that question. It sets out to explain why the economic failures of a modern capitalist economy stem from our system of money and banking, the consequences for the economy as a whole, and how we can end the alchemy. Our ideas about money and banking are just as much a product of our age as the way we conduct our politics and imagine our past. The twentieth-century experience of depression, hyperinflation and war changed both the world and the way economists thought about it. Before the Great Depression of the early 1930s, central banks and governments saw their role as stabilising the financial system and balancing the budget. After the Great Depression, attention turned to policies aimed at maintaining full employment. But post-war confidence that Keynesian ideas – the use of public spending to expand total demand in the economy – would prevent us from repeating the errors of the past was to prove touchingly naive. The use of expansionary policies during the 1960s, exacerbated by the Vietnam War, led to the Great Inflation of the 1970s, accompanied by slow growth and rising unemployment – the combination known as 'stagflation'. The direct consequence was that central banks were reborn as independent institutions committed to price stability. So successful was this that in the 1990s not only did inflation fall to levels unseen for a generation, but central banks and their governors were hailed for inaugurating an era of economic growth with low inflation – the Great Stability or Great Moderation. Politicians worshipped at the altar of finance, bringing gifts in the form of lax regulation and receiving support, and sometimes campaign contributions, in return. Then came the fall: the initial signs that some banks were losing access to markets for short-term borrowing in 2007, the collapse of the industrialised world's banking system in 2008, the Great Recession that followed, and increasingly desperate attempts by policy-makers to engineer a recovery. Today the world economy remains in a depressed state. Enthusiasm for policy stimulus is back in fashion, and the wheel has turned full circle.

The recession is hurting people who were not responsible for our present predicament, and they are, naturally, angry. There is a need to channel that anger into a careful analysis of what went wrong and a determination to put things right. The economy is behaving in ways that we did not expect, and new ideas will be needed if we are to prevent a repetition of the Great Recession and restore prosperity.

Many accounts and memoirs of the crisis have already been published. Their titles are numerous, but they share the same invisible subtitle: 'how I saved the world'. So although in the interests of transparency I should make clear that I was an actor in the drama – Governor of the Bank of England for ten years between 2003 and 2013, during both the Great Stability, the banking crisis itself, the Great Recession that followed, and the start of the recovery – this is not a memoir of the crisis with revelations about private conversations and behind-the-scenes clashes. Of course, those happened – as in any walk of life. But who said what to whom and when can safely, and properly, be left to dispassionate and disinterested historians who can sift and weigh the evidence available to them after sufficient time has elapsed and all the relevant official and unofficial papers have been made available. Instant memoirs, whether of politicians or officials, are usually partial and self-serving. I see little purpose in trying to set the record straight when any account that I gave would naturally also seem self-serving. My own record of events and the accompanying Bank papers will be made available to historians when the twenty-year rule permits their release.

This book is about economic ideas. My time at the Bank of England showed that ideas, for good or ill, do influence governments and their policies. The adoption of inflation targeting in the early 1990s and the granting of independence to the Bank of England in 1997 are prime examples. Economists brought intellectual rigour to economic policy and especially to central banking. But my experience at the Bank also revealed the inadequacies of the 'models' – whether verbal descriptions or mathematical equations – used by economists to explain swings in total spending and production. In particular, such models say nothing about the importance of money and banks and the panoply of financial markets that feature prominently in newspapers and on our television screens. Is there a fundamental weakness in the intellectual economic framework underpinning contemporary thinking?

An exploration of some of these basic issues does not require a technical exposition, and I have stayed away from one. Of course, economists use mathematical and statistical methods to understand a complex world – they would be remiss if they did not. Economics is an intellectual discipline that requires propositions to be not merely plausible but subject to the rigour of a logical proof. And yet there is no mathematics in this book.[2] It is written in (I hope) plain English and draws on examples from real life. Although I would like my fellow economists to read the book in the hope that they will take forward some of the ideas presented here, it is aimed at the reader with no formal training in economics but an interest in the issues.

In the course of this book, I will explain the fundamental causes of the crisis and how the world economy lost its balance; how money emerged in earlier societies and the role it plays today; why the fragility of our financial system stems directly from the fact that banks are the main source of money creation; why central banks need to change the way they respond to crises; why politics and money go hand in hand; why the world will probably face another crisis unless nations pursue different policies; and, most important of all, how we can end the alchemy of our present system of money and banking.

By alchemy I mean the belief that all paper money can be turned into an intrinsically valuable commodity, such as gold, on demand and that money kept in banks can be taken out whenever depositors ask for it. The truth is that money, in all forms, depends on trust in its issuer. Confidence in paper money rests on the ability and willingness of governments not to abuse their power to print money. Bank deposits are backed by long-term risky loans that cannot quickly be converted into money. For centuries, alchemy has been the basis of our system of money and banking.[3] As this book shows, we can end the alchemy without losing the enormous benefits that money and banking contribute to a capitalist economy.

Four concepts are used extensively in the book: disequilibrium, radical uncertainty, the prisoner's dilemma and trust. These concepts will be familiar to many, although the context in which I use them may not. Their significance will become clear as the argument unfolds, but a brief definition and explanation may be helpful at the outset.

Disequilibrium is the absence of a state of balance between the forces acting on a system. As applied to economics, a disequilibrium is a position that is unsustainable, meaning that at some point a large change in the pattern of spending and production will take place as the economy moves to a new equilibrium. The word accurately describes the evolution of the world economy since the fall of the Berlin Wall, which I discuss in Chapter 1.

Radical uncertainty refers to uncertainty so profound that it is impossible to represent the future in terms of a knowable and exhaustive list of outcomes to which we can attach probabilities. Economists conventionally assume that 'rational' people can construct such probabilities. But when businesses invest, they are not rolling dice with known and finite outcomes on the faces; rather they face a future in which the possibilities are both limitless and impossible to imagine. Almost all the things that define modern life, and which we now take for granted, such as cars, aeroplanes, computers and antibiotics, were once unimaginable. The essential challenge facing everyone living in a capitalist economy is the inability to conceive of what the future may hold. The failure to incorporate radical uncertainty into economic theories was one of the factors responsible for the misjudgements that led to the crisis.

The **prisoner's dilemma** may be defined as the difficulty of achieving the best outcome when there are obstacles to cooperation. Imagine two prisoners who have been arrested and kept apart from each other. Both are offered the same deal: if they agree to incriminate the other they will receive a light sentence, but if they refuse to do so they will receive a severe sentence if the other incriminates them. If neither incriminates the other, then both are acquitted.[4] Clearly, the best outcome is for both to remain silent. But if they cannot cooperate the choice is more difficult. The only way to guarantee the avoidance of a severe sentence is to incriminate the other. And if both do so, the outcome is that both receive a light sentence.

But this non-cooperative outcome is inferior to the cooperative outcome. The difficulty of cooperating with each other creates a prisoner's dilemma. Such problems are central to understanding how the economy behaves as a whole (the field known as macroeconomics) and to thinking through both how we got into the crisis and how we can now move towards a sustainable recovery. Many examples will appear in the following pages. Finding a resolution to the prisoner's dilemma problem in a capitalist economy is central to understanding and improving our fortunes.

Trust is the ingredient that makes a market economy work. How could we drive, eat, or even buy and sell, unless we trusted other people? Everyday life would be impossible without trust: we give our credit card details to strangers and eat in restaurants that we have never visited before. Of course, trust is supplemented with regulation – fraud is a crime and there are controls of the conditions in restaurant kitchens – but an economy works more efficiently with trust than without. Trust is part of the answer to the prisoner's dilemma. It is central to the role of money and banks, and to the institutions that manage our economy. Long ago, Confucius emphasised the crucial role of trust in the authorities: 'Three things are necessary for government: weapons, food and trust. If a ruler cannot hold on to all three, he should give up weapons first and food next. Trust should be guarded to the end: without trust we cannot stand.'[5]

Those four ideas run through the book and help us to understand the origin of the alchemy of money and banking and how we can reduce or even eliminate that alchemy.

When I left the Bank of England in 2013, I decided to explore the flaws in both the theory and practice of money and banking, and how they relate to the economy as a whole. I was led deeper and deeper into basic questions about economics. I came to believe that fundamental changes are needed in the way we think about macroeconomics, as well as in the way central banks manage their economies. A key role of a market economy is to link the present and the future, and to coordinate decisions about spending and production not only today but tomorrow and in the years thereafter. Families will save if the interest rate is high enough to overcome their natural impatience to spend today rather than tomorrow. Companies will invest in productive capital if the prospective rate of return exceeds the cost of attracting finance. And economic growth requires saving and investment to add to the stock of productive capital and so increase the potential output of the economy in the future. In a healthy growing economy all three rates – the interest rate on saving, the rate of return on investment, and the rate of growth – are well above zero. Today, however, we are stuck with extraordinarily low interest rates, which discourage saving – the source of future demand – and, if maintained indefinitely, will pull down rates of return on investment, diverting resources into unprofitable projects. Both effects will drag down future growth rates. We are already some way down that road. It seems that our market economy today is not providing an effective link between the present and the future.

I believe there are two reasons for this failure. First, there is an inherent problem in linking a known present with an unknowable future. Radical uncertainty presents a market economy with an impossible challenge – how are we to create markets in goods and services that we cannot at present imagine? Money and banking are part of the response of a market economy to that challenge. Second, the conventional wisdom of economists about how governments and central banks should stabilise the economy gives insufficient weight to the importance of radical uncertainty in generating an occasional large disequilibrium. Crises do not come out of thin air but are the result of the unavoidable mistakes made by people struggling to cope with an unknowable future. Both issues have profound implications and will be explored at greater length in subsequent chapters.

Inevitably, my views reflect the two halves of my career. The first was as an academic, a student in Cambridge, England, and a Kennedy scholar at Harvard in the other Cambridge, followed by teaching positions on both sides of the Atlantic. I experienced at first hand the evolution of macroeconomics from literary exposition – where propositions seemed plausible but never completely convincing – into a mathematical discipline – where propositions were logically convincing but never completely plausible. Only during the crisis of 2007–9 did I look back and understand the nature of the tensions between the surviving disciples of John Maynard Keynes who taught me in the 1960s, primarily Richard Kahn and Joan Robinson, and the influx of mathematicians and scientists into the subject that fuelled the rapid expansion of university economics departments in the same period. The old school 'Keynesians' were mistaken in their view that all wisdom was to be found in the work of one great man, and as a result their influence waned. The new arrivals brought mathematical discipline to a subject that prided itself on its rigour. But the informal analysis of disequilibrium of economies, radical uncertainty, and trust as a solution to the prisoner's dilemma was lost in the enthusiasm for the idea that rational individuals would lead the economy to an efficient equilibrium. It is time to take those concepts more seriously.

The second half of my career comprised twenty-two years at the Bank of England, the oldest continuously functioning central bank in the world, from 1991 to 2013, as Chief Economist, Deputy Governor and then Governor. That certainly gave me a chance to see how money could be managed. I learned, and argued publicly, that this is done best not by relying on gifted individuals to weave their magic, but by designing and building institutions that can be run by people who are merely professionally competent. Of course individuals matter and can make a difference, especially in a crisis. But the power of markets – the expression of hundreds of thousands of investors around the world – is a match for any individual, central banker or politician, who fancies his ability to resist economic arithmetic. As one of President Clinton's advisers remarked, 'I used to think if there was reincarnation, I wanted to come back as the president or the Pope or a .400 baseball hitter. But now I want to come back as the bond market. You can intimidate everybody.'[6] Nothing has diminished the force of that remark since it was made over twenty years ago.

In 2012, I gave the first radio broadcast in peacetime by a Governor of the Bank of England since Montagu Norman delivered a talk on the BBC in March 1939, only months before the outbreak of the Second World War. As Norman left Broadcasting House, he was mobbed by British Social Credits Party demonstrators carrying flags and slogan-boards bearing the words: CONSCRIPT THE BANKERS FIRST! Feelings also ran high in 2012. The consequences of the events of 2007–9 are still unfolding, and anger about their effects on ordinary citizens is not diminishing. That disaster was a long time in the making, and will be just as long in the resolving. But the cost of lost output and employment from our continuing failure to manage money and banking and prevent crises is too high for us to wait for another crisis to occur before we act to protect future generations.

Charles Dickens' novel *A Tale of Two Cities* has not only a very famous opening sentence but an equally famous closing sentence. As Sydney Carton sacrifices himself to the guillotine in the place of another, he reflects: 'It is a far, far better thing that I do, than I have ever done ...' If we can find a way to end the alchemy of the system of money and banking we have inherited then, at least in the sphere of economics, it will indeed be a far, far better thing than we have ever done.

1

THE GOOD, THE BAD
AND THE UGLY

'I think that Capitalism, wisely managed, can probably be made more efficient for attaining economic ends than any alternative system yet in sight.'

John Maynard Keynes, *The End of Laissez-faire* (1926)

'The experience of being disastrously wrong is salutary; no economist should be spared it, and few are.'

John Kenneth Galbraith, *A Life in Our Times* (1982)

History is what happened before you were born. That is why it is so hard to learn lessons from history: the mistakes were made by the previous generation. As a student in the 1960s, I knew why the 1930s were such a bad time. Outdated economic ideas guided the decisions of governments and central banks, while the key individuals were revealed in contemporary photographs as fuddy-duddies who wore whiskers and hats and were ignorant of modern economics. A younger generation, in academia and government, trained in modern economics, would ensure that the Great Depression of the 1930s would never be repeated.

In the 1960s, everything seemed possible. Old ideas and conventions were jettisoned, and a new world beckoned. In economics, an influx of mathematicians, engineers and physicists brought a new scientific approach to what the nineteenth-century philosopher and writer Thomas Carlyle christened the 'dismal science'.[1] It promised not just a better understanding of our economy, but an improved economic performance.

The subsequent fifty years were a mixed experience. Over that period, national income in the advanced world more than doubled, and in the so-called developing world hundreds of millions of people were lifted out of extreme poverty. And yet runaway inflation in the 1970s was followed in 2007–9 by the biggest financial crisis the world has ever seen. How do we make sense of it all? Was the post-war period a success or a failure?

The origins of economic growth

The history of capitalism is one of growth and rising living standards interrupted by financial crises, most of which have emanated from our mismanagement of money and banking. My Chinese colleague spoke an important, indeed profound, truth. The financial crisis of 2007–9 (hereafter 'the crisis') was not the fault of particular individuals or economic policies. Rather, it was merely the latest manifestation of our collective failure to manage the relationship between finance – the structure of money and banking – and a capitalist system. Failure to appreciate this explains why most accounts of the crisis focus on the symptoms and not the underlying causes of what went wrong. The fact that we have not yet got the hang of it does not mean that a capitalist economy is doomed to instability and failure. It means that we need to think harder about how to make it work.

Over many years, a capitalist economy has proved the most successful route to escape poverty and achieve prosperity. Capitalism, as I use the term here, is an economic system in which private owners of capital hire wage-earners to work in their businesses and pay for investment by raising finance from banks and financial markets.[2] The West has built the institutions to support a capitalist system – the rule of law to enforce private contracts and protect property rights, intellectual freedom to innovate and publish new ideas, anti-trust regulation to promote competition and break up monopolies, and collectively financed services and networks, such as education, water, electricity and telecommunications, which provide the infrastructure to support a thriving market economy. Those institutions create a balance between freedom and restraint, and between unfettered competition and regulation. It is a subtle balance that has emerged and evolved over time.[3] And it has transformed our standard of living. Growth at a rate of 2.5 per cent a year – close to the average experienced in North America and Europe since the Second World War – raises real total national income twelvefold over one century, a truly revolutionary outcome.

Over the past two centuries, we have come to take economic growth for granted. Writing in the middle of that extraordinary period of economic change in the mid-eighteenth century, the Scottish philosopher and political economist, Adam Smith, identified the source of the breakout from relative economic stagnation – an era during which productivity (output per head) was broadly constant and any increase resulted from discoveries of new land or other natural resources – to a prolonged period of continuous growth of productivity: specialisation. It was possible for individuals to specialise in particular tasks – the division of labour – and by working with capital equipment to raise their productivity by many times the level achieved by a jack-of-all-trades. To illustrate his argument, Smith employed his now famous example of a pin factory:

> A workman ... could scarce, perhaps, with his utmost industry, make one pin in a day, and certainly could not make twenty. But in the way in which this business is now carried on, not only the whole work is a peculiar trade, but it is divided into a number of branches. One man draws out the wire, another straights it, a third cuts it, a fourth points it, a fifth grinds it at the top for receiving the head ... The important business of making a pin is, in this manner, divided into about eighteen distinct operations, which, in some manufactories, are all performed by distinct hands.[4]

The factory Smith was describing employed ten men and made over 48,000 pins in a day.

The application of technical knowhow to more and more tasks increased specialisation and raised productivity. Specialisation went hand in hand with an even greater need for both a means to exchange the fruits of one's labour for an ever wider variety of goods produced by other specialists – money – and a way to finance the purchase of the capital equipment that made specialisation possible – banks. As each person in the workforce became more specialised, more machinery and capital investment was required to support them and the role of money and banks increased. After a millennium of roughly constant output per person, from the middle of the eighteenth century productivity started, slowly but surely, to rise.[5] Capitalism was, quite literally, producing the goods. Historians will continue to debate why the Industrial Revolution occurred in Britain – population growth, plentiful supplies of coal and iron, supportive institutions, religious beliefs and other factors all feature in recent accounts. But the evolution of money and banking was a necessary condition for the Revolution to take off.

Almost a century later, with the experience of industrialisation and a massive shift of labour from the land to urban factories, socialist writers saw things differently. For Karl Marx and Friedrich Engels the future was clear. Capitalism was a temporary staging post along the journey from feudalism to socialism. In their *Communist Manifesto* of 1848, they put forward their idea of 'scientific socialism' with its deterministic view that capitalism would ultimately collapse and be replaced by socialism or communism. Later, in the first volume of *Das Kapital* (1867), Marx elaborated (at great length) on this thesis and predicted that the owners of capital would become ever richer while excessive capital accumulation would lead to a falling rate of profit, reducing the incentive to invest and leaving the working class immersed in misery. The British industrial working class in the nineteenth century did indeed suffer miserable working conditions, as graphically described by Charles Dickens in his novels. But no sooner had the ink dried on Marx's famous work than the British economy entered a long period of rising real wages (money wages adjusted for the cost of living). Even the two world wars and the intervening Great Depression in the 1930s could not halt rising productivity and real wages, and broadly stable rates of profit. Economic growth and improving living standards became the norm.

But if capitalism did not collapse under the weight of its

own internal contradictions, neither did it provide economic security. During the twentieth century, the extremes of hyper-inflations and depressions eroded both living standards and the accumulated wealth of citizens in many capitalist economies, especially during the Great Depression in the 1930s, when mass unemployment sparked renewed interest in the possibilities of communism and central planning, especially in Europe. The British economist John Maynard Keynes promoted the idea that government intervention to bolster total spending in the economy could restore full employment without the need to resort to fully fledged socialism. After the Second World War, there was a widespread belief that government planning had won the war and could be the means to win the peace. In Britain, as late as 1964 the newly elected Labour government announced a 'National Plan'. Inspired by a rather naive version of Keynesian ideas, it focused on policies to boost the demand for goods and services rather than the ability of the economy to produce them. As the former outstripped the latter, the result was inflation. On the other side of the Atlantic, the growing cost of the Vietnam War in the late 1960s also led to higher inflation.

Rising inflation put pressure on the internationally agreed framework within which countries had traded with each other since the Bretton Woods Agreement of 1944, named after the conference held in the New Hampshire town in July of that year. Designed to allow a war-damaged Europe slowly to rebuild its economy and reintegrate into the world trading system, the agreement created an international monetary system under which countries set their own interest rates but fixed their exchange rates among themselves. For this to be possible, movements of capital between countries had to be severely restricted – otherwise capital would move to where interest rates were highest, making it impossible to maintain either differences in those rates or fixed exchange rates. Exchange controls were ubiquitous, and countries imposed limits on investments in foreign currency. As a student, I remember that no British traveller in the 1960s could take abroad with them more than £50 a year to spend.[6]

The new international institutions, the International Monetary Fund (IMF) and the World Bank, would use funds provided by its members to finance temporary shortages of foreign currency and the investment needed to replace the factories and infrastructure destroyed during the Second World War. Implicit in this framework was the belief that countries would have similar and low rates of inflation. Any loss of competitiveness in one country, as a result of higher inflation than in its trading partners, was assumed to be temporary and would be met by a deflationary policy to restore competitiveness while borrowing from the IMF to finance a short-term trade deficit. But in the late 1960s differences in inflation across countries, especially between the United States and Germany, appeared to be more than temporary, and led to the breakdown of the Bretton Woods system in 1970–1. By the early 1970s, the major economies had moved to a system of 'floating' exchange rates, in which currency values are determined by private sector supply and demand in the markets for foreign exchange.

Inevitably, the early days of floating exchange rates reduced the discipline on countries to pursue low inflation. When the two oil shocks of the 1970s – in 1973, when an embargo by Arab countries led to a quadrupling of prices, and 1979, when prices doubled after disruption to supply following the Iranian Revolution – hit the western world, the result was the Great Inflation, with annual inflation reaching 13 per cent in the United States and 27 per cent in the United Kingdom.[7]

Economic experiments

From the late 1970s onwards, the western world then embarked on what we can now see were three bold experiments to manage money, exchange rates and the banking system better. The first was to give central banks much greater independence in order to bring down and stabilise inflation, subsequently enshrined in the policy of inflation targeting – the goal of national price stability. The second was to allow capital to move freely between countries and encourage a shift to fixed exchange rates both within Europe, culminating in the creation of a monetary union, and in a substantial proportion of the most rapidly growing part of the world economy, particularly China, which fixed its exchange rates against the US dollar – the goal of exchange rate stability. And the third experiment was to remove regulations limiting the activities of the banking and financial system to promote competition and allow banks both to diversify into new products and regions and to expand in size, with the aim of bringing stability to a banking system often threatened in the past by risks that were concentrated either geographically or by line of business – the goal of financial stability.

These three simultaneous experiments might now be best described as having three consequences – the Good, the Bad and the Ugly. The Good was a period between about 1990 and 2007 of unprecedented stability of both output and inflation – the Great Stability. Monetary policy around the world changed radically. Inflation targeting and central bank independence spread to more than thirty countries. And there were significant changes in the dynamics of inflation, which on average became markedly lower, less variable and less persistent.[8]

The Bad was the rise in debt levels. Eliminating exchange rate flexibility in Europe and the emerging markets led to growing trade surpluses and deficits. Some countries saved a great deal while others had to borrow to finance their external deficit. The willingness of the former to save outweighed the willingness of the latter to spend, and so long-term interest rates in the integrated world capital market began to fall. The price of an asset, whether a house, shares in a company or any other claim on the future, is the value today of future expected returns (rents, the value of housing services from living in your own home, or dividends). To calculate that price one must convert future into current values by discounting them at an interest rate. The immediate effect of a fall in interest rates is to raise the prices of assets across the board. So as long-term interest rates in the world fell, the value of assets – especially of houses – rose. And as the values of assets increased, so did the amounts that had to be borrowed to enable people to buy them. Between 1986 and 2006, household debt rose from just under 70 per cent of total household income to almost 120 per cent in the United States and from 90 per cent to around 140 per cent in the United Kingdom.[9]

The Ugly was the development of an extremely fragile banking system. In the USA, Federal banking regulators' increasingly lax interpretation of the provisions to separate commercial and investment banking introduced in the 1933 Banking Act (often known as Glass-Steagall, the senator and representative, respectively, who led the passage of the legislation) reached its inevitable conclusion with the Gramm-Leach-Bliley Act of 1999, which swept away any remaining restrictions on the activities of banks. In the UK, the so-called Big Bang of 1986, which started as a measure to introduce competition into the Stock Exchange, led to takeovers of small stockbroking firms and mergers between commercial banks and securities houses.[10] Banks diversified and expanded rapidly after deregulation. In continental Europe so-called universal banks had long been the norm. The assets of large international banks doubled in the five years before 2008. Trading of new and highly complex financial products among banks meant that they became so closely interconnected that a problem in one would spread rapidly to others, magnifying rather than spreading risk.[11] Banks relied less and less on their own resources to finance lending and became more and more dependent on borrowing.[12] The equity capital of banks – the funds provided by the shareholders of the bank – accounted for a declining proportion of overall funding. Leverage – the ratio of total assets (or liabilities) to the equity capital of a bank – rose to extraordinary levels. On the eve of the crisis, the leverage ratio for many banks was 30 or more, and for some investment banks it was between 40 and 50.[13] A few banks had ratios even higher than that. With a leverage ratio of even 25 it would take a fall of only 4 per cent in the average value of a bank's assets to wipe out the whole of the shareholders' equity and leave it unable to service its debts.

By 2008, the Ugly led the Bad to overwhelm the Good. The crisis – one might say catastrophe – of the events that began to unfold under the gaze of a disbelieving world in 2007 was the failure of all three experiments. Greater stability of output and inflation, although desirable in itself, concealed the build-up of a major disequilibrium in the composition of spending. Some countries were saving too little and borrowing too much to be able to sustain their path of spending in the future, while others saved and lent so much that their consumption was pushed below a sustainable path. Total saving in the world was so high that interest rates, after allowing for inflation, fell to levels incompatible in the long run with a profitable growing market economy. Falling interest rates led to rising asset values and increases in the debt taken out against those more valuable assets. Fixed exchange rates exacerbated the burden of the debts, and in Europe the creation of monetary union in 1999 sapped the strength of many of its economies, as they became increasingly uncompetitive. Large, highly leveraged banks proved unstable and were vulnerable to even a modest loss of confidence, resulting in contagion to other banks and the collapse of the system in 2008.

At their outset the ill-fated nature of the three experiments was not yet visible. On the contrary, during the 1990s the elimination of high and variable inflation, which had undermined market economies in the 1970s, led to a welcome period of macroeconomic stability. The Great Stability, or the Great Moderation as it was dubbed in the United States, was seen – as in many ways it was – as a success for monetary policy. But it was unsustainable. Policy-makers were conscious of problems inherent in the first two experiments, but seemed powerless to do anything about them. At international gatherings, such as those of the IMF, policy-makers would wring their hands about the 'global imbalances' but no one country had any incentive to do anything about it. If a country had, on its own, tried to swim against the tide of falling interest rates, it would have experienced an economic slowdown and rising unemployment without any material impact on either the global economy or the banking system. Even then the prisoner's dilemma was beginning to rear its ugly head.

Nor was it obvious how the unsustainable position of the world economy would come to an end. I remember attending a seminar of economists and policy-makers at the IMF as early as 2002 where the consensus was that there would eventually be a sharp fall in the value of the US dollar, which would produce a change in spending patterns. But long before that could happen, the third experiment ended with the banking crisis of September and October 2008. The shock that some of the biggest and most successful commercial banks in North America and Europe either failed, or were seriously crippled, led to a collapse of confidence which produced the largest fall in world trade since the 1930s. Something had gone seriously wrong.

Opinions differ as to the cause of the crisis. Some see it as a financial panic in which fundamentally sound financial institutions were left short of cash as confidence in the credit-worthiness of banks suddenly changed and professional investors stopped lending to them – a liquidity crisis. Others see it as the inevitable outcome of bad lending decisions by banks – a solvency crisis, in which the true value of banks' assets had fallen by enough to wipe out most of their equity capital, meaning that they might be unable to repay their debts.[14] But almost all accounts of the recent crisis are about the symptoms – the rise and fall of housing markets, the explosion of debt and the excesses of the banking system – rather than the underlying causes of the events that overwhelmed the economies of the industrialised world in 2008.[15] Some even imagine that the crisis was solely an affair of the US financial sector. But unless the events of 2008 are seen in their global economic context, it is hard to make sense of what happened and of the deeper malaise in the world economy.

The story of what happened can be explained in little more than a few pages – everything you need to know but were afraid to ask about the causes of the recent crisis. So here goes.

The story of the crisis

By the start of the twenty-first century it seemed that economic prosperity and democracy went hand in hand. Modern capitalism spawned growing prosperity based on growing trade, free markets and competition, and global banks. In 2008 the system collapsed. To understand why the crisis was so big, and came as such a surprise, we should start at the key turning point – the fall of the Berlin Wall in 1989. At the time it was thought to represent the end of communism, indeed the end of the appeal of socialism and central planning. For some it was the end of history.[16] For most, it represented a victory for free market economics. Contrary to the prediction of Marx, capitalism had displaced communism. Yet who would have believed that the fall of the Wall was not just the end of communism but the beginning of the biggest crisis in capitalism since the Great Depression?

What has happened over the past quarter of a century to bring about this remarkable change of fortune in the position of capitalist economies? After the demise of the socialist model of a planned economy, China, countries of the former Soviet Union and India embraced the international trading system, adding millions of workers each year to the pool of labour around the world producing tradeable, especially manufac-tured, goods. In China alone, over 70 million manufacturing jobs were created during the twenty-first century, far exceeding the 42 million working in manufacturing in 2012 in the United States and Europe combined.[17] The pool of labour supplying the world trading system more than trebled in size. Advanced economies benefited from an influx of cheap consumer goods at the expense of employment in the manufacturing sector.

The aim of the emerging economies was to follow Japan and Korea in pursuing an export-led growth strategy. To stimulate exports, their exchange rates were held down by fixing them at a low level against the US dollar. The strategy worked, especially in the case of China. Its share in world exports rose from 2 per cent to 12 per cent between 1990 and 2013.[18] China and other Asian economies ran large trade surpluses. In other words, they were producing more than they were spending and saving more than they were investing at home. The desire to save was very strong. In the absence of a social safety net, households in China chose to save large proportions of their income to provide self-insurance in the event of unemployment or ill-health, and to finance retirement consumption. Such a high level of saving was exacerbated by the policy from 1980 of limiting most families to one child, making it difficult for parents to rely on their children to provide for them in retirement.[19] Asian economies in general also saved more in order to accumulate large holdings of dollars as insurance in case their banking system ran short of foreign currency, as happened to Korea and other countries in the Asian financial crisis of the 1990s.

In most of the advanced economies of the West, it was the desire to spend that gained the upper hand, as reflected in falling saving rates. Napoleon may (or may not) have described England as a nation of shopkeepers, but it would be more accurate to say that it is a nation that keeps on shopping. Keen though western consumers were on spending, their appetite was not strong enough to offset the even greater wish of emerging economies to save. The consequence was that in the world economy as a whole there was an excess of saving, or in the vivid phrase of Ben Bernanke, Chairman of the Federal Reserve from 2006 to 2014, a 'savings glut' in the new expanded global capital market.[20]

This glut of saving pushed down long-term interest rates around the world. We think of interest rates as being determined by the Federal Reserve, the Bank of England, the European Central Bank (ECB) and other national central banks. That is certainly true for short-term interest rates, those applying to loans for a period of a month or less. Over slightly longer horizons, market interest rates are largely influenced by expectations about the likely actions of central banks. But over longer horizons still, such as a decade or more, interest rates are determined by the balance between spending and saving in the world as a whole, and central banks react to these developments when setting short-term official interest rates. Governments borrow by selling securities or bonds to the market with different periods of maturity, ranging from one month to thirty years or sometimes more. The interest rate at different maturities for such borrowing is known as the yield curve.

Another important distinction is between 'money' and 'real' interest rates. Money interest rates are the usual quoted rate – if you lend $100 and after one year receive $105, the money interest rate is 5 per cent. If over the course of that year the price of the things that you like to buy is expected to rise by 5 per cent, then the 'real' rate of interest you earn is the money rate less the anticipated rate of inflation (in this example the real rate is zero). In recent years, short-term real interest rates have actually been negative because official interest rates have been less than the rate of inflation. And the savings glut pushed down long-term real interest rates to unprecedentedly low levels.[21] In the nineteenth century and most of the twentieth, real rates were positive and moved within a range of 3 to 5 per cent. My estimate is that the average ten-year world real interest rate fell steadily from 4 per cent or so around the fall of the Berlin Wall to 1.5 per cent when the crisis hit, and has since fallen further to around zero.[22] As the Asian economies grew and grew, the volume of saving placed in the world capital market by their savers, including the Chinese government, rose and rose. So not only did those countries add millions of people to the pool of labour producing goods to be sold around the world, depressing real wages in other countries, they added billions of dollars to the pool of saving seeking an outlet, depressing real rates of interest in the global capital market.

Lower real interest rates and higher market prices for assets boosted investment. From the early 1990s onwards, as real interest rates were falling, it appeared profitable to invest in projects with increasingly low real rates of return. On my visits to different towns and cities across the United Kingdom I was continually surprised by the investment in new shopping centres, justified by low rates of interest and projections of unsustainable rates of growth of consumer spending.

For a decade or more after the fall of the Berlin Wall, the effects of the trade surpluses and capital movements seemed wholly benign. Emerging markets grew rapidly and their citizens' income levels started to converge on those of advanced economies. Consumers in advanced economies initially benefited from the lower prices of consumer goods that they imported from emerging economies. Confronted with persistent trade deficits thanks to this growth in imports, the United States, the United Kingdom and some other European countries relied on central banks to achieve steady growth and low inflation.[23] To achieve that, their central banks cut short-term interest rates to boost the growth of money, credit and domestic demand in order to offset the drag on total demand from the trade deficit. So interest rates, both short-term and long-term, were at all-time lows. Such low interest rates, across all maturities, encouraged spending and led it along unsustainable paths in many, if not most, economies.[24] With high levels of saving in Asia and rising debt in the West, saving and investment in a number of large countries, and in the world economy as a whole, got out of kilter and produced a major macroeconomic imbalance or disequilibrium. What started as an imbalance between countries became a disequilibrium within economies.

When the world economy is functioning well, capital normally flows from mature to developing economies where profitable opportunities abound, as happened in the late nineteenth century when Europe invested in Latin America. A strange feature of the savings glut was that because emerging economies were saving more than they were investing at home, they were actually exporting capital to advanced economies where investment opportunities were more limited. In effect, advanced economies were borrowing large sums from the less developed world. The natural direction of capital flows was reversed – capital was being pushed 'uphill'.[25]

Much of those capital flows passed through the western banking system, and this led to the second key development before the crisis – the rapid expansion of bank balance sheets, or in the phrase of Hyun Song Shin, Chief Economist at the Bank for International Settlements, a 'banking glut'.[26] A bank's balance sheet is a list of all the bank's assets and all its liabilities. The former are the value of the loans it has made to customers and other investments. The latter is the value of the deposits and other borrowing that the bank has taken in to finance its operations. The difference between the assets and liabilities to others is the bank's net worth and is the value of the bank to its owners – the shareholders. As western banks extended loans to households and companies, particularly on property, their balance sheets – both assets and liabilities – expanded rapidly.

Bank balance sheets exploded for two reasons. First, low real interest rates meant that asset prices rose around the world. The rise in asset prices induced a corresponding and rational rise in debt levels. Housing provides a good example. The housing stock gradually passes down the generations from old to young. As houses are sold, the older generation invests the proceeds in other financial assets and the younger generation borrows in order to buy the same houses. When house prices rise sharply following a fall in real interest rates, the young have to borrow more than their parents did. The young end up with more debt and the old with more financial assets. The household sector as a whole has a higher ratio of both debt and assets to income. During the Great Stability, banks financed much of the higher borrowing by the young as housing was transferred down the generations, and the balance sheets of banks expanded rapidly.

There was nothing irrational in this – *provided* the belief that real interest rates would stay at that new lower level was itself rational. The market clearly thought it was, and still does. In mid-2015 the ten-year real rate in the industrialised world was close to zero.

There was, however, a second and less benign reason behind the expansion of bank balance sheets. With interest rates so low, financial institutions and investors started to take on more and more risk, in an increasingly desperate hunt for higher returns, without adequate compensation. Investors were slow to adjust and reluctant to accept that, in a world of low interest rates and low inflation, returns on financial assets would also be at historically low levels. Greed and hubris also led them to demand higher returns – such behaviour became known as the 'search for yield'. Central banks warned about the consequences of low interest rates, but by allowing the amount of money in the economy to expand rapidly did little to prevent the search for yield and increased risk-taking.[27] In addition, financial institutions, such as pension funds and insurance companies, were coming under pressure to find ways of making their savings products more attractive and reduce the rising cost of pension provision in the face of falling real interest rates.

Banks played their part in meeting this search for yield. They created a superstructure of ever more complex financial instruments, which were combinations of, and so derived from, more basic contracts such as mortgages and other types of debt – hence their name 'derivatives'. To increase their yield, banks created instruments that comprised highly risky and often opaque structures with obscure names such as 'collateralised debt obligations'. The average rate of return on a risky asset is higher than that on a safe asset, such as a US or UK government bond, to compensate the investor for the additional risk – the additional return is called the risk premium. Although some of the deals offered to investors were close to being fraudulent, the desire for higher returns meant there was no shortage of willing buyers. Only an optimist could believe that the risk premium in the market was adequate to compensate for the risk involved. It was all too close to alchemy.

Both the complexity and the size of financial assets increased markedly. The total assets of US banks, which for a long time had been around one-quarter of annual gross domestic product (GDP, the total value of goods and services produced in the economy), amounted to close to 100 per cent of GDP by the time of the crisis. In Britain, as the main financial centre in Europe, bank assets exceeded 500 per cent of GDP, and they were even larger in Ireland, Switzerland and Iceland. Bank leverage rose to astronomical levels – in some cases to more than 50 to 1; that is, the bank borrowed more than $50 for each dollar of capital provided by its shareholders. The banking system had become extremely fragile. Regulators took an unduly benign view of the expansion of the banking sector because while real interest rates continued to fall, asset prices rose and investors, including banks, made substantial profits. The political climate supported the development of large and highly leveraged global banks, and regulators were under pressure not to impede the expansion of the sector.

The 'savings glut' and the 'banking glut' combined to produce a toxic mix of a serious disequilibrium in the world economy, on the one hand, and an explosion of bank balance sheets, on the other. It was the interaction between the two that made the crisis so severe. Superficially, the position beforehand seemed sustainable. Trade deficits were a fairly stable share of GDP. But the scale of the borrowing meant that the stock of debt – both external and internal – relative to incomes and GDP kept on rising. Domestic spending in countries whose trade balance was in deficit was deliberately boosted to a level that could not be sustained in the long run. Low interest rates were encouraging households to bring forward spending from the future to the present. That, too, could not continue indefinitely – and it didn't. Sooner or later an adjustment was going to be necessary. And the longer it was delayed, the bigger the adjustment would be.

Which would crack first – the confidence of investors in the soundness of the banks, or the continuation of spending on an unsustainable path? Most policy-makers believed that the unsustainable pattern of spending and saving, and the mirror image pattern of external surpluses and deficits, would end with a collapse of the US dollar, as lenders started to doubt the ability of the United States, the United Kingdom and other borrowers to repay. But the political commitment of emerging economies to their export-led growth strategy was extremely strong. And the US dollar – as the world's reserve currency – was a currency in which China, and other emerging markets, were happy to invest, not least because its own currency, the renminbi, was not convertible into other currencies. There seemed no limit to China's willingness to accumulate US dollars. And that has continued unabated – by the end of 2014, China's foreign exchange reserves exceeded $4 trillion.[28] So the dollar remained strong and it was the fragility of bank balance sheets that first revealed the fault lines.

Behind the scenes, the stocks of credits and debits were building in an unsustainable way, like piles of bricks. It is always surprising how many bricks can be piled one on top of another without their collapsing. This truth is embodied in the first law of financial crises: an unsustainable position can continue for far longer than you would believe possible.[29] That was true for the duration of the Great Stability. What happened in 2008 illustrated the second law of financial crises: when an unsustainable position ends it happens faster than you could imagine.

The 'small' event that precipitated the collapse of the pile of bricks occurred on 9 August 2007 when the French bank BNP Paribas announced that it was stopping, temporarily, further redemptions (that is, investors could no longer ask for their money back) from three of its funds that were invested in so-called asset-backed securities (financial instruments that were claims on underlying obligations, such as mortgage payments), citing 'the complete evaporation of liquidity in certain segments of the US securitization market'.[30] Before long, market liquidity in a much wider range of financial instruments dried up. Attention was focused on risky, irresponsible – and even illegal – mortgage lending in the United States. But the underlying financial problem was the vulnerability of the banking system to US sub-prime mortgages – loans to households on low incomes who were highly likely to default.

At the beginning of September, central bank governors from around the world congregated in Basel at their regular bimonthly meeting. Although young wire service reporters hang around outside waiting for an unwary or publicity-seeking governor to confide his or her thoughts, the meetings themselves are always strictly private. A practice had grown up whereby the heads of the bank regulators from around the world met with central bank governors each September. In 2007 the bank regulators were asked whether the US sub-prime mortgage market was sufficiently large to bring down major banks. The answer was an emphatic no. Although the stock of such mortgages was around $1 trillion, potential losses were not large enough to create a problem for the system as a whole. After all, the loss of wealth in the dotcom crash earlier in the decade had been eight times greater.

This time, however, banks had made large bets on the sub-prime market in the form of derivative contracts. Although these bets cancelled each other out for the banking system as a whole, some banks were in the money and others were under water. The problem was that it was impossible for investors, and in some cases even for the banks themselves, to tell one from the other. So all banks came under suspicion. Banks found it difficult, and at times impossible, to raise money that only weeks earlier had been easily available. They stopped lending to each other. LIBOR (the London Inter-Bank Offer Rate) was supposed to be the quoted interest rate at which banks said they could borrow from each other. It became the interest rate at which banks didn't lend to each other.

From the start of the crisis, central banks provided emergency loans, but these amounted to little more than holding a sheet in front of the Emperor – in this case the banking system – to conceal his nakedness. It didn't solve the underlying problem – banks needed not loans but injections of shareholders' capital in order to be able to reduce their extraordinarily high levels of leverage and to absorb losses from the risky investments they had made. From the beginning of 2008, we at the Bank of England began to argue that banks needed extra capital, a lot of extra capital, possibly a hundred billion pounds or more. It wasn't a popular message. There was a deep reluctance in the banking community to admit that leverage was unsustainably high and therefore banks needed either to be recapitalised or to drastically reduce their lending. For the economy as a whole, the former was obviously preferable to the latter.

The system staggered on for a year. Market confidence in banks ebbed and flowed. But on 15 September the long-established investment bank Lehman Brothers failed – its large losses on real-estate lending combined with very high leverage prompted a loss of confidence among the financial institutions that provided it with access to cash. Although hardly surprising given the growing appreciation of the system's underlying fragility over the previous twelve months, the failure of Lehman

Brothers was such a jolt to market sentiment that a run on the US banking system took off at extraordinary speed. The runners were not ordinary depositors but wholesale financial institutions, such as money market funds. The run soon spread to other advanced economies – and so the Great Panic began. Already extremely chilly, the financial waters froze solid. Banks around the world found it impossible to finance themselves because no one knew which banks were safe and which weren't. It was the biggest global financial crisis in history.

Where banks could still borrow, it was only at a very high premium to official rates. Some banks in Europe, which had borrowed large sums at short maturities in US wholesale markets, found that instead of being able to borrow for three months, they could do so only for one month. Then only for a week. And then only for a day. Banks depend on the confidence of their depositors and others who lend to them, and they had lost it. In early October 2008, two UK banks – Royal Bank of Scotland (RBS) and Halifax Bank of Scotland (HBoS) – found themselves unable to get to the end of the day. The Bank of England lent £60 billion to the two banks to avoid a collapse of the banking system.[31] I can still hear the disbelief in the voice of Fred Goodwin, the CEO of the Royal Bank of Scotland, as he explained to me in early October 2008 what was happening to his bank. And Goodwin wasn't the only one to be taken aback. Other central banks took similar action with their own banks.

The Great Panic lasted less than a month from the failure of Lehman Brothers to the announcement of the recapitalisation of the banks – twenty-eight days that shook the world. In October 2008, the finance ministers and governors of the G7 group of seven major industrialised countries (the US, UK, Japan, Canada, France, Germany and Italy) met in Washington DC amid the chaos and fear that followed the failure of Lehman. At that meeting I suggested to Hank Paulson, the US Treasury

Secretary at the time, that we tear up the standard (and rather lengthy) communiqué drafted overnight by the G7 deputies and replace it with a short, succinct statement of solidarity and intent to work together.[32] To his great credit, Paulson took up the idea and the statement was a turning point in the handling of the crisis. At last, there was an acceptance among governments, and among at least some banks, that the crisis reflected not just a shortage of liquidity but a much deeper problem of insufficient capital.

When the western banking system teetered on the verge of collapse, only drastic intervention, including partial nationalisation, saved it from going over the edge. The potential catastrophe of a collapse finally provoked action to recapitalise the banking system, using public money if necessary; the UK was first to respond, followed by the United States and then continental Europe. That action ended the bank run. The problem was that governments ended up guaranteeing all private creditors of the banks, imposing on future taxpayers a burden of unknown magnitude.

Between the autumn of 2008 and the summer of 2009, there was a collapse of confidence and output around the world. World trade fell more rapidly than during the Great Depression of the 1930s. Around ten million jobs were lost in the United States and Europe, almost as many as were employed in US manufacturing prior to the crisis. The period became known as the Great Recession. The economic consequences were seen well beyond countries that had experienced a banking crisis. My opposite numbers in Brazil and India, for example, talked to me about the puzzle of why demand for cars and steel in their countries had 'fallen off a cliff'. For almost a year, the collapse in confidence was global. It seemed that, just as in the 1930s, much of what we had to fear was fear itself. Spending had fallen around the world because people feared that others would no longer go on spending. The situation cried out for a Keynesian policy response in the form of monetary and fiscal stimulus. Central banks and governments duly supplied it, and the policy was endorsed by the summit of the Group of Twenty (G20), which included both industrialised and emerging market economies, in London in May 2009.

The banking crisis itself could be said to have ended when the US Treasury and Federal Reserve announced on 7 May 2009 the results of the stress tests carried out on US banks to see if they were capable of withstanding the losses incurred under a range of adverse scenarios and the amount of new capital which those banks would be required to raise in the market or accept from the US government – $75 billion in total. By the summer of 2009, emerging market economies were starting to recover. But although the banking crisis had ended, the problems of the global economy remained. The shock of the events of 2008, and the subsequent sharp downturn, made western households and businesses reluctant to spend and banks unwilling to lend. Uncertainty prevailed. By 2015 there had still been no return to the growth and confidence experienced during the Great Stability.

This account captures, I believe, the essence of what happened in the run-up to and during the crisis of 2007–9, a journey from the Great Stability through the Great Panic to the Great Recession, but not yet to the Great Recovery. Much of my explanation has appeared in one or other previous account, with widely varying degrees of emphasis, and has become conventional wisdom. But it leaves some big unanswered questions.

Three questions

First, why did all the players involved – governments, central banks, commercial banks, companies, borrowers and lenders – take no action to change direction while steaming ahead on a course destined to lead to serious problems and a major adjustment of the world economy? The three experiments on which the West had embarked were all beginning to fail, and their outcomes – the Good, the Bad and the Ugly – were becoming evident. Of course, big shocks to financial markets, such as a sharp fall in share prices or the failure of a bank, always come as a surprise. Some events are unpredictable, at least in their timing. But the economic path on which the world economy was proceeding was clearly unsustainable. Why was there such inertia before the crisis, and why were concerns about macroeconomic unsustainability not translated into actions by regulators and policy-makers?

Second, why has so little been done to change the underlying factors that can be seen as the causes of the crisis? The alchemy of our present system of money and banking continues. The strange thing is that after arguably the biggest financial crisis in history, nothing much has really changed in terms either of the fundamental structure of banking or the reliance on central banks to restore macroeconomic prosperity. Real interest rates have fallen further. Capital has continued to flow 'uphill'. Industrialised economies have struggled to recover. Output, even if growing slowly, is well below the pre-crisis path. Real wages have continued to stagnate. The same banks dominate Main Street and the high streets of our towns.

There has certainly been a vast effort to change the regulation of banks – in the United States with the Dodd-Frank Wall Street Reform and Consumer Protection Act of 2010, in the United Kingdom with the Banking Act of 2009 and Banking Reform Act of 2013, in Europe with a move towards a common regulatory system in the European Union, and internationally through changes in the way banks are required to finance themselves.[33] These initiatives have made banks more resilient by reducing their leverage and limiting their ability to put highly risky assets on the same balance sheet as deposits from households. But they have not changed the fundamental structure of banking.

The banking and financial crisis of 1931, and the resulting Great Depression, had a dramatic effect on politics and economics at the time and in many ways shaped the intellectual climate of the post-war period. The response to the recent crisis has so far been much more muted. Of course, the immediate impact on many people was dampened by the response of policy-makers, who threw the monetary kitchen sink at the economy to restore demand and output. But as the impact of such policies peters out, and the underlying problems are seen to remain, anger is growing. To many citizens of advanced economies, the recent financial crisis came out of a clear blue sky. For a generation, they had adapted to the discipline of a market economy by accepting reforms to labour markets and, in Europe, the privatisation of ossified state industries, accompanied by the promise of rising productivity and prosperity. Businesses with products that attracted few customers accepted that they should not be supported by the state, and either adapted or closed. Employees accepted that wages might need to fall if conditions deteriorated in the company for which they worked, and the choice would be either lower wages or less employment. And the market economy delivered, as we seemed to reach the Holy Grail of steady economic growth and low inflation. Then came the collapse and the taxpayer bailouts of the very institutions most prominent in advocating market discipline for others – the banks. Why then, in sharp contrast to the 1930s, was there so little enthusiasm for radical reform to our economic system and institutions?

Third, why has weak demand become a deep-seated problem, and one that appears immune to further monetary stimulus? The crisis was not so much a financial earthquake, releasing pressure that had been building up, as a sudden shift to a lower path for demand and output than had seemed normal only a short time earlier, and one that threatens to persist indefinitely. Between the Second World War and 2008, the path of GDP per person in the US and UK fluctuated around a trend growth rate of about 2 per cent a year, with frequent but temporary deviations from that path. Since the crisis, there has been a sharp deviation of output from the previous trend path, such that output is now around 15 per cent below the level that seemed attainable only a few years ago. That gap amounts to around $8500 per person in the US and £4000 per person in the UK – a huge and continuing loss of output.[34] Why have the economic prospects for our grandchildren suddenly deteriorated? When will we see the Great Recovery and what needs to be done to achieve it?

To answer those three questions means going behind and beyond the story of the crisis as told above. It requires a much closer look at the structure of money and banking that we have inherited from the past and at the nature of the disequilibrium in the world economy today. By the end of this book I hope to have suggested some answers.

A capitalist economy is inherently a monetary economy, and, as we shall see, a monetary economy behaves very differently from the textbook description of a market economy, in which households and businesses produce and trade with each other. The reasons for the divergence between the nature of a monetary economy and the textbook model are profound. They derive from the limitations on economic transactions created by radical uncertainty. In practice, buyers and sellers simply cannot write contracts to cover every eventuality, and money and banks evolved as a way of trying to cope with radical uncertainty. Our inability to anticipate all possible eventualities means that we – households, businesses, banks, central banks and governments – will make judgements that turn out to have been 'mistakes'. Those mistakes lie at the heart of any story about financial crises.

Disequilibrium in the world economy

No country is finding it easy to escape from the devastation that followed the collapse of the banking system in the western world in 2008. From 2000 to 2007 the advanced economies grew at an annual average rate of 2.7 per cent. From 2010 to 2014, when those economies should have been rebounding with rapid growth after the sharp fall in output in late 2008 and 2009, GDP rose at an average rate of only 1.8 per cent a year.[35] How can the world economy escape from the comparative stagnation into which it has fallen, despite sharply lower oil prices, since those dramatic days in the autumn of 2008 when central banks stepped in to prevent a complete collapse of the banking system?

After the banking crisis ended in May 2009, confidence in the US banking system was restored. Output started to recover in the emerging economies, and, with the benefit of hindsight, we can see that the falls in output in many of the advanced economies came to an end. A recovery – of sorts – began. Six years later, however, in the middle of 2015, we were still searching for a sustainable recovery despite cuts in interest rates and the printing of electronic money by central banks on an unprecedented scale. Output has started to grow, but only with the support of the prospect of extraordinarily low interest rates for a very long period. Recovery in the United States and United Kingdom has ebbed and flowed, Japan is struggling and the euro area is relying on the stimulus from a lower exchange rate. Growth in China has been slowing for a number of years and its financial system is in trouble. Central banks have thrown everything at their economies, and yet the results have been disappointing. Most sharp economic downturns are followed by sharp recoveries – and the sharper the downturn, the more rapid the recovery. Not this time. So why, after the biggest monetary stimulus the world has ever seen, and six years after the end of the banking crisis, is the world recovery so slow?

Some economists believe that we are experiencing what they call 'secular stagnation', a phrase coined by the American economist Alvin Hansen in his 1938 book *Full Recovery or Stagnation?*[36] Today's American economists, such as Ben Bernanke, Paul Krugman, Kenneth Rogoff and Larry Summers, have been using the more modern literary form of blogging to debate the issue. But it is not exactly clear what they mean by secular stagnation. Does it refer to stagnation of supply or of demand, or indeed both? Growth today seems possible only if interest rates are much lower than normal – at present the long-term real rate of interest is close to zero. The 'natural' real rate is the real rate of interest that generates a level of total spending sufficient to ensure full employment. When asked why demand is weak, economists tend to answer that it is because the natural real rate of interest is negative – in other words, people will spend only when faced with negative real interest rates. And when asked why that is, they reply that it is because demand is insufficient to maintain full employment. The reasoning is circular. Simply restating the phenomenon of secular stagnation in different words and pretending to have offered an explanation does not amount to a theory. Secular stagnation is an important description of the problems afflicting the world economy, but we need a new theory, or narrative, to explain why global demand is so weak and real interest rates are so low.

The conventional analysis used by economists and central

banks is based on the assumption that the economy grows along a steady path from which it occasionally deviates as a result of temporary shocks to demand or supply. Such shocks are called 'headwinds' if negative or 'tailwinds' if positive. Output will return to its full-employment level once the temporary shocks have abated. The role of both monetary policy (interest rates and money supply) and fiscal policy (government spending and taxation) is to speed up the return to the underlying path of steady growth. Applied to current circumstances, the conventional view is that the major economies, such as the United States and the United Kingdom, have been held back by 'headwinds' to which the kind of stimulus to total spending proposed by Keynesians is the right answer until the headwinds in due course abate of their own accord. The statements of the Federal Reserve in recent years are a good example of this viewpoint.

During the Great Stability, this framework seemed adequate to capture the challenges facing policy-makers. But as it became evident, at least to some, that patterns of spending were unsustainable, the inadequacies of the model were revealed, albeit ignored by many policy-makers. What mattered was not just total spending but how it was divided between different types of demand. The factors holding back demand are not just temporary phenomena that will disappear of their own accord but the result of a gradual build-up of a disequilibrium in spending and saving, both within and between countries, which must be corrected before we can return to a strong and sustainable recovery. From its origins in an imbalance between high- and low-saving countries, the disequilibrium has morphed into an internal imbalance of even greater significance between saving and spending within economies. Desired spending is too low to absorb the capacity of our economies to produce goods and services. The result is weak growth and high unemployment (the euro area), falls in productivity growth (US and UK) and potentially large trade surpluses at full employment (Germany, Japan and China). Policy faces much bigger challenges than responding to temporary shocks to demand; it must move the economy to a new equilibrium.

Since the early 1990s, long-term real interest rates have fallen sharply, and this has had enormous implications for all our economies, as described above. Countries such as the United States, United Kingdom and some others in Europe, were faced with what were in effect structural trade deficits. Those deficits – an excess of imports over exports – amounted to a continuing negative drag on demand. So in order to ensure that total demand – domestic demand minus the trade deficit – matched the capacity of their economies to produce, central banks in the deficit countries cut their official interest rates in order to boost domestic demand. That created an imbalance *within* those countries with spending too high relative to current and prospective incomes. In countries with trade surpluses, such as China and Germany, spending was too low relative to likely future incomes. And the imbalance *between* countries – large trade surpluses and deficits – continued.

All this reinforced the determination of central banks to maintain extraordinarily low interest rates. Monetary stimulus via low interest rates works largely by giving incentives to bring forward spending from the future to the present. But this is a short-term effect. After a time, tomorrow becomes today. Then we have to repeat the exercise and bring forward spending from the new tomorrow to the new today. As time passes, we will be digging larger and larger holes in future demand. The result is a self-reinforcing path of weak growth in the economy. What started as an international savings glut has become a major disequilibrium in the world economy. This creates an enormous challenge for monetary policy. Central banks are, in effect, like cyclists pedalling up an ever steeper hill. They have to inject more and more monetary stimulus in order to maintain the same rate of growth of aggregate spending. This problem was building up well before the crisis, and was evident even in the 1990s. It led to a lopsided growth of demand. Rightly or wrongly, central banks took the view that two-speed growth was better than no growth.

Before the crisis, many thought that the Great Stability could continue indefinitely and failed to comprehend that it could not. Their credulity was understandable. After all, GDP as a whole was evolving on a steady path, with growth around historical average rates, and low and stable inflation. But the imbalance in the pattern of spending and saving was far from sustainable, and was leading to the build-up of large stocks of debts. Bad investments were made, encouraged by low real interest rates. The crisis revealed that much of that misplaced investment – residential housing in the United States, Ireland and Spain; commercial property in Britain – was unprofitable, producing losses for borrowers and lenders alike. The impact of the crisis was to make debtors and creditors – households, companies and governments – uncomfortably aware that their previous spending paths had been based on unrealistic assessments of future long-term incomes. So they reduced spending. And central banks then had to cut interest rates yet again to bring more spending forward from the future to the present, and to create more money by purchasing large quantities of assets from the private sector – the practice known as unconventional monetary policy or quantitative easing (QE). There is in fact nothing unconventional about such a practice – as I will explain in Chapter 5, so-called QE was long regarded as a standard tool of monetary policy – but the scale on which it has been implemented is unprecedented. Even so, it has become more and more difficult to persuade households and businesses to bring spending forward once again from an ever bleaker future. After a point, monetary policy confronts diminishing returns. We have reached that point.

The 'headwinds' that the major economies are facing today are not the result of a temporary downward shock to aggregate demand, but of an underlying weakness caused by the earlier bringing forward of spending. Stagnation has resulted from the realisation that domestic spending before the crisis was too high. The focus on short-term stimulus creates a 'paradox of policy'.[37] The policies of Keynesian monetary and fiscal stimulus adopted in the short run in 2008–9 – to encourage consumer spending and borrowing – were necessary then to deal with a dramatic collapse of confidence in the autumn of 2008. The move to inject substantial additional money into the economy was vital to prevent a downward spiral of falling demand and output. It worked. There was no repetition of the Great Depression. The supply of money did not collapse as it had in the United States in the 1930s. But those measures were the absolute opposite of what we needed to do – encourage saving and exports – to correct the underlying disequilibrium. The fact that the recovery is far weaker than we expected, even with the extraordinary monetary stimulus that we have in fact put in place, suggests that something is amiss. We need to tackle the underlying disequilibrium. Easy monetary policy is necessary but it is not sufficient for a sustained recovery. Interest rates today are too high to permit rapid growth of demand in the short run, but too low to be consistent with a proper balance between spending and saving in the long run.

Parallel to these internal imbalances between spending and saving within major economies are the external imbalances between countries. These, too, have not yet been resolved. The sharp fall in demand and output across the world in 2008–9 certainly lowered actual external surpluses and deficits. But surpluses and deficits will re-emerge if countries return to full employment. China's surplus and America's deficit are widening again. Most acute, of course, is the position in the euro area. Germany's trade surplus is now approaching 8 per cent of GDP, and that of the Netherlands is even higher. Those surpluses and the deficits in the periphery countries (the southern members of the euro area with high unemployment) are both consequences of monetary union in Europe.

Correcting the internal and external imbalances will be a long process – the Great Unwinding. It will require many policy changes. The failure to recognise the need for a real adjustment in most major economies, and the continued reliance on monetary policy as the 'only game in town', constitute an error as much of theory as of practice, and are the cause of weak growth today. The underlying problem today is that past mistakes – too much consumption in some countries and too little in others; misdirected investment in most – mean that households have lowered their desired level of consumer spending and businesses are not yet confident that a rebalancing of our economies justifies significant new investment. Low interest rates cannot correct the disequilibrium in the pattern of demand. We are seeing a slow recovery not because the economy is battling temporary headwinds, but as the consequence of a more deep-seated problem.

Although we cannot foresee the future, we can study the past. Recent events, vivid though they are in the memories of participants and spectators alike, are only one episode among the many crises in the history of capitalism. The events of previous crises are an invaluable test bed for new ideas, and I shall refer to several of them in subsequent chapters. An unpredictable future means that there will always be ups and downs in a capitalist economy. But are full-blown crises inevitable? Are they the by-product of the processes that generate economic growth? There are no simple answers to these questions. But they are questions worth asking. Although my Chinese friend was absolutely right in saying that the West had worked out how to use a market economy, with free competition and trade, to raise productivity and standards of living, he was also right to point to our failings in managing money and banking. Such was our obsession with money, and the absurdly high pedestal on which we placed money-men, that we failed to see some of the weaknesses of the system. It would be irresponsible if, through intellectual complacency, we failed to analyse thoroughly the lessons of this and earlier crises, to distinguish between symptoms and causes, and to redesign our institutions to prevent a future generation from suffering in the way that so many are today.

The central idea in this book is that money and banking are particular historical institutions that developed before modern capitalism, and owe a great deal to the technology of earlier times. They permitted the development of a market economy and promised financial alchemy. But in the end it was that financial alchemy that led to their downfall. Money and banking proved to be not a form of alchemy, but the Achilles heel of capitalism – a point of weakness that threatens havoc on a scale that drains the life out of a capitalist economy. Since, however, they are man-made institutions, men – and women – can remake them. To do that we must first analyse how money and banking work today.

2

GOOD AND EVIL:
IN MONEY WE TRUST

'The love of money is the root of all evil.'

1 Timothy, 6:10 (King James Bible)

'Evil is the root of all money.'

Kiyotaki and Moore (2002)

In the United States I studied at Harvard as a Kennedy Scholar.[1] Later in life, I was a member of the interviewing panel to select new scholars. One young man, who was studying theology at Oxford, entered the room and, obviously a little nervous, sat on the chair in front of a line of eminent figures. The chairman, a distinguished philosopher, started by asking, 'Tell me, does God have much of a role in theology these days?' The young man blinked and never recovered. But it made me think that the question one should ask of economists is, 'Does money have much of a role in economics these days?'

Money is misunderstood because it is so familiar, although not as familiar as many of us might wish. Its function in a capitalist economy is complex, and economists have struggled to understand it. It is not even easy to define because the word is used to mean different things: the notes and coins in our wallets, the value of our total wealth, sometimes even the power that wealth confers, as in 'money talks'. Whatever it is, we seem to be in thrall to it. In his Epistle to Timothy, quoted above, St Paul put it more bluntly.

The management of money, in rich and poor countries alike, has been dismal. Governments and central banks may talk about price stability, but they have rarely achieved it. During the 1970s, prices doubled in the United States in ten years and in Britain they doubled in five years. In November 1923, prices in Germany doubled in less than four days and GDP fell by over 15 per cent during the year.[2] That experience helped to undermine the Weimar Republic and contributed to the rise of Nazi totalitarianism.[3] In the film *Cabaret*, set in Berlin in the 1930s, the MC at the Kit Kat Klub performs a song entitled 'Money', which includes the lines:

> A mark, a yen, a buck, or a pound
> Is all that makes the world go around.

Yet in recent years, with central banks printing money like never before (albeit electronically rather than by churning out notes) and a world recovery still elusive, you could be forgiven for thinking that money *doesn't* make the world go round. So what does money do? Why do we need it? And could it eventually disappear?

As Governor of the Bank of England, I would sometimes

visit schools to explain money, especially to the younger pupils. Bemused by the fact that I was actually paid for 'hanging out with my friends' (the only answer I could come up with to their question 'What is a meeting?'), they were nonetheless certain about the value of money. I would hold up a £5 note and ask them what it was. 'Money,' they would scream. 'Surely it's just a piece of paper,' I would reply, and make as if to tear it in two. 'No, you mustn't,' they gasped, as I hesitated and asked them what the difference was between a piece of paper and the paper note in my hand. 'Because you can buy stuff with it,' they explained loudly. And so we went on to discuss the importance of making sure that the amount of stuff you could buy with my note didn't change drastically from one year to the next. They all got the idea that low and stable inflation was a good thing, and that whatever form money takes, it must satisfy two criteria. The first is that money must be accepted by anyone from whom one might wish to buy 'stuff' (the criterion of acceptability). The second is that there is a reasonable degree of predictability as to its value in a future transaction (the criterion of stability).

Most 'stuff' is today bought not with notes and coins, but with cheques, debit and credit cards, and by electronic transfers drawn on interest-bearing bank deposits. Economists have long debated how to measure the amount of money in the economy. But since what is accepted as money changes over time with both technology and economic circumstances, the quest for a precise definition has little point. Some people prefer a narrow definition in which money comprises the notes and deposits issued only by the central bank or government. Others prefer a broad definition that includes deposits issued by private banks and accepted in transactions. Yet others would include unused overdraft facilities that can be spent at the borrower's wish.[4] In normal circumstances the amount of money available for the financing of transactions is better captured by a broad measure, although in a banking crisis, as we shall see, a narrower definition may be more appropriate.

When money satisfies the two criteria of acceptability and stability it can be used as a measuring rod for the value of spending, production and wealth. After the Normans conquered Britain in 1066, they put together an inventory of wealth – houses, cattle and agricultural land – in order to assess the taxable capacity of their new domain. Known as the Domesday Book, the survey (now available online) measured wealth in terms of pounds, shillings and pence, Anglo-Saxon monetary units still in use in my youth before the decimalisation of Britain's currency in 1971.[5]

The view that money is primarily an acceptable medium of exchange – a way to buy stuff – underpins the traditional interpretation of the history of money. Specialisation created the need for people to exchange their own production for that of others. Adam Smith's division of labour did not start with his pin factory. It is as old as the hills, almost literally, with the early specialisation between hunters and cultivators, and the development of a bewildering variety of crafts and skills from early civilisation onwards. Smith described how 'in a nation of hunters, if anyone has a talent for making bows and arrows better than his neighbours he will at first make presents of them, and in return get presents of their game'.[6] A man who spends all day making arrows in order to swap them for meat gives up the possibility of hunting himself for the chance of sharing in a larger catch. To be willing to specialise, the hunter who turns arrow-maker has to be sure that his partner in trade will deliver the 'present' of meat.

Smith explained that 'when the division of labour first began to take place, this power of exchanging must frequently have been very much clogged and embarrassed in its operations.'[7] He was referring to the absence of what economists call a 'double coincidence of wants': the hunter wants arrows and the arrow-maker wants meat. Without that double coincidence, exchange cannot take place through barter. If the arrow-maker wants corn, and the farmer who grows the corn wants meat, then only a sequence of bilateral transactions will satisfy their wants. Since the transactions are separated in time, and probably space, some medium of exchange – money – enters the picture to allow people to engage in their desired trades.

The history of money is, in this view, the story of how we evolved as social animals, trading with each other. It starts with the use as money of commodities – grain and cattle in Egypt and Mesopotamia as early as 9000 BC. Many other commodities, ranging from cowrie shells in Asia to salt in Africa, were deployed as money. It is, of course, costly to hold stocks of commodities with a useful value; salt kept as money cannot be used to preserve meat. Nevertheless, commodities continued to function as money until relatively modern times. Adam Smith wrote about how commodities like 'dried cod at Newfoundland; tobacco in Virginia; sugar in some of our West India colonies' had been used as money and how there was even 'a village in Scotland where it is not uncommon . . . for a workman to carry nails instead of money to the baker's shop or the alehouse'.[8] Commodities that had an intrinsic value were used in communities where trust, either in others or in a social convention such as a monetary token, was limited. In the early days of the penal colony of New South Wales, managed by the British Navy, rum was commonly in use as money, and, during the Second World War, cigarettes were used as money in prisoner-of-war camps.

The cost and inconvenience of using such commodities led to the emergence of precious metals as the dominant form of money. Metals were first used in transactions in ancient

Mesopotamia and Egypt, while metal coins originated in China and the Middle East and were in use no later than the fourth century BC. By 250 BC, standardised coins minted from gold, silver and bronze were widespread throughout the Mediterranean world.

Governments played an important role in regulating the size and weight of coins. Minted by the authorities, and carrying an emblem denoting official authorisation, coins were by far the most convenient form of money. Officially minted coins were supposed to overcome the problem of counterfeits and of the need to weigh precious metals before they could be used in a transaction – the need to protect the physical object used as money has always been essential to its acceptability. Adam Smith's close friend, the chemist Joseph Black, said that while teaching at the University of Edinburgh, where students paid the professors in advance, he was 'obliged to weigh [coins] when strange students come, there being a very large number who bring light guineas, so that I should be defrauded of many pounds every year if I did not act in self-defence against this class of students'.[9] Counterfeiting continues today – indeed, coins are counterfeited more often than banknotes.

The use of standardised coinage was a big step forward. Technology, however, did not stand still. As the English economist David Ricardo wrote in 1816:

The introduction of the precious metals for the purposes of money may with truth be considered as one of the most important steps towards the improvement of commerce, and the arts of civilised life; but it is no less true that, with the advancement of knowledge and science, we discover that it would be another improvement to banish them again from the employment, to which, during a less enlightened period, they had been so advantageously applied.[10]

The drawback of using precious metals as money had been evident since at least the sixteenth century when the first European voyages across the Atlantic led to the discovery of gold and, especially, silver mines in the Americas. The resulting imports of the two metals into Europe produced a dramatic fall in their prices – by around two-thirds. So in terms of gold and silver, the prices of commodities and goods rose sharply. This was the first truly European Great Inflation. Prices increased by a factor of six or so over the sixteenth century as a whole. That experience demonstrated vividly that, whatever form money took, abrupt changes in its supply could undermine the stability of its value.

Even more convenient than coin is, of course, paper money, which has for a long time dominated our monetary system. The earliest banknotes appeared in China in the seventh century AD. Later banknotes from the Ming dynasty in China were made from the bark of mulberry trees – the paper is still soft to the touch today.[11] The penalty for counterfeiting was death – as advertised on the notes themselves.[12] If not backed by gold or some other commodity, paper money is what is known as a pure 'fiat currency' – it has no intrinsic value and, crucially, cannot be exchanged for gold or any other valuable commodity at the central bank. It is useful only insofar as other people accept it at face value in exchange for goods and services, and its value depends upon the trust people have in it. The earliest western experiment with paper money was conducted in the United States – not the new post-revolutionary nation, but the pre-revolutionary colonies on the eastern seaboard. Before American independence, the creation of money was the prerogative of the British government. Thus prevented from minting their own coins, the colonists rightly complained of a lack of money to support commerce.[13] Whatever gold and silver existed in the colonies (sadly there were no gold or silver mines to provide a new supply) rapidly flowed out to pay for a regular excess of imports over exports to England, which resulted from trade restrictions imposed by the mother country. As a consequence, barter systems and commodity monies, such as tobacco, became the main method of exchange in the colonial economies. Students at Harvard College met their bills by paying in 'produce, livestock and pickled meat'.[14] There was a strong incentive to find a way to create a new form of money. In 1690, Massachusetts started to issue paper money and other colonial governments followed. In part the paper money thereby created was backed by explicit promises to redeem the notes in gold or silver at specified future dates, but partly it was a pure fiat currency.[15] This was a monetary experiment on a grand scale. As that great man Benjamin Franklin wrote in 1767:

> Where the Sums so emitted were moderate and did not exceed the Proportion requisite for the Trade of the Colony, such Bills retain'd a fixed Value when compar'd with Silver without Depreciation for many Years ... The too great Quantity has, in some Colonies, occasioned a real depreciation of these Bills, tho made a Legal Tender ... This Injustice is avoided by keeping the Quantity of Paper Currency within due Bounds.[16]

The issuing of such colonial paper money did not, on the whole, prove inflationary.[17] By and large, the colonists understood Franklin's admonitions and created sufficient paper money to meet the needs of commerce but not so much as to generate high inflation.

So far, I have described the traditional view of the history of money. It explains how and why commodity money came into existence, and the role of precious metals as standardised coins. But the replacement of commodity by paper money is more difficult to explain. Of course, it is more convenient to buy stuff with paper, but the paradox of money is that people choose to own something that has no intrinsic value, and pays no interest. Over time people chose to hold less of it, and money today largely comprises bank deposits rather than notes and coin. How did the liabilities of banks come to be used as money? To explain this we need an alternative history of money, one that focuses on the role of money as a store of value.

As early as Roman times, and despite the prevalence of coins, money and credit existed in the form of loan contracts. Wealthy individuals acted as banks by extending loans, with the bank's owner often exploiting personal knowledge of his customers, and those claims on the borrowers were used by the owner to make payments because the recipients could in turn pass them on to pay for their own purchases.[18] The claims met the criterion of acceptability. In medieval Europe, banknotes evolved out of promissory notes – pieces of paper issued as receipts for gold bullion deposited with goldsmiths and other merchants. The paper money so created was backed by the bullion held by the goldsmith. The holder of the paper claim knew that at any time it could be exchanged for gold. As it became clear that most notes were not in fact immediately converted into bullion but were kept in circulation to finance transactions, merchants started to issue notes that were backed by assets other than gold, such as the value of loans made by the merchants to their customers. Provided the holders of the paper notes were content to carry on circulating them, the assets backing those notes could themselves be illiquid, that is, not suitable for conversion quickly or reliably into money. From this practice emerged the system of banking we see today – illiquid assets financed by liquid deposits or banknotes.

The problem with private banks' creation of money is

obvious. Money in the form of private banknotes and deposits is a claim on illiquid assets with an uncertain value. So both its acceptability and stability can from time to time come under threat. The nature of the problem was illustrated by the experience of 'free banking' in the United States, when banknotes were issued by private banks and not central government (the Federal Reserve did not start operating until 1914). The so-called 'free banking' era lasted from 1836, when the renewal of the charter of the Second Bank of the United States was vetoed by President Andrew Jackson, until 1863, when the Civil War led to the passing of several National Bank Acts, which imposed taxes on the new issue of banknotes. During that period, most states allowed free entry into banking. For banks, loans are assets and banknotes and deposits are liabilities; the opposite is true for their customers. Hundreds of private banks made loans and financed themselves by taking deposits and printing banknotes. Their assets were holdings of gold and the value of the loans they had extended, and their liabilities were banknotes and deposits, the former typically comprising a larger proportion of liabilities than the latter.[19]

In principle, banknotes issued by private banks were exchangeable on demand for gold at the bank's head office at face value, and were backed by a mixture of gold (or silver) and the value of the loan assets held by the bank. But when banknotes were exchanged at significant distances from the head office of the issuing bank, they often traded in the secondary market at discounts to their face value.[20] Banknote Reporters – special newspapers that published the latest prices of different banknotes – sprang up to provide information on the value of unfamiliar notes. The discounts varied not only with distance from the head office, but also across banks and, over time, according to perceptions about the creditworthiness and vulnerability to withdrawals of the bank at that moment.

In 1839, an enterprising Philadelphia businessman, Mr Van Court, started to publish what became known as *Van Court's Counterfeit Detector and Bank Note List*. It contained his measures of the discount in Philadelphia, then second only to New York as a financial centre, of different banknotes issued by the many hundreds of banks around the United States. For banks from Alabama, the average discount in Philadelphia varied from 1.8 per cent in 1853 to 25 per cent in 1842, and the maximum discount for a single bank was 50 per cent. Connecticut, a state with many more banks than Alabama, had several banks with discounts of over 50 per cent, but on average its banks rarely suffered a discount of more than 1 per cent. Illinois banks, by contrast, regularly experienced average discounts of well over 50 per cent.[21] During the era of 'free banking' many banks failed and there were frequent financial crises.

The interesting feature of free banking was that it revealed the inherent tension between the use of bank liabilities as money, which requires that notes or deposits exchange at face value, and the risky nature of bank assets. If banknotes in the nineteenth century were exchanged at face value there was a serious risk that the underlying assets might one day be inadequate to support that valuation. There was also the possibility that the owners of banks would issue too many notes, invest in risky assets and, if necessary, shut down the bank and disappear. Worried about such risks, consumers accepted banknotes only at a discount. But since the discount fluctuated over time, the value of banknotes as a means of payment was diminished.

Banknotes were a store of (uncertain) value. If the prices of banknotes always correctly valued the assets of the bank, then the holders of the notes could not be defrauded by over-issue of paper money. But they would in effect have become like shareholders, with a claim on the underlying assets of the bank that varied in value over time. So the value of banknotes as money, with the accompanying requirements of acceptability and stability, was sharply reduced.

The tension inherent in the use of private bank liabilities as money led inexorably to the regulation of banks and, after the experiences with 'free banking', to the creation of the Federal Reserve System as America's central bank. After the Great Depression, the introduction of deposit insurance, with the creation of the Federal Deposit Insurance Corporation (FDIC) in 1933, largely eliminated the risk to ordinary depositors. By transferring the risks to the taxpayer, deposit insurance reduced the likelihood of depositors running on their banks, but it cemented the role of banks as the main creators of money in the form of bank deposits with banknotes issued solely by government.

This alternative view of the history of money has the merit of explaining why bank deposits have come to comprise the vast majority of the money supply. They have an intrinsic value and offer a positive, if small, rate of return (either explicitly as interest, or, in the case of current accounts, implicitly in the form of subsidised money transmission services). As a result, they dominate the value of notes and coin in circulation. Over the past century, the amount of money in the US economy – defined broadly – has remained roughly stable as a proportion of GDP, at around two-thirds, and the share of bank deposits in total money has also been roughly constant at around 90 per cent. Gold and silver, which a hundred years ago amounted to around 10 per cent of total money and were of equal importance to notes and coin, are no longer counted as money. The share of bank deposits in total money is even higher in other major countries, at 91 per cent in the euro area, 93 per cent in Japan and no less than 97 per cent in the United Kingdom.[22] What is striking about these figures is that the production of money has become an enterprise of the private sector. The amount of money in the economy is determined less by the need to buy 'stuff' and more by the supply of credit created by private sector banks responding to the demand from borrowers. In normal times, changes in the supply of credit will be driven by changes in the demand from borrowers to which banks react, and in turn those developments will reflect the influence of the interest rate set by the central bank. So the fact that banks are the main creator of money does not prevent a central bank from being the major influence on the amount of money in the economy. Credit booms are less the result of irresponsible lending by banks and more the outcome of optimism on the part of borrowers, aided and abetted by low interest rates and competition between banks to meet customers' demands.[23] In a crisis, however, changes in the supply of credit may reflect a shift in the willingness of banks to lend, or the market to fund banks, as perceptions of the soundness of the banks are revised downwards. In those circumstances, it is much harder for a central bank to offset the contraction of money by stimulating demand for borrowing, as events since 2008 have shown.

In its role as an acceptable medium of exchange, money is not only necessary, it is a social good. As the historian of Rome, Edward Gibbon, expressed it: 'The value of money has been established by general consent to express our wants and our property, as letters were invented to express our ideas; and both these institutions, by giving more active energy to the powers and passions of human nature, have contributed to multiply the objects they were designed to represent.'[24] But the amount of money created by a private banking system may not always correspond to the amount that is socially desirable. Indeed, where the former exceeds the latter there is a risk of financial excess and inflation, and where the former falls short of the latter there is a risk of a financial crisis. Should money be created privately or publicly? The answer depends on how the choice affects the twin criteria of acceptability and stability.

Acceptability in good and bad times

The traditional view of the history of money stresses the importance of acceptability in transactions for 'stuff' – purchases of goods and services. Far more important, however, in a modern economy is the acceptability of money in financial transactions, including the making or repaying of loans, or the buying and selling of financial assets. In situations of extreme uncertainty, some forms of money may no longer be accepted as a means of payment. Cheques, for example, may be refused if there is doubt about the solvency of the bank on which they are drawn.[25] In October 2008, the Bank of England saw a sharp rise in the demand for £50 notes as confidence in banks fell – matched by a rise in sales of home safes![26] Moreover, in periods of great uncertainty, the amount of money people want to hold as a liquid store of value may rise sharply. To fulfil its functions, money needs to be acceptable in bad times as well as good, and to be available in sufficient quantities. That is why there is a very close link between money and liquidity, where the latter is the property of a non-monetary asset to be convertible into money quickly and at little cost. Some assets are more liquid than others; for example, stocks and shares of large companies are liquid, houses are not.

Before the recent crisis, financial experts believed that the 'deep and liquid' markets in which most financial assets were traded meant that there would always be sufficient access to liquidity. That illusion was destroyed by the events of 2007 and 2008. Some of the 'deep and liquid' markets simply closed, not to reopen for many years (mortgage-backed securities, for example, which are discussed in Chapter 4). Others became suddenly illiquid, with a large difference between the price at which one could buy and the price at which one could sell, such as commercial paper issued by non-financial companies (essentially an IOU promising to pay a fixed sum at a specified date a few months hence). It became clear that the only truly liquid assets were cash and bank deposits. As the latter shrank when banks began to stop lending, the Bank of England and the Federal Reserve stepped in to boost total deposits in the banking system. They did this by creating 'emergency money' with which to buy large quantities of paper assets (primarily government securities) from the non-bank private sector.

When a central bank buys or sells assets it adds to or subtracts from the supply of money. Someone (usually a financial institution in an auction) who sells $1 million of government bonds to the Federal Reserve, receives a cheque drawn on the Fed. When that cheque is deposited in the person's own bank account, which increases by $1 million, the bank presents the cheque to the Federal Reserve, which then credits the bank with $1 million in its reserve account at the central bank. The immediate effect is that both the money supply and central bank reserves rise by $1 million. The same argument holds in reverse when the central bank wants to reduce the money supply. Changing the amount of money in the economy in this fashion using electronic transactions is simpler and faster than printing notes. But it is creating money just the same. It boosts the money supply by increasing bank deposits.

The sharp increase in the demand for liquidity in 2007–8 was met by the creation of more central bank reserves. This was not because households, companies or banks wanted more money to buy 'stuff', but because central bank money was a store of liquidity that offered protection against a very uncertain future for the banking system. Inherent in this role for money is that its demand is liable to sudden and unexpected swings, and it is to such changes that the supply of emergency money must respond. The creation of emergency money adds to the total stock of central bank reserves and notes and coin – known as the 'monetary base'.

Sharp changes in the balance between the demand for and supply of liquidity can cause havoc in the economy. The key advantage of man-made money is that its supply can be increased or decreased rapidly in response to a sudden change in demand. Such an ability is a virtue, not a vice, of paper or electronic money. When there is a sudden increase in the demand for liquidity it is imperative to increase the supply of the asset that constitutes liquidity in order to prevent a damaging rise in the price of that asset and a corresponding fall in the price of goods and services in the economy. Because gold was in limited supply, those countries that used gold as their monetary standard in the late 1920s and early 1930s suffered falling prices (deflation).[27] A sudden fall in the general level of prices tends to go hand-in-hand with a fall in spending today, as households and companies wait to buy things more cheaply tomorrow. The ability to expand the supply of money in times of crisis is essential to avoid a depression. A crisis could, in fact, be defined as a set of circumstances in which the demand for liquidity suddenly jumps.

What the experience of emergency money reveals is that the private sector will not always be able to meet the demand for acceptable money. In bad times, governments may need to issue assets which will be regarded as both acceptable in making payments and reliable as a store of value. To leave the production of money solely to the private sector is to create a hostage to fortune. But there must be confidence in the process that generates changes in money. In an era of paper money, that amounts to trust in the central bank or government that controls money creation.

Stability of the value of money

The second criterion for money to be able to perform its functions in a capitalist economy is that its value – its purchasing power in terms of goods and services – must be in some sense stable. Defining price stability in a world where new goods and services come along that were not available before is a hazardous undertaking. Official statisticians are always adding new entries to the basket of goods and services that they use to calculate the average price level and measure inflation. And they also remove goods and services that no longer account for much of our spending. In 2014, the Office for National Statistics in the UK removed DVD recorders and gardeners' fees from the Consumer Price Index and replaced them by films streamed over the Internet and fresh fruit snacking pots. Leaving measurement issues to one side, the big question is whether governments can be trusted to maintain the value of money.

Since the Civil War, dollar coins in the United States have exhibited the words 'In God We Trust', and the motto has appeared on dollar bills since 1957.[28] Trust is fundamental to the acceptability, and so the value, of money. But it is trust not in God but in the issuer of money, usually governments, that determines its value. And that trust has been sorely tried over the centuries. Whether clipping the coinage (shaving some of the precious metal from the edge of the coin), devaluing the currency or restricting the convertibility of notes into gold, governments, east and west, north and south, have found ways to renege on their promises. It is an old tradition. As Sir William Hunter of the Indian Civil Service wrote in 1868, in his study of Bengal:

> The coinage, the refuse of twenty different dynasties and petty potentates, had been clipped, drilled, filed, scooped out, sweated, counterfeited, and changed from its original value by every process of debasement devised by Hindu ingenuity during a space of four hundred years. The smallest

coin could not change hands, without an elaborate calculation as to the amount to be deducted from its nominal value.
This calculation, it need hardly be said, was always in favour
of the stronger party.

Much of the financial history of the past 150 years is the
story of unsuccessful attempts to maintain the value of money.
The willingness of governments to debase the currency has
been illustrated many times – indeed, almost all paper currencies have suffered a massive loss of value, through intention or
incompetence, at one time or another – including in medieval
China, France during the Revolutionary period, the revolutionary war in the United States with its Continental currency,
the American Civil War with the greenback dollar, Germany
in the 1920s under the Weimar Republic, Eastern Europe following the collapse of the Soviet Union, and, most recently,
Zimbabwe in 2008 and North Korea in 2009.[29] Less dramatically, many industrialised countries, including the United States
and the United Kingdom, experienced the Great Inflation of
the 1970s.

In a democracy, people cannot be forced to use paper money,
although after the French Revolution the Jacobins had a try.
They made it a capital offence to use commodities as money.
This was a desperate and unsustainable action resulting from
the Jacobin policy of debasing their paper money – the *assignat*
and *mandat* – to make up for a collapse in tax revenues and to
finance a war against Prussia. And a few years later, in 1815
when Napoleon, after his defeat at Waterloo, was travelling
back to Paris to rally his forces, an innkeeper at Rocroi refused
to accept a chit for 300 francs as payment for dinner for the
Emperor's entourage, demanding payment in gold instead – 'as
sure a sign as any of Napoleon's waning authority'.[30]

When a government is in crisis, there is usually an exodus

from the paper money it issues, a collapse of the currency and 'hyperinflation' – which is usually defined as a period in which the monthly rate of inflation goes above 50 per cent. That may not sound so bad, but it is equivalent to an annual rate of inflation of well over 1000 per cent. Perhaps the simplest definition of a hyperinflation is when it becomes impossible to keep track of the inflation rate. In the worst hyperinflations the peak *monthly* inflation rate was several million per cent. It is easier to measure such hyperinflations by the length of time it takes for prices to double (in *hours*). At the peak of the hyperinflation in Germany, in November 1923, prices doubled every three and a half days. No wonder people paid for their lunch at the beginning of the meal. Printers, busy producing more and more notes, went bankrupt because their machinery wore out sooner than expected and they could not accumulate sufficient reserves to invest in new equipment. The economy collapsed.[31] At the end of the First World War, in November 1918, a gold mark (the standard on which paper money was based) was worth 2.02 paper marks. By November 1923, one gold mark was worth one trillion paper marks![32]

That experience shaped German attitudes to inflation, and the memory lingers today. But it was by no means the worst hyperinflation on record. That was in Hungary in July 1946 when prices, in terms of the pengö currency, doubled every fifteen hours. There are poignant photographs showing children in Germany playing with bricks made out of worthless paper marks and of street cleaners in post-war Hungary sweeping away piles of pengö notes because it was not worth the effort of picking them up from the pavement.

There is a natural tendency to think of hyperinflations as belonging to the history books. Far from it. The second worst hyperinflation in history took place in Zimbabwe during the first decade of this century. Few economies have collapsed quite so spectacularly as that of Zimbabwe. As inflation rose to absurd levels, citizens abandoned the local currency and started to use foreign currencies. Once some did, others followed – an instance of good money driving out bad. The sale of pre-paid minutes of mobile phone time also flourished as a substitute currency, as it did in a number of other African countries. Inflation peaked in November 2008, at which point prices were doubling every day. The use of other currencies, especially the US dollar, became official policy in early 2009. As a result, inflation quickly dropped to single digits and economic growth resumed.

All of these hyperinflations were caused by the excessive printing of money to finance government deficits that had been allowed to spiral out of control. But even in countries with more stable institutions, such as the United Kingdom and United States, inflation has eroded the value of money over the past century.[33] Both countries saw price stability in the nineteenth century, only to experience significant inflation in the twentieth century when prices accelerated rapidly, especially in the immediate aftermath of the First World War and in the later post-war period. The experience of the two countries was broadly similar until the 1970s, when even more rapid inflation in Britain led to a divergence of their price levels. But over the past twenty-five years or so, annual inflation has come under control and averaged close to 2 per cent, which is the current inflation target in the United States, the United Kingdom, the euro area and Japan. Other countries, too, have experienced high inflation; few can match the record of Switzerland, which has experienced an average inflation rate of only 2.2 per cent a year since 1880.

Why has money been so difficult to manage? Part of the answer is the failure of political institutions to avoid the temptation to create money either as a source of revenue or a way to court popularity by engineering a short-term boost to the economy before the resulting rise in inflation becomes apparent. But there have also been significant advances in our understanding of how to manage money. The creation of independent central banks, with a clear mandate to maintain the value of the currency in terms of a representative basket of goods and services (inflation targeting), proved successful in stabilising inflation in the 1990s and early 2000s during the Great Stability. The conquering of inflation across the industrialised world over the past twenty-five years was a major achievement in the management of money, and one, despite the financial crisis, not to be underrated. It was the result of successful institutional design (see Chapter 5).

Nevertheless, designing a system of monetary management that is capable of achieving price stability – providing the right amount of money in good times – and coping with crises – providing the right amount and quality of emergency money in bad times – is by no means straightforward. Neither the private nor the public sector has an unblemished record in striking a balance. That is why over the years, and right up until today, there are those who continue to search for a *deus ex machina* to provide monetary stability.

Gold versus paper

For some the answer is gold. Indeed, in the United States there is a degree of political support for a constitutional amendment to abolish the Federal Reserve Board and allow money supply to be determined by an automatic link to gold.[34] Few debates in economic history have attracted so much passion as that of the merits of gold versus paper as the basis for our monetary system. Two hundred years ago, William Cobbett railed against the iniquities of paper money and the policies of successive

British governments that had broken the link with gold during the Napoleonic Wars. He edited *The Political Register*, a radical newspaper, and used as his motto 'Put me on a gridiron and broil me alive if I am wrong'! He was obviously not an economist. In 1828 he published a book, written while imprisoned for treasonous libel, entitled *PAPER AGAINST GOLD; or, The History and Mystery of the Bank of England, of the Debt, of the Stocks, of the Sinking Fund, and of all the other tricks and contrivances, carried on by the means of Paper Money.*

The book lives up to its title. As the author points out,

The time is now come, when every man in this kingdom ought to make himself, if possible, well acquainted with all matters belonging to the *Paper-Money System*. It is that System, which has mainly contributed towards our present miseries; and, indeed, without that System those miseries never could have existed in any thing approaching towards their present degree. In all countries, where a *Paper-Money*, that is to say, a paper which could not, at any moment, be converted into Gold and Silver, has ever existed; in all countries, where this has been the case, the consequence, first or last, has always been great and general misery.

Gold has held a special position as money down the centuries and across the globe. The Egyptians used gold bars as a medium of exchange as far back as the fourth millennium BC. Even when paper money came into existence, its acceptance usually depended on its convertibility into gold. Major currencies were readily convertible into gold at a fixed exchange rate – the 'gold standard', as it was called. A country on the gold standard promised to exchange its notes and coin for gold at a fixed price. When a country joined the gold standard its exchange rate against other member countries became fixed. If the exchange rate of, say, the US dollar against the French franc were to fall, then it would be cheaper for American importers of French goods to pay in gold than in depreciated dollars. Gold would flow to France. The US would have less gold to back its supply of paper dollars, which would then contract, pushing up the value of the dollar until it returned to its official price in terms of gold. Although the cost of transporting gold allowed small fluctuations in exchange rates before physical movements of gold became attractive, the automatic nature of such movements kept exchange rates in line.

For most of the nineteenth century, and right up until the early 1930s, the price of gold was fixed at $20.65 per ounce.[35] The Great Depression saw a revaluation of gold to around $35 an ounce, where it stayed until 1971, when the United States abandoned the policy of a fixed dollar price of gold. Inflationary pressures in the US, stemming in part from the Vietnam War, put downward pressure on the dollar. Rather than face the recessionary consequences of the need to lower wages and prices to maintain a fixed rate against gold and other major currencies, President Nixon decided to break the link between the dollar and gold for good. The price of gold (per ounce) then rose steadily to around $160 in the inflationary 1970s, moved higher in the 1980s, and fell back only in the 1990s as inflation was conquered. But from around 2000 it rose steadily again, reaching a peak of almost $1800 in 2011 before falling back to below $1100 by late 2015.[36] The price of gold is not only volatile but highly sensitive to changes in sentiment about the ability of governments to control their monetary system.

The tension between paper and gold as the basis for our monetary system was revealed to me every day during my time at the Bank of England. The Governor's office leads on to a small garden in which are planted a number of mulberry trees. The reasons for choosing that type of tree were twofold. First, it was

a deliberate homage to the use of their bark in the production of
early Chinese banknotes. Second, mulberry trees grow in shallow soil. The soil in the garden had to be shallow because only
a couple of feet below was the ceiling of the enormous vault in
which the large gold reserves held by the Bank of England were
stored. Paper and gold were linked by the trees in this small
garden. The garden – and the Bank – had hedged their bets.

The persistent attraction of gold as an acceptable medium
of exchange in any set of circumstances stems from the fact
that, apart from new mining, its supply is fixed, independent of
human decision, and its weight and value can easily be checked.
New mining adds only a small amount to the total stock of gold
each year. Today, gold mining uses highly advanced technology to dig gigantic open pits. Arguably the largest hole in the
ground anywhere in the world is the Super Pit at Kalgoorlie
in Western Australia. After around fifteen years, the diggers in
Kalgoorlie have created a hole that is 4.5 kilometres in length,
1.2 kilometres wide and 500 metres deep. Excavating this hole
has yielded 27 million cubic metres of earth which, after pro-
cessing with acid, has yielded just 10 cubic metres of gold.[37]
Those few cubic metres were, however, worth around US$8
billion at the prices of early 2015. The investment paid off.
Nevertheless, the 200 tonnes of gold mined from this extraordinary hole is small compared with the 5.5 thousand tonnes
(the vast majority of it owned by foreign governments and not
the UK), worth US$235 billion, that sat in the vaults under-
neath my office in the Bank of England and the 6700 tonnes,
worth almost US$300 billion, in the vault of the Federal
Reserve Bank of New York in downtown Manhattan.[38]

For centuries gold has been the most widely accepted form
of payment. It is independent of government, and, ironically,
governments themselves want to hold reserves in gold because
they do not trust other countries to maintain the real value of

claims denominated in their own paper currency. But despite its attractions, gold suffers from two major drawbacks as money. First, it is extremely heavy and inconvenient to use, and even when gold coins were used widely by travellers (in the way that we might use travellers' cheques or credit cards today), coins of smaller denominations were usually made out of metals such as bronze or copper.

The second drawback is more fundamental. The attraction of gold to many – namely that its supply cannot easily be expanded by governments – is in fact a serious weakness. In times of financial crisis, paper money can be created quickly and easily when the demand for liquidity is high; not so the supply of gold. Almost invariably, the gold standard was suspended during a financial panic. The most notorious example was in Britain in 1797 during the wars against Revolutionary France, arguably the first financial crisis in a modern economy. An attempted invasion by 1200 French soldiers was thwarted but added to public concern about the value of paper money; a rush to gold ensued. With the Bank of England's gold reserves disappearing fast, William Pitt the Younger slapped an order of the Privy Council on the Bank, suspending the convertibility of notes into gold. The printing of notes was stepped up, and the result was inflation and a series of wonderful cartoons by James Gillray. One showed the Bank as a lady of a certain age being violated by the Prime Minister as he tries to get at her gold.[39] It was the origin of the Bank's later nickname, the Old Lady of Threadneedle Street. Convertibility into gold resumed in 1821 and was maintained right through until the First World War.

In normal times, the problem with the gold standard was that, with gold in effectively fixed supply, economic growth meant upward pressure on the price of gold in terms of goods and services. Since the dollar (and sterling) price of gold was fixed, there was, conversely, downward pressure on the dollar (and sterling) prices of goods and services. That deflationary pressure, squeezing wages and profits, pushed down activity and employment. The commitment to gold was seen as a battle between bankers and financial interests, on the one hand, and working people, on the other. Never was this expressed so forcefully as by William Jennings Bryan, the three-time losing Democratic presidential candidate, who concluded his speech to the party convention in 1896 with the words 'you shall not crucify mankind upon a cross of gold'.[40]

Keynes's famous description of gold as 'a barbarous relic' was apposite.[41] What was especially 'barbarous' was the decision in the 1920s to impose substantial deflation on economies in order to go back to the gold standard at the same parities as existed before the First World War. It is certainly arguable that a return to a different set of parities might have enabled a system of fixed exchange rates to be retained, while not putting those economies through a period of deflation which, in the event, led not only to the Great Depression but to the inevitable abandonment of the gold standard itself, starting with Britain in 1931. But breaking the link to gold made it possible to expand the supply of money, and countries were then free to adopt looser monetary policies at home – an appropriate response to the world of the Great Depression. The search for a reliable anchor for the monetary system has continued ever since.

Following the 2008 crisis, both the Federal Reserve and the Bank of England expanded the supply of money sharply in order to meet a sudden increase in demand for liquidity. If the money supply had been determined solely by the available quantity of gold in the world, then neither central bank would have found it easy to prevent a depression. To be sure, enthusiasts of gold and critics of paper money argue that crises would be much less frequent in the absence of discretionary monetary interventions by governments and their central banks.[42] But the history of nineteenth-century America, before the creation of the Federal Reserve, does not suggest that a world without central banks would be free of crises. The choice between basing our monetary unit of account on either gold or paper money managed by a central bank has largely been resolved in favour of the latter, partly because of the advantages of discretion in controlling the supply of liquidity during a crisis and partly because of the success in conquering inflation during the 1990s.

But for many, the crisis of 2007–9 is evidence of the continuing folly of central banks and the attractions of an automatic standard for the value of money. And if actions speak louder than words, it is striking that most advanced economies still maintain significant quantities of gold in their official reserves of foreign currencies and commodity money. By far the largest holders of gold are the United States (over 8000 tonnes, comprising 72 per cent of its total reserves of gold and foreign exchange) and the euro area (10,784 tonnes, accounting for 57 per cent of total reserves). China's holdings have been rising and are now over 1000 tonnes. By contrast, the United Kingdom has only 310 tonnes (11.6 per cent of total reserves) and Japan 765 tonnes (2.5 per cent of total reserves).[43]

Gold has the advantage that its supply is not dependent on unpredictable human institutions. Its disadvantage is precisely the same – namely that when a discretionary increase in the supply of money would be advantageous to overcome a sudden panic, gold cannot play that role. The evolution of a framework for the issue of paper money, culminating in the 1990s inflation-targeting regime, showed signs of success. But it is still too early to judge whether democratic societies have managed to create sustainable regimes to manage paper money, avoiding the deflationary impact of fixed-supply commodity money on the one hand, and the dangers of excessive inflation from discretionary control of money supply on the other.

Economists and money

In recent years, many economists have been reluctant to use the word 'money'. If one is very clever, it is indeed possible to talk about monetary policy without using the word 'money'. The interesting question is why anyone would want to. The explanation largely lies in a pervasive ideological split between 'Keynesian' and 'monetarist' economists, which dominated debates on economic policy in the post-war period until inflation had been conquered in the 1990s, but has flared up again with the experience of stagnation since 2008. Monetarists, like Milton Friedman of the University of Chicago, believed that the solution to inflation, and the key to stabilising the economy more generally, was to control the rate of increase of the money supply. Friedman pointed to the collapse of the money supply during the Great Depression and advocated a fixed percentage increase in the money supply each year.[44] Keynesians believed that fiscal policy was more powerful in controlling the economy, and doubted whether there was a close link between changes in the money supply and movements in the economy. Yet John Maynard Keynes was a monetary economist, and the full title of his *magnum opus* – published in 1936 and which transformed debates about macroeconomic policy after the Great Depression – is *The General Theory of Employment, Interest and Money*. Whether monetarist or Keynesian, no economist should ignore the significance of money, even if they disagree about what its role is.

For over two centuries, economists have struggled to provide a rigorous theoretical basis for the role of money, and have largely failed. It is a striking fact that as economics has become more and more sophisticated, it has had less and less to say about money. The apparently obvious idea, articulated by David Hume in the eighteenth century, that the level of prices reflects the balance between the demand for and supply of money has been described by the Nobel Laureate Christopher Sims as 'obsolete'.[45] And even the existence of money has proved something of a mystery for economic theorists. As the eminent Cambridge economist, the late Professor Frank Hahn, wrote: 'the most serious challenge that the existence of money poses to the theorist is this: the best developed model of the economy cannot find room for it'.[46]

Why is modern economics unable to explain why money exists? It is the result of a particular view of competitive markets. Adam Smith's 'invisible hand' – the notion that the impersonal forces of competition among a large number of people pursuing their own self-interest would guide resources to activities where they would be used as efficiently as possible – was a beautiful idea. But if the 'hand' was invisible, what exactly did it correspond to in the world? For over two hundred years, economists tried to formalise Smith's proposition and discover under exactly what conditions a competitive market economy would allocate resources efficiently. In the nineteenth century, important contributions came from Frenchman Léon Walras, who taught in Lausanne, and Englishman Alfred Marshall, who taught in Cambridge. Then, in the early 1950s, two economists, Kenneth Arrow and Gerard Debreu, both working in America, finally produced a rigorous explanation of the invisible hand (for which they were subsequently awarded the Nobel Prize).[47] They imagined a hypothetical grand auction held at the beginning of time in which bids are made for every possible good and service that people might want to buy or sell at all possible future dates. The process continues until every market has cleared (that is, demand equals supply) with prices, demands and supplies of all goods and services determined in the auction. Life then starts and time unfolds. Because the auction at the beginning of time has done its job, no market needs to reopen in the future. There are, therefore, no further transactions once life starts. Everything has been settled during the initial auction, and all people have to do is to deliver the services, such as employment, for which they have contracted and take delivery of the goods and services that they purchased in the auction. There is no need for something called money to act as either a medium of exchange (the 'double coincidence of wants' problem is circumvented by the auction), a store of value (there is no requirement for a reserve of savings), or indeed an absolute standard of value (consumers bidding in the auction need only know the relative prices of different goods and services, including labour). Money has no place in an economy with the grand auction.

Central to the Arrow–Debreu view of the world is a special way of dealing with uncertainty about the future. When bidding in the auction, consumers must bid not only for the good they want – lunch in their favourite Manhattan restaurant, say – and the date on which they want it – next Tuesday – but also for the 'state of the world' in which they wish to purchase it. For example, if the restaurant is outdoors you might bid high for a table if next Tuesday were to be sunny and perhaps zero for a table if it were cold or wet. Market-clearing prices are likely to be high in the former 'state of the world' and low in the latter. The key point is that all transactions can be made in advance because it is possible, in this theoretical view, to identify all relevant states of the world and make the auction contingent on them. In other words, radical uncertainty is ruled out by assumption.

Obviously, there are many ways in which the world is very far removed from this abstract description, apart from the obvious impracticability of organising the grand auction. Two are of particular importance – the need for institutions to police a market economy, and the nature of uncertainty.

The importance of trust

In the theoretical world of the auction economy, people are assumed to fulfil their previously contracted obligations to work and consume. But some people might be tempted to renege on their obligations – for example, to stay at home and enjoy leisure instead of working.[48] So there is a strong motive to find a mechanism or institution whereby contracts may be enforced. In practice we rely heavily on the legal system – hugely expensive though it is – to enforce a wide array of contracts. But we also rely on a mechanism that plays an important role in the economic life of all successful societies – trust. The absence of trust leads to economic inefficiency. As the philosopher Onora O'Neill, Chair of the UK Equality and Human Rights Commission, put it in 2002, 'It isn't only rulers and governments who prize and need trust. Each of us and every profession and every institution needs trust. We need it because we have to be able to rely on others acting as they say that they will, and because we need others to accept that we will act as we say we will.'[49]

Economists mistrust trust. They believe that people will pursue their own self-interest given the incentives they face. Finding a cooperative outcome when confronted with the prisoner's dilemma inherent in the short-term advantage of reneging on a contract is difficult. Shame, ostracism and loss of honour are all ways in which a society can penalise the individualistic pursuit of self-interest when it leads everyone to be worse off. The creation of a social ethic or code of behaviour is a means of escaping the prisoner's dilemma.

The consequences of the absence of trust for our ability to exchange goods and services is well illustrated (both in novels such as John le Carré's *Smiley's People* and in reality) by the exchanges of spies during the Cold War. The two sides would approach each other from opposite ends of the Glienicke Bridge, which connected East Germany and West Berlin across the River Havel at Potsdam, meeting in the middle to exchange their prisoners. A classic exchange requiring a 'double coincidence of wants', it was an instance of pure barter.

Trust in others can make it possible for one party to deliver goods and services to another at one date and receive an agreed delivery of other goods and services at a later date. Some economists have argued that the role of money is to embody and cement that trust. Imagine a world in which each generation lives for only two periods, and is in turn succeeded by the next generation. Each generation wishes to work in the first period of life and then enjoy retirement in the second. The economic challenge is to ensure that each young generation hands over part of its earned income to the retired older generation, hoping or believing that in turn their children will do the same for them. There is a potentially profitable trade between successive younger and older generations, but one that is difficult to enforce. Money might be a way to solve this problem, by supporting a convention under which the younger generation saves in the form of 'tokens' that it carries forward into retirement in order to purchase goods and services from the new younger generation.[50] Such tokens, or money, could be called a dollar or 100 dollars, or for that matter a mark, a yen, a buck or a pound. As long as everyone continues to believe that tokens will continue to be acceptable in future, everyone can be better off. The use of money facilitates the trust that is necessary to reach the best possible outcome.[51] More generally, our inability to make credible pre-commitments, or to trust each other, explains why 'evil is the root of all money', to use the phrase coined by the economists Nobuhiro Kiyotaki and John Moore quoted at the beginning of the chapter.[52]

The blunt truth, however, is that the implicit intergenerational cooperation that represents the best outcome is supported by trust, not money.[53] If the younger generation decides not to support the elder, the existence of tokens will make no difference. And if the older generation has invested in, say, housing, they too could renege on the implicit intergenerational transfer by 'consuming' the value of their housing capital by selling it to foreigners or a minority of the wealthy, leaving the young unable to afford to buy the housing stock. That is exactly the intergenerational bargain on which, David Willetts argues, the post-war baby-boomer generation has reneged.[54] Trust obviates the need for money, and money without trust has no value. Perhaps it is trust that makes the world go round.

Money and radical uncertainty

The second big difference between the real world and the grand auction is the nature of uncertainty. The auction requires both that we have an exhaustive and complete list of all possible future outcomes so that we can write contracts contingent on all these states, and that we know the probabilities of different outcomes so that we can work out how much to bid for each contingent good or service at each point in the future. But the essence of a capitalist economy is that we cannot imagine today all the new ideas and products that will be discovered in future. If the future is unknowable, then we simply do not know and it is pointless to pretend otherwise.

In 1972, while Joel Grey, as the MC in *Cabaret*, was singing about money making the world go round, the computer for the whole of Cambridge University was less powerful than that in my smartphone today. The handheld devices we now take for granted were simply unimaginable then. And even if someone had been able to write down a list of possible outcomes that included these developments, I rather doubt that it would have been easy to add to that list all the events that have subsequently occurred in the world, including the fall of the Berlin Wall, the Arab Spring, and other occurrences that were relevant to the profitability of investments and the path of the world economy. Investment is driven by the imagination of individuals who can see opportunities invisible to the rest of us. Their risks are largely uninsurable. Risk-taking by entrepreneurs is an intuitive gamble, not a cool appraisal of expected returns based on a scientific assessment of the probabilities of a known and finite number of possibilities.

How then can people cope with the unimaginable and uninsurable? We may not have a clear idea about the goods and services that we will want to buy in the future, but we know that we need a way to carry forward claims of purchasing power from the present to the future in a form that is generalised in the sense that we do not have to decide today on what we will spend tomorrow. Money gives us the ability to exchange labour today for generalised purchasing power in the future. That is why many savings contracts are denominated in money terms. We do not invest in a bank account that offers us a fixed number of television sets or foreign holidays in the future. We expect to earn an interest rate defined as a percentage increase in the amount of money in our account. Money is not principally a means of buying 'stuff' but a way of coping with an uncertain future. We do not know which new goods and services will exist in future, nor what their relative prices will be. There is no auction mechanism today that will allow us to discover that. Maintaining a reserve of purchasing power denominated in a monetary unit reduces the risk from placing one's eggs in the basket containing only contracts that can be written today. Although we cannot literally insure against the uninsurable, we can try to keep our options open by holding claims on future purchasing power in a general monetary unit of account. Any savings account on which the returns were fixed in money terms would suffice; even a promise of a fixed pension might seem to offer a claim on future purchasing power. But in times of financial stress only money claims issued and guaranteed by government will fully serve the purpose. And in anticipation of the unexpected in a world of radical uncertainty, money does therefore play a special role.

Could a market economy make do without money? It probably could in a simple world where we purchased items for immediate consumption and we all lived in close proximity. In medieval times, village or town markets, often held once a week, played very much that role. But our demand for a growing variety of goods and services outstripped the supply available in a given, small locality long ago. A glance at the Amazon website suggests that we want everything, and we want it now. And the market, whether Amazon or another firm, supplies it. In this more complex world, where people save for, and borrow against, an unknowable future, money plays a special, indeed unique, role. Money is a specific feature of a capitalist economy. Over the centuries, money has evolved from a means of payment designed to circumvent the limitations of a simple barter system to a liquid reserve essential to the operation of a capitalist economy in a real world with an unknowable future.

Money oils the wheels of commerce and finances transactions. There needs to be sufficient money to support the steady expansion of economic activity, but not so much as to generate inflation. Only then can money operate as a credible common measuring rod, whether in the Domesday Book or in modern estimates of gross domestic product. Expanding the amount of money in the economy can be either good or bad, depending on the circumstances. Printing paper money can, as described in Goethe's famous play *Faust*, be a stimulus to production when times are bad.[55] But the alchemy of money creation fosters the illusion of unbounded pleasure and the temptation to issue so much money in good times that the result is not prosperity but rising inflation, leading to economic chaos and the destruction of prosperity. Few countries suffered more from this pact with the devil than Goethe's own homeland in the hyperinflation of 1923.

In normal times, a wide range of assets may be accepted as money. In a crisis, central bank money is the ultimate means of payment and store of value. Although gold is unlikely ever to regain its position at the centre of monetary management, it is a store of wealth that is universally acceptable. Other assets, such as bank deposits, which do function as money in good times, may become illiquid as a result of a loss of confidence in their acceptability, and so in a crisis, sufficient 'emergency money' needs to be supplied to meet the demand for liquidity. These two roles for money – in 'good' and 'bad' times – are usually discussed and implemented separately, with the first being seen as 'monetary policy' and the second as 'financial policy'. That compartmentalisation of the different reasons for a central bank to supply money contributed to the failure to understand the evolving problems of the major economies prior to the crisis.

During the twentieth century, governments allowed the creation of money to become the by-product of the process of credit creation. Most money today is created by private sector institutions – banks. This is the most serious fault line in the management of money in our societies today. In his 'cross of gold' speech, William Jennings Bryan spoke passionately about the evils of the gold standard – the needs of Main Street should come before those of Wall Street. But almost forgotten are the most important sentences in the speech: 'We believe that the right to coin money and issue money is a function of government. We believe it is a part of sovereignty and can no more with safety be delegated to private individuals than can the power to make penal statutes or levy laws for taxation ... the issue of money is a function of the government and the banks should go out of the governing business.' He was consciously reiterating Thomas Jefferson, who said in 1809, 'the issuing power should be taken from the banks and restored to the people, to whom it properly belongs'.[56]

Why have governments allowed money – a public good – to fall under private control? To answer that, we need to understand the role of banks.

❦

3

INNOCENCE LOST:
ALCHEMY AND BANKING

'Was ist ein Einbruch in eine Bank gegen die Gründung einer Bank?' (What is robbing a bank compared with founding a bank?)

Bertolt Brecht, *Die Dreigroschenoper*
(*The Threepenny Opera*), Act 3 Scene 3 (1928)

'"Splendid financiering" is not legitimate banking, and "splendid financiers" in banking are generally either humbugs or rascals.'

Hugh McCulloch, Comptroller
of the Currency, December 1863

In his account of the origins of the First World War, the historian Max Hastings quotes an exchange that took place in 1910 between a student and the commandant of the British Army staff college. Surely, the student suggested, only 'inconceivable stupidity on the part of statesmen' could precipitate a general European war. Brigadier-General Henry Wilson replied, 'Inconceivable stupidity is just what you're going to get.'[1]

Many would argue that 'inconceivable stupidity' was also the cause of the recent financial crisis – bankers were wicked and central bankers incompetent. Of course, the extraordinary events surrounding the start and evolution of the crisis took many by surprise, as did those that initiated the First World War. But the crisis of 2007–9 is not a story about individuals, entertaining though that portrayal might be. To see Dick Fuld, CEO of Lehman Brothers, or Fred Goodwin, CEO of the Royal Bank of Scotland, as the villains who undermined our financial system is a caricature that may satisfy our desire to name and blame – if difficult in practice to shame – but fails to get to grips with why so many people, so many banks, and so many countries took decisions that, with the benefit of hindsight, appear mistaken. Rather, it is a story about deeper forces shaping the constraints that governed the actions of individuals.

No doubt there were bankers who were indeed wicked and central bankers who were incompetent, though the vast majority of both whom I met during the crisis were neither. It would be both arrogant and complacent to assume that all the problems generated in money and banking arose because our predecessors, let alone our contemporaries, fell prey to 'inconceivable stupidity'. Rather, like everyone else, they naturally responded to the incentives they faced. As individuals, they tried to behave in what they saw as a rational manner, but the collective outcome was disastrous. Because they could not affect the behaviour of others, all the key actors in the drama were understandably acting in their own self-interest – given the actions of everyone else. Since, for one reason or another, they could not cooperate with the other players, they all ended up worse off – an example of the prisoner's dilemma.

Banks, too, faced a prisoner's dilemma. If, before the crisis, they had exited the riskier types of lending, stopped buying complex derivative instruments and reduced their leverage, they would, in the short term, have earned lower profits than their competitors. The chief executive would likely have lost his job, and other staff defected to banks willing to take risks and pay higher bonuses, well before the wisdom of the new strategy had become evident. Even understanding the risks, it was safer to follow the crowd. The most famous – now infamous – statement of this dilemma was that of Chuck Prince, the CEO of Citigroup (at the time the biggest bank in the world), who said before the crisis, 'As long as the music is playing, you've got to get up and dance. We're still dancing.'[2] He kept on dancing until the music did eventually stop in November 2007, and at that point he lost his job. Had he stopped dancing to the music of risk four years earlier, when he became CEO, I doubt that he would have survived that long. So it is less 'inconceivable stupidity' than the inherent difficulty of finding a way to a cooperative solution that was the main challenge facing bankers and other economic actors before the crisis. After the event it may seem easy to see how the crisis could have been avoided by some set of actions, but no one at the time had any incentive to take them.

During the crisis, I found that the study of earlier periods was more illuminating than any amount of econometric modelling (that is, the application of empirical statistical methods to economic data).[3] The crisis did not exactly mirror any one episode in the past, but there were uncanny parallels with many such episodes. It was natural for American commentators to look back to the Great Depression of the early 1930s – the previous major episode of bank failures in North America – and

Ben Bernanke, a long-time scholar of that period, brought to discussions among central bank governors a valuable historical perspective on the problems we faced. The collapse of the banking system in the United States in the 1930s was so severe that President Franklin Roosevelt, only a week after his inauguration in March 1933, announced a bank holiday (which lasted a week), shutting the banks to provide a breathing space during which confidence could be restored.[4] In his first fireside chat on the wireless, he talked about 'a bad banking situation', and continued:

> Some of our bankers have shown themselves either incompetent or dishonest in their handling of the people's funds. This was of course not true in the vast majority of our banks but it was true in enough of them to shock the people of the United States for a time into a sense of insecurity and to put them in a frame of mind where they did not differentiate but seemed to assume that an act of a comparative few had tainted them all.[5]

In 2008 we too had a 'bad banking situation', and since then evidence of the repeated scandals of 'a comparative few' have indeed 'tainted them all'.

Banks are part of our daily life. Most of us use them regularly, either to obtain cash, pay bills or take out loans. But banks are also dangerous. They are at the heart of the alchemy of our financial system. As described in Chapter 2, banks are the main source of money creation. They create deposits as a by-product of making loans to risky borrowers. Those deposits are used as money. Banks are able to transform short-term liabilities into long-term assets; in essence, they borrow short and lend long. They are, therefore, vulnerable to any crisis of confidence, real or imagined. The failure in 2008 of several large international banks, threatening not only to bring down the international financial system but to lead us back to another Great Depression, is hardly an isolated incident. Banking crises have been frequent down the years, occurring almost once a decade in Britain and the United States in the nineteenth and twentieth centuries. In one of the earliest crises, in Britain in 1825, many of the patterns apparent in the recent crisis could be seen almost two hundred years earlier: rapid expansion in overseas lending, a stock market boom, a central bank trying to restore price stability, a collapse of the banking system, concern about the interconnectedness of banks, the absence of effective regulation, official purchases of government bonds and drastic intervention by the central bank – the Bank of England – to lend to banks in distress. A familiar story

Banks are also highly visible. In New York, London and any major city, they dominate the skyline. Even on the other side of the world, far from the epicentre of the financial crisis, the names of the tallest buildings you can see from Auckland Harbour in New Zealand are dominated by global financial institutions: HSBC, Citi, Rabobank, ANZ, Westpac, AIG, Zurich, PWC, Deloitte, Ernst & Young. And the historic head-quarters of English cricket at Lord's in London is now sponsored by the American firm J.P. Morgan. Banks are visible not only in our physical but also in our financial architecture. They are huge players in the global economy. The biggest bank in the world is ICBC from China. In an age where inequality is prominent, it is remarkable how equal global banks are in terms of size. Among the twenty biggest banks in the world, the ratio of the assets of the largest to the smallest is little more than two to one.[6]

Taken together, however, these twenty banks accounted for assets of $42 trillion in 2014, compared with world GDP of around $80 trillion, and for almost 40 per cent of total world-wide bank assets.[7] In the league table of countries that are home to the top banks in the world, China, France and the USA share the leading position with four each, followed by Japan and the UK with three each, and one each in Germany and Spain. Of the largest fifty banks in the world, ten are from China and the rest are in the major industrialised countries.[8]

Size isn't everything, although it helps. As Macheath pointed out in Brecht's *Threepenny Opera*, why rob a bank and risk imprisonment when you could start a bank and create money? Both robbers and founders are attracted to banks because that is usually where the money is. But in September 2008 the money wasn't there. Banks were losing money hand over fist as people who had been willing to lend them large sums suddenly refused to make new loans. Unlike the frequent bank runs in the nineteenth century, when individual depositors occasionally panicked and withdrew their funds, the change of heart had come from other financial institutions, wholesale investors such as money market and hedge funds. Unable to replace these sources of funding, banks had to call in loans, sell assets, and, in some cases, seek funding from their central bank. Before the crisis, banks could borrow at the finest interest rates. During the crisis, the rates at which banks could borrow rose very sharply and in some cases funds were not available at any price – a case of innocence lost. Almost all the largest banks in the world received direct or indirect support ('bailouts') from their governments.

Much of the expansion of the banking system described in Chapter 1 resulted from the explosion of so-called derivative instruments (explained more fully in Chapter 4), based on the application of mathematics to finance. It is difficult not to be reminded of the *Titanic* – a marvel of modern engineering whose failure and sinking was unthinkable. But when the *Titanic* sank, at least only one ship was lost and not an entire fleet. In 2008 the whole banking system was at risk.

There has always been a fine dividing line between the respectable activities of traditional banking, managing the deposits of and lending prudently to established customers, and the 'splendid financiering' of those who cross the boundary into more dubious practices. While the chief executives of the world's largest banks were reaching for the sky – literally, in their suites at the top of the new skyscrapers that housed their headquarters – some of their employees were at the same time plumbing the depths of banking by rigging the markets in which they traded. The modern exponents of 'splendid financiering' – investment banks – have been described as, on the one hand, inventing new financial instruments that are 'socially useless' and, on the other, of 'doing God's work'.[9] With their global reach, their receipt of bailouts from taxpayers, and involvement in seemingly never-ending scandals, it is hardly surprising that banks are unpopular. Some bankers of my acquaintance are reluctant to admit their profession in polite company – certainly innocence lost. As the quotations at the head of the chapter illustrate, 'twas ever thus.

In 1873, the English political economist and editor of *The Economist*, Walter Bagehot, published a book that was to become a bible for those interested in how to handle financial crises. *Lombard Street*, a highly successful account of banking and the money market, explained how the Bank of England could and should have prevented earlier banking collapses by the provision of temporary financial support until the crisis had passed. As Bagehot knew only too well, banking crises are endemic to a market economy. Although his description of a central bank's responsibility as a 'lender of last resort' has entered the textbooks, and was frequently cited as justification for their lending by central bankers during 2008–9, it is in need of updating. Banking has changed almost out of recognition since Bagehot's time.

Changes in banking since Bagehot

For almost a century after Bagehot wrote his classic work, the size of the banking sector, relative to GDP, was broadly stable. But, over the past fifty years, bank balance sheets have grown so fast that the size and concentration of banks, and the risks they undertake, would be unrecognisable to him. J.P. Morgan today accounts for almost the same proportion of US banking as all of the top ten banks put together in 1960.[10]

The size of the US banking industry measured in terms of total assets has grown from around 20 per cent of annual GDP one hundred years ago to around 100 per cent today. In the UK, a medium-sized economy with a large international banking centre, the expansion is even more marked, from around 50 per cent of GDP to over 500 per cent. Most of this expansion has taken place over the past thirty years, and has been accompanied by increasing concentration: the largest institutions have expanded the most. Today, the assets of the top ten banks in the US amount to over 60 per cent of GDP, six times larger than the top ten fifty years ago. In the UK, the asset holdings of the top ten banks amount to over 450 per cent of GDP, with Barclays and HSBC both having assets in excess of UK GDP.

While banks' balance sheets have exploded, so have the risks associated with them. Bagehot would have been used to banks with leverage ratios (total assets to equity capital) of around six to one.[11] In the years immediately prior to the crisis, leverage in the banking system of the industrialised world increased to astronomical levels.[12]

How did banks find themselves in such a precarious position? Without a banking system our economy would grind to a halt with people unable to receive wages and salaries, pay bills, service loans and make other transactions. Banking is at the heart of the 'payments system'. As with the supply of electricity, its importance to the economy is much greater than is reflected in the number of its employees or its contribution to GDP. Because of its critical role in the infrastructure of the economy, markets correctly believed that no government could let a bank fail, since that would cause immense disruption to everyone's ability to make and receive payments. Creditors were willing to lend to banks at lower interest rates than would otherwise have been on offer because they were confident – correctly as it turned out – that even if things went wrong taxpayers would see them right.

When all the functions of the financial system are so closely interconnected, any problems that arise can end up playing havoc with services vital to the operation of the economy – the payments system, the role of money and the provision of working capital to industry. If such functions are materially threatened, governments will never be able to sit idly by. Institutions supplying those services are quite simply too important to fail.[13] Everyone knows it. So highly risky banking institutions enjoy implicit public sector support. In turn, the implicit subsidy incentivises banks to take on yet more risk. In good times, banks took the benefits for their employees and shareholders, while in bad times the taxpayer bore the costs. For the banks, it was a case of heads I win, tails you – the taxpayer – lose. Greater risk begets greater size, greater importance to the functioning of the economy, higher implicit public subsidies, and yet larger incentives to take risk – described by Martin Wolf of the *Financial Times* as the 'financial doomsday machine'.[14] All banks, and large ones in particular, benefited from an implicit taxpayer guarantee, enabling them to borrow cheaply to finance their lending.

Although the implicit subsidy was not new, banks were able to exploit its existence to borrow more, and resorted to the use of ever more short-term finance from institutions (known as wholesale funding) in addition to deposits from individual or business customers. The average maturity – the length of life of a loan – of wholesale funding issued by banks declined by two-thirds in the UK and by around three-quarters in the US over the thirty years prior to the crisis – at the same time as reliance on such funding increased. As a result, banks ran a higher degree of mismatch than in the past between the long-dated maturities of their assets, such as loans to companies and households, and the short-term maturities of the funding to finance their lending, often from hedge funds.

Cheap funding fuelled lending. And as the banks got bigger, so did the implicit subsidy – the IMF estimated that in 2011 the cost of the implicit subsidy in the major economies was of the order of $200–300 billion. The bigger banks became, the more they were seen as too important to fail, and the surer markets became that the taxpayer would bail them out. But there are only so many good loans and investments to be made. Banks made increasingly risky investments. To make matters worse, they started making huge bets with each other on whether loans that had already been made would be repaid. As some of those loans went bad, the bets generated large losses. To cap it all, banks held only small quantities of liquid assets on their balance sheets, so they were utterly exposed if some of the short-term funding dried up. In less than fifty years, the share of highly liquid assets held by UK banks declined from around a third of their assets to less than 2 per cent.[15] In the US the share had fallen to below 1 per cent just before the crisis.

The turning point came when the size of the balance sheet of the financial sector became divorced from the activities of households and companies. During the 1980s, a combination of deregulation and the invention of derivatives had two effects. First, it separated the scale of bank balance sheets from the scale of the real household and business activities in the economy. Lending to companies is limited by the amount they wish to borrow. But there is no corresponding limit on the size of transactions in derivative financial instruments, and most buying and selling of derivatives is carried out by large banks and hedge funds. The gross market value of derivatives has fallen since the crisis, but at just over $20 trillion at the end of 2014 it was still around one-half of the assets of the largest twenty banks in the world (and of the same order of magnitude as total lending to households and businesses).[16]

Second, the focus of much of banking changed from making loans, which requires a careful local assessment of potential borrowers, to trading securities, which involves a centralised operation to make and monitor transactions. The rise of US investment banks played a large part in that development. Commercial and investment banking, separated after the Glass-Steagall Act, were merged in large conglomerate banks after the repeal of Glass-Steagall in 1999 by the Gramm-Leach-Bliley Act. Standalone investment banks that were previously organised as partnerships turned themselves into limited liability companies – Morgan Stanley in 1975, Lehmans in 1982 and Goldman Sachs in 1999. Even traditional mutual building societies in Britain (the UK equivalent of US savings and loan associations) decided to convert into limited companies in order to be free to engage in a wider range of banking activities, and every single one that did so from 1990 onwards failed in the crisis.[17]

Those two developments altered the business model and the culture of our largest banks. Size became an objective because a bank that was clearly too important and too big to fail was able to borrow more cheaply, and even a small advantage in funding costs meant that it could offer cheaper loans to its customers. That enabled such a bank to expand more rapidly than its rivals in a virtuous circle of growth. So the size of the financial sector grew and grew. Along the way it included a massive expansion of trading in new and complex financial instruments, covering activities such as sub-prime mortgage lending. When I visited New York in December 2003, I found all the major banks worrying about whether they should either emulate Citigroup's strategy of using its size to obtain a comparative advantage in funding costs or abandon the aim of global reach and try to become a niche player in particular markets. Inevitably, perhaps, when the crisis came it was Citi that required a large bailout. Although it fell from grace in dramatic fashion, the fact that it wasn't allowed to fail vindicated the original strategy.

Before the crisis, banks paid large salaries and bonuses to people who created and analysed new products that could be sold to their clients. But not enough resources were devoted to assessing the riskiness of the balance sheet as a whole. With a growing proportion of bank activity deriving from the trading of complex instruments, it was difficult to work out how big the risks actually were. Certainly, no investor could have done so from the information made available by the banks in their accounts or any other published source. Nor did the banks themselves seem to understand the risks they were taking. And if that was the case, there was not much hope that the regulators, relying on information provided by the banks, could get to grips with the potential scale of the risk.

The expansion of trading rather than traditional lending also altered the culture of banking. New ways of making money relied on recruiting extremely clever individuals – mathematicians, physicists and engineers – whose job was to invent and price new financial instruments, and who were then lost to their former professions. Economists, who love being clever, applauded the application of mathematics to finance and the resulting explosion of transactions in derivatives. Sadly, the growth of trading led also to an erosion of ethical standards. There was a view that being very clever was a justification for

making money out of people who were less clever.[18] This attitude encouraged the arrogance of the traders who rigged and
fixed prices in what were thought to be competitive markets.
Almost all the major banks have been dragged into one or more
misconduct scandals. Whether selling oversized mortgages to
poor people in the US, selling inappropriate pension and other
financial products to millions of people in the UK, rigging foreign exchange and other markets in which banks' own traders
were operating around the world, failing to stop overseas subsidiaries in places as far apart as Mexico and Switzerland from
engaging in money laundering and tax evasion, there seemed
no end to the revelations about what banks had been doing.
By 2015, the total fines imposed on banks worldwide since the
banking crisis ended in 2009 amounted to around $300 bil-
lion – a staggering figure.[19]

Bad behaviour by talented young men is often associated
with the sporting world. But it applies equally to the world of
finance, and is not a recent phenomenon. As long ago as 1905,
the young John Maynard Keynes wrote to his friend Lytton
Strachey: 'I want to manage a railway or organise a Trust, or at
least swindle the investing public; it is so easy and fascinating
to master the principles of these things.'[20] It is a small step from
the expression of superiority in a private letter to the public
expression of contempt seen on the trading floor. Keynes was,
however, badly burned twice by misjudgements in the timing
of his buying and selling activities. Towards the end of his
investing career he mellowed and put less faith in speculative
investments, writing: 'As time goes on, I get more and more
convinced that the right method in investment is to put fairly
large sums into enterprises which one thinks one knows something about.'[21] Perhaps the enormous losses banks incurred in
the crisis, and the fines levied by regulators around the world,
will bring a similar change of heart in banking.

Banks and other financial intermediaries create wealth by providing valuable services to their customers. But there is always the risk that they create the illusion of wealth – in the extreme case of the fraudster Bernie Madoff and his funds there was quite a long period when the perception of wealth was substantially higher than the reality.[22] More generally, many of the substantial bonuses that were paid as a result of trading in derivatives reflected not profits earned in the past year but the capitalised value of a stream of profits projected years into the future. Such accounting proved more destructive than creative.

It is clear that the size, nature and culture of banking have changed considerably since the days of Walter Bagehot. To analyse the implications of those changes we need to step back and ask why banks are special.

What is a bank?

What is a bank? The answer may seem obvious. It was actor and comedian Bob Hope who said that a bank is 'a place that will lend you money if you can prove that you don't need it'.[23] But most borrowers from banks do need the money. A growing economy requires new investment to add to the stock of capital (plant and machinery, inventories and buildings, including offices and housing) which, when harnessed to the labour force and supply of raw materials, produces the output that we call GDP. And that investment is financed from the supply of savings from both home and foreign savers.

Savings can be transferred to investors, whether businesses or households, in several ways. Businesses can retain profits to reinvest rather than distributing them as dividends; they can sell new issues of shares or bonds directly to savers; or they can borrow from banks. Equity, bond and bank finance are the essential building blocks of the methods companies use to finance themselves – although they can be combined in complex ways. Several factors influence the form in which savings are transformed into investment, including the tax treatment of different forms of saving and the willingness of savers to take risk. But perhaps the most important factor concerns the difficulty of assessing and monitoring the potential and actual profitability of investment projects. Equity finance (whether the sale of new shares or the retention of profits by companies) requires careful and continuous monitoring of a company's activities. In contrast, one attraction of loan (whether bond or bank) as opposed to equity finance is that monitoring is required only when the borrower fails to make a scheduled payment.

Companies large enough to be quoted on a stock exchange produce annual accounts showing profits, as well as assets and liabilities, which are verified by independent auditors and scrutinised by an army of analysts.[24] Savers who do not wish to rely on such public information can choose to invest in an array of financial intermediaries, such as mutual, pension and hedge funds or insurance companies. In that case, savers are relying on the judgement of the managers of the intermediary. Perhaps the most famous example of such a manager is Warren Buffett, whose company Berkshire Hathaway has an enviable track record of purchasing businesses that are well run and highly profitable. People who bought shares in Berkshire Hathaway, and held onto them, have seen the value of their investments steadily rise.[25] Someone who invested $1000 in Berkshire Hathaway in 1985 would by the middle of 2015 have an investment worth $161,000, a compound annual rate of return of almost 17 per cent. By relying on the judgement of Buffett and his colleagues, such investors did not themselves need to monitor the businesses in which they were investing. Over the past century, financial intermediaries have grown enormously as the wealth of the middle classes has increased. Substantial amounts of wealth are now invested through pension funds, and even house purchases can be financed by sharing the equity in the home with an intermediary.

Banks are a particular type of financial intermediary which provide loan finance to businesses and households. They are particularly well placed to monitor their borrowers' cash flows because they can observe the movements into and out of the bank accounts of the people to whom they lend. In most jurisdictions, the legal definition of a bank is an institution that takes deposits from households and businesses. A bank can raise finance by taking in or creating deposits, issuing other debt instruments and increasing equity invested in the bank. In the days of Walter Bagehot, banks' assets mainly comprised loans and holdings of government debt and their liabilities consisted of deposits and shareholders' equity. Banks today have more complex balance sheets, although the similarities remain. Consider a simplified version of the balance sheet of Bank of America at the end of 2014. Its assets comprised $139 billion of cash (including reserves held at the Federal Reserve), $867 billion of loans to businesses and households, and $1099 billion of financial investments, together with the value of buildings and other real assets. Total assets were $2105 billion.[26] Liabilities comprised $1119 billion of deposits, $743 billion in other forms of borrowing and $243 billion of shareholders' equity capital, giving total liabilities of $2105 billion. In fact, shareholders' equity is simply what is left after all other liabilities have been deducted from the value of total assets.

Two features of the balance sheet are striking. First, loans comprise only around 40 per cent of the bank's assets. Second, although deposits clearly exceed loans, other types of borrowing provide a significant source of finance. There is clearly more to Bank of America than taking in deposits from households and businesses and making loans.

What is it that makes banks special? The distinguishing feature of a bank is that its assets are mostly long-term, illiquid and risky, whereas its liabilities are short-term, liquid and perceived as safe. Returns on risky long-term assets are normally much higher than the returns which the bank has to offer on its safe short-term liabilities. So banking is highly profitable. Unfortunately, the notion that a bank can offer safe returns on deposits that can be withdrawn at a moment's notice by using them to finance long-term illiquid risky investments is, as common sense would suggest, generally false. The transformation of short-term liabilities into long-term assets – borrowing short to lend long – is known as maturity transformation. And the creation of deposits, which are regarded by the depositors as safe, into loans which, by their nature, are inherently risky constitutes risk transformation. Banks combine maturity and risk transformation. This is what makes them special. Moreover, when a bank makes a loan, it creates a deposit of equal value in the account of the borrower. That deposit can be withdrawn on demand and used to make payments. It is money. As explained in Chapter 2, most money today comprises bank deposits.

The transmutation of bank deposits – money – with a safe value into illiquid risky investments is the alchemy of money and banking. Despite innumerable banking crises, belief in the alchemy persists. Economists have shown great ingenuity in coming up with explanations of how the alchemy of money and banking works, and in suggesting some special synergy between bank assets and liabilities. The idea that risk transformation might be possible is based on the view that regional or national banks can diversify their lending across a large number of loans on which the risks are uncorrelated – that is, if a particular loan goes sour, it does not do so in circumstances when other loans also perform poorly. By making a large

number of such loans, the bank supposedly avoids any real risk
to the loan portfolio as a whole.

Unfortunately, experience suggests that the world does not
behave in this way. In normal times, it may be true that the
profits on loans to some businesses and households can be used
to pay for defaults by others. When there are large swings in
the economy, however, then the fates of different businesses
move together. Such risk makes the value of the assets of a bank
uncertain and prone to volatility. In the post-war period, most
of the banking system's large losses have occurred during times
of recession and often on property loans that have gone sour.

People believed in alchemy because, so it was argued, depositors would never all choose to withdraw their money at the
same time. If depositors' requirements to make payments or
obtain liquidity were, when averaged over a large number of
depositors, a predictable flow, then deposits could provide a
reliable source of long-term funding. But if a sizeable group of
depositors were to withdraw funds at the same time, the bank
would be forced either to demand immediate repayment of the
loans it had made, resulting in a fire sale of the borrowers' assets
that might realise less than the amount owed to the bank – or
to default on the claims of depositors.

Such a system is fragile for two reasons. First, most banks,
especially in recent years, have financed themselves with rather
small amounts of shareholders' equity. The result is that even a
small item of bad news about the value of a bank's assets might
put the value of deposits at risk. Concerns about the size of
potential losses would leave depositors scurrying for the door.
Second, even without bad news concerning the loan book, if
any group of depositors started to withdraw their money it
would be rational for other depositors to join the queue and
get their money out before the bank had to start calling in
loans, with the attendant risk of a loss to the depositors at the

end of the queue. A run on the bank is self-fulfilling. And a run on its liquidity reserves can bring a bank down in short order.[27]

A bank run is likely either if there is a loss of confidence in the value of the bank's assets or an unusually high demand for liquidity. In the first case, the run may be specific to a particular bank if, for example, there was a suggestion of fraudulent activity by its managers. In the second case, a change in perception of the value of bank assets more widely might lead to a suspicion of all banks and lead to a general increase in demand for liquidity. Only an increase in overall liquidity of the system will meet this demand. An individual bank will find it difficult to obtain more liquidity when all banks are scrambling for cash. In the extreme case where depositors flee the bank in large numbers, the resulting run on the bank can bring down not only that particular bank but create a sense of panic that spreads to other banks, leading to a collapse of the banking system. It was to avoid just such a panic that central banks lent hundreds of billions of dollars to commercial banks in 2008.

The basic problem with the alchemy of the banking system is that it is irrational for one person to place trust in a bank if others do not. And it is rational to be concerned about whether a bank can make good its promise to return a deposit on demand when radical uncertainty means that it is impossible to know how big might be the losses on loans. Four ways have been suggested to deal with this problem.

First, banks might suspend withdrawal of deposits in the face of a potential bank run. Banks could just shut their doors for a few days until the crisis has subsided. Of course, for a bank to close its doors, even if only because of a temporary shortage of liquidity, would send a signal that might lead to a loss of confidence on the part of depositors. It might only encourage a run to start sooner than would otherwise be the case, and if suspensions were regarded as potentially likely, then bank deposits would no longer function effectively as money.

Second, governments could guarantee bank deposits to remove the incentive to join a bank run. Deposit insurance is now a common feature of most advanced economies' banking systems. Nevertheless, the insurance provided is not fully comprehensive, and on occasions that has created difficulties. In 2007, when the UK bank Northern Rock failed, individual depositors joined a bank run because their deposits were insured only up to a limit and not for their full value. The run stopped only when the UK government belatedly announced a taxpayer guarantee of the deposits. In 2008, financial institutions withdrew their funds from US banks or their new equivalents, known as 'shadow' banks, because those deposits were not insured. The Federal Reserve stepped in to provide a degree of guarantee to stop the run. The provision of deposit insurance is a subsidy and an incentive to risk-taking by banks. It is no panacea, although, as I will argue in Chapter 7, in a world of radical uncertainty some government insurance is probably inevitable.

Third, the benefits of limited liability – the system we take for granted today in which shareholders' losses are limited to their initial investment – could be revoked for the shareholders of banks. In modern times, limited liability originated in the nineteenth century as companies sought to find capital on a scale adequate to finance the expansion of railways and new industrial plants. In the case of banks, unlimited liability would mean that shareholders were responsible for all losses, providing assurance to depositors and making a bank run less likely. In the United States, between 1865 and 1934 (when deposit insurance was introduced), bank shareholders were subject to 'double liability' – in the event of failure they were liable to lose not merely their equity stake but also an additional amount corresponding to the initial value subscribed for the shares they held, which could be used to repay depositors and other creditors. During this period, claims on shareholders in failed banks were quite successful in producing resources to pay out depositors.[28] Following numerous bank failures during the Great Depression, however, limited liability was extended to banks, and reliance placed on deposit insurance to deter runs.

In Britain, the death knell of unlimited liability came somewhat sooner with the failure of the City of Glasgow Bank, the third largest bank in the UK, in October 1878.[29] The bank had been badly managed and its accounts falsified. Following a report that revealed serious problems with the accounts, other banks withdrew their support for City of Glasgow and it closed its doors. Later that month, the directors were arrested and charged with fraud. With a promptness that seems remarkable by today's standards, the directors went on trial the following January, were convicted and sent to prison. It was left to the shareholders to meet the costs of supporting the depositors. Not only individual shareholders but also the trustees of private trusts which owned shares in the bank were personally liable for the losses, and 80 per cent of them went bankrupt. The plight of the shareholders aroused widespread public concern and the government introduced legislation to permit banks to convert to limited liability status.

The Economist magazine backed the legislation, citing the difficult position in which many innocent shareholders found themselves: 'an examination of the share lists of most of our banks exhibits a very large – almost an incredible – number of spinsters and widows, a considerable sprinkling of Clergymen and Dissenting Ministers, professional men, and others, whose occupations do not appear likely to have enabled them to accumulate much wealth ... Out of the whole number more than one third are women.'[30] Admirable though such diversity might seem today, it was seen then as evidence of the vulnerability of small investors. Spinsters and widows, let alone dissenting ministers, could not be expected to monitor and control bank executives. By August 1879, with commendable speed, the Banking and Joint Stock Companies Act, covering little more than three pages, had been passed by Parliament, requiring the publication of audited accounts and permitting banks to take advantage of limited liability.

It seems impossible to imagine now that unlimited liability could be restored. Yet limited liability in a bank with only a small margin of equity capital means that the owners have incentives to take risks – to 'gamble for resurrection' – because they receive all of the profits when the gamble pays off, whereas their downside exposure is limited. That is not in the best interest of the company as a whole. During the crisis, the chairman of one of Britain's largest banks told me of his frustration that he was supposed to act solely in the interests of shareholders and not also in the interests of bondholders and depositors. After the crisis I asked a senior member of Goldman Sachs why he believed that their attitude towards risk management was an example for others to follow. The answer was simple: for a century Goldman Sachs had been a partnership and so every partner had an incentive to help monitor and manage the risks of the firm, a culture that had survived its transition to limited liability company status in 1999. In investment banking, the partnership form of business has much to be said for it. Those who manage other people's money are more careless than when managing their own.

Fourth, central banks could replace lost deposits by providing official loans to a bank experiencing a run. It would, in the phrase that has become only too well known, act as a 'lender of last resort'. If banks experienced a run then the central bank could supply liquidity to enable each individual bank to meet its depositors' demands until the panic subsided and confidence returned. And if the crisis were a purely temporary one and the bank were solvent – in the sense that its assets could be sold once the crisis was over for an amount greater than the value of its liabilities – this 'lender of last resort' policy would achieve the objective of stabilising the banking system.

Flooding the system with liquidity has been seen by many economists, officials and politicians as the answer to almost any financial crisis. But it is never easy to distinguish between a liquidity and a solvency problem. In only a matter of days, a shortage of liquidity can turn into a solvency question. Banks will always claim that their problems result solely from illi-quidity rather than a fall in the value of their assets. And the distinction between liquidity and solvency is one that may be observable only after a detailed examination of a bank's balance sheet, difficult for the authorities and impossible for investors. In September 2007, the consensus was that the crisis was solely one of liquidity. But it quickly became clear that it was in fact a crisis of solvency, and that a solution would require the com-bined efforts of central banks and taxpayers.

The failure before the crisis was a lapse into hubris – we came to believe that crises created by maturity and risk transforma-tion on a massive scale were problems that no longer applied to modern banking, that they belonged to an era in which people wore top hats. There was an inability to see through the veil of modern finance to the fact that the balance sheets of too many banks were an accident waiting to happen, with levels of lever-age on a scale that could not resist even the slightest tremor to confidence about the uncertain value of bank assets. For all the clever innovation in the world of finance, its vulnerability was, and remains, the extraordinary levels of leverage. Pretending that deposits are safe when they are invested in long-term risky assets is an illusion. Without a sufficiently large cushion of equity capital available to absorb losses, or the implicit support of the taxpayer, deposits are inherently risky. The attempt to transform risky assets into riskless liabilities is indeed a form of alchemy.

Risk in the system and interconnectedness

Given that banks are inherently fragile, it is not surprising that there have been frequent banking crises. The failure of any one bank can cause serious problems for its depositors, other creditors, and its shareholders. But what really matters for the economy is the risk inherent in the banking system as a whole. Risk in the system is not measured by an average of the risks of each individual bank. The simplest way to see this is to consider an artificial but striking example. Borrowing short to lend long creates risk. Suppose that there are one hundred banks in the economy. The first bank issues demand deposits (that is, deposits that are instantly convertible into cash) and invests in securities issued by other banks with a maturity of six months. The second bank issues liabilities comprising securities with a maturity of six months and invests in bank securities with a maturity of twelve months. And so on. The one hundredth bank issues liabilities with a maturity of forty-nine and a half years and invests in non-bank securities with a maturity of fifty years. Bank regulators are asked to check that each bank is not exposed to an excessive degree of maturity transformation. Since, in this example, that is only six months for each bank, the regulators report a satisfactory compliance with restrictions on the degree to which banks are allowed to borrow short and lend long. But the banking system as a whole is creating demand deposits and investing in long-term securities with a maturity of fifty years. There is massive maturity transformation in the banking system as a whole. This example is clearly artificial – although before the crisis banks did transact extensively with each other in similar ways – but it illustrates the need to examine the system rather than individual banks.[31]

The question of interconnectedness is not restricted to links within the banking system. Since the crisis a great deal of attention has been paid to the need for banks to issue liabilities that can absorb losses in bad times without the need for taxpayer support. This is the basis of calls for banks to issue either more equity or special 'bail-inable' bonds that can be converted to equity capital when substantial losses arise. Such proposals have much merit, but they beg one very important question. Who are the people or institutions who hold the equity and debt that are supposed to absorb losses? If they are pension funds or insurance companies, which play a crucial role in the management of household savings, then it is far from obvious that they are best placed to absorb the risks generated in the banking system. This takes us back to the fundamental question posed by the alchemy of the banking system – we all want deposits to be safe and yet we also want to finance risky investment projects. How do we square the circle? In other words, we need to look at the financial sector as a whole, and not just the formal banking system.

In the run-up to the crisis, new institutions grew up to form a so-called 'shadow banking' system. In the US it became larger in terms of gross assets than the traditional banking sector, especially between 2002 and 2007, largely because it was free of much of the regulation that applied to banks. There is no clear definition of what constitutes 'shadow banking', but it clearly includes money market funds – mutual funds that issued liabilities equivalent to demand deposits and invested in short-term debt securities such as US Treasury bills and commercial paper.

Money market funds were created in the United States as a way of getting around so-called Regulation Q, which until

2011 limited the interest rates that banks could offer on their accounts. They were an attractive alternative to bank accounts. Such funds – and hence the owners of their liabilities – were exposed to risk because the value of the securities in which they invested was liable to fluctuate. But the investors were led to believe that the value of their funds was safe. By the time the crisis hit, such funds had total liabilities repayable on demand of over $7 trillion. And they lent significant amounts to banks, both directly and indirectly through other intermediaries.

It was because they were a significant source of funding for the conventional banking system that the Federal Reserve took action to prevent the failure of money market funds in the autumn of 2008 when, after the failure of Lehman Brothers, concern about the ability of such funds to hold their value led to a run on them.[32] In Europe and Japan, money market funds did not grow to the same extent because banks had more free-dom to pay interest, and since the crisis, unlike in the US, such funds have had to choose between being regulated as banks or becoming genuine mutual funds with a risk to the capital value of investors' money.

At one time or another, almost all non-bank financial insti-tutions have been described as shadow banks. In some cases, such as special purpose vehicles set up by banks themselves, the description is merited. Those vehicles were legal entities, such as limited liability companies, set up for the sole purpose of issuing short-term commercial paper, not dissimilar to bank deposits, and purchasing longer-term securities, such as bundles of mortgages, created by the banks themselves.[33] In essence, they were off-balance-sheet extensions of banks, and during the crisis many were taken back on to the balance sheet of their parent bank. Entities such as hedge funds and other bodies carrying out fund management are also sometimes described as examples of shadow banking. But since they do not issue demand deposits, the comparison with banks is much less convincing. The challenge posed by shadow banks is to ensure that institutions engaging in the alchemy of banking are regulated appropriately, and I shall return to this issue in Chapter 7.

Financial engineering allows banks and shadow banks to manufacture additional assets almost without limit. This has had two consequences. First, the new instruments created are traded largely among big financial institutions and so the financial system has become enormously more interconnected. The failure of one firm causes trouble for the others. This means that promoting the stability of the system as a whole by regulating individual institutions is much less likely to be successful than hitherto. As in the stylised example described above, maturity and risk mismatch can grow through chains of transactions among banks and shadow banks without any significant amount being located in any one institution. Shadow banks posed as big a risk to the stability of the financial sector as conventional banks. Second, although many of these positions even out when the financial system is seen as a whole, gross balance sheets are not restricted by the scale of the real economy, and so banks and shadow banks were able to expand at a remarkable pace. When the crisis began in 2007, no one knew which banks were most exposed to risk. Almost no institution was immune from suspicion, the result of the knock-on consequences so eloquently described by Bagehot when he wrote:

At first, incipient panic amounts to a kind of vague conversation: Is A.B. as good as he used to be? Has not C.D. lost money? and a thousand such questions. A hundred people are talked about, and a thousand think, 'Am I talked about, or am I not?' 'Is my credit as good as it used to be, or is it less?' And every day, as a panic grows, this floating suspicion becomes both more intense and more diffused; it attacks more persons; and attacks them all more virulently than at first. All men of experience, therefore, try to 'strengthen themselves,' as it is called, in the early stage of a panic; they borrow money while they can; they come to their banker and offer bills for discount, which commonly they would not have offered for days or weeks to come. And if the merchant be a regular customer, a banker does not like to refuse, because if he does he will be said, or may be said, to be in want of money, and so may attract the panic to himself.[34]

The risk premium – the rate of return required by investors over and above the return on safe government debt of the same maturity – on loans even to large banks rose very sharply during the crisis. For most banks the risk premiums on their unsecured debt had more than trebled by October 2008 relative to their levels at the start of 2007. All banks, irrespective of the precise nature of their business and balance sheet, were tarred with the same brush. Even today, risk premiums are higher than before the crisis.

Size of the banking sector

The size, concentration and riskiness of banks have increased in extraordinary fashion over recent decades – as described above – and would be unrecognisable to Bagehot. A banking and financial sector is essential to economic growth. Many poor countries need a growing financial sector as they develop, and many poor people around the world will need greater access to financial facilities. But is the banking sector now too large?

Size has advantages, and not just for big banks themselves. A system comprising a few large nationwide banks may be more resilient than one consisting of a large number of small local banks. In the 1930s, the United States saw the failure of almost 10,000 banks – 4000 in 1933 alone. It was the regional fragmentation of American banking that proved so vulnerable to the downturn because there were limited opportunities to set losses in one area or industry against profits in others. The loss of so many banks was devastating to small businesses in general and agriculture in particular, and exacerbated the depression in the economy. In contrast, the UK did not experience a banking crisis during the Great Depression. One reason was the tradition of national branch banking with its greater resilience and, it is fair to say, a high degree of oligopoly, which restrained competitive pressures on banks to lend in more optimistic times.

A similar benefit from size can be seen in the experience of Canada, a country with a long history of remarkably few banking crises.[35] Canada has a small number of banks (now five) and is not an international financial centre.[36] Those two factors have stood it in good stead and explain the comparatively good performance of Canadian banking during the recent crisis.

Those advantages of size relate to the composition of the banking sector and its concentration. There are three reasons to believe that, before the crisis, the banking sector as a whole became too large. First, because bank deposits are used as money, their failure can prevent people paying bills and receiving wages, so undermining the payments system. That is why governments are unwilling to allow banks, other than small ones, to fail. Banks, as we have seen, are too important to fail. The implicit guarantee of bank liabilities amounts to an effective subsidy, allowing banks to raise finance more cheaply than other entities in the private sector. Depositors and others who lend money to banks believe that they are in effect lending to the government.[37] The belief that when in trouble banks will be bailed out by the state because they are too important to fail leads to an implicit subsidy, which means a larger banking system than is justified by the underlying economics.

Second, many of the examples of high personal remuneration, especially in the form of bonuses, in the financial sector reflect not high productivity but what economists call rent-seeking behaviour. In other words, the remuneration is far higher than is necessary to persuade people to work in the industry. Financial markets are places where delusion and greed find common cause. Many of the transactions in complex financial instruments are zero-sum – a clever trader makes money out of a less clever one. Such activity diverts talent from professions where the social returns are high, such as teaching, to those, such as finance, where the private return exceeds, often substantially, the social return.

Third, financial capital is attracted into the industry by the appearance that there are high profits to be made. Sometimes these are overstated, especially on long-term financial contracts. As mentioned earlier, a common way of exploiting normal accounting conventions for derivative and other complex transactions was to report as current income the present value of expected future cash flows, even though they had not yet been received. Some of those practices reminds me of certain football clubs, which would sell the right to future gate receipts and season ticket sales to outside investors and then report the proceeds as money available for current spending. Indeed, the practice of converting a stream of future profits into a capitalised present value was one of the ways in which Enron, the American energy company that went bankrupt in December 2001, misled the market.[38] The exaggeration of the profitability of complex transactions represented by these accounting practices provides misleading incentives to the use of capital in the banking industry.

For those reasons, when the crisis hit, banks had grown

to a size where it was risky to the system as a whole to allow them to be subject to normal market disciplines, where they had become almost impossible to manage (as the growing revelations of misconduct by most large banks have revealed), and where they were immune to the usual due process of law out of fear of the consequence of their failure for the financial system as a whole. Banks had become too big to fail, too big to sail, and too big to jail. And in some countries, the size of the banking sector had increased to the point where it was beyond the ability of the state to provide bailouts without damaging its own financial reputation – for example in Iceland and Ireland – and it proved a near thing in Switzerland and the UK. The fate of the Bank of Scotland (which in 2001 evolved into HBoS) and the Royal Bank of Scotland, founded in 1695 and 1727 respectively, encapsulates the problems of British banking. Between 2000 and 2008, the exposure of HBoS to commercial property rose by 600 per cent, resulting in a potentially large loss if asset prices were to fall. RBS's exposure to commercial property also rose rapidly, at an annualised rate of 21 per cent, and the fragility of its balance sheet was exacerbated by the ill-timed acquisition of the Dutch bank ABN Amro in the autumn of 2007. Both had to be rescued by the taxpayer, in the form of the Bank of England and the government, in 2008. Millions of passengers in Europe arriving at airport gates emblazoned with the letters RBS are reminded daily not of the successes of UK banking but of its failures.

By 2008, too many banks were an accident waiting to happen. When the banking system failed in September of that year, not even massive injections of both liquidity and capital by the state could prevent a devastating decline of confidence and output around the world. So it is imperative that we find an answer to the question of how to make our banking system safer.

The attempt to link the creation of money, in the form of bank deposits, to the financing of long-term risky investments seems attractive in normal times because the alchemy it represents conceals the true cost of the arrangement. Only when the inherent fragility is revealed by a crisis do the costs become apparent. The demand for a safe reserve of purchasing power in the form of money can increase hugely and suddenly in times of crisis. But banks and even governments cannot create safe assets. To understand the demand for safe assets, and the extent to which our banking system as presently constituted can respond to that demand, requires a deeper analysis of the nature of uncertainty.

4

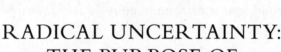

RADICAL UNCERTAINTY: THE PURPOSE OF FINANCIAL MARKETS

And what you do not know is the only thing you know
And what you own is what you do not own
And where you are is where you are not.

T.S. Eliot, 'East Coker', *The Four Quartets*

'You've got to expect the unexpected.'

Paul Lambert, Aston Villa manager,
press conference, 22 November 2013

Are we really capable of expecting the unexpected?[1] In 1998, the hedge fund Long-Term Capital Management (LTCM) failed, although its senior management team comprised two Nobel Laureates in Economic Science, Myron Scholes and Robert Merton, and an experienced practitioner in financial markets, John Meriwether. Their strategy, successful at first, was to create a highly leveraged fund that bought large amounts of one asset and sold equally large amounts of a slightly different asset (for example, government bonds of slightly different maturities), so as to exploit anomalies in the pricing of those assets. The return on each transaction was tiny but done on a sufficiently large scale, it generated huge profits.

The choice of assets was based on sophisticated statistical analysis of high-frequency data over a decade or more. But the data, although voluminous, covered only a short period of history, and when a rare but significant event – the Russian default and devaluation in the summer of 1998 – occurred, past correlations proved a poor guide to asset returns. LTCM failed. Its management argued, in hindsight almost certainly correctly, that given sufficient time they would be able to work their way through the losses to a position of positive net worth. But if you start with a portfolio worth less than nothing, you have to persuade your creditors to allow you to continue. As usually happens in such circumstances, the creditors called a halt. The lesson is that no amount of sophisticated statistical analysis is a match for the historical experience that 'stuff happens'. At the heart of modern macroeconomics is the same illusion that uncertainty can be confined to the mathematical manipulation of known probabilities. To understand and weather booms and slumps requires a different approach to thinking about uncertainty.

The illusion of certainty

Risk, luck, fate, uncertainty, probability theory – we all have names for the game of chance. Most decisions in life involve risk. Sometimes we embrace it, as when we enjoy a bet on the Grand National or the Super Bowl, and sometimes we avoid it, as when we insure our houses against fire. The playing of the hand we are dealt can be a pleasure in a game of bridge and a burden in life. We accept that Lady Luck has her part to play in our personal lives. But we cling to the 'illusion of certainty' in monetary matters. There is a seemingly insatiable demand for economic forecasts. Newspapers and television are only too willing to print the latest forecast of, say, national income with a degree of precision that beggars belief and far exceeds the ability of statisticians to measure it. And at the end of each year prizes are awarded to the forecasters who turned out to be the most accurate. It makes as much sense as it would to award the Fields Medal in mathematics to the winner of the National Lottery.

No economic forecaster has ever been able to match Edmund Halley, who in 1682 made calculations predicting that the comet then visible in the skies would return seventy-six years later. It did – on Christmas Day 1758. Fortunately the length of the economic cycle – the duration of the expansion and subsequent contraction of the economy before it returns to its normal levels of output and employment – is shorter than the periodicity of Halley's Comet – although if it goes on increasing at its present rate even that might not be true. But Halley was able to rely on scientific laws; economic predictions are inherently less reliable because they depend upon human behaviour.

Despite the repeated inability of economic forecasting models to predict accurately, there is a persistent belief that there is, if only we could find it, a 'model' of the economy that will produce forecasts that are exactly right. When giving evidence to the Treasury Select Committee in the House of Commons, I would sometimes respond to questions by saying, 'I don't know, I don't have a crystal ball.' Such an answer outraged many Members of Parliament. They thought it was my job to have an official crystal ball in order to tell them what the future held. Any attempt to explain that not only could I not forecast the future, but neither could they, and nor for that matter could anyone else, was regarded with disbelief. Down the ages, quack doctors selling patent medicines and astrologers selling predictions have been in strong demand. Added to their number today are economists selling forecasts, reflecting a desire for certainty that is as irrational as it is understandable.

Why are we so reluctant to accept that the future is outside our control? The reluctance to give adequate prominence to risks may reflect the fact that many of us feel uncomfortable with formal statements of probabilities. Probability theory is a relatively recent development in our intellectual history, dating back to a flowering of ideas in Europe around 1660 produced by Blaise Pascal, Gottfried Leibniz, Christiaan Huygens and others. Despite advances since then, statistical thinking remains prone to confusion and is often avoided. Television weather forecasts in Britain rarely employ the language of probabilities used by the meteorologists themselves. Professor Gerd Gigerenzer, a psychologist and Director of the Max Planck Institute for Human Development in Berlin, who studies the mental processes that actually underlie decisions in practice, has demonstrated in a series of studies how poorly doctors, lawyers and other professionals understand probabilities.[2] At the start of the crisis in August 2007, the Chief Financial Officer of Goldman Sachs, David Viniar, said that the losses suffered on one of their hedge funds implied that 'we were seeing things that were 25-standard deviation moves, several days in a row'.[3] That certainly is extreme, since such moves should occur even less often than once every 13 billion years, or the time elapsed since the creation of the universe!

In times of genuine uncertainty, even the most hard-bitten financiers become disorientated. And despite Seneca's maxim that 'luck never made a man wise', airport bookshops continue to stock titles on how to become rich written by successful investors and entrepreneurs who are confident that their success is the result of outstanding business acumen rather than good fortune. Matthew Syed, a former table tennis international, argued that sporting success reflected practice more than talent – the result of 'hitting a million balls'.[4] His thesis was widely hailed, in part because it gave us back the feeling that we could be in control of our destiny. Clearly, practice is crucial to success, but as Ed Smith, the writer and former England cricketer, explained, chance, or simply luck, plays a big role in both sporting and personal life – 'stuff happens'.[5] The desire for certainty and control over our destiny is a deep-seated human characteristic.

The difficulty we have in confronting uncertainty, and our strong desire to control our own lives, lead to seemingly irrational decisions. After the terrorist attacks on New York on 11 September 2001, many Americans stopped flying for a period and drove instead. Traffic on interstate highways rose 5 per cent in the three months after the attack, and it took a year before normal patterns of travel were resumed. In that period, around 1600 Americans lost their lives in road accidents because of the switch from flying to driving, some 50 per cent of the death toll incurred on 9/11 itself.[6] Such behaviour might appear irrational. After the attacks, airline security was drastically tightened. But how were people to assess the risk of flying in a world of new uncertainties? They opted for a form of transport more directly under their own control, even if it turned out to be more dangerous.

Coping with unquantifiable uncertainties outside our control is a challenge to our mental discipline. We are tempted to put blind faith in experts who claim certainty. We rely on extrapolations of the past. If house prices have risen each year for a long period, it seems natural to conclude that they will go on rising.[7] Such beliefs can fuel a continuing rise in prices until some external event confronts those beliefs with reality. Much statistical analysis in economics – the use of econometrics – relies on the assumption that past correlations will continue to hold in the future because the underlying 'model' generating observations of economic data remains unchanged. But if the model is wrong, observed correlations will prove a poor guide to the future, as LTCM discovered. Neither house prices nor any other asset price are likely to rise indefinitely, relative to a measure of incomes. Failure to understand the context in which correlations are observed leads to false conclusions. The steady fall in long-term real interest rates since 1990 was always likely to lead to a continuing rise in house and other asset prices. But it was never plausible that such a fall could continue indefinitely. Similarly, before the crisis, banks appeared to be well capitalised and had little trouble attracting funds, until one day they couldn't. It is difficult to cope with the complexity of the world, and so we fall prey to the illusion of certainty. An example from the stock market illustrates the problem.

The stock market is volatile and difficult, if not impossible, to predict over short periods. At the beginning of any particular week the chance of the market rising over the following week is roughly the same as the chance of its falling. So if I were to predict the direction of the market movement correctly for five successive weeks, you might think that I knew something you didn't. Indeed, you might be willing to subscribe to an investment service with that sort of track record. How might one create the illusion of clairvoyance? Select around six thousand names and addresses from the London or New York telephone directory. Divide the names into two groups. To the first group, send a letter predicting that the market will rise over the coming week. To the second, write predicting a fall in the market. At the end of the week keep the three thousand or so names who were given the correct prediction and discard the others. Divide those names in turn into two groups. To the first, predict a rise in the market and to the second, a fall. Repeat this process for five weeks, at which point there will be around 200 people to whom the following letter could be sent: 'You may well have been sceptical when you received our first letter, but by now you will know that we have indeed found the secret of predicting successfully the direction of movement of the stock market. You know that our method really works. To subscribe to our investment service please send £5000 by return.'

My publisher has insisted that I make clear that I am not encouraging any reader to set up such a scheme. But the example illustrates that the interpretation of *ex post* outcomes depends critically on understanding the context from which the observations were drawn. In complicated situations that may require imagination of a high order. The wish for certainty and the belief that it exists are seductive and dangerous. The desire to resolve the cause of apparently inexplicable events means that people can easily be misled into believing a false story by a failure to appreciate the context from which the events they observe are drawn. Coping with uncertainty is by no means straightforward, even for the most highly trained professionals. As Voltaire put it, 'Doubt is not a pleasant condition, but certainty is an absurd one.'[8]

The two types of uncertainty

In coming to terms with an unknowable future, it is helpful to use the distinction between risk and uncertainty introduced in 1921 by the American economist Frank Knight.[9] Risk concerns events, like your house catching fire, where it is possible to define precisely the nature of the future outcome and to assign a probability to the occurrence of that event based on past experience. With risk it is then possible to write contracts that can be defined in terms of observable outcomes and to make judgements about how much we would pay to take out insurance against that event. Many random events take the form of risk, and that is why there is a large industry supplying insurance against fire, theft, accidents and death. Uncertainty, by contrast, concerns events where it is not possible to define, or even imagine, all possible future outcomes, and to which probabilities cannot therefore be assigned. Such eventualities are uninsurable, and many unpredictable events take this form. A capitalist economy generates previously unimaginable ideas, new products and new technologies. For example, a friend decides to open a software business and asks you to be an investor. It may be difficult to assess the value of the software product and impossible to assign probabilities to its success or failure.

The distinction between risk and uncertainty can be illustrated by human mortality. 'In this world nothing can be said to be certain, except death and taxes,' wrote Benjamin Franklin in 1789. It is clear, however, that there is indeed substantial uncertainty about both the likely date of our death and the contributions or taxes required to pay for our pensions. Longevity risk – the probabilities of dying at different ages – can be assessed by looking at the experience of others. In England and Wales in 2012 the most common age of death for women was eighty-seven, but of course most died at different ages. Because those frequencies of death at different ages are observable, individual risk – that we will die either earlier or later than the average for our peers – can be insured by taking out life insurance against early death or by purchasing an annuity to insure against later death.

There is, however, also genuine or 'radical' uncertainty

about the average length of life of people belonging to different generations. Average longevity has increased over time, with a remarkable reduction in infant mortality during the twentieth century and a more recent fall in mortality at later ages. A woman who was sixty in 1902, and subject to that year's mortality rates, would have expected to live for another fourteen and a half years. By 2012 that expectation had increased to over twenty-five years. Changes in average longevity have proved hard to predict. In 1798, the English cleric and scholar Thomas Malthus wrote that 'with regard to the duration of human life, there does not appear to have existed, from the earliest ages of the world, to the present moment, the smallest permanent symptom, or indication, of increasing prolongation'.[10] That past experience was to prove a poor predictor of the future. In 1798, life expectancy in Britain was around forty. Today it is over eighty, and even higher for women. We simply do not know how life expectancy will change in the future.[11] Developments in medical science, especially the results of stem-cell research, may enhance the prospects for life expectancy radically, and new infectious diseases may have the opposite effect. Good judgement rather than statistical extrapolation is key to making assessments about changes not only in longevity but in many economic and social variables.

Economists typically think about risk rather than radical uncertainty. They see the future as a game of chance in which we know all the outcomes that might emerge and the odds of each of them, even though we cannot predict the roll of the dice. In that world, because all future outcomes can be defined, it is theoretically possible to hold the grand economic auction described in Chapter 2, leading to efficient decisions about what to produce and consume.[12] Although such an auction would, of course, be impossible to organise in practice, the real failure of the auction model is more profound. If we cannot imagine the goods and services that may exist in the future, nor conceive of all the eventualities that may befall us, then it is impossible to define the markets that are required by the auction model. Radical uncertainty drives a gaping hole through the idea of complete and competitive markets. Even if the markets that do exist are competitive, many crucial markets for future goods and services are absent. When IBM launched its personal computer (the 'PC') in 1981, there were no markets in the products that subsequently displaced it in the consumer marketplace, such as laptop and tablet devices. Neither producers nor consumers can know what options will be available to them in the future, and so they cannot express preferences in markets that might provide a guide to investment decisions. The markets are simply missing. And how tedious it would be if we could imagine what the future holds. Uncertainty – radical uncertainty – is the spice of life.

Coping strategies as rational behaviour under uncertainty

In a world of pure risk, where we can list possible future events and attach probabilities to them, there is a traditional view among economists of what constitutes rational behaviour – the so-called 'optimising' model. According to this view, individuals first evaluate each possible future outcome in terms of its impact on their well-being or 'utility', and then weight each utility by the probability of the event to which it is attached, so deriving the average or 'expected utility' from a given set of actions. People are assumed to choose their actions (for example, how much to save today) in order to reach the highest level of 'expected utility'.[13] Such optimising behaviour in a world of risk has proved a useful tool in analysing the impact of government interventions in markets and the provision of insurance against known risks. Choosing between different models of car, how many hours to work, how much to pay for insurance against an identifiable event – all such decisions, and there are many of them, can be analysed perfectly well within the conventional framework of economic risk and hence the traditional economists' optimising framework. As the imperial power of the social sciences, economics has extended its reach to theories of marriage patterns, divorce and childbearing. It is striking, however, that such economic analysis is largely concerned with areas of economic choice where risk rather than uncertainty is the norm.[14]

The main defence of the theory of optimising behaviour is the one provided by Milton Friedman in 1953, when he compared people making economic decisions with billiards or snooker players who do not understand Newtonian mechanics, but play as if they did.[15] This 'as if' argument has been powerful in persuading economists that people behave as if they carried out immensely complex mathematical calculations – rather as if they were computers playing chess. But we know that when computers play chess, they do so differently from human beings. The former make millions of calculations; the latter make intuitive leaps of imagination. And that should be a warning of the limitations of the economic calculus underlying traditional economic theories. Human capacity for making conscious calculations is bounded, but the ability of the human brain to engage in lateral thinking is well developed. People are better than computers at recognising faces. Most of my economist colleagues have had their deepest insights through the use of intuition, and have deployed logical mathematical proofs to demonstrate to others why that intuition is correct. But the original insight did not come from making a mathematical calculation.

And it appears that cricketers and baseball players are the same, only more so. If, like calculating billiards players, fielders followed the dictates of Newtonian mechanics, they would observe the ball hit high in the air, compute where it would land, run in a straight line, stand still and catch the ball. Careful video observations have revealed that neither cricketers nor baseball players do that.[16] Rather, they seem to follow a simple rule of thumb: watch the ball and keep the angle between it and the horizon constant.[17] It can be shown that this rule of thumb means that fielders will run, not in a straight line but in an arc, and will end up catching the ball while still running. That pattern of behaviour is exactly what the videos have shown. Traditional optimising behaviour is replaced by a rule of thumb that is simple to follow and robust to the complexities of swirling winds and atmospheric resistance of the ball, a practice sustained by experience.

More generally, in a world of radical uncertainty, where it is not possible to compute the 'expected utility' of an action, there is no such thing as optimising behaviour. The fundamental point about radical uncertainty is that if we don't know what the future might hold, we don't know, and there is no point pretending otherwise. Right through his life, John Maynard Keynes was convinced that radical uncertainty, as it has become known, was the driving force behind the behaviour of a capitalist economy. As he explained, drawing on Knight's distinction between the two types of uncertainty, there is an essential difference between a game of roulette or predicting the weather, on the one hand, and the prospect of war or the scope of new inventions, on the other. Of the latter, he wrote: 'About these matters there is no scientific basis on which to form any calculable probability whatever. We simply do not know.'[18]

The language of optimisation is seductive. But humans do not optimise; they cope. They respond and adapt to new surroundings, new stimuli and new challenges. The concept of coping behaviour does not, however, mean that people are irrational. On the contrary, coping is an entirely rational response to the recognition that the world is uncertain. There is no need to abandon the conventional assumptions of economists that people prefer more consumption, or profit, to less, and that their choices display a degree of consistency.[19] The strength of economics as a social science is the belief that people will attempt to behave rationally. The challenge is to work out how a rational person might cope with radical uncertainty. People aren't dumb. It is just that in a world of radical uncertainty even smart people do not find it easy to know what it means to behave in a smart manner.

The main challenge to the economists' assumption of optimising behaviour comes from 'behavioural economics', a relatively new field often associated with Daniel Kahneman, Richard Thaler and Amos Tversky.[20] It studies the emotional and psychological dimensions of economic choices.[21] Behavioural economics has identified an impressive array of cognitive biases in the way people behave in practice. For example, people are observed both to display overconfidence in their ability to judge probabilities and to underestimate the likelihood of rare events. But behavioural economics assumes that deviations from traditional optimising behaviour result from the fact that humans are hardwired to behave in a way that is 'irrational'. Daniel Kahneman suggested that decisions are made by two different systems in the mind: one fast and intuitive, the other slower, deliberate, and closer to optimising behaviour.[22] In this way he was able to explain aspects of behaviour that appear anomalous in the traditional approach.

But simply patching up the optimising model by making the decision process more complicated – adding an intuitive to a rational self – in order to explain particular observed anomalies does not mean that it is likely to perform better in explaining future behaviour. The gold standard of scientific tests is prediction. Consider the problem of trying to explain the movement of the stock market over the past year. By taking into account more variables and more detail from that year, we would be able to 'explain' a larger proportion of the movement. But much of that would reflect the accidental quirks of the past year rather than any underlying structure of the stock market. A complicated explanation of the past makes it no more likely that we can predict the stock market over the coming year than simply tossing a coin. Many smart people have tried and failed to beat the market. Information is quickly incorporated into stock prices, and explaining why prices moved in the past is no basis on which to predict the future. The stock market is a good example of the tendency of economists 'to excel in hindsight (fitting) but fail in foresight (prediction)'.[23]

The danger in the assumption of behavioural economics that people are intrinsically irrational is that it leads to the view that governments should intervene to correct 'biases' in individual decisions or to 'nudge' them towards optimal outcomes. But why do we feel able to classify behaviour as irrational? Are policy-makers more rational than the voters whose behaviour they wish to modify? I prefer to assume that neither group is stupid but that both are struggling to cope with a challenging environment. After the crisis, the earlier belief that competitive markets were efficient and yielded rational valuations of assets was replaced by a conviction that financial markets were not merely inefficient but reflected irrational behaviour that produced 'bubbles' in asset prices and excessive demand for credit. Both views are extreme. Of course, emotions play an important part in economic decisions, especially in financial markets. Professor David Tuckett of University College, London, interviewed a large number of investment managers in different financial centres to discover what motivated them when making their decisions about how to invest large sums of money. Out of this came a theory of 'emotional finance'. Rather than viewing unconscious emotions and conscious reasoning as two systems in conflict, Tuckett sees them as engaging in a continuous two-way communication. As he argues, 'emotion exists to help economic human actors when reason alone is insufficient'.[24] In other words, emotions help us to cope with an unknowable future and should not be seen as 'irrational'.

The problem with behavioural economics is that it does not confront the deep question of what it means to be rational when the assumptions of the traditional optimising model fail to hold. Individuals are not compelled to be driven by impulses, but nor are they living in a world for which there is a single optimising solution to each problem. If we do not know how the world works, there is no unique right answer, only a problem of coping with the unknown. A different way of thinking about behaviour as neither irrational nor the product of a constrained optimisation problem is, I believe, helpful in understanding what happened both before and after the crisis. In other words, we need an alternative to both optimising behaviour and behavioural economics.

What does it mean to be rational in a world of radical uncertainty? Once we are liberated from the view that there is a single optimising solution, rules of thumb – technically known as heuristics – are better seen as rational ways to cope with an unknowable future.[25] A heuristic is a decision rule that deliberately ignores information. It does so not just because humans are not computers, but because it is rational to ignore information when we do not understand how the world works. As is clear from the example of trying to explain and then predict the stock market, getting lost in the thickets of the past conceals the big picture. Ignoring information is rational when it is likely to be of little help in solving the problem we confront – sometimes less is more. Heuristics are not deviations from the true optimal solution but essential parts of a toolkit to cope with the unknown.

An eye surgeon of my acquaintance told me how his patients responded when he explained to them, as was his duty, the risks of a surgical procedure. Half of the patients had already made up their mind before entering the room, based on their attitude towards risk, irrespective of the probabilities of different outcomes. And the other half made up their mind by listening carefully to the doctor and then making the decision on the basis not of reported probabilities but on their own judgement of the character and personality of the man in front of them. In the words of Frank Knight, 'The ultimate logic, or psychology, of these deliberations is obscure, a part of the scientifically unfathomable mystery of life and mind. We must simply fall back upon a "capacity" in the intelligent animal to form more or less correct judgements about things, an intuitive sense of values.'[26] A coping strategy is a way of capturing that unfathomable mystery. Humans are not pre-programmed to solve complex mathematical optimising problems, because it is impossible to know in advance which problems they will need to solve. But they are programmed to learn and to adapt. Coping strategies are the natural, even perhaps genetic response to the need to adapt to an uncertain world. They are, in Gigerenzer's phrase, 'ecologically rational'; that is, they are decision processes that are well suited to the environment in which they are used.[27] In that sense, in a world of radical uncertainty they are more rational than the economists' assumption of optimising behaviour.

A coping strategy comprises three elements – a *categorisation* of problems into those that are amenable to optimising behaviour and those that are not; a set of rules of thumb, or *heuristics*, to cope with the latter class of problems; and a *narrative*. The set of heuristics may comprise one or several rules of thumb to deal with different problems within the class. Each heuristic is a rule for making decisions which ignores much of the information used in optimising behaviour in order to provide a quick and robust decision. It is specific to the environment in which it is used. The narrative is a story that integrates the most important pieces of information in order to provide a basis for choosing the heuristic and the motive for a decision. Narratives compel us to action, and so play a big part in decisions taken under conditions of radical uncertainty. When we cannot write down a mathematical model with numerical probabilities, we can nevertheless think and talk about the future in qualitative terms.

The heuristic must be operational and the narrative believable. Coping strategies are not universal solutions to all problems in all environments but robust and rational ways of responding to particular problems. When things go wrong, as in the crisis, the cause is not necessarily irrational behaviour, nor an external shock, but possibly a mismatch between the chosen heuristic and the environment. In Chapter 8 I shall use these ideas to describe the continuation of unsustainable levels of borrowing and spending before the crisis.

Two real-life examples from financial markets show what this abstract description of decision-making means in practice. The first concerns J.P. Morgan and its British-born banker Sir Dennis Weatherstone, who started as a bookkeeper at the age of sixteen and rose to become CEO in 1990. The challenge was how to decide which of the many new and obscure financial products suggested by the traders and mathematicians on its staff the firm should sell to its clients. With no past history for the performance of those products, there was no basis for judging which ones were likely to be effective. The new products were an example of radical uncertainty. The strategy

Weatherstone employed was to make sure that any new product was understood by senior management. The narrative underlying the strategy was that if the product could be explained in a conversation among senior managers then there was less risk that something might go badly wrong. Weatherstone, I was told, would give the inventors three slots of fifteen minutes to explain the product to him. If at the end of that he still did not understand the product, the firm would not sell it.[28] In 2008 there must have been many executives who wished they had followed Weatherstone's heuristic.

Just before Barings Bank, one of the oldest banks in the world, collapsed in 1995 under the weight of losses of $1.4 billion caused by a rogue derivatives trader, Nick Leeson, in its Singapore branch, the senior managers in London told the Bank of England that they were pleased with the trading results but slightly puzzled as to how its Singapore business had earned such a large profit. A useful heuristic for managers and regulators alike is to probe not only those parts of a business that are losing a lot of money but also those that are making a lot.

The second example is the problem of how to regulate a bank. If a bank fails and is unable to meet its obligations to depositors and bondholders, the ensuing chaos may lead to a loss of confidence in other banks and disrupt the system of payments of wages and bills in the economy as a whole. To limit the risk of failure of a bank, regulators (the Federal Reserve, the Federal Deposit Insurance Corporation and the Office of the Comptroller of the Currency in the United States, the Bank of England in the United Kingdom, and the European Central Bank in the euro area) insist that a bank finances itself with a minimum amount of equity capital contributed by its shareholders. In that way, the bank has some capital that can absorb any losses that might arise, so reducing the risk of failure. The amount of equity capital the bank is required to issue – known as its 'capital requirement' – is related to the riskiness of the bank's activities.

At first sight this seems eminently sensible. The riskier a bank's assets, the more likely it is that the bank will fail unless it has sufficient equity to absorb losses. Internationally agreed standards set the capital requirement as a proportion of its 'risk-weighted assets', where each type of asset on the bank's balance sheet is weighted by a measure of its riskiness.[29] For example, debt issued by governments has a zero weight, meaning that banks are not required to have any equity to support that type of asset. The justification for the zero weight is that governments are assumed not to default on their debt – an assumption that might have looked reasonable when the standards were drawn up after long negotiations among many countries, but looked decidedly odd during the euro area crisis from 2012 onwards. Risk weights derived from statistical studies of the past, moreover, proved highly misleading in the crisis. For example, past data had suggested that mortgages were a relatively safe asset for banks to own, and yet in the crisis they turned out to be the source of large losses. It is extremely difficult, if not impossible, to judge how the riskiness of different assets will change in the future. The appropriate risk weights can change abruptly and suddenly, especially in a crisis, and are an example of radical uncertainty, not risk, despite the words used by regulators.

Risk-weighted capital requirements appealed to many of my international colleagues because risk was explicitly incorporated into the calculation. But if the nature of the uncertainty is unknown, then the use of such measures can be highly misleading. It is better to be roughly right than precisely wrong, and to use a simple but more robust measure of required capital. Heuristics are better than so-called optimising solutions that assume the wrong model. In the case of bank regulation, it is better to use a measure of leverage rather than a ratio of capital to risk-weighted assets. Leverage ratios measure capital relative to total (unweighted) assets. A Bank of England study of 116 large global banks during the crisis (of which 74 survived and 42 failed) found that the simple but robust leverage ratio was better at predicting which banks would fail than the more sophisticated risk-weighted measures of capital.[30]

The most extreme example was Northern Rock, which failed in the autumn of 2007. At the start of that year, Northern Rock had the highest ratio of capital to risk-weighted assets of any major bank in Britain, so much so that it was proposing to return capital to its shareholders because they had no need of it – under the regulations. At the same time, the bank's leverage ratio was extraordinarily high at between 60 to 1 and 80 to 1.[31] The reason for this remarkable discrepancy between the two measures of capital ratios was that the international standards assumed that mortgages were an extremely safe form of lending and Northern Rock did little else. But Northern Rock had been selling its mortgage loans to other investors rather than holding them on its own balance sheet. When the market for such transactions closed in the late summer of 2007, the bank could no longer obtain funds to finance its assets. The initial threat to Northern Rock did not come from volatility in the value of its mortgages but from the risk that its short-term creditors would withdraw their funds, leaving the bank high and dry. And that is what happened after the shock to markets in August 2007. The bank was left exposed as it tried to find alternative, and more expensive, sources of funding, which were not forthcoming to an institution with such a high leverage ratio. Keeping your eye on the leverage ratio is the banking equivalent of the rule of thumb used by baseball and cricket players. The heuristic of keeping the leverage ratio below some critical level is designed to deal with a situation where we know that we don't know how to measure the risks facing a bank. That is where the regulators and executives of the big banks went wrong.

Financial markets and derivatives

Coping strategies are especially important in financial markets because these markets are a link between the present and the future. Radical uncertainty is the key to understanding not just money and banks but financial markets in general. Of all the actors in recent economic history, the most infamous, revered and reviled in turn, were 'the markets'. I wish I had a pound (or even a dollar or a euro) for each time I had to listen to a politician explain, always in an infuriated tone, that 'the markets' didn't understand. But markets are not people. They are an impersonal mechanism by which many different real agents – such as businesses, banks, investors, pension funds and indeed governments – interact in the buying and selling of foreign exchange, loans, stocks and bonds, and, increasingly, a bewildering variety of new financial instruments. What is the purpose of all these financial markets? They channel household savings into business investment, at home and abroad. They make it possible to share risk by giving us the opportunity to insure, hedge, or even speculate, against future events. And they provide continuous valuations – a financial running commentary – of the myriad activities that make up our economy.

Equity, debt and insurance are the basic financial contracts underpinning our economy. A corporate stock is a claim on the earnings of a company in all future eventualities and provides an uncertain stream of dividends over an indefinite future. A loan made today is a claim on repayment of principal and interest over a fixed number of years in all states, except when the borrower defaults. An insurance contract yields payments under specified contingencies at unknown dates in the future. The estimated total value of stocks and bonds around the world is somewhere between $150 and $180 trillion. The total 'global financial stock' of marketable instruments plus loans must be well over $200 trillion. Much of this represents the value of the finance raised by governments, households and companies to fund their expenditure, both current and capital. Finance is essential to the ability to invest in real capital assets – houses, factories, railroads, sewers and a host of private and public infrastructure. Even a cursory glance at economic history shows the importance of a banking and financial sector able to channel household savings into investment projects, to share the risks resulting from those investments, to manage our wealth, and to enable us to do mundane things such as pay our bills. The absence of a proper financial sector handicaps development and was well illustrated by the inefficiencies of centrally planned economies.

Over the past twenty years, a wide range of new and complex financial instruments has emerged, expanding dramatically the scale of financial markets. These new instruments are elaborate combinations of the more traditional debt, equity and insurance contracts, and as such they are known as 'derivative' instruments. They package streams of future returns on a wide variety of investments, ranging from housing to foreign exchange. They are claims on returns generated by the underlying basic financial contracts and play a valuable role of filling in gaps in markets, offering new ways both to hedge risks and speculate on future price movements of the underlying contracts, such as stock prices. Derivatives typically involve little up-front payment and are a contract between two parties to exchange a flow of returns or commodities in the future. The principle of derivative instruments is simple, but if you want to make it complicated there are many lawyers, and investment bankers who will help you – at a (significant) price.

Examples of derivative instruments include forward and futures contracts (the purchase of a commodity to be delivered at a future date), options (the right to buy, or sell, a basic contract such as a stock at a given price on or before a given date), and swaps (where two parties exchange a stream of cash flows in different currencies or for different profiles of interest payments to hedge their other exposures). Many of these instruments have real practical value. For example, the Wimbledon tennis championships receives payments in dollars for broadcast rights in the United States. But almost all the costs of running the tournament are in pounds sterling, which creates a risk from unknown future movements in the pound–dollar exchange rate. That risk can be reduced, at a price, by contracting today to sell dollars for pounds at a specific date in the future and at a particular exchange rate. Many, if not most, companies benefit from similar transactions.[32]

During the crisis more complicated derivative instruments, as well as bundles of underlying assets packaged up and sold as 'securitised' instruments, acquired a certain notoriety because the failure to understand their true nature brought down banks and even AIG, a large American insurance company. These included credit default swaps (CDS, where the seller agrees to compensate the buyer in the event of default of some named party), mortgage-backed securities (MBS, a claim on the payments made on a bundle of many hundreds of mortgages, sold to the market by the originator of the mortgages, often a bank), and collateralised debt obligations (CDO, a claim on the cash flows from a set of bonds or other assets that is divided into tranches so that the lower tranches absorb losses first and the higher last, with investors able to choose in which tranches to invest). All of these complex instruments were legitimate financial contracts to create and sell. But the buyer needed to be aware of what he or she was getting. In their New Year sale the London store Harrods used to offer socks at half price – provided you bought a fixed package of five. When you got home you would discover at least one pair you would never wear (in my case, orange socks). The set of five pairs was rather like a CDO that bundled socks instead of sub-prime mortgages – a legitimate tactic by a sharp salesman.[33]

Talented mathematicians were recruited by banks to invent and market even more complicated instruments that often only they really understood. And even the mathematicians did not fully appreciate that all their sophisticated calculations could take into account only observable risk and not unquantifiable uncertainty. Crucially, since derivatives are not basic contracts representing economic activity but synthetic instruments, there is no limit on the size of the exposure – and the potential losses – that can be created. The scale of exposure inherent in derivatives can be many multiples of the value of the underlying equity or debt claims. In Chapter 1, I described how, at the start of the crisis in 2007, regulators drew comfort from the fact that the size of the basic contracts in sub-prime mortgages was too small to bankrupt the banking system. But the magnitude of the derivative instruments built on sub-prime mortgages was many times greater and led to enormous exposures and losses. It is rather like watching two old men playing chess in the sun for a bet of $10, as one can in Washington Square in New York, and then realising that they are watched by a crowd of bankers who are taking bets on the result to the tune of millions of dollars. The scope for introducing risk into the system rather than sharing it around is obvious. And that is why Warren Buffett described derivatives as 'financial weapons of mass destruction'.[34]

All of this was pointed out to the financial services industry by central bankers and regulators before the crisis.[35] Why, then, did derivatives grow so quickly? One answer is that betting is more addictive than chess, and the trading mentality fed on itself. Derivatives also allowed a stream of expected future profits, which might or might not be realised, to be capitalised into current values and show up in trading profits, so permitting large bonuses to be paid today out of a highly uncertain future prospect. But another answer is that derivatives do have real value when used in the right way – to reduce, not create risk. Many companies and institutions want to hedge (that is, insure against) risk associated with future shifts in the prices of commodities, changes in interest and exchange rates, and other economic variables. Derivatives also create financing options that may not exist in conventional debt markets. Consider investor A, who would like to purchase a bundle of mortgages (an MBS) but can pay for it only by borrowing short term. That creates a risk that when the loan must be repaid it may be either expensive or indeed impossible to take out another loan, as happened to many borrowers in the crisis. Writing a derivative contract with an investor B, under which A pays B fixed amounts over the life of the contract and in return receives the cash flows from the mortgages, amounts to locking in the finance for the purchase of the MBS, which is then used as collateral. Derivatives provide alternative ways to borrow.[36]

Much of the impetus for the creation of a wide range of derivative financial instruments, including options, was the belief that by adding more and more markets a gain to society would be achieved by the effective 'completion' of markets in order to mimic the auction economy described in Chapter 2. In that fictional world of the grand auction, financial markets are redundant. The prices and quantities of every transaction for goods and services, including labour services, are set in the auction, and so financial assets are no more than synthetic packages of those basic components. In reality, where markets for many of those goods and services are missing, as they inevitably are in a world of radical uncertainty, financial markets play a significant role. They can – up to a point – substitute for some of those missing markets. In so doing, they have created the illusion that markets provide almost unlimited ways to cope with uncertainty.

In fact, filling in the gaps between existing markets may serve a valuable purpose, but it cannot deal with the problem of how to create a market in something we cannot imagine. Derivatives do not offer insurance against radical uncertainty. Auctions cannot be held nor contracts written on unimaginable outcomes. As Frank Knight put it, 'it is this *true uncertainty* which by preventing the theoretically perfect outworking of the tendencies of competition gives the characteristic form of "enterprise" to economic organisation as a whole and accounts for the peculiar income of the entrepreneur'.[37] In other words, radical uncertainty is the precondition of a capitalist economy.

Used carefully, derivatives can reduce risk. But the very complexity and obscurity of derivatives can mislead the unwary into thinking that they are hedging risks while in fact they remain exposed to great uncertainty and huge potential losses in the event of even a small change in underlying asset prices. It all brings to mind the previously untold story of what happened when financial markets arrived on a desert island I visited recently, following in the footsteps of Robinson Crusoe.

The parable of financial markets on a desert island

Sitting on his desert island, Robinson Crusoe would have been astonished to learn of the miracles of modern technology and the importance we attach today to financial markets. His descendants, however, learned the hard way. The effects of the explosion of derivative instruments in the financial sector are well captured by the sad story of what happened to that unfortunate island when it inadvertently allowed banking to overtake fishing as its principal activity.

In the beginning, fishing with rods was the only economic activity on the island. Then nets came into use, produced by specialist net-makers. For fishermen, nets were an investment and a banking system came into being to accept deposits, which were then lent to net-makers. The subsequent sale of nets enabled the loans to be repaid. All was going well on the desert island, until one day a banker had a bright idea. Instead of holding on to the loans and paying interest to depositors, he decided, the bank would package together a number of the loans made to net-makers and sell them as a new financial instrument: net-backed securities (NBSs). By selling NBSs to savers, it was possible for the banks to finance further loans and to stop worrying about whether the fishermen would catch enough fish to buy the nets, so enabling the net-makers to repay the loans. That was now the problem of the people who had bought the NBSs.

Some clever islanders with a mathematical bent realised that it was possible to go one step further. They 'sliced and diced' the various NBSs to create new synthetic securities that would allow investors to choose in which quality of net-maker (in the impressive language of the financial advisers, in which tranche of the returns) to invest. These collateralised debt obligations (CDOs) proved highly fashionable. So some of the clever and more mathematically inclined fishermen joined the bank. They created even more complex securities – CDO-squared and even higher orders were not uncommon. Some people were hired to act as 'rating agencies' to demonstrate that the securities were not as risky as might have been feared.

All this activity was rather exciting. The clever people involved in creating and trading the new securities worked out that it was possible to make bets on future fish catches without putting up much capital. As trading in these instruments proceeded, and people's views about the size of the future fish catch changed, so the values of the new securities went up and down. By adopting the modern accounting convention of valuing the new instruments by 'marking to market' – that is, valuing assets at the latest observed price and including all changes in asset values as profits – optimism about the future, whether justified or not, created large recorded profits from the trading of these new securities. In effect, anticipated future profits were capitalised and turned into current profits. From those large reported profits, the clever people paid themselves large bonuses. They acquired more and more claims on the catch of fish. As the wages of people in the financial sector rose, the wages of fishermen fell. There was much concern about rising inequality. But it was explained by the result of the market – trading required high skills. This was undoubtedly true.

The financial sector grew in size, the incomes earned by those in it reached levels not seen before on the island, and there was great admiration for the talents of those who had created such a vibrant and expanding sector. Some visionary islanders even suggested that if only they could find a trading partner across the sea, then it would be sensible for the island to abandon fishing and devote itself entirely to financial activity. Ordinary fishermen felt rather left behind, but they too had to admire the ability of financiers to create such apparently profitable activity and be so successful. Even the community leaders were envious of the power that accrued to the financial sector, and there developed a close, and, in the eyes of many, none-too-healthy relationship between the island's political leaders and the financial sector.

Then one day it all collapsed. The expansion of trading activity had reduced the supply of labour to fishing. Some people started to question whether the old man in the tree, known as the National Statistician, was right to count the profits on these trading activities – which, for a while, had more than offset the reduction in the production of fish – as GDP. As a result, a few people expressed doubts about the underlying value of many of these new financial securities. To meet their obligations, some of the banks started to sell the securities for money. That led to a downward spiral in the prices of these assets, and to concerns about the solvency of some of the banks. Markets in the securities closed, as no one was willing to take the other side. Liquidity disappeared. Banks had nothing with which to create new money. Panic set in, and the demand for liquidity soared. But the supply of liquidity fell. The banks failed and were taken into communal ownership while some of the clever people were employed to disentangle the web of complex interrelationships and contracts between the banks.

Everyone on the island felt let down. The cult of finance had led to the contraction of a successful fishing industry. Too many talented people had been sucked into trading which, with the benefit of hindsight, was little more than a zero-sum activity generating little or no output. How could so many people have been taken in by the new world of finance?

After a painful post-mortem, it was agreed that the banking system should go back to its traditional role of accepting deposits and financing loans to net-makers. More people needed to work in fishing, and to invest in the making of nets to enhance the future catch of fish. Clever people realised that their reputation would in future be enhanced by adding to the social value of production rather than diverting resources from other people's pockets into their own. Some of them even moved out of finance into teaching. They recognised that they had a responsibility to write the history of this episode, and to convey it to future generations, in order to prevent a repetition of the near disaster.

The illusion of liquidity

Radical uncertainty also leads to another problem in financial markets – the illusion of liquidity. In the world of the grand auction, liquidity is not an issue. Prices are determined in the auction, and then, as time passes, the commitments entered into are fulfilled. Markets don't reopen. In reality, of course, markets do reopen; financial markets, in particular, remain open almost continuously with buyers and sellers coordinating through an intermediary – a shop-keeper or 'market-maker' – who holds some stock to bridge the time between the arrival of a buyer and a seller. Such continuous trading is particularly important in financial markets, and I shall return to it later in the chapter. Market-makers offer the opportunity to transact immediately once a decision to buy or sell has been taken. Many financial centres boast that their markets are 'deep and liquid'. By that they mean that investors can quickly sell their financial assets, with only a very small reduction, if any, in the price, in order to obtain money.

Liquidity is the quality of 'immediacy'.[38] For liquidity to be valuable it must be reliable. One aspect of the alchemy of financial markets is the belief that markets are always liquid. It is an illusion because the underlying assets (the physical assets and goodwill of a company, for example) are themselves usually illiquid, and liquidity depends on a continuing supply of buyers and sellers on opposite sides of the market. Radical uncertainty can disrupt that supply. Markets can be liquid one day and illiquid the next, as happened on 19 October 1987 ('Black Monday') when the Dow Jones Industrial Average fell 23 per cent in a day and the market-makers temporarily disappeared because they were worried about the risk of buying at one price and being able to sell only at a much lower price a short time later.

Liquidity also waxed and waned regularly during the year from September 2007 to September 2008. The liquid MBS market, for example, became highly illiquid when investors realised that house prices could go down as well as up. Their claims were now dependent on the circumstances of the individuals whose mortgages had been bundled into the MBSs rather than the value of the houses taken as collateral. Investors discovered that they knew very little about the borrowers on whose payments they depended. One MBS was no longer a good substitute for another. Liquidity dried up because it became difficult to value bundles of mortgages without knowing much more about the characteristics of the borrowers.

None of this should really have been surprising. Radical uncertainty makes it likely that from time to time there is a revision in the narrative guiding investor behaviour, or in the coping strategy as a whole, leading to sharp changes in traders' perception of values and willingness to buy or sell financial assets. A market that was previously characterised by a steady flow of trades may see a disappearance of activity. The behaviour of the LIBOR market (in which banks would lend to each other for short periods, say three months, at the London Inter-Bank Offer Rate) in the crisis brought this home forcefully. Banks supplied to a panel daily quotes of the interest rate at which they believed they could borrow from each other. LIBOR was set by the panel broadly as an average of the quotes received.[39] During the crisis, LIBOR became unstable, with large swings in the rate from day to day and from month to month. What became apparent was how few transactions there were in the interbank lending market at a number of maturities. Even well after the crisis, in 2011, there was little borrowing between banks at maturities of four months and above in sterling and above six months in dollars.[40] With few or no transactions taking place, it was difficult and at times impossible for banks to know what rate to quote. Indeed, once markets realised that different banks had different risks of failure then the whole concept of a single interbank borrowing rate became meaningless. Does this matter? Yes – because LIBOR is used as a reference rate in drawing up derivative contracts worth trillions of dollars. The benchmark interest rate used in those contracts had shallow foundations and in a storm it just blew down.

Amid the smoke created by the inability to define LIBOR during the crisis, it became possible for some traders in banks to collude and submit quotes designed to benefit them directly. Regulators later discovered evidence of manipulation and submission of 'false' quotes, and the so-called LIBOR scandal led to the fining of firms and individuals.[41] But at times in 2007–8 there were so few transactions in the interbank market that any quote submitted would have been hypothetical. An understandable response by some banks was to withdraw from the panel to which quotes were reported, only to discover that while being investigated by regulators for the submission of false quotes, they were also being told that they had to keep submitting quotes with no basis in reality. LIBOR has had its day.[42] Liquidity is not a permanent feature of financial markets. Places that boast of deep and liquid markets, the financial equivalent of an infinity pool, should be aware that their depth is variable, with a long shallow end that is sometimes drained.

In the 1980s, economists debated with some passion whether the stock market was 'rational' or 'irrational'. Three participants in the debate were subsequently awarded Nobel Prizes in Economic Science.[43] One of them, Robert Shiller, argued that it was impossible to explain the volatility of stock prices by reference to the volatility of the dividend stream that is the return to stocks. Others argued that expectations of large surprises in the distant future, not captured in the data for dividends in any observable sample, justifies the volatility apparent in stock markets. The issue can never be resolved, for the simple reason that in a world of radical uncertainty it is impossible to know what the future holds and therefore whether or not any particular valuation is rational, only whether it seems to embody a wise or a foolish judgement. Stock prices move around because investors are trying to cope with an unknowable future. Their judgements about future profits can be highly unstable. This instability is fundamental to a capitalist economy.

The Austrian economist Joseph Schumpeter coined the phrase 'creative destruction' for the way a capitalist economy promotes investment in new ideas and ventures, undermining investments in earlier undertakings.[44] Sometimes the message from the markets provides a helpful signal to businesses about when and in what directions to invest. On other occasions, the message tells us about the psychological nervousness, or even panic, among investors. Keynes's description of the stock market has become famous:

... professional investment may be likened to those newspaper competitions in which the competitors have to pick out the six prettiest faces from a hundred photographs, the prize being awarded to the competitor whose choice most nearly corresponds to the average preferences of the competitors as a whole; so that each competitor has to pick, not those faces which he himself finds prettiest, but those which he thinks likeliest to catch the fancy of the other competitors, all of whom are looking at the problem from the same point of view. It is not a case of choosing those which, to the best of one's judgment, are really the prettiest, nor even those which average opinion genuinely thinks the prettiest. We have reached the third degree where we devote our intelligences to anticipating what average opinion expects the average opinion to be. And there are some, I believe, who practise the fourth, fifth and higher degrees.[45]

Narratives play an important role in the coping strategies of investors. Under radical uncertainty, market prices are determined not by objective fundamentals but by narratives about fundamentals.[46] Those stories can be influenced by important players, such as central banks and governments, but also by changes in intellectual fashion or a realisation that the existing story is misleading – as happened in the crises of 1914, when the narrative that war was inconceivable was replaced by the narrative that it was here and would be won, and 2008, when the narrative that previous spending paths were sustainable was replaced by the narrative that they were not (see Chapter 8 for a fuller exposition of this point).

In today's stock market, the competitors trying to second- (or third-) guess market sentiment have been replaced by computers. Over one-half of orders are driven by computer algorithms – mathematical formulae that tell the computer when to buy or sell. Because stock exchanges have made it possible for some extremely large 'high frequency' traders to pay for faster access to the exchange, the computers of such firms can watch the order flow and then send in their own orders microseconds ahead of other traders, so jumping the queue and getting to the market before the price turns against them.[47] Such behaviour is called 'front-running'. It imposes a 'tax' on the transactions of other investors who are less fleet of foot, and encourages investment in expensive technology, not to incorporate new information in market prices, but to exploit information about other people's orders.

There is no social benefit in allowing some traders preferential access to knowledge of the overall balance between orders to buy and sell. One way of eliminating the 'tax' on ordinary investors would be to change the system of trading on organised exchanges to electronic auctions held once an hour, once a minute, or even once a day, depending on the nature of the stock being traded.[48] Moving to auctions separated by intervals chosen to match the likely arrival of relevant news, as opposed to supposedly real-time trading in which some investors can move (very slightly) faster than others, has much to commend it. It is already the case that much trading is carried out close to the opening and closing of the trading day, as investors want to transact when there are many other buyers and sellers so that their own orders have less of an influence on price.[49]

By their very nature, moreover, algorithms cannot easily change their strategy in the light of new information; so far only humans can rewrite the algorithms, and that requires not raw computing power but judgement.

Under radical uncertainty, investors make judgements, perhaps based on a coping strategy, and with the benefit of hindsight these are sometimes described as 'mistakes'. But beliefs change, and who is to know which beliefs are correct? The valuations in financial markets are for the moment. They change quickly, and sometimes violently, reflecting uncertain knowledge of the future. Investors are simply people trying to cope with an unknowable future and behave, as we all do in such situations, sometimes cautiously, sometimes erratically, but always in a fog of uncertainty.

We too can learn from the experience of Robinson Crusoe's descendants. Finance should support, not overshadow, the real economy. Financial markets can help us to cope with an uncertain future provided we do not succumb to the danger of believing that uncertainty has been turned into calculable risk. Central to a capitalist economy is the fact that the future cannot be seen as a game of chance in which the only source of uncertainty is on which number the wheel of fortune will come to rest. The future is simply unknowable. And in a capitalist economy, money, banking and financial markets are institutions that have evolved to provide a way of coping with an unpredictable future. They are the real-world substitute for the economic theorist's concept of a grand auction.

For that reason, a capitalist economy is inherently a monetary economy. Money has a special role. Provided that there is sufficient trust that its value will be maintained from one period to the next, it offers a means by which one can park generalised purchasing power, to be used in the future when unimaginable events occur. Money gives us the ability to exchange labour today for generalised purchasing power in the future. That is why many savings contracts are denominated in money terms. We expect to earn an interest rate defined as a percentage increase in the amount of money in our account. Money is not just a means of buying 'stuff' but a way of dealing with an uncertain future. A rise in the desire for a reserve of generalised future purchasing power lowers spending today, and can lead to a recession or even a depression.

The struggle to cope with radical uncertainty affects not just investors, businesses and households but also the institutions set up to deal with collective problems such as money creation. Central banks, arguably the most important such institutions, need a coping strategy too.

5

HEROES AND VILLAINS:
THE ROLE OF CENTRAL BANKS

'There have been three great inventions since the
beginning of time: fire, the wheel, and central banking.'

Will Rogers, American actor
and social commentator, 1920

'I promise on *demand* to pay,' affords,
A sort of fascinating sounding words;
And if I'm not the most deceiv'd on earth,
The *sound* they make is nearly all they're worth.

Anonymous, *The Siege of Paternoster Row*, 1826

Before the crisis, I was wandering around the stacks of the
London Library one evening (not something I was able to
do after the crisis started) when my eye was caught by a title:
The Old Lady Unveiled. How could such a risqué title have

found its way into the section on money and central banks? I soon discovered that the book, not held in any other library of which I was aware, was a devastating critique of the Bank of England. Written during the Great Depression, it began:

> The object of this book is to awaken the public to the truth that the Bank of England, commonly believed to be the most disinterested and patriotic of the nation's institutions, has been since its foundation during the reign of William of Orange a private and long-sustained effort in lucrative mumbo jumbo.[1]

Many would say that little has changed in the world of central banks. Certainly, they are more lucrative than ever, making large profits from their enormously expanded balance sheets. Although mumbo-jumbo surfaces from time to time, plain speaking is now very much the order of the day, with central bank governors giving press conferences, testifying regularly before Congress or Parliament, and appearing on television.

The cult of celebrity has reached even the gloomy halls of central banking. President Clinton was once asked by a journalist what it was like to be the most powerful man in the world. Pointing to Andrea Mitchell, White House correspondent for NBC, he replied, 'Ask her. She's married to him.' Her husband was Alan Greenspan, then Chairman of the Federal Reserve. Put on its cover by *Time* magazine as the key member of the 'Committee to Save the World', lionised by former presidential candidate John McCain (who said in one of the debates, 'I would not only reappoint Mr Greenspan – if Mr Greenspan should happen to die, God forbid, I would do like they did in the movie, *Weekend at Bernie's*. I'd prop him up and put a pair of dark glasses on him and keep him as long as we could'), and subsequently vilified on stage and screen (not to mention in print) as the architect of the financial crisis of 2008, Alan Greenspan is unrecognisable, in either guise, as the thoughtful and careful central banker I knew. So it is vital to strip away the magic and mystique of central bankers and see them for who they really are: people. Only then can we ensure that the system in which individuals operate provides the right incentives to behave in a way that leads to the best outcomes for the rest of us.

Attempts by central bankers, such as Ben Bernanke, who followed Greenspan, to take personality out of central banking met with limited success or outright failure. In his bestseller *The Lords of Finance*, Liaquat Ahmed describes the four shadowy central bank governors who led the world into, and eventually out of, the Great Depression. Eighty years later, the equivalent group of governors, of which I was one, confronted an equally difficult challenge. But the difference was that in the build-up to the crisis that started in 2007, central banks had come out of the shadows into the sunlight. They were embarking on a journey from mystery and mystique to transparency and openness. In the 1990s, central banks, if not their governors, became financial idols. The governors themselves saw it differently. We took to heart Keynes's advice, 'If economists could manage to get themselves thought of as humble, competent people, on a level with dentists, that would be splendid!'[2] Our goal was to make monetary policy as boring as possible.

It is fair to say that we failed in our ambition. You would have to be a hermit on a desert island to describe the past decade as boring. Around the world, central banks were thrust into the spotlight of controversy as the world plunged into its worst ever banking and financial crisis. Money and banking may seem boring technical topics. But they generate more than enough excitement when things go wrong. Rapid inflation can quickly turn into catastrophic hyperinflation, as in Weimar

Germany in the 1920s, and deflation can lead to economic stagnation, as in Japan in the lost decade of the 1990s – and, as many fear, in other parts of the industrialised world today. In 2008 the banking crisis dominated the news.

If money and banks are almost as old as *Homo sapiens*, central banks are the new kids on the block. As institutions go, most central banks are youthful. Indeed, the reputation of central banks as wise and disciplined institutions, in contrast with the wild excesses of finance ministries, belies their respective ages. The first central bank was the Riksbank in Sweden, set up in 1668. To celebrate its tercentenary it endowed the Nobel Prize in Economic Science. But the Riksbank did not acquire its name until 1867 and was really only a commercial bank until 1897.[3] The oldest central bank in continuous existence, the Bank of England, opened for business in 1694 to help the government finance military expenditure. Its tercentenary was a more low-key event: it held a concert and published a book of conference proceedings. Next came the Bank of Spain in 1782 and the Banque de France (founded by Napoleon) in 1800, followed by the Bank of Finland in December 1811 (well before the central bank of Russia, of which Finland was then a part, in 1860).

The United States had two false starts in central banking – with the First Bank of the United States between 1791 and 1811 and the Second Bank of the United States between 1816 and 1836 – before Congress legislated in 1913 to set up the Federal Reserve, which opened for business in 1914.[4] A year after the 1907 financial crisis, when a panic in New York led to a fall in the Stock Exchange of 50 per cent and numerous bank failures, Congress set up the National Monetary Commission to report on 'what changes are necessary or desirable in the monetary system of the United States'. Before recommending the establishment of the Federal Reserve System – a plan which it described as 'essentially an American system, scientific in its methods, and democratic in its control' – the Commission produced twenty-two volumes on monetary and banking systems elsewhere, especially in Europe. A complete set sits proudly in the Governor's anteroom in the Bank of England. The authors noted that 'the important place which the Bank of England holds in the financial world is due to the wisdom of the men who have controlled its operations and not to any legislative enactments'. They did not therefore see the Bank of England as a model, instead recommending the creation of an institution framed by legislation and responsible to Congress. After the Great Depression, further changes were made in the way the Federal Reserve operated, with greater powers for the board in Washington and the introduction of a clear national interest-rate policy.

Older central banks often had their origins as commercial banks and made the transition from private to public institutions as a result of their dominant position in their home banking market. For that reason they were deeply unpopular because they were seen as exploiting that position. From the outset, each time the Bank of England charter came due for renewal, a torrent of pamphlets condemned its privileged position. The Bank Charter Act of 1844, which gave the Bank the exclusive right to issue new banknotes, unleashed a new surge of anti-Bank sentiment. The Bank's directors were variously described as 'torpid as toads' and 'priests of Moloch's blood-stained altar'.[5] Whatever criticisms were directed at central bankers during the crisis, we could console ourselves that they were more moderate in tone.

When, in 1832, President Andrew Jackson vetoed the renewal of the charter of the Second Bank of the United States, he argued that Congress had no constitutional right to delegate the issuance of paper money to any other body:

It is maintained by some that the Bank is a means of executing the constitutional power 'to coin money and regulate the value thereof.' Congress have established a mint to coin money and passed laws to regulate the value thereof. The money so coined, with its value so regulated, and such foreign coins as Congress may adopt are the only currency known to the Constitution. *But if they have other power to regulate the currency, it was conferred to be exercised by themselves, and not to be transferred to a corporation.* If the bank be established for that purpose, with a charter unalterable without its consent, Congress have parted with their power for a term of years, during which the Constitution is a dead letter. It is neither necessary nor proper to transfer its legislative power to such a bank, and therefore unconstitutional.[6]

After the experience of banking crises in the late nineteenth and early twentieth centuries, Congress was persuaded that a central bank was both constitutional and a good idea. What led to the change in view? During the era of free banking, described in Chapter 2, the US had no central bank. Banknotes issued by commercial banks often traded at a discount to their face value. That made them less useful as money that could be used to buy stuff or as a store of value. There were concerns that banks might issue too many notes in order to exploit the lack of information among depositors about the solvency of the bank. And when there was a crisis in the banking system there was no central authority to restore confidence – in 1907 the task of putting together a consortium of banks to support their weaker brethren fell to John Pierpont Morgan, founder of the eponymous bank. In a similar fashion, the German Reichsbank was set up in 1876, not to coincide with unification of the country in 1871 but in response to a financial crisis in 1873. Central banks acquired their modern role as the result of experiences of earlier monetary and banking crises. The position of central banks that started life as commercial banks developed into that of first among equals, organising occasional rescues and acting in effect as the secretary of the club of banks, above the competitive fray in which other banks were engaged.[7]

By the twentieth century, central banks were gradually evolving into today's powerful institutions, responsible for managing the money supply and overseeing the banking system. Concern about the power of central banks remains a popular political position on both left and right, as expressed by the slogan 'end the Fed'.[8] Central banks were seen as heroes for delivering the decade of the Great Stability and for preventing a relapse into a second Great Depression after 2008. They were seen as villains for having failed to rein in the excesses of the banking system in the first place and then for creating money on a massive scale. Compared with the late 1990s and early 2000s when their reputation peaked, central banks are now on the back foot, defending their hard-won independence from the ambitions of politicians of all colours. When the Federal Reserve reached its centenary it felt obliged to describe the event as 'marking' rather than celebrating the milestone, and relied on charitable donations rather than its own funds to finance the accompanying exhibition in the American Museum of Finance on Wall Street. Even the courts are getting in on the action – Judge Thomas C. Wheeler of the United States Court of Federal Claims ruled in June 2015 that the Federal Reserve had acted beyond its legal authority in taking a large equity stake in the insurance company AIG in return for a bailout of the company during October 2008.[9] In Germany, the Federal Constitutional Court has expressed reservations about proposals by the European Central Bank to purchase the sovereign debt of some periphery members of the euro area.[10] Yet despite these challenges to their authority, governments have relied more and more on central banks – especially the Federal Reserve, the European Central Bank, the Bank of Japan and the Bank of England – to deliver a recovery from the Great Recession.

Experience has demonstrated the importance of a public body – normally the central bank – responsible for two key aspects of the management of money in a capitalist economy. The first is to ensure that in good times the amount of money grows at a rate sufficient to maintain broad stability of the value of money, and the second is to ensure that in bad times the amount of money grows at a rate sufficient to provide the liquidity – a reserve of future purchasing power – required to meet unpredictable swings in the demand for it by the private sector (see Chapters 2 and 3 respectively). Those two functions are rather simple to state, if hard to carry out. They correspond to the twin objectives of price stability and the provision of liquidity by a 'lender of last resort'.

Price stability – inflation targeting as a coping strategy

Eighteenth-century thinkers, such as David Hume and Adam Smith, understood the relationship between the amount of money in circulation and the prices at which goods and services were bought and sold: 'if we consider any kingdom by itself, it is evident, that the greater or less plenty of money is of no consequence; since the prices of commodities are always proportioned to the plenty of money'.[11] In the long run, more money means higher prices. The quantity theory of money, later refined and popularised by the American economists Irving Fisher and Milton Friedman, had been born.

Over the years, governments have been unable to resist the temptation to debase the currency, and, with the advent of paper money, to print as much of it as possible to finance their expenditures. Lenin is alleged to have remarked that the best

way to destroy capitalism is to debauch the currency. To judge
by the subsequent experience in Europe after the First World
War, he was right. Even where market economies survived,
inflation was a problem. In the twenty-five years before the
Bank of England adopted an inflation target in 1992, prices rose
by over 750 per cent, more than over the previous two hundred
and fifty years.[12] Inflation was simply taken for granted. Price
stability seemed an unlikely state of affairs.

Alan Greenspan, former Chairman of the Fed, defined price
stability as when 'inflation is so low and stable over time that
it does not materially enter into the decisions of households
and firms'.[13] Alan Blinder, the Princeton economist who was
Greenspan's deputy at the Federal Reserve Board, put it even
more clearly. Price stability, he said, was 'when ordinary people
stop talking and worrying about inflation'.[14] In recent years,
we have started to take price stability for granted; so much so
that some people have become exercised about the possibility
of deflation – when prices fall. Deflation is just as damaging
as inflation. In AD 274 the Roman emperor Aurelian tried to
restore the integrity of the coinage, which had been adulterated
by workmen in the mint. Aurelian exchanged bad money for
good, and ordered the destruction of all accounts drawn up
in the devalued currency. Prices fell overnight. Gibbon, in his
History of the Decline and Fall of the Roman Empire, observed that
'a temporary grievance of such a nature can scarcely excite and
support a serious civil war'.[15] And in the long run the operation
did restore the value of money. But in the short run it caused
hardship. Taking the Keynesian view that in the long run we
are all dead, the population at the time rose in insurrection.
Many of them found that they were dead in the short run as
well; seven thousand soldiers and countless civilians perished
during the suppression of the uprising.

In more modern times, governments, even if they profess

a belief in price stability, have found themselves tempted to depart from the path of righteousness in order to obtain a short-term benefit by stimulating the economy prior to an election in the hope that the inflationary cost will become apparent to the electorate only after the vote. Once having given in to temptation, they are faced with an unpalatable choice between a recession to bring inflation back down again, or high and possibly accelerating inflation. Taken together, the verdict of economics, history and common sense is that both inflation and deflation are costly. Giving a central bank the exclusive right to issue paper money raises the question of how we can prevent the abuse of the power to issue money. We cannot commit future generations – or even ourselves – to a particular policy. So how can we design an institution to create the reasonable expectation that money will retain its value?

By tying the currency to the mast of gold it seemed that price stability over a long period was attainable, as indeed it was for much of the nineteenth century. But even the gold standard could not override national sovereignty, and, when the costs (in terms of lost output and employment) of adhering to the standard appeared too high, governments suspended the con-vertibility of their currency into gold, as happened on several occasions in Britain and other European countries in the nine-teenth century during financial crises. There was an underlying need to find a way to retain domestic control over the supply of money and liquidity while at the same time retaining a long-term commitment to price stability.

Unfortunately, the switch from a fixed rule, such as the gold standard, to the use of unfettered discretion led to the failure to control inflation, culminating in the Great Inflation of the 1970s. Attention turned to the idea of delegating monetary policy to independent central banks with a clear mandate to achieve price stability. Central banks were not born with independence, they had it thrust upon them − literally, in the case of Germany when, after the Second World War, the Allies imposed the model of an independent central bank. The movement towards independence gathered pace in the 1990s as a reaction to the Great Inflation. The Bank of England and the Bank of Japan were made independent in 1997, the Swedish Riksbank in 1999, and in the same year the independent European Central Bank was set up, influenced by the track record of the Bundesbank in Germany which had, since its creation in 1957, achieved lower inflation than in other industrialised countries.[16]

Of course central banks may themselves be tempted to court popularity. One riposte to that concern is that central bankers are different from politicians. Central bankers who have the determination and strength of purpose to 'take the punch bowl away just when the party is getting going', in Federal Reserve Chairman McChesney Martin's memorable phrase, clearly have the right stuff − so why don't they 'just do it'?[17] It would be nice to think that all central bankers were made of the right stuff, and maybe they are. But there is no need to rely on our ability to identify superhuman individuals. Instead, the answer is to devise an incentive structure for the individuals appointed to run central banks.

If the elected government, or its advisers, understood exactly how the economy worked then it could write a contract specifying precisely what the central bank should do in each possible state of the world that might arise in the future. Monetary policy could then be delegated to an independent central bank tasked with implementing the contract. There are two problems with this idea. First, governments might be tempted to tear up the contract in precisely the same circumstances that they themselves would give in to the temptation to allow inflation to rise. Second, in a world of radical uncertainty we cannot write a detailed contract covering all possible future events. The future is literally undescribable. Economists have tended to devote more attention to the first of these problems than the second. I am inclined to think that the reverse should be the case. Coping with temptation is easier than coping with the entirely unknown.

Our inability to identify in advance the challenges that will arise in managing money means that it is sensible, indeed unavoidable, to grant the central bank a degree of discretion in responding to unfolding events. This is the basic idea behind inflation targeting, which originated in New Zealand in 1990. The idea soon spread to Canada in 1991 and the United Kingdom in 1992. The aim was to hold the central bank to account for achieving a numerical target for inflation over a specified period. Central banks were given discretion over the extent to which they responded to short-run movements in inflation.

Such movements are unpredictable. Prices and wages do not adjust instantaneously to clear markets whenever demand and supply are out of balance. Firms change prices only irregularly in response to changes in demand; wages adjust only slowly as labour market conditions alter; and expectations are updated only slowly as new information is received. Such 'frictions' or 'rigidities' introduce time lags into the process by which changes in money lead to changes in prices. These lags in the adjustment of prices and wages to changes in demand – so-called 'nominal rigidities' – and lags in the adjustment of expectations to changes in inflation – 'expectational rigidities' – generate short-run relationships between money, activity and inflation.[18] Monetary policy affects output and employment in the short run and prices in the long run. Central banks care about both. This is captured by the so-called dual mandate of the Federal Reserve, which states its objectives as maximum employment and stable prices.[19] The overriding concern of central banks is not to eliminate fluctuations in consumer price inflation from year to year, but to reduce the degree of uncertainty over the price level in the long run. People will then stop worrying about inflation.

An inflation-targeting monetary policy is a combination of two elements: (a) a target for inflation in the medium term and (b) a response to economic shocks in the short term. From time to time shocks – to oil prices or the exchange rate, for example – will move inflation away from its desired long-term level, and the policy question is how quickly it should be brought back. The answer depends on the relative costs of deviations of inflation from the target and of unemployment from its long-term equilibrium level, and central banks have discretion in making that judgement. From this perspective there is no essential difference between the actions of a central bank with a Fed-style dual mandate and a central bank with a single mandate to meet an inflation target. What is crucial is that households and businesses believe that prices will be stable in the long run.

Inflation targeting has been highly successful, both in its primary aim and as a way of ensuring the democratic accountability of powerful public institutions. Some economists have argued that central banks should be compelled to set policy according to a 'policy rule' set by legislators, or at a minimum to explain why their chosen policy deviates from that implied by the rule. Monetary policy rules have become a major area of research.[20] Perhaps the most famous is the so-called Taylor rule, named after John Taylor of Stanford University. The Taylor rule implies that interest rates should rise if inflation is above its target and output is above its trend level, and fall when the converse is true. In 2014, Representatives Scott Garrett and Bill Huizenga introduced a bill that would require the Federal Reserve to provide Congress with 'a clear rule to describe the course of monetary policy'.[21] Such a rule would be a mathematical formula showing how the Fed would adjust interest rates in response to changes in the economy.

Although it is clearly desirable for the Federal Reserve to be held directly accountable to Congress for its actions, the fundamental flaw in this proposal is that there is no timeless rule that is likely to remain optimal for long. Since our understanding of the economy is incomplete and constantly evolving, sometimes in small steps, sometimes in big leaps, any monetary policy rule judged to be optimal today is likely to be displaced by a new and improved version tomorrow. Whatever rule might be mandated in legislation would be superseded by new research within a year.

A good example was the experience of the Federal Reserve and the Bank of England during 2013 and 2014, when they announced the rate of unemployment at which they would start to consider raising interest rates. What looked in 2013 a plausible unemployment rate that would trigger a rise in interest rates turned out to be much less plausible by 2014, when unemployment had fallen faster than expected without signs of a pick-up in inflation. Monetary policy in practice is characterised by a continuous process of learning. Learning from experience means that it is sensible to be prepared to deviate from a rule constructed even a year or two ago. Rather, the onus should be on the central bank to justify its behaviour in terms of presenting convincing economic arguments and evidence for them. Accountability and transparency are superior to the use of a fixed rule.

Delegating policy to an independent central bank operating under a well-specified regime of 'constrained discretion' was seen as the answer to the unappealing choice between adopting a fixed rule and giving unfettered discretion to an independent body. Such a framework required a clear definition of the constraints to be imposed on central banks. One was a numerical target for inflation, and a second was the establishment of a regime under which central banks could be held accountable for their decisions. From the outset, inflation targeting was conceived as a means by which central banks could improve the credibility and predictability of monetary policy.

Since its adoption in New Zealand, Canada and the United Kingdom in the early 1990s, inflation targeting has spread to more than thirty countries around the world.[22] The big central banks now all have an inflation target of 2 per cent, with the Federal Reserve adopting it in 2012 and the Bank of Japan in 2013. In the language of Chapter 4, delegating monetary policy to an independent central bank with an inflation target is a coping strategy. Its clarity and simplicity mean that the target provides a natural heuristic for central banks and the private sector alike. The heuristic for the former is to set policy such that expected inflation is equal to the target rate, and for the latter it is to expect inflation equal to the target rate. Since expectations of inflation have a major influence on the setting of wages and prices, and hence on inflation itself, anchoring expectations on the target is a key element of any credible monetary policy. And the heuristic frees the central bank from having to commit to any one particular model of the economy when making its judgement about the likely future path of inflation. The great attraction of an inflation target is that it is a framework that does not have to be changed each time we learn something new about how the economy behaves.

Inflation targeting is about making and communicating decisions. It is not a new theory of how money and interest rates affect the economy. But, by anchoring inflation expectations on the target, it can in theory reduce the variability and persistence of inflationary shocks – and has done so in practice. And it has done so without pretending to commit to a rule that is incredible because it is not expected to last.

Old problems and new instruments

There are, however, deeper reasons to ask why central banks should worry only about consumer price inflation rather than the state of the real economy. Inflation targeting is designed to mimic the behaviour of a competitive market economy, one that exhibits none of the nominal or expectational rigidities that prevent prices from adjusting immediately. This makes perfect sense within the confines of the conventional economic models used by central banks. But those models take no account of radical uncertainty. And the problem that central banks need to confront is whether there are other significant imperfections in the economy that justify departing from an inflation target. Confronted with radical uncertainty, it is natural that households and businesses make occasional 'mistakes', for example about their future incomes, and realise their errors only after a considerable time lag. Such mistakes can accumulate into substantial deviations of spending and output from a sustainable path, even though they may have little impact on inflation in the short run. This is not the outcome of short-run rigidities but of misjudgements about the nature of the future.

The practical significance of this question has been highlighted by the current disequilibrium in the world economy. Should central banks take responsibility for trying to correct such mistakes before households and businesses come to a true appreciation of the situation, or should they stay focused solely on targeting inflation a year or two ahead? Did central banks contribute significantly to the crisis by not trying to correct the big mistakes made by the private sector? To suggest that monetary policy has the purpose of preventing the economy from getting into an unsustainable position is tantamount to arguing that central banks should, on occasions, target the real equilibrium of the economy and not just price stability – a much deeper and more difficult question than that of whether a central bank should have a dual or a single mandate. The fundamental question is whether central banks should take responsibility for preventing substantial deviations of real variables, such as spending and output, from their normal levels, because the cost of permitting the continuation of a large and growing disequilibrium is a crash at some point in the future, followed by economic stagnation and persistently low inflation.

The proper role of a central bank in guiding the economy is, therefore, a thorny and controversial issue. I shall return to it in a concrete context in Chapters 8 and 9, where I ask whether central banks could have prevented or reduced the severity of the crisis by following a different monetary policy, and consider what they should do today. Related concerns about the desirability of inflation targeting have been raised by those who believe that central banks should focus at least as much on 'financial stability' as on 'price stability', meaning that monetary policy can and should try to affect much more than just short-run movements in inflation. The difficulty with this proposition is that failure to achieve financial stability covers a multitude of sins. It may reflect the consequence for asset prices of 'mistakes' by economic agents – the rapid increases often loosely described as 'bubbles'. Or it may reflect excessive fragility in the banking sector resulting from excessively high leverage and interconnectedness. The appropriate policy response depends on the cause of the instability. The provision of an appropriate amount of 'emergency money' (see below) can ameliorate the immediate consequences, but to prevent instability arising may require either action on monetary policy or a change in the structure of the banking sector. Rather than thinking deeply about the framework for monetary policy or radical change in banking, policy-makers have sought new instruments to deal with the potential causes of financial instability. The most important such instruments go under the name of 'macro-prudential policies'.

Macro-prudential instruments include direct controls on financial markets – for example, setting limits on the size of mortgage loans relative to incomes – and indirect controls – such as requiring banks to use more equity finance if they increase lending to areas that are judged particularly risky. These quantitative controls are equivalent to setting different interest rates for different types of transaction. At the Bank of England, the Monetary Policy Committee decides on the level of the official short-term interest rate (Bank Rate) and a new committee, the Financial Policy Committee, set up in 2011, decides on the macro-prudential measures that act as add-ons. The distinction between monetary and macro-prudential policies is not clear-cut. A crude way of thinking about the difference is that the former is about the amount of money in the economy and the latter is about the allocation of credit across sectors.

Before the crisis, central banks believed that their role was not to enter into the allocation of resources, but rather to guide the economy by sending price signals (in the form of interest rates) about the appropriate relative prices of spending today and in the future. Today, the use of measures to intervene in particular asset markets is all the rage. But the scope for tensions between the two sets of decisions is evident. For example, in the Swedish Riksbank from 2010 to 2013 there was a sharp, and often bitter, division between two groups. The first wanted to raise interest rates because of concerns about the pace at which house prices and indebtedness were rising. The second thought that responsibility for dealing with the housing market should be left with the supervisory authority, which, as it happened, was more relaxed about housing developments than were the majority in the central bank.

Quantitative restrictions on credit are by no means a new policy instrument. They were deployed in many advanced economies in the 1950s and 1960s, and still play a role in many emerging and developing economies. As banking and financial markets were liberalised in the advanced economies in the 1970s and 1980s, and opened up to foreign competition, most of these controls were scrapped. Although central banks can determine interest rates in their own currency, they cannot easily restrict the lending activities of foreign banks. Cooperation between regulators has been improved since those days, but how far macro-prudential measures will be successful in today's world of borderless capital markets remains an open question. Nimbleness and the ability to respond quickly to events are important features of interest-rate policy. It will be more difficult to act, and to defend and explain rapid changes in restrictions on lending (for example, the maximum ratio of a mortgage loan to the value of the house) than in interest rates.

Out of a political consensus on the importance of ensuring monetary stability emerged an agreement that democratic societies would delegate to an unelected central bank the power to set interest rates, even though this would have effects on the distribution of income and wealth. But the entry of central banks into the field of direct controls on mortgages and lending more generally is bound to raise the question of whether this is taking delegation too far. It is possible to debate the merits of intervening in the market allocation of credit to help, for example, first-time homeowners and small businesses. But decisions on that type of interference with the market should properly be left to elected politicians with a mandate to take such action. It is hard to see why central banks should want the power to intervene in the microeconomic allocation of credit. If, as has happened over the past twenty years, saving and spending get out of kilter, then central banks will come under increasing pressure to intervene in particular financial markets to correct so-called distortions, which are in fact the result of a macro-economic disequilibrium. And 'distortions' and 'excesses' will then pop up in other markets. Down that road lies a degree of intrusion into individual decisions on saving and credit that is incompatible with an innovative market economy.

Amid the post-crisis confusion about whether central banks should focus solely on price stability, or whether they should take responsibility for guiding the economy to a new equilibrium, or deal with potential 'bubbles' in asset prices, one might be forgiven for thinking that central bankers should follow the example of the Church of England in making a general confession: we have not targeted those things which we ought to have targeted and we have targeted those things which we ought not to have targeted, and there is no health in the economy.[23]

Expectations and communications

When I joined the Bank of England in 1991, I asked the legendary American central banker Paul Volcker for one word of advice. He looked down at me from his great height (a foot taller than I) and said, 'Mystique.'[24] He was talking about the importance of businesses, households and financiers having confidence in the central bank. Today that confidence has to be earned in a much more transparent way. During my time at the Bank of England, it became apparent that politicians and central bank governors were on a divergent path. As they try to make an impression on the electorate, politicians have become taller and taller, whereas central bank governors have become shorter and shorter. Paul Volcker was followed by Alan Greenspan, Ben

Bernanke and Janet Yellen, a steady decline in height. At the Bank of England, Gordon Richardson, the counterpart of Paul Volcker during the 1980s debt crisis, was followed by Robin Leigh Pemberton, Eddie George, myself and Mark Carney. It is evident that central banks have come to rely less on height and hauteur and more on transparency and the ability to look the average person straight in the eye.[25]

Businesses and households base their decisions on expectations of the future, and so the way we expect monetary policy to be conducted in the future affects economic outcomes today. Consider a simple and stark example. Suppose that there were no frictions or time lags in the way the economy responded to changes in monetary policy. Imagine a central bank which, in those conditions, was successful in controlling inflation perfectly by responding to all shocks instantaneously. The outcome would be a constant inflation rate. Interest rates would move around but with no apparent link to or effect on inflation. To an observer – whether journalist or econometrician – interest-rate changes would appear to have little to do with inflation. The central bank would appear to be behaving almost randomly. By assumption, that inference would be false. Indeed, if people did expect the central bank to behave randomly, then the behaviour of households and firms would change and inflation would no longer be stable.

This observation leads to what we might call the Maradona theory of interest rates. The great Argentine footballer, Diego Maradona, is not usually associated with the theory of monetary policy. But his performance against England in the World Cup in Mexico City in June 1986 when he scored twice is a perfect illustration of my point. Maradona's first 'hand of God' goal, when he deliberately punched the ball into the England net unseen by the referee, was obviously against the rules. He was lucky to get away with it. His second and quite brilliant goal, however, was an example of the power of expectations. Maradona ran sixty yards from inside his own half, beating five players before shooting into the English goal. The truly remarkable thing, however, is that, as cameras positioned above the stadium showed, Maradona ran virtually in a straight line. How can you beat five players by running in a straight line? The answer is that the English defenders reacted to what they expected Maradona to do. Because they expected Maradona to move either left or right, he was able to go straight on.

Monetary policy works in a similar way. Market interest rates react to what the central bank is expected to do. In recent years there have been periods in which central banks have been able to influence the path of the economy without making large moves in official interest rates. They headed in a straight line for their goals. How was that possible? Because financial markets did not expect interest rates to remain constant. They expected that rates would move either up or down. Those expectations were sufficient – at times – to stabilise private spending while official interest rates in fact moved very little. An example of the Maradona theory of interest rates in action was seen in the UK in 2002. During that year the Bank of England was able to achieve its inflation target by moving in a straight line with unchanged official interest rates. But, although interest rates scarcely moved, expectations of future interest rates – as revealed in market interest rates – did move around as the economic outlook changed from the expectation of a swift recovery to worries about a protracted slowdown. And in turn those changes in expected future rates affected activity and inflation. In other words, monetary policy was able to respond by less than would otherwise have been necessary because it affected expectations.

Of course, if developments in the economy continue to evolve in the same direction then interest rates will eventually have to move and follow expectations. It should be clear that, just as Maradona could not hope to score in every game by running towards goal in a straight line, so monetary policy cannot hope to meet the inflation target by leaving official interest rates unchanged indefinitely. Rates must always be set in a way that is consistent with the overall strategy of keeping inflation on track to meet the target; sometimes that will imply changes in rates, at other times not. But the key point is that the power of expectations about future rates can often be more important than the current level of the official interest rate itself.

Because the expectation of what central banks might do has become as important as their immediate actions, if not more so, an entire industry of private sector central bank watchers has grown up. They now comment ceaselessly on when the Federal Reserve or other central banks will change interest rates. But they are like characters in a John le Carré novel, working in the shadows and inhabiting a world of double-talk, coded language and private vocabulary. One of the aims of central banks has been to put this industry out of business and to move to a world of simple, clear language. The advent of inflation targeting saw a move from the old central banking tradition of mystery and mystique to openness and transparency. The old world was illustrated by Lord Cunliffe, the Governor of the Bank of England during the First World War, who, when giving evidence before a Royal Commission on the size of the Bank of England's gold and foreign exchange reserves, replied that they were 'very, very considerable'. When pressed by the commission to give an approximate figure, he replied that he would be 'very, very reluctant to add to what he had said'. Today the figures are published monthly. Until February 1994, believe it or not, the Federal Reserve did not even reveal what the official interest rate was, or whether it had changed. Analysts and researchers had to infer from market interest rates whether or not the Federal Reserve had changed policy. Today, the Federal Reserve publishes the decision of each meeting along with minutes of the discussion and reasons for its actions.

Transparency is, however, not an end in itself. Any requirement for transparency in a central bank's deliberations should have the aim of improving the quality of its decisions. The publication of the minutes of meetings of the policy boards of central banks, as well as of regular monetary policy reports or inflation reports, has provided information both to guide expectations as to how the central bank will respond to future events and to explain past decisions. They are the basis for accountability. But the publication of transcripts of meetings can inhibit free and open discussion, and the style of meetings of the Federal Open Market Committee has undoubtedly changed since such transcripts were first disclosed in 1994; prepared formal statements are read out, while the important private discussions take place at earlier, often bilateral, meetings.[26] In any policy setting, there has to be room for private conversations. There are limits to the desirable degree of transparency.

It is also important for central banks to be honest about what they do not know. A case in point was the recent, and rather short-lived, experiment in 'forward guidance' adopted by the Federal Reserve and the Bank of England in 2013. Both central banks wanted to provide more information about the likely future path of official interest rates. In the first instance, this was a laudable attempt to reduce uncertainty about how they might respond to developments in the economy. But it soon became an attempt to predict the future path of interest rates.

They were not the first to be tempted down this path. For some years, the Reserve Bank of New Zealand and the Swedish Riksbank have published forecasts of their own policy rates. This has not been an entirely happy experience, especially in the latter case when the markets did not believe, correctly as it turned out, the Riksbank's forecasts about its own policy actions. The danger is that markets and commentators read too much into central bank forecasts of their own future actions. When, as is almost inevitable, the future turns out to contain surprises, interest rates will deviate from the forecast path. Although the latter is not intended to represent a commitment by the central bank to pursue that path, it is only too easy to paint it as such.

In turn, central banks were reluctant to concede that the path should be adjusted. The confidence that central banks wanted the private sector to have in their forecasts was not consistent with the inherent degree of uncertainty surrounding those forecasts. To retain credibility, it is important that central banks do not claim to know more than they in fact do. And it is clear that central banks are not able to provide accurate forecasts of their own actions. Policy must confront the fact that 'stuff happens'. Making forecasts is inherently difficult. They always turn out to be wrong. The most egregious example of wrong forecasts by central banks was the prediction before the crisis that the Great Stability would continue. Central banks were using forecasting models that ignored the lessons explored in Chapter 4.

New problems and old instruments

Until recently, central banks thought of monetary policy in terms of setting interest rates rather than fixing the supply of money. The two are, of course, closely related. Reducing interest rates stimulates the demand for borrowing and if banks increase their lending, the supply of bank deposits rises. That pushes up the money supply. But frequent and volatile shifts in the demand for money have led central banks to choose interest rates as their principal policy instrument.

Instabilities in the demand for money are not new. In the

early years of the Bank of England, there were unexpected shifts in the demand for money and credit resulting from the uncertain arrival times in the Port of London of ships laden with commodities from all over the world. The uncertainty derived from changes in the direction and speed of the wind carrying ships up the Thames. To cope with this, the Court Room of the Bank of England contained a wind dial linked to a weather vane on the roof, which provided an accurate guide to these shifts in money demand – the weather vane is there to this day, and it still works. If only monetary policy could be as scientific today!

To prevent a repetition of the Great Depression, central banks during 2008 and 2009 cut interest rates virtually to zero, at which point influencing the supply of money directly was the only remaining monetary instrument. The new problem they faced was what to do when interest rates are zero and cannot be lowered any further. When official interest rates have reached zero, modern Keynesians draw the conclusion that monetary policy is impotent and only fiscal policy can return the economy to full employment. Central banks did not accept this proposition, and took steps to expand the money supply.

My own explanation was simple. For most of the post-war period, governors of the Bank of England had been trying to prevent the amount of money in the economy from growing too quickly. If it were to expand at a rate much faster than the ability of the economy to grow, then the result would be inflation. But the problem facing the Bank in 2009 was that the amount of money in the economy available to finance spending was actually falling. The reason was that banks had begun to contract their balance sheets by refusing to roll over loans and no longer making new ones, thus reducing their total assets. The automatic counterpart on the liabilities side was a corresponding reduction in deposits as loans were repaid. Since most money comprises bank deposits, the fall in deposits meant that the amount of money available to finance spending actually fell. If left unchecked, that threatened a depression. So the task of the Bank was to ensure that the amount of money in the economy grew neither too quickly nor too slowly.

In the particular circumstances of 2009, that meant creating more money. It did not create inflation for two reasons. First, the increase in the supply of money was matched by a sharp increase in the demand for highly liquid reserves on the part of the banking system and the economy more generally. Second, the total supply of broad money, including bank deposits, rose only moderately. The 'emergency money' created by the Bank was necessary to prevent a fall in the total money supply. It was precisely because the demand for money and liquidity changed so sharply that monetary developments mattered. It is ironic, therefore, that economists who believe that money matters (for example, Milton Friedman) argue that 'the demand for money is highly stable', whereas Keynesian economists argue that money does not matter because its demand is unstable.[27] Both groups are wrong – money really matters when there are large and unpredictable jumps in the demand for it.

The method used to create money was to buy government bonds from the private sector in return for money.[28] Those bond purchases were described by many commentators as 'unconventional' monetary policies and became known as 'quantitative easing', or QE. They were regarded as new-fangled and untried. If history is what happened before you were born, then many of the commentators must be extremely young. For open market operations to exchange money for government securities have long been a traditional tool of central banks, and were used regularly in the UK during the 1980s, when they were given the descriptions 'overfunding' and 'underfunding'.[29] What was new in the crisis was the sheer scale of the bond purchases – £375 billion by the Bank of England, almost 20 per cent of GDP, and $2.7 trillion by the Federal Reserve, around 15 per cent of GDP. The need for purchases on such a scale reflected the fact that since government and central banks control directly only a small proportion of the money supply – less than 10 per cent, as we saw in Chapter 2 – a large percentage increase in the printing of money is required to create even a moderate increase in the total money supply.

Economists produced convoluted explanations of how and why this extra money might affect the economy through changes in risk premiums and other arcane aspects of the financial system.[30] Ben Bernanke, then Chairman of the Federal Reserve, said in January 2014 that 'the problem with QE is it works in practice, but it doesn't work in theory'.[31] Perhaps there was a problem with the theory.

How does QE work? Such asset purchases inject money into the portfolios of the private sector. Those investors, such as pension funds and insurance companies, who have sold bonds to the central bank will reallocate their higher money holdings among all possible other assets, such as common stocks, corporate bonds and foreign investments. Those purchases change the prices of private sector financial assets, which in turn affects wealth and spending. For example, if investors use their new-found money to buy corporate bonds, the higher price of those bonds will correspond to a reduction in their yield and hence the cost to companies of obtaining finance for new investment.

So, extremely low official interest rates do not exhaust the ammunition of central banks. But when interest rates at all maturities, from one month right out to thirty years or more, have fallen to zero, then money and long-term government bonds become perfect substitutes (they are both government promises to pay which offer zero interest), and the creation of one by buying the other makes no difference. To be sure, a number of advanced countries are close to that position, though none has yet quite reached it. Central bank official interest rates are virtually at zero in many countries. Long-term bond rates, by contrast, as measured by yields on ten-year bonds, are still above zero. In late 2015, bond yields were around 2 per cent in the United States and most other advanced economies, apart from Germany and Japan, where rates were around 1 per cent and 0.5 per cent respectively. Only in Switzerland, of the major economies, were ten-year bond yields slightly negative.

When the yield curve is completely flat, central banks may still create money by purchasing assets other than government bonds – either private sector assets, such as corporate bonds, or overseas currencies (the latter was the main strategy pursued by the Swiss National Bank in a vain attempt to prevent a sharp appreciation of the Swiss franc against the euro). But this means taking on credit risk of a very different kind from that involved in monetary policy, which is limited to buying and selling government bonds of different maturities, and has long been accepted as a legitimate role for central banks. Taking on credit risk, which ultimately falls on taxpayers, means that monetary policy is entering the world of fiscal policy. At this point, it is for governments to take the responsibility of deciding which sectors of the economy should be favoured over others. To be sure, there are circumstances in which the central bank and government, working together, can improve matters. For example, in the midst of the crisis some financial markets (for short-term commercial paper, for example) seized up, and both the Bank of England and the Federal Reserve intervened for a short period as a market-maker of last resort until those markets returned to some semblance of normality. But those crisis conditions in financial markets ended a long time ago. The challenge today is to deal with a period of prolonged weakness in demand.

It is not that monetary policy is completely impotent when

central bank interest rates are close to zero. It is that monetary policy runs into diminishing returns; although continually falling real interest rates encourage households to bring forward spending from the future to the present, there comes a point when they are reluctant to sacrifice more and more future spending to increase current spending. I shall return to this quandary in Chapter 9.

Now that official interest rates are virtually at zero, an even more extreme version of forward guidance has been proposed by some economists as a way of stimulating the economy.[32] The idea is that central banks should promise to allow inflation to go above their normal target at some point in the medium term so that real interest rates – nominal rates less expected inflation – can fall to more negative levels, so stimulating spending. This is a counsel of despair and is literally incredible. Suppose businesses and markets believed that inflation would indeed be higher in the future and that the resulting lower real interest rate did indeed stimulate recovery. The central bank would then be faced with the following dilemma. Should it proceed to allow inflation to rise above the target despite the recovery, or should it be grateful for the recovery and then set policy to keep inflation on track to meet the target? It is not hard to see that for any central bank governor the latter would be more attractive than the former. Markets will anticipate that reaction and so not believe that inflation will be allowed to rise above target. But then real interest rates will not fall and the recovery will not take place. The strategy of promising to generate an inflationary boom is 'time inconsistent'; in other words, what you say you will do in the future is not what you will want to do when you get there.

If it really were thought desirable to generate an inflationary boom in order to bring down real interest rates, then there would be a much simpler answer – abolish independent central banks and return interest-rate decisions to government. Markets would then certainly expect higher inflation in future. But we would be back to where we started, when central banks were handed independent responsibility for controlling inflation.

Inflation is not a beast that can be killed once and for all. Success is a matter of the patient application of policies designed to maintain price stability. Central bankers are like doctors – they need to be on top of the latest technical developments, have several years of experience and a good bedside manner. Even then, it may be impossible to do much more than avoid big mistakes and promote a healthy way of living. Stability is like dieting – it is no good alternating between binge and starvation, boom and bust. It is necessary to follow a few principles consistently and in a sustained manner. Inflation targeting represented a healthy way of living for central banks charged with the task of ensuring monetary stability.[33] Accountability and transparency provide the incentives for central banks to meet the inflation target. Such a framework of 'constrained discretion' is far removed from the world of 1930, when the Deputy Governor of the Bank of England explained to the Macmillan Committee that 'it is a dangerous thing to start to give reasons'.[34]

An event in 2007 illustrates the change in the way in which monetary policy was conducted after inflation targeting was introduced and independence was granted to the Bank of England. At 12 noon on Thursday 10 May, Tony Blair announced his resignation as Prime Minister after ten years at Number Ten. At exactly the same moment the Bank of England announced an increase in interest rates of 0.25 percentage points. Nothing could symbolise more vividly the change in the monetary regime in Britain than that conjunction. Before the Bank of England became independent it would have been inconceivable that interest rates would have risen on a day when there was an important government announcement.

Monetary policy in bad times – emergency money

No central banker should be spared the experience of a financial crisis, and few are. Since 2008, central banks have reoriented their focus towards financial stability and, with inflation low and often below their target, have placed less emphasis on monetary stability. To some extent this change of focus is a return to the historical origins of central banks. It has gone hand in hand with the view that the instruments available to central banks need to be extended well beyond those used during the Great Stability. Inevitably, attention turned to refining the instruments designed and deployed in the dark days of 2008 and after, and to the macro-prudential powers discussed above. What has been missing, however, from this broader vision of central banks is a coherent unifying framework within which to analyse policies in both good and bad times, and especially in the best and worst of times. I shall try to show that an integrated framework can be constructed and, indeed, is necessary if we are to challenge the alchemy of our current system.

As I described in Chapter 3, banks borrow short and lend long. This leaves them open to runs by the people who make short-term unsecured loans to banks. In theory, this could be the result of a temporary shortage of cash in the bank. But often it is related to concerns about losses on the loans the bank has made. Because depositors cannot easily coordinate their actions, if a run begins it is rational to join it. As many depositors discovered in nineteenth-century America, being last at the counter is a recipe for leaving empty-handed. Banks are inherently unstable.

Over the past 150 years the conventional wisdom has been that central banks should stand ready to be the 'lender of last resort' (LOLR) and supply liquidity to the banking system when the public loses confidence in one or more banks. It is a little-known, though not uninteresting, fact that the Wimbledon Championships are viewed in more countries than belong to the International Monetary Fund, and they are certainly more entertaining than the Annual Meetings of the IMF. Just a stone's throw from Centre Court is the house in which Walter Bagehot wrote his classic study of central banking, *Lombard Street*. Setting out the doctrine of the LOLR – lend freely against good collateral at a penalty rate to banks facing a run – it became the bible for central bankers wondering how to respond to financial crises. Ben Bernanke at the Federal Reserve, and other central bank governors, often referred to Bagehot when explaining the measures they had taken to support banks during the recent crisis.[35]

Although the policy is widely attributed to Bagehot, it can be traced back to Henry Thornton in *An Enquiry into the Nature and Effects of the Paper Credit of Great Britain* published in 1802, in which he writes: 'if any one bank fails, a general run upon the neighbouring ones is apt to take place, which, if not checked in the beginning by pouring into the circulation a large quantity of gold, leads to very extensive mischief'.[36] And even before that, in response to the first financial crisis in the United States – the panic of 1792 – Alexander Hamilton, then US Treasury Secretary, intervened to stem the crisis and in so doing was arguably the first person to discover the benefits of a LOLR.[37] He certainly was the first in a long line of US Treasury Secretaries who believed in bailouts.

When Bagehot wrote his seminal work, there were no Wimbledon Championships and banking was very different from the global industry we see today. His vision of a central bank playing the role of LOLR was inspired by the banking crises in London in 1825, 1836, 1847 and 1866. After the end of the Napoleonic Wars, Britain experienced a period of prosperity and the banks were sufficiently carried away that they invested in widely speculative ventures in Latin America, including the country of Poyais that turned out not to exist. In 1825, although many banks failed, the Bank of England, albeit belatedly, was able to stem the resulting panic; as described by one of my predecessors as Governor, Jeremiah Harman, it lent 'by every possible means, and in modes that we had never adopted before . . . and we were not upon some occasions over nice; seeing the dreadful state in which the public were, we rendered every assistance in our power'.[38] That description was later used by Bagehot to illustrate the proposition that liquidity support is not designed to save an individual bank but is carried out in the collective interest of the system as a whole. In doing that, the central bank may need to take strong and unpopular action. The Bank also issued around one million £1 notes, which helped to ease the crisis when gold ran short – an early example of the creation of 'emergency money'.

Of particular significance to Bagehot was the failure of Overend, Gurney & Co., an erstwhile competitor of the Bank of England. On Thursday 10 May 1866 the bank announced that it would immediately suspend its activities following a severe run. As *The Bankers' Magazine* put it at the time, the announcement generated 'the greatest possible excitement in the City'.[39] The Bank of England lent unprecedented sums to other banking houses, but it did not step in to prevent the failure of Overend, Gurney itself. For several years, there had been concerns about the health of Overend, Gurney and the reaction when it became a public company in 1865 had been decidedly mixed. But it was more than three years after its collapse when it emerged that the directors of the company, who stood trial on charges of fraud, had published a false prospectus concealing the fact that the firm had been, in essence, bankrupt before it went public. The bank had expanded out of its traditional business of short-term lending in the money market into activities closer to present-day investment banking, becoming an investor in railways and ships, among other things. Despite the scale of lending by the Bank of England, other banks failed and a recession followed.

From his vantage point as editor of *The Economist*, Bagehot observed the 1866 crisis and drew the conclusion that when faced with a sudden and large increase in the demand for liquidity by the public, in other words a bank run – a 'panic' – the responsibility of the central bank was to meet it: 'a panic, in a word, is a species of neuralgia, and according to the rules of science you must not starve it'.[40] One of the unique roles of central banks is the ability to create 'liquidity'.[41] Banks create money, but if people lose faith in banks, the ultimate form of money is that created by the central bank – provided it is backed by the tax-raising power of a solvent government. In Germany in October 1923, as the hyperinflation was nearing its peak, the government was close to insolvent with only 1 per cent of its expenditure financed by taxation. Commercial banks have accounts at the central bank, and in a crisis, the central bank can lend to them against the collateral of their assets. Bagehot's doctrine was that in a crisis central banks should lend freely against the security of good collateral, at an interest rate above normal levels to ensure that the central bank was the lender of last resort not the lender of first resort. What Overend, Gurney revealed to Bagehot was that, although in a crisis it might be difficult to know whether a bank was solvent, it was nevertheless safe for the central bank to lend against good collateral.

His view has since become the conventional wisdom. So much so, that the phrase 'lender of last resort' is widely misused to refer to any action that deals with a financial crisis by dousing the fire with a massive injection of liquidity. It is used to urge the European Central Bank to lend to sovereign governments within the euro area, and to imply that the IMF should lend to any country in difficulty; I have even heard it used by sports teams in financial trouble who believe that the league in which they play should bail them out. The expressions 'lender of last resort' and 'bailout' have become synonymous. It is only a matter of time before there is a demand for a LOLR for the Bank of Mum and Dad. Bagehot's argument was very different. In essence, the problem was that the banking system was an intermediary financing illiquid assets by promising instant liquidity to depositors. For the economy as a whole, the promise cannot be met. When enough depositors want their money back, the banking system cannot provide it. If this additional demand for liquidity is temporary, then the provision of emergency money by the central bank can tide the system over until the panic subsides. But if the assets have genuinely lost value, then the central bank must be careful not to subsidise insolvent undertakings. The problem is that in a world of radical uncertainty it is never clear whether a bank is solvent or insolvent, and in a crisis there is rarely time to find out. Actions by a LOLR can prevent a liquidity problem turning into a solvency problem, although not all solvency problems can be converted into liquidity problems by LOLR lending, as governments have painfully discovered in recent times.

Even in Bagehot's time, however, his views attracted sceptics. Thomas Hankey, a former Governor of the Bank of England, published a book just one year after the failure of Overend, Gurney in which he recognised the alchemy of the banking system: 'the mercantile and Banking community must be undeceived in the idea that promises to pay at a future date can be converted into an immediate payment without a supply of ready money adequate for that purpose'.[42] If banks came to rely on the Bank of England to bail them out when in difficulty, then they would take excessive risks and abandon 'sound principles of banking'.[43] They would run down their liquid assets, relying instead on cheap central bank insurance – and that is exactly what happened before the recent crisis. The provision of insurance without a proper charge is an incentive to take excessive risks – in modern jargon, it creates 'moral hazard'. Both Bagehot and Hankey were right, in their own way. Once a panic has started, the provision of liquidity to others can prevent widespread contagion. But the design of the LOLR mechanism must be thought through carefully beforehand in order to avoid incentives to excessive risk-taking. As time passed, it became easier to flood the system with liquidity when problems arose than to design a framework that would counter moral hazard.

If Bagehot's ideas grew out of his study of earlier financial crises, can we too learn from financial episodes after 1866? Milton Friedman and Anna Schwartz, in their monumental study of the monetary history of the United States, laid the blame for the depth of the Great Depression on the Federal Reserve for failing to create sufficient money and act as a lender of last resort to the many banks that subsequently failed.[44] During that period the money supply fell by around 30 per cent. The Fed was culpable for failing to prevent that contraction of the supply of money, rather than for failing to meet a sudden increase in the demand for liquidity. For lessons on the LOLR role, a more relevant historical episode is the financial crisis at the beginning of the First World War and the creation in unusual circumstances of emergency money.[45]

The centenary of the First World War witnessed a veritable blizzard of new books on that dreadful conflict – almost as many as on the recent financial crisis. Few people have drawn comparisons between the two episodes. But the outbreak of the First World War saw the biggest financial crisis in Europe, at least until the events of 2008, and an equally severe crisis in New York, albeit that the Great Depression was a bigger economic crisis in terms of its impact on output and unemployment. An examination of the crisis of 1914, and in particular of the difference between the outcome in London and New York, throws light not only on our recent experience but on financial crises more generally. After September 2007, when the latest banking crisis began, I often publicly compared current events with those of 1914. Yet I found that few people knew much about the financial crisis of 1914. Even the war memoirs of the Chancellor of the Exchequer at the time, David Lloyd George, devote only fourteen out of 2108 pages to the financial crisis he faced.

So what happened in 1914? Historians have long documented the prevailing disbelief in the likelihood of a European war. Among other things, the economic cost would simply be too high. Complacency among financial policy-makers showed in the failure of both governments and markets to take seriously the likelihood and economic consequences of such a war. Just two days before Britain declared war in August 1914, the Governor of the Bank of England, Lord Cunliffe, was lunching on the yacht of the wealthy and well-connected Clark family, moored off the west coast of Scotland. As Kenneth Clark, the art historian, wrote in his memoirs, 'On the second he [Cunliffe] lunched with us on the yacht. I had fallen in love with his daughter, who had red hair and wore a monocle, and so was glad to be present. "There's talk of a war," said Lord Cunliffe, "but it won't happen. The Germans haven't got the credits." I was much impressed.'[46] John Maynard Keynes too was not immune to the mood of the moment when, on 24 June 1914, he wrote to the Treasury: 'In a modern panic it is improbable that the big banks will come to grief.'[47] Gaspar Ferrer, the key adviser to Lord Revelstoke, the Chairman of Barings Bank, said later: 'The war came like a bolt from the blue.'[48] Even after the assassination of Archduke Franz Ferdinand (heir to the Austro-Hungarian throne) in Sarajevo on 28 June 1914, there was barely a ripple in London markets. It was almost a month before financial markets woke up to the significance of the unfolding political events, and it was the ultimatum from Austria to Serbia (demanding that Serbia take draconian steps to suppress the expression of nationalist opinions) on 23 July that finally changed sentiment.

The next two weeks saw panic in markets and among banks. European stock markets fell sharply, and several were closed. There was a flight to safety, especially to cash, and liquidity dried up in all major markets, including those for foreign exchange, stocks and shares. Three-month interest rates more than doubled. At 10.15 a.m. on Friday 31 July the London Stock Exchange was closed in order to postpone settlement of transactions and thereby prevent a wave of failures among its members as prices plummeted.

That same day, lines formed in Threadneedle Street outside the Bank of England as depositors queued, as was their right, to convert deposits or notes into gold sovereigns, which commercial banks would not provide to them. As Keynes later put it, 'the banks revived for a few days the old state, of which hardly a living Englishman had a memory, in which the man who had £50 in a stocking was better off than the man who had £50 in a bank'.[49]

Meanwhile, on the other side of the Atlantic, the position was no less precarious. Europeans had begun to sell their investments on Wall Street and convert the dollars they received into gold to bring back to Europe. The dollar fell sharply. What happened over the next few weeks, however, was to result in New York displacing London as the money centre of the world. Although the Federal Reserve System had been created by Congress in December 1913, nominations to the Federal Reserve Board stalled in the Senate Banking Committee, and it met for the first time only in August 1914. So although

William McAdoo, as Treasury Secretary (and, coincidentally, the son-in-law of President Woodrow Wilson), was also the first Chairman of the Board, the Fed did not enter the playing field until after the financial crisis had come and gone. As a result, in 1914 the major decisions in dealing with the crisis were taken not by central banks but by the respective finance ministers – Treasury Secretary McAdoo and Chancellor of the Exchequer Lloyd George.

Despite falls in stock prices of around 10 per cent earlier in the week, a meeting of bankers on the evening of Thursday 30 July had seen no reason for closing the New York Stock Exchange. But McAdoo intervened and, worried that if New York remained the only open exchange European investors would take the opportunity to sell and repatriate gold, ordered the exchange to close on Friday 31 July, a matter of hours after the closure of the London Stock Exchange.[50] As it was, there were substantial outflows of gold from New York to Europe during that final week of July. The start of the First World War saw the end of the period during which most countries had fixed the price of their currency in terms of gold (and hence to each other) – the gold standard. In Europe the demands of wartime finance led governments to suspend the convertibility of paper into gold and conserve their holdings of bullion. If the United States could retain its fixed rate between the dollar and gold then it could aspire to be the world's financial leader; in 1914 the British pound sterling and not the US dollar was the safe haven currency. From McAdoo's perspective, it was no time to allow large withdrawals of gold that might force America off the gold standard.

Back in London, on the following day, Saturday 1 August, Basil Blackett, then a Treasury civil servant, wrote to John Maynard Keynes: 'I tried to get hold of you yesterday and today, but found you were not in town. I wanted to pick your brains for your country's benefit and thought you might enjoy the process. If by any chance you could spare time to see me on Monday I should be grateful, but I fear the decisions will all have been taken by then.'[51] Keynes lost no time. On Sunday he rode down from Cambridge in the sidecar of his brother-in-law's motorcycle and went straight to the Treasury.

While Keynes and Blackett were conferring in Whitehall, McAdoo left Washington by train to meet with more than twenty senior bankers in the Vanderbilt Hotel in New York. All those present were desperate to avoid a repetition of the panic in 1907 when a run on the Knickerbocker Trust Company led to the suspension of cash withdrawals. During that earlier crisis, John Pierpoint Morgan had added to his fame by organising a private consortium of banks to lend to banks under suspicion, so averting a major collapse of the banking system, though other banks did suspend payments and there was a sharp contraction of the US economy. From that experience came the impetus to create the Federal Reserve System, which would be able to lend to banks that were temporarily short of funds – to act as a lender of last resort – obviating the need for a Morgan or similar to organise a private consortium to prevent a banking failure. But with the Federal Reserve not yet in operation, what could McAdoo offer the bankers in the Vanderbilt?

Out of the 1907 crisis came another solution to the problems of 1914. The Aldrich-Vreeland Act of 1908 permitted banks to deposit government bonds or short-term paper issued by American companies with the US Treasury and receive 'emergency notes' in return. Emergency banknotes, embossed with each bank's own name and logo, worth $500 million were printed in advance and stored with the Treasury in a new underground vault. Here was a source of emergency money that could be distributed to banks in exchange for collateral without the need for a central bank. There was a limit on the value of the notes that could be obtained of 90 per cent of the value of the bonds and 75 per cent of the value of commercial paper deposited by the banks with the US Treasury. And there was a tax on the value of the emergency notes drawn.

At his meeting with bankers on Sunday 2 August 1914, McAdoo found men in urgent need of emergency currency, and plenty of it. The emergency money began arriving in New York on Monday 3 August, and the printing presses operated around the clock to print additional money. The fact that the Bank of England was not immune from the possibility of a run by depositors energised the American financial community to support the creation of this emergency money. In contrast with 1907, when the money supply fell by over 10 per cent, in 1914 the creation of emergency money allowed the money supply to rise at an annual rate of around 10 per cent. Demand for emergency money peaked at the end of October 1914 and fell gradually, disappearing altogether by the middle of 1915. Despite the absence of any help from the new Federal Reserve Board, not yet up and running, McAdoo had shown how a government could act as a lender of last resort.

In London, Monday 3 August was, fortunately perhaps, a bank holiday. Britain declared war on Tuesday 4 August. The bank holiday was extended by an additional three days. During that first week of August, a series of extraordinary measures was introduced by the Treasury and the Bank of England. The UK government decided to intervene and use taxpayers' money on an unprecedented scale in a mission to 'save the City'. The problem was that London had made, as was then usual, large short-term loans by 'accepting' or guaranteeing – for a price – loans to borrowers on the continent of Europe. Such guarantees could be traded and were known as bills of exchange. In normal times those bills could be bought and sold in the London market. As Lloyd George put it, 'the crackle of a bill on London with the signature of one of the great accepting houses was as good as the ring of gold in any port throughout the civilised world'.[52] With the onset of war in Europe, providing guarantees had become risky. London banks had underwritten loans that were not being repaid when due and might never be. As Lloyd George went on, 'when the delicate financial cobweb was likely to be torn into shreds by the rude hand of war, London was inevitably thrown into panic'.[53]

The first measure – on the Tuesday – was emergency legislation to impose a moratorium on all London bills of exchange for one month. Three days later this became a general moratorium. Debts, except for wages, and taxes and debts owed by foreigners, could not be enforced. The legislation provided that, if necessary, the moratorium extended to bank deposits. This provided temporary relief but did not tackle the underlying solvency problem.

Unfortunately, unlike in 1825, the Bank did not have sufficient stores in its vaults to meet the sudden increased demand for low denomination notes as gold coin was conserved to rebuild the nation's gold reserves. So the second measure to be taken – on the Thursday – was the passage in one day of the Currency and Bank Notes Act, allowing the Treasury to print special £1 notes, to a much lower standard – in the interests of speed – than the Bank of England would have accepted. This amounted to temporary removal of the limits on the fiduciary note issue of the Bank of England, and required the suspension of the Bank Charter Act of 1844, as had previously happened in 1847, 1857 and 1866. Britain had not learned from the US experience in 1907 and had printed no store of emergency money to distribute in a crisis.

Third, on Friday 7 August the government decided that the bank holiday should end and the banks reopened. The crisis had been contained, if not solved. As Keynes put it later:

In the dark and uncertain days, which seemed to divide by an interminable period the last Thursday of July from the first Thursday of August, the City was like a very sick man, dazed and feverish, called in to prescribe for his own case. Its great houses, suspecting the worst, could not then gauge exactly how ill they really were; and the leaders of the City were many of them too much overwhelmed by the dangers, to which they saw their own fortunes and good name exposed, to have much wits left for the public interest and safety.[54]

In the weeks that followed, measures were taken to deal with the underlying insolvency problem in London. In wartime conditions, debtors on the Continent would be unable to repay London banks, discount houses, and other institutions that had accepted bills, and hence many of the assets held by British financial houses would lose their value, leaving those institutions insolvent. As a contemporary author described the position: 'the banking system, was, to put it quite bluntly – "bust". They could not pay what they owed. They had not the money. The outbreak of the War at once revealed the hopeless make-believe of the whole pass-the-buck debt-generating process.'[55] Over five months, Chancellor of the Exchequer Lloyd George and Treasury officials recapitalised the City. The Bank of England purchased a large volume of bills amounting to around 20 per cent of total assets held on bank and other financial balance sheets in London, all potential losses being indemnified by the government on behalf of the taxpayer. The Bank bought one-third of the entire stock of bills, amounting to some 5.3 per cent of GDP. As Lloyd George admitted in his memoirs, by offering the guarantee the government had 'temporarily assumed immense liabilities'.[56] He took the risk of losses on the assets he guaranteed without seeking any compensation. It was a gamble that could have been taken only in wartime.

It worked. The City was saved. When the recapitalisation was complete, the Stock Exchange was able to reopen on Monday 4 January 1915, and the assembled financiers sang all three verses of the National Anthem. The financial crisis 'was over'.

Across the Atlantic, McAdoo's problem was different. It was widely understood that the conflict in Europe would lead to higher prices and volumes of exports of American commodities. The Great War strengthened the US economy. The US banking system faced no solvency problem. But to reopen the Stock Exchange would lead to a resumption of sales of stocks by Europeans anxious to convert dollars into gold, which could then be shipped back to Europe. The solution was to increase European demand for dollars. And the way to do that was to meet the increased European demand for US exports arising from war needs.

To supply that demand more ships were required, and two factors ensured their availability. The first was the creation of the US Bureau of War Risk Insurance in August 1914 to insure American-registered vessels against war damage. The second was the unexpected announcement in October that Britain would not regard cargoes of cotton (essential for the production of explosives) destined for Germany as contraband and they would therefore not be at risk of seizure. Exports of cotton, and agricultural commodities more generally, grew rapidly. The New York Stock Exchange reopened on 15 December 1914. The link between the dollar and gold was maintained. The US government, unlike its British counterpart, had no need to assume 'immense liabilities' to solve the challenges to its financial system. Within a matter of months the dollar had begun its inexorable rise to become the dominant international currency and in due course the United States would replace Britain as the world's leading financial power.

Two broad lessons emerge from the experience of 1914. The first is that the key function of the monetary authorities, whether as government or central bank, is to determine the supply of money in both good times and bad. In 1914 McAdoo had the advantage that the crisis of 1907 had alerted the US authorities to the need to prepare a stock of emergency money, whereas the British had forgotten the events of 1825. It was another example of a law that I saw on many occasions – countries learn only from their own mistakes and not from those of others (the failure of the UK to develop a resolution regime for failing banks despite US experience in the 1930s was another). The second is that a crisis will not be resolved by the provision of liquidity if there is also an underlying solvency problem; in other words, a shortage of capital available to absorb losses and prevent default. In 1914, London had a solvency issue and New York did not. In 2008, the turning point of the crisis was when governments were eventually persuaded that the banking system was suffering from a shortage not just of liquidity but of capital, and had to be recapitalised, forcibly if necessary.[57]

The concept of 'emergency money' is important. It captures the need for a sudden increase in money when there is a sharp rise in the demand for liquidity. A jump in the demand for liquidity can arise for many reasons, including a loss of confidence in the public sector itself. Not long after McAdoo was sending banknotes to New York, local and regional governments in Germany began printing new banknotes: *Notgeld*, the German word for emergency money. In Germany (and also in France and Belgium) the war had led to a sharp increase in the demand for, and hence the value of, metal. Coins made out of metal disappeared because their face value as minted coinage was less than their value to producers of armaments.

Soon there was a big shortage of small change. In response, and in the absence of a centralised solution, local and regional communities began to print low-denomination banknotes. The temptation to use *Notgeld* to promote their local communities proved irresistible, and 'regional memories and loyalties revived, and found an exuberant, colourful expression of local identity and civic pride'.[58] The designs included serious scenes, featuring people such as Luther and Goethe, as well as amusing stories of life at the seaside. In the end, no central bank can act as a LOLR unless there is confidence in the government that underwrites it.

Banks today are very different from banks in Bagehot's time or during most of the twentieth century. They are much bigger, their assets are more complex and difficult to value, they hold far fewer liquid assets, they finance themselves with far less equity capital, and they wield greater political power. As a result, the maxim 'lend freely against good collateral at a penalty rate' is outdated. This creates two problems for the LOLR role envisaged by Bagehot.

First, the definition of 'good collateral'. Both Alexander Hamilton and Walter Bagehot knew that the authorities could lend against the security of government stock. They could not know whether the banks to which they might consider lending were solvent or not, but that did not matter if they could lend against good collateral. Until well into the post-war period, banks held around 30 per cent of their assets in the form of government securities, most of them short-term and all of them liquid. In that world, the central bank could lend $100 against the value of stock of $100. Today, however, bank assets comprise largely illiquid and often unmarketable assets such as loans or complex financial instruments. Such illiquid assets can be turned into good collateral if the central bank lends only a proportion of the value of those assets. If a commercial bank wants to borrow $100 from the central bank, it will therefore have to provide collateral worth more than $100, so that if for some reason it cannot repay the loan there is a suitable margin to provide confidence to the central bank that it will be able to sell those assets for at least the value of the loan. The difference between the amount lent by the central bank and the value of the collateral offered in return is described as the 'haircut' on that type of collateral. In practice, haircuts range from only a percentage point or two, when the collateral takes the form of highly liquid financial assets such as government bonds, to very high haircuts, of 50 per cent or more, in the case of individual loans on which little information is available.

When the European Central Bank lent several hundred billion euros to banks all over Europe in December 2011 and February 2012, many thought that the crisis in the euro area was solved. They were soon to be disillusioned. Although the ECB was willing to lend for three years at a very low interest rate, it still expected banks to repay those loans. A bank that had too little capital to absorb likely future losses was still too risky to attract funding from the private market. So unless the ECB was to provide a permanent source of funding, European banks remained an accident waiting to happen. Moreover, like any central bank, the ECB would lend only against good collateral. What that meant in practice was that banks had to provide the ECB with collateral in the form of claims on their loans before the ECB would provide them with cash. Many of those loans were far from 'good'. So the ECB would lend only a proportion of the estimated value of the loans surrendered by banks. In the operation in February 2012, the haircuts on some of those loans amounted to 60 per cent of their face value. In other words, banks surrendering such loans would receive just 40 per cent of their face value in cash. Only in that way could the ECB be confident that the collateral they received would be sufficient to compensate for the failure of a bank to repay its loan.

But that created a serious problem for those in the market, such as pension funds and insurance companies, who were thinking of lending to banks. For as the ECB increased its lending to banks, so a larger and larger proportion of the assets of those banks were encumbered by claims on them in the name of the ECB. The proportion of a bank's assets available to act as collateral for debt provided by the market diminished. So the cost of unsecured funding – loans made without the security of collateral – to banks started to rise. Banks depend on financing a sufficiently high proportion of their balance sheet by unsecured funding, such as deposits or securities issued to pension funds and insurance companies, to enable them to function. Any attempt to fund the whole balance sheet in secured form – borrowing against collateral – could work only if the haircut required by those lending to the bank was literally zero.

Consider the simple hypothetical example of a bank with $100 million in total assets, financed by $90 million of short-term deposits and $10 million of equity capital. Suppose that for some reason $30 million of deposits are withdrawn, and the bank turns to the central bank for temporary liquidity support. In order to protect itself and, ultimately, taxpayers, the central bank decides that the appropriate haircut on pledged collateral is 25 per cent. The bank must then pledge $40 million of assets as collateral to the central bank so that after the haircut it will receive cash loans of $30 million. The bank has maintained its funding but the remaining depositors, who have a prior claim over shareholders, can see that there are only $60 million of assets left to support $60 million of deposits, whereas before there were $100 million of assets to support $90 million of deposits. And the effect of the haircut is to impose an upper limit of $75 million on the LOLR assistance that can be made available.

When the Bank of England lent to Northern Rock in 2007, it was possible to predict when the LOLR assistance would reach its maximum limit. The limit was duly reached on the date predicted and the government had to take over the financing of the bank and the associated credit risk. The more a central bank lends, the lower the proportion of assets to deposits available to support loans from the private sector. A LOLR supplies temporary funding but at the expense of increasing the incentive for a run by the private sector depositors or short-term creditors. In extreme cases, the LOLR is the Judas kiss for banks forced to turn to the central bank for support.

The second problem with the LOLR role is that banks may be reluctant to accept assistance because of the implied stigma from the revelation that they are in need of liquidity support. The information revealed to the market by the decision to accept central bank liquidity may damage the ability of the bank to obtain funding from elsewhere – partly because of the information itself and partly because of the Judas kiss effect in reducing available collateral – and so make it reluctant to turn to the central bank. This turned out to be a major problem in 2007 and 2008, when attempts to provide liquidity led to great caution on the part of banks reluctant to give a signal that they were in need of support. As a result, central banks created auction facilities in which banks could bid anonymously for liquidity.

But the LOLR must be ready to supply liquidity at any moment, and auctions cannot be organised on a continuous basis. At the height of the crisis, weekly auctions played a useful purpose, but they still needed to be supplemented by direct LOLR when banks experienced an urgent need for additional liquidity. In an effort to overcome the problem of stigma, central banks have traditionally been reluctant to publish details of institutions benefiting from access to special lending until the need for such support has come to an end. Delayed reporting of access by banks to central bank facilities helps to reduce the stigma problem. For example, in 2008, the details of the support for Royal Bank of Scotland and HBoS, although approved by the Chancellor of the Exchequer, were not revealed publicly until many months later when there was no longer any need for such secrecy. Legislators, however, are keen to impose greater disclosure requirements on such facilities. Details of those accessing the central bank 'discount window', at which banks can exchange collateral for money, are published, if at all, only after some delay. In the United States, Congress has mandated the publication of the names of all borrowers at the Federal Reserve discount window no later than two years after they borrow.

The stigma problem is not new. In 1914, there were concerns 'about the potential reputational damage of borrowing from the Bank of England' if it became known to others that advantage had been taken of such a facility.[59] Equally, the creation of emergency money in the United States under the Aldrich-Vreeland Act of 1908 was an opportunity not used by banks until the collective crisis of July 1914. No such emergency money had ever been demanded by a bank until the events of the summer of 1914. As the Comptroller of the Currency warned when the Act was passed, 'the issue of so-called emergency notes ... would at once be a confession of weakness and a danger signal that no bank would dare make until in desperate condition'.[60] And, as the financial historian William Silber later wrote, 'Emergency currency lost its stigma during the first week of August as the Great War threatened major banks throughout the country.'[61] There is no simple or, for that matter, complex solution to this problem, which continues to trouble the designers of central bank liquidity facilities. The importance of stigma is that over the course of history, the reluctance of banks to be seen to accept support from the central bank has probably meant that the size of LOLR operations has probably been too little and too late, exacerbating the severity of crises. Central banks cannot afford to be 'over nice'.

Aware of the importance of 'lending freely' in a crisis, and the problems caused by the need to lend against good collateral and at a penalty rate, central banks and governments have relaxed the conditions of a traditional Bagehotian lender of last resort and turned to bailouts. This creates risks to taxpayers and incentives for banks to expand the alchemy of the system. The solution is to convert the crisis function of the lender of last resort into a regime that determines the amount a bank can borrow in both good times and bad, and ensures that a bank will have posted sufficient collateral in good times that it will have access to liquidity in bad times adequate to meet the demands of short-term creditors. I will explain how this works in Chapter 7.

The future of central banks

Despite some ups and downs, central banks are starting this century well ahead of where they were a century ago. There are more of them, and they have greater power and influence. But has their reputation peaked? Will future historians look back on central banks as a phenomenon largely of the twentieth century? Although central banks have matured, they have not yet reached old age. But their extinction cannot be ruled out altogether. Societies have managed without central banks in the past.

Before the crisis, central banking seemed rather simple. There was a single objective – price stability – and a successful framework within which to make decisions on interest rates – inflation targeting. It seemed a successful coping strategy. Communication became more important, and central banks moved from mystery and mystique to transparency and open-ness. During the crisis, however, many of those assumptions were challenged, as we learned how inadequate our under-standing of the economy and the financial system was. There is more to managing the economy than hitting a target for con-sumer price inflation. Most of the models used by central banks to forecast the economy proved deficient in explaining the dis-equilibrium in their own and the world economy, as described in Chapter 1. As a result, policy-makers failed to realise that the period of low inflation and steady growth during the Great Stability was unsustainable, and would probably come to an end with a crash of some sort.

Central banks have a role to play in changing the heuristic used by households and businesses when they see a serious disequilibrium building up. In such circumstances, what is required is a clear and convincing explanation of why it may be desirable to allow inflation to run above or below target for a period in order to restore a sustainable path for the economy. It would be a big mistake to jettison inflation targeting altogether. It is a valuable heuristic for central banks, provided there is room to deviate when circumstances demand.

The crisis also brought home the importance of the frame-work for liquidity provision to the banking system. Because both banking and central banks have changed out of all recog-nition since Bagehot wrote his book, it is time to reassess the old doctrines. The Bagehotian lender of last resort is a concept in need of reform. A number of new ideas and instruments were developed on the hoof during the crisis and undoubtedly some will persist. But what has been missing is an integrated single framework within which to analyse the provision of money by central banks in both good and bad times. Such a framework is the key to ending the alchemy of our monetary and financial system, and I shall return to this question in Chapter 7.

Despite those problems, the surprising outcome has been that central banks have been handed greater responsibilities than before the crisis. The Bank of England I left behind was twice as big as the one I inherited. There is a risk in expecting more from central banks than they can, in fact, deliver. Some people seem to believe that central banks are the answer to all of our economic problems – the 'only game in town'. Any central bank that allows itself to be described as the 'only game in town' would be well advised to get out of town. In the end, expecting too much from central banks will produce disillusionment with the central bank independence that played such an important role in the conquering of inflation. With careful design of the mandate for central banks they can continue to be one of the three great inventions since the beginning of time.

Appreciation of central banks' actions was well captured by a pamphleteer in the middle of the eighteenth century:

> There certainly never was a body of men that has contributed more to the Publick Safety and Emolument than the Bank of England, and yet even this great, this useful Company, has not escaped the invectives of malicious tongues ... This flourishing and opulent Company has upon every emergency always cheerfully and readily supplied the necessities of the Nation ... and it may very truly be said that they have in many critical and important conjunctures relieved this Nation out of the greatest difficulties, if not absolutely saved it from ruin.[62]

The popularity of central banks has waxed and waned over the past couple of centuries. One point, however, stands out from that history. The freedom of a central bank to act in a crisis depends on its legitimacy. In turn that requires a clear mandate providing the assurance for the legislature to delegate powers to an independent central bank. Democratic legitimacy has been built up over the years, in part through greater transparency and accountability, and works at national level. It is far from clear, however, that any democratic mandate can function at a supranational level. The attempt to break the link between money and nations has always been fraught with difficulty.

6

MARRIAGE AND DIVORCE:
MONEY AND NATIONS

'So they [the government] go on in strange paradox,
decided only to be undecided, resolved to be irresolute,
adamant for drift, solid for fluidity, all-powerful to be
impotent.'

Sir Winston Churchill,
Hansard, 12 November 1936

'Elections change nothing. There are rules.'

Wolfgang Schäuble,
German finance minister, 31 January 2015

What is the relationship between money and nations?
From the role that money plays both in normal periods and, even more, in times of crisis, it is clear that there is
an intimate link between the nation state and the money that

circulates within it. That link runs very deep. The main building of the International Monetary Fund in Washington DC is shaped roughly as an ellipse. As you walk around the corridor on the top floor, on one side are symbols of each of the member nations. On the opposite side are display cabinets of the banknotes used by those countries. There is a remarkable, almost uncanny, one-to-one relationship between nations and their currencies. Money and nations go hand in hand.

Should this surprise us? Is it a natural state of affairs? Although money moves across frontiers at ever-increasing speed, we are no closer to the world currency that idealists like Walter Bagehot imagined in the nineteenth century. Economists have typically looked to economic factors as determining currency arrangements. They argue that we should expect to see fewer currencies than countries because at least some countries will see advantages in forming a currency union with others. The novel idea that money and nations are not synonymous, and that an 'optimum currency area' could encompass several nations, or regions within nations, was popularised by the Canadian economist Robert Mundell in 1961.[1] Sharing a currency reduces the transaction costs of trade within the union. If each of the fifty states in the USA used its own dollar then the cost of doing business across states would be much greater than it is today. Just as there is a federal system of weights and measures, so the dollar is the single monetary unit of account. But whereas there are single international systems of weights and measures for time, length and weight (the last expressed in two forms: imperial and metric), there is no single world currency.

Sharing a currency means pooling monetary sovereignty – accepting a single official interest rate throughout the union. How restrictive and costly that constraint is depends on the degree to which countries would choose different interest rates if they were free to do so. If one country wants to raise rates – because demand is strong and might push up inflation – and another wants to lower rates – because it is facing weak demand, pushing inflation down – then tensions will arise between the members of a currency union. Such 'asymmetric shocks' to demand require, within the union, a flexible labour market encompassing the entire area so that labour can move easily from a country with little demand for it to a country where demand is high.

In contrast, retaining a separate currency means that it is possible to use movements in the exchange rate to coordinate in terms of foreign currency the changes in domestic wages and prices that are necessary following shocks to competitiveness, and to respond to a local fall in demand. In that way it is possible to avoid the high rates of unemployment that might otherwise be required to decrease wages and prices in domestic currency in a decentralised market economy. Experience of the inter-war period across Europe showed that exchange rate changes were more effective than either government edict or mass unemployment in coordinating necessary reductions in real wages.

'Optimal' currency areas comprise countries or regions that experience similar shocks and have a single labour market. They also share similar attitudes to inflation. These embrace the choice of a long-run average inflation target, decisions on the trade-off between inflation and employment in the short run, and credibility in the eyes of markets in delivering those objectives.[2] Far from being solely economic, such factors are highly political. So we should not be surprised that currency arrangements are determined as much by political as by economic factors.

Money and nations are both important social institutions with a long history. As the historian Linda Colley has written, nation states are:

synthetic and imperfect creations and subject to change, and
most have been the result of violent conflict at some stage . . .
In order to persist and cohere, states usually require effective
political institutions, a degree of material well-being, efficient means of defence against external enemies, mechanisms
for maintaining internal order and, very often, some kind of
religious or ideological underpinning.[3]

Much the same could be said of money. As John Stuart Mill put
it in the nineteenth century, 'so much of barbarism, however,
still remains in the transactions of most civilised nations, that
almost all independent countries choose to assert their nation-
ality by having, to their own inconvenience and that of their
neighbours, a peculiar currency of their own'.[4] As if to illustrate
the point, on 14 November 2014, the extremist militant group
Islamic State announced that it intended to issue its own currency, comprising coins made of precious metal, to help create
a new country – the caliphate.[5]

More often than not, force was the factor that brought about
the domain of empires and their subsequent destruction, creating new nation states in the process. It is important not to see
either nations or their monies as fixed. Much of what we now
take for granted in the identity and composition of nation states
was far from obvious at earlier times – we should not only look
through the back window but imagine also peering through
the front windscreen to try to understand what did determine
the creation of currencies and the nations in which they were
used. There has been a remarkable expansion of the number
of countries in the world during the post-war period. Today,
there are 196 countries in the world (the 193 members of the
United Nations plus Kosovo, Taiwan and the Vatican) and
188 members of the International Monetary Fund. And there
are around 150 currencies in use in those countries.[6] Back in

1945 when those organisations were founded, there were far fewer countries – fifty-one members of the United Nations and twenty-nine members of the IMF – and a correspondingly smaller number of currencies. Of course in 1945 there were more countries than members of the United Nations. Adjusting for that, the number of countries has still more than doubled in little more than half a century. The increase in the number of nation states reflects the process of decolonisation and the fragmentation of former nation states created by force or by delegates at peace conferences who did not represent the area. One might expect that the expansion of international trade, and the growing use of the English language in finance and commerce, would have strengthened the case for common currency areas and led to a reduction in the number of currencies. That has evidently not been the case.

Monetary unions have a chequered history. There have been many successful marriages, and a number of spectacular divorces. The welding of the North American colonies into the United States of America, with a single currency and a collective federal fiscal policy, guided by the determination of the then Treasury Secretary Alexander Hamilton, is one of the most successful unions. The Continental Congress authorised the issuance of the US dollar in August 1786, and the status of the dollar as the unit of account throughout the new republic was established by the Coinage Act of 1792. The importance of the dollar rose with American economic and political power. In 1871 the Meiji government of Japan adopted a new currency – the yen – which has since become one of the world's major currencies. And one of the oldest currencies in the world, the pound sterling, the origins of which are lost in the mists of time, became the currency of the United Kingdom after the Acts of Union between England, including Wales, and Scotland in 1707.[7]

There have also been a number of break-ups of monetary unions. When empires or nations split up, the associated monetary union also tends to dissolve. That was true of the Roman Empire, the Austro-Hungarian Empire and, more recently, the Soviet Union.[8] When the latter broke up in 1991, the IMF recommended that the successor states continue to use the rouble. But within a short time, they had all adopted new currencies. Less spectacularly, but no less completely, when the British Empire metamorphosed into the British Commonwealth during the post-war period, the sterling area faded away. When Czechoslovakia was divided into the Czech Republic and Slovakia in 1993, the two new states soon moved to distinguish their currencies, and in 2009 Slovakia joined the euro area. That was a relatively amicable divorce. Much less happy was the break-up of Yugoslavia in the 1990s, ultimately into seven successor states, each with its own monetary arrangements.[9]

Monetary unions comprising more than one sovereign state all ran into trouble. In 1866 the Latin Monetary Union (LMU), comprising France, Belgium, Italy and Switzerland, and from 1868 also Spain and Greece, was formed. It fell foul of the temptation of one part of the union to create money in its own interests rather than those of the area as a whole. The LMU was based on a bimetallic standard that set currency values in terms of fixed quantities of gold or silver, with a fixed price of silver in terms of gold. When the market price of silver fell, some member states started to export silver coins and exchange them for gold in order to exploit the difference between the official and market price of the two precious metals. In effect, they were debasing the currency for their own benefit. Not surprisingly, the resulting lack of trust between its members undermined political support for the LMU and from 1878 it was little more than an agreement to conform to the gold standard.[10] Inspired by the example of the LMU, Sweden and

Denmark set up the Scandinavian Monetary Union in 1873, with Norway joining two years later. It came to an end in 1914 when Sweden decided to abandon the gold standard.

The case of Ireland is also telling. After the Easter Rising of 1916, and the subsequent political and military struggle, Irish independence became a reality. The 1921 Anglo-Irish Treaty recognised the Irish Free State but implied that it would remain part of the British Empire. That interpretation was not accepted in Dublin, although the new Free State continued to use sterling as its currency. It made no attempt to design or issue banknotes because those printed by the Bank of England, at that time a private company, did not depict the UK sovereign.[11] When distinctive Irish coins were introduced in 1928, with inscriptions entirely in the Irish language and depictions of animals instead of British heraldry and the King's head, they 'were intended to be unambiguous in declaring a distinct Irish identity and in announcing the arrival of a new sovereign state to the community of nations'.[12] Following independence, the Irish Republic maintained an informal monetary union with the United Kingdom but left in 1979, first to cohabit with and then formalise its relationship with the euro area.

None of the decisions to join and then leave those monetary unions had much to do with the concept of 'optimum currency areas'. Whatever the efficiency considerations, it makes little sense to remain in a currency union with partners who do not share the same objectives and commitment for the management of money. The choice of which money to use is a political act.

Three examples illustrate the complex relationship between money and nations. The first is monetary union in Europe – an example of many countries with a single currency. It is the obvious counter to the post-war trend of fragmentation and its fate will affect the whole world economy. As a marriage of currencies accompanied by no tying of the political knot, it is developing into a battle between political will and economic reality. The second is very different in scale and scope, but no less interesting. It concerns the currency arrangements in Iraq before and after the invasion in 2003, an example of one country with two currencies. And the third relates to the new currency arrangements that might have emerged from the referendum on Scottish independence held in 2014 had the result been 'yes' rather than the actual 'no'.

European Monetary Union

European Monetary Union (EMU) is the most ambitious project undertaken in monetary history. Launched in 1999, it now comprises nineteen members.[13] It was, and is, a great economic and political experiment. No monetary union has survived unless it has also developed into a political union, and the latter usually came before the former, as when a single currency followed the unification of Germany under Bismarck. EMU has not proved to be an easy marriage, with the enterprise trying to navigate a safe passage between the Scylla of political ideals and the Charybdis of economic arithmetic. Since concerns about the Greek economy emerged in late 2009, there has been a series of crises to which the European authorities have responded by trying to build the foundations of a more enduring political union. But the diverging economic performance of the member countries has led to tensions about the appropriate design of any such development. The European Central Bank has found itself in the middle of a political debate and been forced to take what are in essence political decisions in order to hold the monetary union together.

Almost 150 years ago, Walter Bagehot overestimated the longevity of the Latin Monetary Union when he wrote that 'Before long, all Europe, save England, will have one money.'[14]

Monetary union in Europe has always been about France and Germany. In 1929, Gustav Stresemann, a politician in the Weimar Republic and a recipient of the Nobel Peace Prize for his attempts to achieve reconciliation between the two countries, recommended a European currency to the League of Nations. And during the German occupation of France in the Second World War, the head of the bank Société Générale, Henri Ardant, at a reception at the German Embassy in Paris, expressed 'his hopes that Germany would set up a single customs zone in Europe and create a single European currency'.[15]

After the war, proposals for a single currency were planted in the fertile soil of European integration. During that period, several attempts were made to link exchange rates in Europe, of which the most serious was the Exchange Rate Mechanism (ERM). One of the reasons so many countries wished to join the ERM in the 1980s was the belief that by linking their exchange rate to the Deutschmark they would inherit the same commitment to price stability as had been demonstrated by the Bundesbank over many years. But the mechanism broke down first in 1992, when the UK and Italy left it under the pressure of currency speculation, and then more completely in 1993 when the bands within which currencies were permitted to fluctuate against each other were widened to such an extent that the mechanism was ineffective. It did so for two reasons. First, markets saw that countries did not in fact all have the same commitment to price stability; some, when push came to shove, showed themselves unwilling to pay the price to maintain an indefinite commitment to a fixed exchange rate against the Deutschmark. Second, and especially following German reunification, economic conditions in Germany were very different from those in other countries, and different monetary policies were self-evidently appropriate.

The move to European Monetary Union in the 1990s was

designed to overcome the weaknesses of a fixed exchange-rate system by making a permanent commitment to a common currency, the euro. From the German point of view, this had the major disadvantage that the political culture surrounding the management of money would now be determined by a larger group of nations and no longer by the history and experience of Germany itself. Creating a monetary union of separate sovereign states was and remains an enormous gamble, one that required a high degree of mutual trust to be successful. As its founders were aware, there is no successful example of a currency union among independent states that have not gravitated to a high degree of political union. Of course, all great historic steps are gambles. But not all gambles result in historic steps forward. Before the euro was launched, the view in Germany was that monetary union should follow political union only with a time lag, and a long one at that. Elsewhere, especially in southern Europe, the view was that the creation of monetary union would lead to crises that would force the pace of political union.[16] Everything that has happened since has confirmed the wisdom of the former view and the risks of the latter. How long this marriage will last is something known only to the partners themselves; outsiders cannot easily judge the state of the relationship.

A century ago, Mrs Patrick Campbell, a British actress and close friend of George Bernard Shaw, suggested that a married union represented 'the deep, deep peace of the double-bed after the hurly-burly of the chaise-longue'.[17] During the long engagement among the European partners prior to the creation of the euro, culminating in attempts to consummate the relationship by fixing exchange rates through the ill-fated ERM, there was plenty of hurly-burly. But whatever description the members of EMU would give to the first fifteen years of their marriage, it is unlikely to be a deep, deep peace.

To celebrate the launch of monetary union a glamorous ceremony was held in June 1998 for the assembled European elite at the Alte Oper (the old opera house) in Frankfurt, featuring the Irish *Riverdance* performers.[18] It was no time to remind them of the difficulties in persuading the peoples of Europe, with their different languages, histories and cultures, to accept the massive sacrifice of national sovereignty required to create a stable economic and monetary union. Ten years later, on a very hot day in June 2008, the elite reassembled in the Alte Oper, this time for a concert of a more traditional and less exuberant kind, to celebrate the first decade of the euro. Within two years the euro area found itself deep in crisis.

The basic problem with a monetary union among differing nation states is strikingly simple. Starting with differences in expected inflation rates – the result of a long history of differences in actual inflation – a single interest rate leads inexorably to divergences in competitiveness. Some countries entered European Monetary Union with a higher rate of wage and cost inflation than others. The real interest rate (the common nominal rate of interest less the expected rate of inflation) was therefore lower in these countries than in others with lower inflation. That lower real rate stimulated demand and pushed up wage and price inflation further. Instead of being able to use differing interest rates to bring inflation to the same level, some countries found their divergences exacerbated by the single rate. The best measure of 'inflation', which captures a country's international competitiveness, is the GDP deflator – a measure of the average price of all the goods and services produced within a country. From the start of monetary union until 2013, prices on this measure rose by 16 per cent in Germany, 25 per cent in France, 33 per cent in Greece, 34 per cent in Italy, 37 per cent in Portugal, and 40 per cent in Spain.[19] So although the birth of the euro brought about some initial convergence of expected inflation rates, the consequence of a single interest rate was to generate subsequent divergence of inflation outcomes.

The resulting loss of competitiveness among the southern members of the union against Germany is large, even allowing for some overvaluation of the Deutschmark when it was subsumed into the euro. It increased full-employment trade deficits (the excess of imports over exports when a country is operating at full employment) in countries where competitiveness was being lost, and increased trade surpluses in those where it was being gained. Those surpluses and deficits are at the heart of the problem today. Trade deficits have to be financed by borrowing from abroad, and trade surpluses are invested overseas. Countries like Germany have become large creditors, with a trade surplus in 2015 approaching 8 per cent of GDP, and countries in the southern periphery are substantial debtors. Although much of Germany's trade surplus is with non-euro area countries, its exchange rate is held down by membership of the euro area, resulting in an unsustainable trade position. Because of sharp reductions in the level of domestic demand, which have cut imports, the trade deficits of periphery countries have fallen sharply since the global financial crisis, and are now broadly in balance. But unless there is a significant improvement in external competitiveness, they will re-emerge if domestic demand picks up and full employment is restored. When the crisis hit in 2008, employment levels were much higher than today and the trade deficits of Portugal and Spain were around 6 per cent of GDP and in Greece around 11 per cent of GDP. Restoring competitiveness within a monetary union (where there are no intra-union exchange rates to adjust) is a long, difficult and painful process that places strains on a democratic society.

Tensions are inevitable where political identity is aligned with differences between creditors and debtors. None of this has anything to do with the fiscal policies adopted by countries before or after the creation of monetary union. Most of today's fiscal problems are the result of falling demand and output, partly as a result of the downturn in the world economy following the crisis of 2007–9 and partly because the downturn has been exacerbated in the periphery countries by the loss of competitiveness. Fiscal problems have been largely consequences, not causes of the crisis of the euro area.

The crisis in the euro area started in Greece at the end of 2009, when a new government elected in October revealed that the previous administration had been under-reporting the budget deficit, resulting in an increase in the estimated deficit from around 7 per cent of GDP to almost 13 per cent (later revised up to 15 per cent). Trust in the accuracy of Greek statistics, never high, was further damaged. It seemed that Greece had been admitted to the euro area on false pretences. The problem became more serious during 2010 when Greece found itself increasingly unable to borrow from global financial markets and turned to its partners in Europe for emergency loans. At the beginning of May the first of many emergency summits of euro area leaders met in Brussels, and it was agreed to set up a €500 billion fund to bail out Greece and other countries that might find themselves in difficulty. But the crisis did not really subside over the following year. Countries with trade deficits were finding it difficult to borrow from abroad, and the interest rates at which their governments could borrow rose sharply, not only but especially in Greece. As foreign banks and hedge funds withdrew their money, the sharp reduction in those inflows of money to the periphery countries necessitated an equally sharp reduction in the excess of imports over exports. With no ability to use a depreciation of the currency to stimulate exports, the only way to close the gap was to reduce imports. Reductions in government spending and increases in taxes lowered domestic demand and imports. As a result, output fell precipitously.

In July 2011, the euro area crisis took a turn for the worse. It was increasingly difficult to pretend that the problems of countries such as Greece were solely a shortage of temporary liquidity rather than a question of underlying solvency and loss of competitiveness. Yields on the sovereign debt (that is, government bonds) issued by Greece, Ireland and Portugal reached near record highs, making new borrowing very expensive, and Portugal joined Greece in having its debt downgraded to junk status (meaning that the debt was judged by the rating agencies to be a highly speculative investment and therefore not one suitable for a range of funds, including many overseas pension funds). Soon Italy was drawn in, not least because government debt there, at €1.7 trillion, amounted to the third largest in the world, comfortably exceeding the resources available through existing euro area rescue funds.

The summer of 2011 was the start of a six-month period during which governments and commentators regularly called for Germany to act decisively and in an overwhelming show of force to demonstrate its unequivocal support for the continuation of the euro. Unfortunately for Germany, the decisive action envisaged by others was for it to provide sufficient money to enable the periphery countries to regain market confidence. Those countries still had insufficient export revenues to pay for imports and the servicing of overseas debt. Since they also had little access to private markets, the solution envisaged by many was to ask for very significant transfers from German taxpayers to the southern members of the euro area. It was never likely that Germany would be willing to make such a commitment, and certainly Angela Merkel, Germany's Chancellor, was in no rush to do so.

Monetary union was starting to challenge democratic governments elected by their own citizens. A secret letter, leaked later, signed by both the outgoing and incoming ECB presidents, Jean-Claude Trichet and Mario Draghi respectively, was sent to the Italian Prime Minister, Silvio Berlusconi, on 5 August 2011. It demanded that Mr Berlusconi make drastic cuts in public expenditure, open up public services, and enact a number of reforms, including changes to pay-bargaining and employment laws. The letter went well beyond the usual remit of central banks. When its contents became public, Berlusconi's authority was weakened, and after losing his parliamentary majority, he resigned on 12 November. A technocratic Prime Minister was appointed in his place: Mario Monti, a highly respected economist and former European Commissioner. From personal experience, I know that it would have been difficult to find anyone better than Mario Monti to lead Italy in such difficult circumstances. Yet he had not been elected, and had no parliamentary majority. His ability to put in place reforms to improve the supply-side performance of the Italian economy was limited, and his proposals met stiff resistance from numerous interest groups, including lawyers, taxi drivers and, indeed, members of parliament.

Politicians in the euro area believed that they were fighting a battle against the markets. One very senior euro area politician had said at a meeting I attended that 'we will show the markets that we shall prevail'. The strategy adopted by the new President of the ECB, Mario Draghi, who replaced Jean-Claude Trichet on 1 November 2011, was to avoid, as far as possible, controversial purchases of sovereign bonds and instead to channel support directly to the banking system because any immediate threat to the euro would be visible in a run on a major euro area bank. By the following February, the spotlight was back on Greece. Although for years Greece had suffered from incompetent and corrupt governments, which made it difficult for its partners in the euro area to sympathise, the mood inside the country was captured by Archbishop Hieronymos of

Athens, who wrote to the Greek Prime Minister setting out the concerns of the Church:

> Our hearts are shattered and our minds are blurred by recent events in our country. Decent people are losing their jobs, even their homes, from one day to the next. Homelessness and hunger – phenomena last seen in times of foreign occupation – are reaching nightmare proportions. The unemployed are growing by the thousands every day ... Young people – the best minds of our country – are migrating abroad ... Those making decisions are ignoring the voices of those in despair, the voices of the Greeks. Unfortunately, we cannot find a response – neither to explain what has happened, nor to the demands made by foreigners. Indeed, foreigners' insistence on failed recipes is suspect at best. And their claims against our national sovereignty are provocative. The exhaustion of the people cannot be ignored.[20]

Greece became the first major European country to experience a depression on the scale of the 1930s Great Depression in the United States. Between 1929 and 1933, total output in the US fell by 27 per cent. In Greece, output fell between 2007 and 2015 by slightly more than that, and domestic spending (consumption and investment in both private and public sectors) by no less than 35 per cent, an outcome I would never as a student in the 1960s have imagined possible with our new-found understanding of how to prevent depressions. There were, and remain, many inefficiencies in the Greek economy. But in the absence of political union, decisions about them are for the citizens of Greece. In March 2012, Greece defaulted on, or to be precise 'restructured', its debt. The restructuring transferred much of the debt from private to public sector creditors. By 2015, around 80 per cent of Greek sovereign debt was owed to public sector institutions elsewhere in the EU or to the International Monetary Fund. Monetary union, far from leading to greater political integration, was proving the most divisive development in post-war Europe.

By the end of July 2012, exit from the euro for Greece and perhaps others was becoming accepted as likely. The ECB, the European Commission and the German government had plans for how to handle a Greek exit. It was widely assumed that exit would imply the imposition of capital controls in Greece, and probably a bank holiday to allow the government to nationalise many, if not most, of the local banks. Then came the démarche that transformed market sentiment. At a Global Investment Conference on 26 July to mark the start of the London Olympic Games, I chaired a panel of central bank governors. One of them was Mario Draghi. As he stood up to make his remarks, I noticed that, unusually, he did not intend to read from a prepared text. The ECB would, he said, 'do whatever it takes to preserve the euro. And believe me, it will be enough.'[21]

His words reverberated around the world, but just as important was the joint statement made the following day by Chancellor Merkel and President Hollande, indicating their full commitment to the euro and support for Draghi's intention. It was clear that the ECB would buy, or was actively considering buying, Spanish and Italian sovereign debt. Spanish ten-year bond yields fell back from 7.6 per cent to below 7 per cent. Bank shares in the euro area rose between 5 and 10 per cent on the day. It was the start of a marked change in sentiment that was to result in significant falls in sovereign bond yields over the next two years. By the end of 2014, ten-year yields in Greece had fallen from 25 per cent to just over 8 per cent, Portuguese bond yields from over 11 per cent to under 3 per cent, and those in Spain from over 6 per cent to below 2 per cent. Indeed, by the end of 2014 Spain was able to borrow more cheaply than the United States government. Draghi's commitment had obviously done the trick.

But it had also raised a serious problem. The mandate of the ECB does not extend to fiscal transfers. And it was obvious from comments made both publicly and privately that the Bundesbank was strongly opposed to any selective purchases of sovereign debt, which it believed might well be unconstitutional.[22] Certainly, on the face of it, it is hard to reconcile the sovereign debt purchase programme with the 'no bailout' clause in the European Treaty. So it was some weeks before the ECB announced a programme of Outright Monetary Transactions to allow it to buy the government bonds of periphery countries in return for requests from them for assistance from the new European Stability Mechanism (ESM). By 2015, no purchases had been made. Overall, however, the Draghi promise to 'do whatever it takes' brought a sense of calm to financial markets and an end to a long series of crisis weekends. It appeared that Germany had abandoned the idea of a Greek exit from the euro. Investors from outside the euro area were seduced into buying financial assets, particularly sovereign debt, in the periphery countries, bond yields fell further and the ECB was able to reduce its lending to banks.

But the purchase of sovereign debt by overseas investors pushed up the value of the euro. Its effective rate would rise around 10 per cent over the next two years. That led to the next challenge for the euro – in France. The higher exchange rate of the euro exacerbated the loss of competitiveness that had been increasingly evident in the French economy. Unemployment rose and activity stagnated. It was all very well for countries like Greece or Portugal to suffer substantial falls in output, but it was unthinkable politically for France to suffer the same fate. The euro was born out of Franco-German cooperation; divisions between the two would be fatal to the project.

By early 2015, the ECB had decided to embark on a programme of monetary expansion, following the example of the Federal Reserve and the Bank of England some six years earlier. In January of that year it announced a programme of bond purchases to expand its balance sheet back to its previous peak some two years earlier. The aim was clear – to lower the value of the euro. And its initial effect was to do just that. The euro fell to its lowest level against the dollar for more than a decade.

January also saw the election in Greece of a new government, led by the Syriza party, committed to reducing the burden of austerity imposed on the country by the much-disliked 'troika' of the European Central Bank, European Commission and International Monetary Fund. Fruitless negotiations ensued, with all the focus on the country's debt-servicing obligations, which had been significantly reduced by the earlier debt restructuring and rescheduling, rather than on the underlying cause of the problem of weak demand, namely the inability of Greece to find a new lower real exchange rate through devaluation.

Within the confines of monetary union, the route to a lower real exchange rate is via an 'internal devaluation', which entails sustained mass unemployment in order to bring down wages and prices in those sectors of the economy that produce tradeable goods and services. Unemployment remains extremely high in a number of euro area countries. By the autumn of 2015, the unemployment rate was over 10 per cent in France, around 12 per cent in Italy and Portugal, 22 per cent in Spain and 25 per cent in Greece. Depressingly, youth (under-twenty-five) unemployment was close to 50 per cent in both Greece and Spain.[23] In recent years several hundred thousand young people have emigrated from Greece, Italy, Portugal and Spain.[24] By contrast, the overall unemployment rate had fallen to 5 per cent in both the United States and United Kingdom, and to similar low levels in the euro area countries with trade surpluses; the rate stood at 6.9 per cent in the Netherlands and just 4.5 per cent in Germany.

Increasingly acrimonious negotiations between Greece and its partners in the euro area led to a breakdown of negotiations in the summer of 2015. Greek banks were shut on Monday 29 June following a decision by the ECB to cap lender of last resort support to them. Cash payments from ATMs were limited to €60 a day and the economy started to grind to a halt. On 30 June, Greece became the first advanced economy to default on a payment due to the IMF. A few days later, on Sunday 5 July, in a national referendum, the people of Greece rejected by a large majority the proposals of their 'partners' in Europe for further austerity in return for a further bailout. Yet the leaders of the euro area reacted to the referendum result by demanding even tougher proposals for reforms from the Greek government. There was no prospect for growth in Greece without substantial debt relief. In practice, that would mean significant losses for taxpayers in Germany and other euro area countries.

By July 2015, it was clear that neither side was prepared to contemplate a Greek withdrawal from the euro. On 13 July, after all-night negotiations, an agreement was reached under which Greece accepted virtually all the creditors' demands for reforms – including, bizarrely, the introduction of Sunday trading hours – in return for additional finance in the form of loans of some €87 billion and the promise of discussions on some debt restructuring. Since the agreement implied an increase in Greece's already unsustainable debt burden and no measures to boost overall demand, it was unclear why either side saw any benefit to it other than preserving the shackles of euro membership. The Greek Prime Minister, Mr Tsipras, called the proposals 'irrational' but said he was willing to implement them to 'avoid disaster for the country'.[25]

Within twenty-four hours the IMF published a report that, given its position over the previous four years, belatedly recognised the obvious. It stated that 'Greece's debt can now only be made sustainable through debt relief measures that go far beyond what Europe has been willing to consider so far', and pointed out that since debt was expected to peak at around 200 per cent of GDP over the following two years, it would be necessary to extend by thirty years the grace period for debt repayment to the rest of the euro area or to make explicit annual transfers to Greece.[26] The rug had been pulled from under the German position that monetary union did not require transfers from creditors to debtors. The spectre of crisis eased after the Syriza government consolidated its position in elections unexpectedly called in September 2015, albeit on the lowest turnout in a Greek election since the restoration of democracy in 1974. Quite how the agreement would restore growth of the Greek economy was unclear, and the underlying problems of lack of competitiveness and unsustainable debt remain.

The approach being followed by the ECB is a 'finger in the dyke' strategy. Of necessity, it adopts the policy best suited to help the country most likely either to exit the euro in the near future or to suffer politically from continuing membership. When Greece was in danger of exit, sovereign debt was forgiven; when other periphery countries were in danger, it bought sovereign debt from those countries in order to bring down their bond yields; and when France was facing a deeper downturn, it adopted a policy of general sovereign bond purchases and money creation to lower the value of the euro. As a result, the ECB has had to choose between allowing the euro to fail and becoming a politicised institution. Naturally, it chose the latter. In years to come that may return to haunt the bank if there are attacks on its independence for straying into political territory.

Before the Treaty on European Union, signed in Maastricht

in 1992, the Bundesbank argued that monetary union required the degree of solidarity characteristic of a nation: 'all for one and one for all'.[27] The experience of monetary union has not demonstrated that degree of solidarity and trust. That is hardly surprising given that for Germany today interest rates are too low – and their savers are losing money – whereas in the periphery countries real interest rates are too high, exacerbating the depression. Keeping the show on the road is a challenge to which the ECB has so far successfully risen. But it begs the question of how a longer-lasting solution to the travails of the euro area can be found.

The economics of such an answer are straightforward. The real challenge is not the state of the public finances but a country's external competitiveness. So the euro area must pursue one, or some combination of, the following four ways forward:

1 Continue with high unemployment in the periphery countries until wages and prices have fallen enough to restore the loss in competitiveness. Since the full-employment trade deficits of these countries are still significant, further reductions will be painful to achieve. Unemployment is already at very high levels in these countries. In small countries, for which a floating exchange rate may seem too risky, such a route may be the only option.

2 Create a period of high inflation in Germany and other countries in surplus, while restraining wages and prices in the periphery, to eliminate the differences in competitiveness between north and south. That would require a marked fall in the euro for a long period, which would be unpopular in both Germany, whose savers would earn an even lower return on their assets than at present, and the rest of the world, which would interpret the fall as a hostile move.

3 Abandon the attempt to restore competitiveness within the euro area, and accept the need for *indefinite* and explicit transfers from the north to the south to finance the full-employment trade deficits in the periphery countries and to service external debt. Such transfers could well exceed 5 per cent of the GDP of the countries in the north, and would require significant conditions to be imposed on the periphery countries to limit the extent of those transfers.[28] Moreover, there is no popular support for transfers on such a scale in either donor or recipient countries.

4 Accept a partial or total break-up of the euro area.

I shall return to the prospects for these alternative ways of dealing with the problem in Chapter 9. When confronted with such a range of unpalatable choices, the leaders of Europe react by saying, 'We don't like any of them.' So they have responded by muddling through and adopting the coping strategy of Mr Micawber (in Charles Dickens' *David Copperfield*), waiting for something to turn up. Since the future is wholly unpredictable, it is certainly possible that something might turn up. But it is hard to believe that it would be an improvement on facing up to the problem and providing a sustainable economic basis for monetary union. The euro is no longer a means to an end, but the end itself. Given the strength of their political commitment to the project, one can sympathise with the dilemma in which those leaders find themselves. They are essentially following the views of John Maynard Keynes who, when confronted with the prospect of war in the 1930s, wrote:

We do not know what the future will bring, except that it will be quite different from anything we could predict. I have said in another context that it is a disadvantage of 'the long run' that in the long run we are all dead. But I could have said equally well that it is a great advantage of 'the short run' that in the short run we are all alive. Life and history are made up of short runs. If we are at peace in the short run that is something. The best we can do is put off disaster, if only in the hope, which is not necessarily a remote one, that something will turn up.[29]

The problem with the Mr Micawber strategy, however, is that whatever else may turn up, it is unlikely to be the economy.

For perfectly understandable reasons, Germany is unwilling to sign up to permanent, or at least indefinite, transfers of the kind that characterise most existing monetary unions (say between northern and southern Italy, or between different states of the United States). It is equally unenthusiastic about either higher inflation or a break-up of the monetary union. Yet trying to restore competitiveness by continued depression does not seem likely to succeed – it didn't in the 1920s after the return to the gold standard. Many commentators seem to believe in the 'progress through crisis' doctrine for Europe. Fred Bergsten, who served as Assistant Secretary for International Affairs during the Carter administration, argued the case when he said in 2014 that 'Germany would pay whatever was necessary, repeat whatever was necessary, to preserve the euro'.[30] That proposition is yet to be tested. But if other member countries come to believe it, then any semblance of fiscal discipline will be lost unless Germany takes control of their economies.

Policies dictated by Brussels and Frankfurt, and supported by policy-makers in Washington, have imposed enormous costs on citizens throughout Europe. The inability of governments to prevent high unemployment and avoid reductions in living standards has led to disillusionment. It was predictable that many voters would seek salvation in parties outside the mainstream. The European elections in 2014 and the Greek elections of 2015 were testimony enough. Putting the cart before the horse – setting up a monetary union before a political union – has forced the ECB to behave like a supranational fiscal authority. But neither it nor governments have a mandate to create a transfer or political union – voters do not want it. The bond market may be powerful, but the belief that a monetary crisis will provoke rapid steps to political union is pie in the sky.

Some German economists would like to return to the original idea of monetary union – with a strict implementation of the no-bailout clause in the European Treaty and the Stability and Growth Pact (SGP), which is a set of rules governing the fiscal policies of member countries of the European Union adopted in 1998–9. Among them is the man who more than anyone else made a success of the European Central Bank, Otmar Issing, its first Chief Economist. As he wrote in 2015, 'Economically and politically, relaxing the no bail-out clause would open the door for a massive violation of the principle of no taxation without representation, creating strong movement toward a transfer union without democratic legitimacy.'[31] But politicians in Europe seem immune to such powerful arguments. The treaty was ignored in the past, and would be again. The reason is that European monetary union is a political, not a constitutional project. As in many instances of nation-building, constitutions play an important role. They legitimise and popularise the essential strands of political ideology that bind people into their 'nation'. The European Treaty contains a number of provisions relating to monetary and fiscal policy to support the monetary union, including a prohibition on the direct financing of governments (Article 123), the no-bailout clause, which makes it illegal for one member to assume the debts of another (Article 125), limits on government deficits and debt (Article 126), and the SGP to enforce the limits on deficits and debt (secondary legislation based on Articles 121 and 126). Although those provisions had the appearance of binding treaty commitments, in times of crisis the treaty was simply ignored or reinterpreted according to the political needs of the moment. For example, in 2003 France and Germany ignored the constraints of the SGP and neither ministers nor the European institutions took any action. A similar reaction occurred in 2014–15 when the economic problems facing France and Italy demanded a relaxation of the constraints of the SGP. After 2010, the no bailout clause was quietly forgotten in the need to restructure Greek debt. The treaty seems to mean whatever the politicians in the big countries want it to mean.

People around Europe quite like the idea of the euro – but they don't like what it is doing to them. As someone once said to me, he wouldn't mind if the UK adopted the euro provided that we could keep our own interest rate. Misunderstanding of the economics of a monetary union is widespread. Just as the internal imbalances between spending and saving within major economies remain, as I discussed in Chapter 1, so do the external imbalances between economies. The sharp fall in demand and output across the world in 2008–9 did lower external surpluses and deficits. But full employment surpluses and deficits remain. Germany's trade surplus is approaching 8 per cent of GDP. To argue, as the German finance minister did, that this is helpful to the euro area as a whole because the German surplus offsets deficits elsewhere is to misunderstand the economic consequences of monetary union.[32] Germany's surplus and the deficits in the periphery countries are two sides of the same coin, and can be managed only by adopting one or more of the four solutions set out above.

The European experience over the past fifteen years or

so suggests three main lessons for the relationship between nations and monetary unions. First, it is sensible to ensure that all partners in a monetary union have fully converged on the same underlying rates of wage and price inflation before they are permitted to join. Although this was the intention of the monetary union in Europe, political pressures led to the admission of countries where inflation rates had not fully converged. Second, once a union has been created, it is important to monitor and prevent the emergence of divergences in wage and price inflation before they lead to losses of competitiveness, which can be reversed only by long periods of mass unemployment. To its credit, the European Central Bank issued many warnings about this, but they were ignored. Third, future economic shocks are inherently unpredictable and monetary union will come under great strain unless there is a high degree of mutual trust and willingness to make transfers to countries that have suffered major shocks. That requires a degree of political integration that is absent in Europe today. Substantial powers have been transferred to European institutions, but democratic legitimacy remains in the hands of national governments.

The crisis of European Monetary Union will drag on, and it cannot be resolved without confronting either the supranational ambitions of the European Union or the democratic nature of sovereign national governments. One or other will have to give way. Muddling through may continue for some while, but eventually the choice between a return to national monies and democratic control, or a clear and abrupt transfer of political sovereignty to a European government cannot be avoided.[33] European leaders, including the British, have for many years failed to make clear the nature of this choice to their peoples, for fear of being seen to rock the boat and thereby lose influence. The leaders of the smaller countries, in particular, have been cowed by threats from the centre, on the one hand, and by the prospect of jobs in European institutions when they stand down from national office on the other. Voters in a growing number of countries have turned away from centre-left and centre-right parties towards more extreme parties that still respect national sovereignty. There is a limit to the economic pain that can be imposed in the pursuit of a federal Europe without a political counter-reaction.

Iraq between the Gulf Wars

The second example illustrating the complex relationship between money and nations is the remarkable story of currency arrangements in Iraq between the First and Second Gulf Wars. It is the unusual story of one country with two currencies, or, perhaps more accurately, a country divided into two halves, one of which had a government and a badly run currency and the other, which had no government but a stable currency.

At the time of the First Gulf War in 1991, the Iraqi currency was the dinar. Following the war, Iraq was divided into two parts that were politically, militarily and economically separate from each other: southern Iraq was under the control of Saddam Hussein, and northern Iraq, protected by a no-fly zone north of the 36th Parallel, became a *de facto* Kurdish protectorate. In the south, Saddam's regime struggled to cope with UN sanctions, and resorted to printing money to finance growing budget deficits. Unable to import notes printed abroad because of sanctions, the official Iraqi government started to print new notes that bore Saddam's image. These were known as 'Saddam' dinars. Citizens had three weeks to exchange old notes for new. So many notes were eventually printed that the face value of cash in circulation jumped from 22 billion dinars at the end of 1991 to 584 billion only four years later. Inflation soared to an average of about 250 per cent a year over the same period.

In the north, however, people were given no opportunity to exchange their banknotes. So the new Saddam dinar did not circulate in the north, and people continued to use the old dinar notes. These were known as the 'Swiss' dinar – so-called because although the notes had been printed by the British company De La Rue, the plates had been manufactured in Switzerland. The Swiss dinar developed a life of its own and in effect became the new currency in the north – a successful coping strategy. No Swiss dinar notes were issued after 1989, and since the region had no issuing authority there was at most a fixed, and probably a declining money stock in the north. As a result, the Saddam and Swiss dinars developed into two separate currencies.

For ten years, therefore, until the invasion in 2003 by the United States and its coalition partners, Iraq had two currencies. In the south the Saddam dinar was issued by the official government of Iraq. In the north the Swiss dinar circulated, even though backed by no formal government or central bank, nor any law of legal tender. For a fiat currency this was an unusual situation. Whatever gave the Swiss dinar its value did not derive from the official Iraqi government, nor indeed from any other government.[34]

Although there was little or no trade between northern and southern Iraq, both the Swiss and Saddam dinars were traded against the US dollar. After 1993, the implied cross-exchange rate between Swiss and Saddam dinars rose in value from parity to around 300 Saddam dinars to each Swiss dinar by the time Saddam was deposed in 2003.[35] The appreciation of the Swiss dinar was clearly a consequence of the evolution of the actual and expected money supplies in the two territories: the supply of Saddam dinars rose rapidly, whereas the supply of Swiss dinars was fixed.

What is less obvious is the interesting behaviour of the Swiss dinar against the US dollar. After fluctuating in the 1990s, the Swiss dinar rose sharply against the US dollar from the middle of 2002 as the prospect of an end to the Saddam regime increased. It rose from around eighteen to the dollar in May 2002 to about six to the dollar by the beginning of May 2003, when the war ended. That appreciation reflected expectations about two factors: first, the durability of the political and military separation of Kurdish from Saddam-controlled Iraq and, second, the likelihood that a new institution would be established governing monetary policy in Iraq as a whole and would retrospectively back the value of the Swiss dinar. The political complexion of northern Iraq led to the assumption that the currency used there would have value once regime change had occurred. In other words, the value of the Swiss dinar had everything to do with politics and nothing to do with the economic policies of the government issuing the Swiss dinar, because no such government existed.

The crucial role of the political regime is illustrated by the behaviour of the exchange rate in the light of beliefs about a likely invasion and its consequences. At the time, financial market traders could, believe it or not, buy and sell futures contracts related to the fate of Saddam Hussein. One such contract paid out $1 if Saddam was deposed by the end of June 2003 and nothing otherwise. The price of the contract, which lay between $1 and zero, was a measure of how expectations about the political order in Iraq were evolving, and traders could bet on the outcome by buying or selling as many contracts as the market would bear. As the chance of Saddam's regime being deposed (and the price of the contract) increased, the Swiss dinar appreciated against the dollar. Later, another futures contract paid $1 if Saddam was captured by the end of December 2003, and nothing otherwise. As the chance of this happening (and the price of the contract) fell during

2003, with Saddam still missing, the Swiss dinar fell against the dollar. It rose again just before Saddam's capture on 13 December 2003.

After American and other coalition forces assumed control of Iraq in July 2003, the head of the Coalition Provisional Authority, Paul Bremer, announced that a new Iraqi dinar would be printed and exchanged for the two existing currencies at a rate that implied that one Swiss dinar was worth 150 Saddam dinars. The exchange was to take place over the period from October to the following January. The new dinars, like the Swiss, were printed by De La Rue in a very short space of time using plants in Britain and several other countries, and were flown into Iraq on twenty-two flights using Boeing 747s and other aeroplanes. The 150-dinar parity was barely half the rate the Swiss dinar reached at its peak. But it was above both the average rate that had prevailed over the previous six years, and the rate that would equalise the purchasing power of the two currencies. For example, around the time when the new conversion rate was being determined, it was estimated that 128 Saddam dinars to the Swiss dinar would equalise the wages of an engineer in the two parts of Iraq, 100 would equate the price of the shoes he wore to work, and 133 the price of his suit.[36] The new Iraqi dinar has remained fixed against the US dollar since, with the exception of the period between December 2006 and December 2008, when the Central Bank of Iraq steadily revalued the currency to prevent a rise in inflation, so that after two years it had appreciated by around 20 per cent.

The circulation of Swiss dinars in Kurdish-controlled Iraq during the 1990s was a market solution to the problem of devising a medium of exchange in the absence of a government with the power to issue currency. Changes in the relative price of Swiss and Saddam dinars show that the value of money depends on beliefs about the probability of survival of the institutions that define the state itself, and not just the policies pursued by the current government. The recent monetary history of Iraq is a telling example of the importance of political stability and the consequences of its absence.

Interestingly, a similar issue arose during the Second World War in the French overseas territories, which were divided between Vichy France and the Free French under Charles de Gaulle. In French Equatorial Africa, Cameroon and other French territories in sub-Saharan Africa, the right to issue banknotes had been vested in the Banque de l'Afrique Occidentale (BAO), which was under Vichy control until 1943. But as Free France began to acquire Vichy territory, it operated a different currency policy – namely, an exchange rate fixed to the pound sterling. So 'francs' meant different things in the two sets of territories, even though the notes were at first indistinguishable. Naturally, this created opportunities for making money by exchanging franc notes into foreign currency in one region and then reversing the exchange in the other. To prevent such activity, in 1941 Free France set up the Caisse Centrale de la France, operating from the Bank of England, as the issuer of its own banknotes and coins.[37] Notes issued by the BAO were exchanged at par for those of the Caisse Centrale in the summer of 1942, and were no longer legal tender. The Free French notes advertised their origin by incorporating in their design a phoenix and the 'Marianne de Londres' as symbols of freedom.

In the very different circumstances of both Iraq and the French overseas territories, the value of the currency depended very much on beliefs about the future political arrangements of the 'nation' that would stand behind it. There is clearly much more to the value of money than the economic issues that dominate the financial pages in the press.

An independent Scotland

The third example of the relationship between money and statehood concerns a country considering a divorce from its partner and the end of a long-standing monetary union. On 18 September 2014, the people of Scotland were asked in a referendum, 'Should Scotland be an independent country?' With a high turnout of 85 per cent, they rejected the proposition by 55 per cent to 45. Much of the referendum campaign centred on the choice of currency arrangements for a newly independent Scotland. The Yes campaign was reluctant to spell out a clear answer to the question of which currency would be used in the event of independence; the No campaign made a series of unsubstantiated claims about the difficulty of finding a satisfactory solution to the question. In fact there was a simple answer which, interestingly, neither side was prepared to spell out, each for its own reasons.

The original vision of the Scottish nationalists, put forward before the crisis, was of an arc of prosperity encompassing Ireland, Iceland and Scotland, within the euro, and with a large and successful banking sector in all three countries. After the crisis hit in 2008, it became clear that the vision was an illusion: Iceland and Ireland were overwhelmed by the cost of supporting a banking sector that had grown far too big for any small country to support, the euro was struggling to survive, and the two British banks that required substantial recapitalisation by the state (Royal Bank of Scotland and Halifax Bank of Scotland, the latter of which became part of Lloyds), and so by taxpayers in the UK as a whole, were both Scottish. Joining the euro was no longer a credible option. Nor was a new Scottish currency that would have floated against sterling and the euro in what had become turbulent monetary waters. With such a large proportion of trade and economic activity taking place with the rest of the UK, the next option was to peg a new Scottish currency to the pound sterling through a currency board. That would have required potentially unlimited reserves of sterling to convince markets that there was no risk to the peg. And that in turn would have meant a large borrowing programme in sterling – not an attractive prospect for a newly independent country trying to convince markets of its fiscal prudence.

So, by the time of the referendum, the Yes campaign proposed that in the event of independence there should be a formal monetary union with the residual United Kingdom, maintaining existing arrangements but with additional representation for Scotland in decision-making on monetary policy at the Bank of England. The No campaign flatly rejected this arrangement and ruled out any possibility of a monetary union, citing the experience of monetary union in Europe, which had shown the need for fiscal rules governing the newly independent country that would undermine the case for independence. The Yes campaign responded by pointing out that, whatever had been said during the campaign, the morning after a vote in favour of independence would be a new situation in which negotiating positions would change. Because the referendum was lost, this was never put to the test. But a formal monetary union cannot occur without the explicit agreement of both Scotland and the residual United Kingdom, and, given the demands of the former and the opposition of the latter, it seems most unlikely that this would have been forthcoming.

When the referendum took place, the currency question remained unresolved. But there was an answer. The simple and straightforward solution was 'sterlingisation'. Following a 'yes' vote, the Scottish government could have announced the next day that an independent Scotland had no intention of issuing its own currency and that all contracts denominated in sterling would always be legally honoured in sterling. There would be no formal currency union. Scotland would simply go on using sterling. Nothing would change. The Yes campaign could not, however, openly advocate such a solution, because it would have made clear that independence would give Scotland no real say over its monetary arrangements – they would be borrowed from England, exactly as they are today, because the relative size of the two economies means that interest rates are largely unaffected by conditions in Scotland. Politically, sterlingisation would have provided an answer to the currency question, but it would have taken the edge off the case for an independent Scotland.

The No campaign was also misleading. To admit that there was a simple and straightforward answer to the currency question would have undermined its argument that independence would be an economic disaster. That proposition was always implausible. There are many small and successful countries in the world, and there is no reason why Scotland could not have joined them. The case for and against the Union is more to do with identity than economics, the political costs of breaking up a three-hundred-year partnership, and whether Scotland needs full independence to manage its own domestic affairs when it already has substantial devolved powers. After the referendum, the Westminster Parliament moved rapidly to grant further powers to the Scottish Parliament.

Sterlingisation is a perfectly reasonable policy for a country that is happy to accept the economic consequences of a fixed exchange rate with sterling, but does not have the option of joining a formal monetary union with the UK. The attraction to Scotland of such a solution is that nothing significant would need to change. Many banknotes issued by banks in Scotland already have distinctive national designs, and the same could occur with coins if another symbol of Scottish identity was desired, as in Ireland following independence.[38]

Dollarisation has worked well for countries looking for a safe haven in stormy monetary conditions – including Cambodia, Ecuador and Panama – and sterlingisation would work for Scotland.[39] It would be the right solution because Scotland has successfully lived in a currency union with England and Wales for three hundred years. Current expectations of inflation and wage settlements are consistent with an enduring exchange rate link. Scotland would not be joining, as were the members of European Monetary Union, a new currency arrangement. Scotland has less need than in the past for subsidies from England to offset adverse shocks specific to Scotland because changes in the industrial structure of both Scotland and England, with the decline of heavy manufacturing and mining and the decreasing contribution from North Sea oil, mean that the two economies tend to move together. Nor would Scotland be faced with a substantial burden in the event of another banking failure. It is true that under sterlingisation major banks in an independent Scotland would have to unscrew the brass plates at their legal headquarters in Edinburgh and move them to London. Effectively, Scotland would have only foreign banks. As a consequence, Scotland would need no ability to act as a lender of last resort to those banks. That role would continue to be performed by the Bank of England, just as it does today for UK banks, such as Barclays, with overseas banking operations. But there is no reason to suppose that there would be any significant change in the number or location of jobs in banks in Scotland – the economic incentives to locate jobs in different places would be unchanged.[40]

Of course, it is always possible that over decades the economic links between the two former partners could diminish. But that is for the distant future; in the short term, sterlingisation is a perfectly feasible solution. In brief, despite the positions of the two sides, the currency question does not need to be at the centre of the debate on the future of Scotland. Independence was, and remains, a question about political identity. Until that issue is resolved, and this writer would be extremely sad to see Scotland choose to leave the Union, the fate of the United Kingdom will remain uncertain. In the General Election of 2015, the Scottish Nationalists won fifty-six out of fifty-nine seats in Scotland. So independence will remain a live issue. If, for example, the UK as a whole were in the future to vote to leave the European Union, while in Scotland a majority voted to remain a member, the clamour for independence would be even more difficult to resist than in 2014.

What do these three examples tell us about the relationship between nations and monies? As we saw in Chapter 2, the key role of governments is to supply the right amount of money in good times in order to avoid the extremes of hyperinflation on the one hand, and depression on the other, and to create emergency money in bad times. In both cases that involves political judgements in the face of radical uncertainty. In good times, monetary policy combines an inflation target, whether implicit or explicit, with a policy for how quickly to react to temporary disturbances to inflation and growth. Judgements about the desirable long-term inflation rate, and the trade-offs between inflation and output in the short term, are inherently political. In bad times, decisions about how much emergency money to create and to whom it should be distributed are highly political, as the popular anger following the financial bailout of banks in the crisis revealed. Institutions, whether national or supranational, are important ways of embodying these political judgements so that monetary management, in good times and bad, can be effective. Moreover, trust in government is a crucial component of successful monetary arrangements.

Traditional economic arguments about 'optimum currency areas' – trading off the loss of flexibility in adjusting to
shocks from having your own currency against the greater
trade intensity that stems from an integrated monetary area –
played only a minor role in shaping monetary arrangements in
Europe, Iraq and Scotland. Monetary integration in Europe
was driven by a political agenda, and in some cases a belief
that economic problems flowing from the common currency
would force faster political integration. In Iraq, market prices
revealed the importance of political institutions in determining
the value of a currency. And in the debate leading up to the
Scottish referendum, neither side was prepared to embrace the
obvious economic solution to the currency question for fear
that it would undermine their political case. In both Iraq and
Scotland the immediate questions have been answered. But in
the euro area the fight for survival has become a battle between
politicians and arithmetic. Although the future outcome is
unknowable, history is on the side of arithmetic. The tragedy of
monetary union in Europe is not that it might collapse but that,
given the degree of political commitment among the leaders of
Europe, it might continue, bringing economic stagnation to the
largest currency bloc in the world and holding back recovery
of the wider world economy. It is at the heart of the disequilibrium in the world today.

The French ambition to curtail the economic power of
Germany, and especially its central bank the Bundesbank, by
drawing it into a monetary union that would be controlled by
French civil servants has failed. The French economy is weaker
than that of Germany, and monetary union has increased,
not reduced, Germany's political dominance. Responsibility
for the economic conditions in other member states will be
laid at the door of Germany. The idea of a federal union was
intended to represent the birth of a new Europe, born out of

the common experience of defeat and occupation during the Second World War among all the original members of the European Economic Community. Attempts to recreate the Holy Roman Empire have often appealed to a European elite, but have foundered on the resistance of its peoples. The relationship between nations and their money reflects politics more than economics. And the same applies to the relationship between nations and their banks.

❦

7

INNOCENCE REGAINED: REFORMING MONEY AND BANKING

'How is it possible to expect that Mankind will take advice, when they will not so much as take warning?'

Jonathan Swift, 'Thoughts on Various Subjects', 1703

'We call upon every man who professes to be animated with the principles of the democracy, to assist in accomplishing the great work of redeeming this country from the curse of our bad bank system.'

William Leggett, *Evening Post*, 6 August 1834

For centuries, alchemy has been the basis of our system of money and banking. Governments pretended that paper money could be turned into gold even when there was more of the former than the latter. Banks pretended that short-term riskless deposits could be used to finance long-term risky investments. In both cases, the alchemy is the apparent transformation of risk into safety. For much of the time the alchemy seemed to work. From time to time, however, people realised that the Emperor had far fewer clothes than the Masters of the Universe wanted us to believe. Once confidence in the value of money or the soundness of banks was lost, there was a monetary or banking crisis. As Bagehot wrote in *Lombard Street*, 'The peculiar essence of our financial system is an unprecedented trust between man and man; and when that trust is much weakened by hidden causes, a small accident may greatly hurt it, and a great accident for a moment may almost destroy it.'[1] For a society to base its financial system on alchemy is a poor advertisement for its rationality. The key to ending the alchemy is to ensure that the risks involved in money and banking are correctly identified and borne by those who enjoy the benefits from our financial system.

How can we regain the innocence and trust in banking that, as described in Chapter 3, was lost over a long period in which crises became accepted as an inevitable feature of the financial landscape? Many English children used to be brought up on John Bunyan's *Pilgrim's Progress*, published in 1678 – a religious allegory telling the story of the trials and tribulations of Christian's long and difficult journey from his home in the City of Destruction to find the Celestial City on Mount Zion, passing on the way through the Slough of Despond, Hill Difficulty, Vanity Fair, Hill Lucre and Doubting Castle. Much less well known and less well-read than Bunyan's book is *The Political Pilgrim's Progress*, published in 1839.[2] It is the story of the journey of Radical from the City of Plunder to the City of Reform. In the City of Plunder:

Its people seemed active, industrious, and enterprising; but there appeared a singular custom amongst them, which greatly marred their social happiness and unanimity, and this was, that nearly one half of the inhabitants made a practice of putting their hands into the pockets of the other half, and taking their money from them. There was a *law*, indeed, for this singular custom ... fortified by a thing called '*government*' [which] always vehemently affirmed that the mode of making one half of the people work for and support the other half, was the very perfection of human wisdom.[3]

Like Christian, Radical faces many trials and tribulations while passing through many of the same places, particularly Vanity Fair. In that den of iniquity, with his friend Common-sense, Radical is shown the Paperkite-Buildings:

Here the people seemed to talk an altogether new language, different from anything that Pilgrim had hitherto heard in this metropolis. There was an everlasting chatter, like the incessant crowings of a rookery, about stocks, funds, omnium, scrip, debentures, rentes, metalliques, discounts, premiums, exchequer bills, shares, accounts, balances, advances, consols, India stock, bank stock, exchanges, set-tling days, bear and bull accounts, lame ducks, pressures, panics, long annuities, bar gold, bullion, coin, mint prices &c. The agitation and anxiety amongst the moving throng of the *Buildings* were exceedingly interesting. The people were all exchanging bits of paper, one with another; and this act was designated by the phrase of 'the circulating medium', on which many large volumes of books had been written, and which was considered as an occult science in that part of the country.[4]

But when he finally reaches his goal, Radical finds that in the City of Reform 'there was no such thing as a stock exchange or a saving bank, or a bank note for any sum under FIFTY pounds'.[5]

Drawing inspiration from Radical, we might well ask how we can find our way to the City of Reform. The pretence that the illiquid real assets of an economy – the factories, capital equipment, houses and offices – can suddenly be converted into money or liquidity is the essence of the alchemy of the present system. Banks and other financial intermediaries will always try to finance illiquid assets by issuing liquid liabilities because they make profits by paying less on the latter than they earn on the former. That is why, although money is a public good, the bulk of its supply is provided by commercial banks. The problem is that the liquidity promised to investors or depositors can be supplied only if at each moment a small number of people wish to convert their claim on the bank into cash. Liquidity simply disappears if everyone wishes to convert their claim into money at the same time. What may be possible for a small number of people is self-evidently impossible for the community as a whole. And the problem is made worse by the fact that if a depositor believes that others are likely to try to take their money out, it is rational for him or her to do the same and get to the front of the queue as soon as possible – a bank run. Runs reflect the underlying alchemy and make the system unstable.

Liquidity is an illusion; here one day, gone the next. It reminds me of those attractive soap bubbles that one can blow into the air. From a distance, they look appealing. But if you ever try to hold them in your hand, they disappear in a trice. And whenever at the same time many people try to convert their assets into a liquid form, they often discover that liquidity has disappeared without trace. When there is a sudden jump in the demand for liquidity and investors rush to convert their claims on illiquid assets into money, the result is usually a crisis, exposing the alchemy for what it is. Liquidity is, however, only one aspect of the alchemy of our present system. Risk, and its impact on the solvency of banks, is the other. And in the recent crisis, concern about solvency was the main driver of the liquidity problems facing banks. When creditors started to worry that bank equity was insufficient to absorb potential losses, they decided that it was better to get out while the going was good. Concerns about solvency, especially in a world of radical uncertainty, generate bank runs. To reduce or eliminate alchemy, we need a joint set of measures to deal with both solvency and liquidity problems.

If a market economy is to function efficiently, businesses and households need a secure mechanism by which to pay their bills and receive wages and salaries. Ordinary current accounts are not vehicles for speculative investments and it is important that they have a stable value in terms of money, in which payments are denominated. But if a bank has assets that are highly risky, as many of its loans may be, then it is alchemy to pretend that deposits can be secure. So governments decided to guarantee deposits, first by creating deposit insurance and then in the recent crisis by extending blanket guarantees to all bank creditors. Because of their importance to the economy, and their political power, banks had become too important to fail. And the larger they became, the more likely it was that the government would bail them out in times of difficulty. Central banks lent vast sums to commercial banks. That stopped the rot, in the sense of removing the incentive to run on a bank, but at the cost of shifting the risk of the assets of banks on to taxpayers. In the case of Ireland, it almost bankrupted the country.

The toxic nexus between limited liability, deposit insurance and lender of last resort means that there is a massive implicit subsidy to risk-taking by banks. After the 1980s, when banking was liberalised, the degree of alchemy, and hence of subsidy, inherent in the risk and maturity transformation in the system increased. No individual bank could easily walk away from the temptation to exploit the subsidy. Each bank faced a prisoner's dilemma. Only by running down its holdings of liquid assets, and financing itself as cheaply as possible by short-term debt, could it keep up with the rising profitability of its peers.

In short, compared with a century or even fifty years ago, banks have been financing themselves with too little equity and holding too few liquid assets. Before the crisis, equity was insufficient to absorb potential losses from the risks being taken, which meant that it was more likely that depositors or other short-term creditors would think about running on the bank in the wake of bad news. And in the event of a run, there were insufficient liquid assets to enable the bank to douse the flames by paying out. Even governments recognised that something had to change.

Official sector reforms

Since the crisis, the official sector has been hyperactive. Both at the national and international level, regulators have been tightening up on the freedoms given to banks in respect of how they finance themselves, their structure and their conduct. At the international level, a concerted effort has been made by the major countries in the G20, working through the Basel Committee of the Bank for International Settlements, to rectify some of the pre-crisis failures in regulation. The minimum amount of equity a bank must use to finance itself, known as its capital requirement, has been raised, and banks also have to hold a minimum level of liquid assets related to the deposits and other short-term financing that could run from the bank within thirty days, known as the liquidity coverage ratio. Regulators are also conscious of the need to look outside the boundaries of the traditional banking sector to see if elements of alchemy are appearing in the 'shadow' banking sector, and to conduct stress tests to see if banks are capable of withstanding the losses incurred due to particular adverse scenarios.

The Financial Stability Board, a group of officials from the G20, is leading work both on these investigations and on the challenge posed by the potential failure of banks that operate across borders. Nationally, regulators in countries such as Sweden, Switzerland and the United States have imposed additional capital requirements over and above the internationally agreed minimum. Countries such as the United Kingdom and United States have introduced legislation to separate, or ring-fence, basic banking operations from the more complex trading activities of investment banking.[6] And most countries have either improved or introduced special bankruptcy arrangements – known as resolution mechanisms – to enable a bank in trouble to continue to provide essential services to its depositors while its finances are being sorted out and, if necessary, to facilitate a speedy transfer of depositors from a failing to a profitable bank. That represents a significant shift of opinion since before the crisis, when most countries were primarily concerned to ensure that their banking system was not weighed down by heavier regulation than in other countries. Ensuring a safer banking system is now seen as in a country's self-interest. And national regulators, often working together, have pursued cases of misconduct by bank employees and levied substantial fines, as described in Chapter 3, as well as restricting compensation of bank executives.

Moreover, the market itself has imposed its own discipline on banks and other financial institutions. As a result, the banking system has changed a great deal since 2008. The largest banks have become smaller; the balance sheet of Goldman Sachs in 2015 was around one quarter smaller than in 2007. Investment banking is not as profitable now as it was when asset prices were rising in the wake of falling real interest rates. Many banks have cut back on the size of their investment banking operations and some, such as Citigroup and Bank of America, have sold their proprietary trading desks, which bought and sold investments on their own account, and turned themselves back into more traditional commercial banks.

Is all this enough? I fear not, and for one simple reason. Radical uncertainty means that sentiment towards financial firms can change so quickly that regulations which appear too burdensome one moment seem too lenient the next. The experience of 2007–8 illustrates what can happen. Let's ask the following question: how much equity finance does a bank need to issue in order to persuade potential creditors that it is safe for them to lend to the bank? Before the crisis, the answer was hardly any at all. Markets were content to lend large sums to banks at low interest rates, even though banks were highly leveraged. After 2008, the answer was a very large amount. Not even the new higher levels of capital mandated by regulators were sufficient to ensure that markets were happy to restore previous levels and pricing of funding. The innocence that was lost during the crisis was proving very expensive to regain. For investors, the narrative about the wisdom of lending to banks had changed. So it is extremely difficult to know the appropriate level of equity finance a bank should be required to use in a world where alchemy is still a characteristic of the banking system. And the right answer can change from one day to the next. In 2012, the Spanish bank Bankia reported a risk-weighted capital ratio of over 10 per cent, well above the regulatory minimum; three months later it required a capital injection of €25 billion.

Two further aspects of current regulation are difficult to reconcile with radical uncertainty. The first is that official capital requirements are calculated with respect to estimates of the riskiness of different assets on a bank's balance sheet. As described in Chapter 4, each type of asset is given a risk weight, agreed by international regulators, and this is used to calculate the overall amount of equity a bank must issue. Mortgage lending, for example, was thought on the basis of past experience to be relatively safe, and was given a low risk weight. Sovereign debt was believed to be so safe that it was given a zero risk weight, meaning that banks did not have to raise any equity finance in respect of such investments and so had no additional capacity to absorb losses on them. So complex did the system become that banks were allowed to propose their own internal models to calculate risk weights. It turned out that some banks had very different estimates of the riskiness of the same assets than others, undermining confidence in the fairness of the regulations.[7]

The people who designed those risk weights did so after careful thought and an evaluation of past experience. But they simply did not imagine how risky mortgage lending and the sovereign debt of countries such as Greece would become during the crisis, nor how large were the risks inherent in much more complicated financial instruments. Rather than lambast the regulators for not anticipating those events, it is more sensible to recognise that the pretence that it is possible to calibrate risk weights is an illusion. The need for banks to use equity to absorb losses is most important in precisely those circumstances where something wholly unexpected occurs and previous calculations of risk weights are irrelevant. That is why, during the crisis, a measure of equity relative to total assets was a much better indication of safety than equity relative to total risk-weighted assets. Risk weights in the design of capital regulation seem attractive at first sight, but they break in our hands when we try to use them. A simple leverage ratio is a more robust measure for regulatory purposes.

The second problematic aspect of current regulation concerns the requirement for banks to hold a minimum level of liquid assets – the liquidity coverage ratio – so that they can withstand an unusually high demand for the repayment of debt or deposits. I chaired the meetings that eventually agreed on the definition of the ratio. The discussions were overshadowed by one major conceptual problem. How could we define assets that were always liquid? Before the crisis, it seemed obvious that government debt was a safe and liquid asset. But experience showed that the sovereign debt of some countries was far from safe and liquid. Moreover, other countries, such as Australia, had managed their public finances so carefully that there was simply too little government debt outstanding to supply the demand for liquid assets. It seemed rather odd to penalise well-managed countries for not issuing large amounts of government debt! At heart, the problem was the failure to recognise that in a world of radical uncertainty only the central bank can create liquidity, and so liquidity regulation has to be seamlessly integrated with a central bank's function as the lender of last resort.

None of this means that the extraordinary efforts of regulators in recent years to improve the system have been a mistake. But they are in danger of failing to see the wood for the trees. Regulation has become extraordinarily complex, and in ways that do not go to the heart of the problem of alchemy. The objective of detail in regulation is to bring clarity, not to leave regulators and regulated alike uncertain about the current state of the law.[8] Much of the complexity reflects pressure from financial firms. By encouraging a culture in which compliance with detailed regulations is a defence against a charge of wrong-doing, bankers and regulators have colluded in a self-defeating spiral of complexity. No capitalist economy can prosper without sufficient certainty about the way that rights and obligations will be interpreted and enforced. Arbitrary regulatory judgements impose what is effectively a high tax on all investments and savings. The fact that it was in England that the Industrial Revolution began was in part the result of a stable and predictable framework for doing business with others. As the father of English commercial law, Lord Mansfield, put it in 1761 as the Industrial Revolution was gathering pace: 'The daily negotiations and property of merchants ought not to depend upon subtleties and niceties; but upon rules easily learned and easily retained, because they are the dictates of common sense, drawn from the truth of the case.'[9]

Not many people can easily absorb and retain the totality of current financial regulation, and those who try are not left with the impression that it is common sense. The Dodd-Frank Act passed in the US in 2010 contained 2300 pages, with many thousands of pages more expected to cover the detailed rules that will follow, whereas the Glass-Steagall Act of 1933, which separated commercial and investment banking, covered a mere thirty-seven pages.[10] In Britain, the Prudential Regulation Authority and the Financial Conduct Authority have combined rulebooks exceeding ten thousand pages.[11] Such complexity feeds on itself and brings the system into disrepute. Efforts to comply with financial regulation are a barrier to new small firms trying to enter the financial sector, and, in advanced countries, result in the employment of several hundred thousand people. To employ such a large number of talented people to cope with complex regulation constitutes a large 'dead-weight' cost to society.

As we saw in Chapter 4, complexity is an inefficient way of coping with radical uncertainty. Can we do better?

More radical reforms

Frenetic activity among the official community cannot conceal the fact that, although much useful repair to the fabric of regulation has been made, nothing fundamental has changed. The alchemy of our banking system remains. Since the bank bailouts in most advanced economies were huge, it is surprising that more has not been done since the crisis to address the fundamental problem. The scale of central bank lending to a relatively small number of financial institutions was so large that one could have paraphrased Winston Churchill by saying that never in the field of financial endeavour had so much been owed by so few to so many – and with so little radical reform. Of course, governments, financial regulators and central banks are all well aware of the nature of the problem, but official efforts to tackle it are in stark contrast with more radical ideas proposed, albeit never implemented, by earlier generations of economists.

Even though the degree of alchemy of the banking system was much less fifty or more years ago than it is today, it is interesting that many of the most distinguished economists of the first half of the twentieth century believed in forcing banks to hold sufficient liquid assets as reserves to back 100 per cent of their deposits. They recommended ending the system of 'fractional reserve banking', under which banks create deposits to finance risky lending and so have insufficient safe cash reserves to back their deposits.[12] The elimination of fractional reserve banking was a proposal put forward in 1933 as the 'Chicago Plan'.[13] The proponents of the plan included the brilliant American monetary theorist Irving Fisher and a distinguished group of economists at Chicago such as Frank Knight, Henry Simons and Paul Douglas; later support came from right across the spectrum of post-war economists, ranging from Milton Friedman to James Tobin and Hyman Minsky.[14] Interestingly, John Maynard Keynes was not part of this group, largely because Britain did not experience a banking crisis in the 1930s and his focus was on restoring output and employment.[15] More recently, a number of economists have proposed variations on the same theme: John Cochrane from Chicago, Jaromir Benes and Michael Kumhof from the IMF, the British economists Andrew Jackson, Ben Dyson and John Kay, Laurence Kotlikoff from Boston and the distinguished *FT* commentator Martin Wolf.[16]

There are two ways of looking at these radical approaches to banking reform, one by focusing on the banks' assets and the other on their liabilities. The essence of the Chicago Plan was to force banks to hold 100 per cent liquid reserves against deposits. Reserves would include only safe assets, such as government securities or reserves held with the central bank. In this way there would be no reason for anyone to run on a bank, and even if some people did withdraw their deposits there would be no incentive for others to join them, because there would always be sufficient funds to support the remaining deposits.

So far, so good. But who would perform the many functions that banks carry out today, especially lending to businesses and households, so enabling them to build factories and purchase homes? In other words, who would finance the transfer of existing assets and bear the risk involved in financing new investment? That relates to the liabilities of banks under such radical reforms. If deposits must be backed with safe government securities, then it follows logically that all other assets, essentially risky loans to the private sector, must be financed by issuing equity or long-term debt, which would absorb any losses arising from those risky assets. As a result, this approach would, in effect, separate safe and liquid 'narrow' banks, carrying out payment services, from risky and illiquid 'wide' banks performing all other activities.[17] It would be illegal for wide banks, including the 'shadow' banking sector, to issue demand, or even short-term, deposits.[18]

The great advantage of reforms such as the Chicago Plan is that bank runs and the instability they create would disappear as a source of fragility. The Chicago Plan breaks the link between the creation of money and the creation of credit. Lending to the real economy would be made by wide banks and financed by equity or long-term debt, not through the creation of money. Money would once again become a true public good with its supply determined by the government or central bank.[19] Governments would not have to fight against the swings in money creation or destruction that automatically occur today when banks decide to expand or contract credit. It was the sharp fall in credit and money after 2008 that led to the massive expansion of money via quantitative easing. As Irving Fisher put it, 'We could leave the banks free ... to lend money as they please, provided we no longer allowed them to manufacture the money which they lend ... In short: nationalize money but do not nationalize banking.'[20] And the clarity and passion of Fisher in the 1930s are echoed in the arguments of John Cochrane and Martin Wolf today. Such reforms would indeed eliminate the alchemy in our banking system, which the official reform agenda fails to tackle.

So why hasn't the idea been implemented? One explanation is that it would eliminate the implicit subsidy to banking that results from the 'too important to fail' nature of most banks. Banks will lobby hard against such a reform. To protect the system of making payments, as crucial to the daily functioning of the economy as electricity is to our daily lives, governments will always guarantee the value of bank accounts used to make payments, and it is therefore in the interest of banks to find ways of putting risky assets on to the same balance sheet as deposits. More importantly, however, eliminating alchemy in this particular way has some other disadvantages. First, the transition from where we are today to complete separation of narrow and wide banks could be disruptive, forcing a costly reorganisation of the structure and balance sheet of existing institutions. It would be easy for the banking community to portray such a move as unwarranted interference in the management of private banks, and even the much more limited ring-fencing adopted in the UK has come under attack for precisely this reason.

Second, the complete separation of banks into two extreme types – narrow and wide – denies the chance to exploit potential economic benefits from allowing financial intermediaries to explore and develop different ways of linking savers, with a preference for safety and liquidity, and borrowers, with a desire to borrow flexibly and over a long period. Constraining financial intermediation would mean that the cost of financing investment in plant and equipment, houses and other real assets would be higher. The potential efficiencies in using different ways of bringing savers and investors together would be lost by legally mandating a complete prohibition on the financing of risky assets by safe deposits – provided that we could find other ways, as I discuss below, of following a path that would lead to the end of alchemy.

Third, and most important of all, radical uncertainty means that it is impossible for the market to provide insurance against all possible contingencies, and one role of governments is to provide catastrophic insurance when something wholly unexpected happens. Ending alchemy does not in itself eliminate large fluctuations in spending and production. In a world of radical uncertainty, where it is possible that households and businesses will make significant 'mistakes' about the future profitability of investment, there is always a risk of unexpected sharp changes in total spending.

Ensuring that money creation is restored to government through the requirement for narrow banks to back all deposits with government securities does stop the possibility that runs on the banking and shadow banking sectors will transmit shocks at rapid speed right across the financial sector, as happened to such devastating effect in 2008. But the risk from unexpected events is then focused on the prices of assets held directly by households and businesses and on the solvency of wide banks. It would be possible for governments to stand back and allow the prices of real assets and claims on those assets, including the prices of the bonds and equity of wide banks, to take the hit. As discussed in Chapter 5 and again in Chapter 9, one of the most difficult issues in monetary policy today is the extent to which central banks should intervene in these asset markets – either to prevent an 'excessive' rise in asset prices in the first place or to support prices when they fall sharply. It is difficult because the case for intervention rests on the view that the central bank knows better than other people when market prices reflect 'mistakes'. I am not sure that their track record justifies an optimistic judgement of the ability of central banks to see the rocks ahead and steer the economy around them. Providing emergency money to meet a sharp jump in the demand for liquidity and central bank reserves is one thing; impeding a move of the economy, and asset prices, to a new equilibrium quite another.

But there is a somewhat more compelling argument for the provision of catastrophe insurance to financial intermediaries. It stems from the importance of debt finance in the financing of the real economy. Since the crisis it has become fashionable to obsess about the role of debt – and it is indeed a good idea not to owe too much in case an unpleasant surprise leads to financial embarrassment. But debt has a special role, especially when held against collateral; that is, when the lender takes a claim on assets owned by the borrower that act as a guarantee of the loan in the event of a failure to repay. The lender will typically lend only a proportion of the value of the collateral, applying a haircut to cover the risk that if the borrower defaults the collateral will still be sufficient to repay the debt. The more liquid and less volatile the collateral, the lower the value of the haircut.

Debt finance of this kind means that the lender does not need to monitor carefully the twists and turns of the venture to which the loan was extended – which may be well-nigh impossible in the case of small or complex businesses – but only the value of the collateral. That is why many small businesses find it difficult to obtain equity finance and their owners have to pledge the value of their home as collateral when borrowing. It is also why banks find lending to students unappealing: it is difficult to monitor their ability to repay and they can offer little by way of collateral. Collateral is valuable precisely because its value does not depend upon the borrower's creditworthiness. The extension of debt backed by collateral helps to overcome the pervasive lack of information about borrowers' creditworthiness.[21] It oils the wheels of those parts of the economy that other sources of finance, such as equity, cannot reach. And one of the key roles of financial intermediaries is to lend against collateral.

Collateralised borrowing is, therefore, an important feature of the financial system, and it will survive the elimination of the incentive to run on deposits and other short-term unsecured debt. Although wide banks cannot create money in the form of deposits, they can still borrow short and lend long. In both cases they use collateral. They lend to households and businesses against real assets, and they borrow against financial securities created for the purpose, which give the impression to purchasers of bank debt of being liquid and safe but ultimately are backed by the long-term loans and other assets of the bank. A large quantity of paper claims on underlying assets has been constructed to satisfy the demand for collateral. In this way, even wide banks create a degree of alchemy. When unexpectedly bad news arrives, collateral falls in value and is perceived as more volatile and less liquid than before. Lenders will want more collateral to continue or roll over existing loans. Borrowers, whether businesses or banks themselves, may be forced to sell assets in order to replace withdrawn loan facilities, and the attempt by all borrowers to obtain sufficient collateral creates a multiplier effect, driving down asset prices further. All this is very much worse in a banking and financial system where runs can occur. But it would not be entirely absent in a world of wide banks. It would create a demand for governments or central banks to provide catastrophic insurance in the form of supporting the value and liquidity of collateral. Undoubtedly, one of the motives for the bailouts of the creditors of banks and other financial firms in 2008 was the conviction that failures of such firms would cause the financial system as a whole to freeze up and contract the availability of credit to the real economy. As former US Treasury Secretary Timothy Geithner wrote in his memoirs, 'the only way for crisis responders to stop a financial panic is to remove the incentives for panic, which means preventing messy collapses of systemic firms, assuring creditors of financial institutions that their loans will be repaid, and ... exposing taxpayers to more short-term risk'.[22]

Whatever the merits of the actions taken in 2008, there is no doubt that an observer could say wryly, 'I wouldn't start from here.' Runs on conventional and shadow banking systems alike led to a collapse of both. The size and cost of creditor bailouts were increased significantly by the inadequate amounts of equity available to absorb losses in the banking system. And attempts to provide liquidity insurance through central bank facilities as the lender of last resort failed to penalise banks that took advantage of such support, not least because to collect insurance premiums when paying out on the policy is rather late in the day and might have made matters worse. The system in place before the crisis provided many incentives for banks to structure themselves in a way that made a crisis more likely – and that is exactly what concern about 'moral hazard' means. Standing ready to do whatever it takes to keep the financial system functioning is not enough. The system itself has to be designed carefully in order to reduce the frequency and severity of crises. There is a case for the provision of catastrophic insurance – but not unconditionally and not in the way that was forced on policy-makers in the circumstances of 2008.

Some commentators have taken issue with concerns about moral hazard, arguing, by analogy, that fire departments put out fires started by people who smoke in bed. But as a society we supplement fire services by strict regulations to make it less likely that fires will start. We need to do the same in the financial sector. Too much thinking about how to respond to crises, especially in the United States, has focused on throwing money at the problem once the fire has broken out. We need to anticipate the problem. There is wisdom in the Roman saying '*Si vis pacem, para bellum*' – if you want peace, prepare for war.

Can we find a way of retaining the attractive feature of the Chicago Plan – that it ends bank runs – while at the same time reducing alchemy in the wider banking system? Or, to put it another way, can we reduce the cost of eliminating alchemy?

A new approach – the pawnbroker for all seasons

The way forward is to recognise that the prohibition on the creation of money by private banks is not likely to be sufficient to eliminate alchemy in our financial system. Radical uncertainty means that the provision of catastrophic insurance in some circumstances is desirable. Bagehot's concept of a lender of last resort is, in some key respects, outdated. He understood that it was impossible in a crisis to tell whether a bank was or was not solvent, but that would not matter if the central bank could lend against 'good collateral'. In his day, and until relatively recently, banks held large amounts of government securities and secure private commercial paper on their balance sheets. Good collateral was in plentiful supply. But when banks ran down their holdings of liquid assets, that all changed. The result was that in the crisis there was not enough good collateral and central banks had to take 'bad' collateral in the form of risky and illiquid assets on which haircuts, often large ones, had to be imposed to avoid risk to taxpayers. In consequence, central banks could lend only a proportion of the liquid funds that a bank might need. As described in Chapter 5, central bank lending encumbers the balance sheet, reducing the collateral available for other creditors, thereby encouraging them not to roll over their loans to the bank.

The essential problem with the traditional LOLR is that, in the presence of alchemy, the only way to provide sufficient liquidity in a crisis is to lend against bad collateral – at inadequate haircuts and low or zero penalty rates. Announcing in advance that it will follow Bagehot's rule – lend freely against good collateral at a penalty rate – will not prevent a central bank from wanting to deviate from it once a crisis hits. Anticipating that, banks have every incentive to run down their holdings of liquid assets and to finance themselves with large amounts of debt, and that is what they did. It is not enough to respond to the crisis by throwing money at the system to douse the fire while reciting Bagehot; ensuring that banks face incentives to prepare in normal times for access to liquidity in bad times matters just as much.

It is time to replace the lender of last resort by the pawn-broker for all seasons (PFAS). A pawnbroker is someone who is prepared to lend to almost anyone who pledges collateral sufficient to cover the value of a loan – someone who is desperate for cash today might borrow $25 against a gold watch. Since 2008, central banks have become used to lending against a much wider range of collateral than hitherto, and it is difficult to imagine that they will be able to supply liquidity insurance without continuing to do so. In the spirit of not letting a good crisis go to waste, I think it is possible to build on two of the most important developments in central banking since the crisis – the expansion of lending against wider collateral and the creation of money by quantitative easing – to construct a new role for a central bank as such a pawnbroker. I stress this point because so many proposals for reform create alarm among bankers, and often therefore governments, since they are a step into the unknown. In contrast, the idea of PFAS is a natural extension of measures already introduced.

When there is a sudden jump in the demand for liquidity, the pawnbroker for all seasons will supply liquidity, or emergency money, against illiquid and risky assets. Only a central bank on behalf of the government can do this. But it will do so within a framework that eliminates the incentive for bank runs. The idea of the PFAS is a coping strategy in the face of radical uncertainty.

Inspiration for the principle of a PFAS can be drawn from the American journalist William Leggett, who wrote in an article in the *New York Evening Post* in December 1834:

Let the [current] law be repealed; let a law be substituted, requiring simply that *any person* entering into banking business shall be required to lodge with some officer designated in the law, real estate, or other approved security, to the full amount of the notes which he might desire to issue ... Banking, established on this foundation, would be liable to none of the evils arising from panic; for each holder of a note would, in point of fact, hold a title-deed of property to the full value of its amount.[23]

The aim of the PFAS is threefold. First, to ensure that all deposits are backed by either actual cash or a guaranteed contingent claim on reserves at the central bank. Second, to ensure that the provision of liquidity insurance is mandatory and paid for upfront. Third, to design a system which in effect imposes a tax on the degree of alchemy in our financial system – private financial intermediaries should bear the social costs of alchemy.[24]

The basic principle is to ensure that banks will always have sufficient access to cash to meet the demands of depositors and others supplying short-term unsecured debt. The key is to look at both sides of a bank's balance sheet. Start with its assets. Each bank would decide how much of its assets it would position in advance at the central bank – that is, how much of the relevant assets the central bank would be allowed to examine and which would then be available for use as collateral.[25] For each type of asset the central bank would calculate the haircut it would apply when deciding how much cash it would lend against that asset. Adding up all assets that had been pre-positioned, it would then be clear how much central bank money the bank would be entitled to borrow at any instant. Because these arrangements would have been put in place well ahead of any crisis, there would be no difficulty in the central bank agreeing to lend at a moment's notice. The assessment of collateral, and the calculation of haircuts, have become routine since the crisis and would become a normal function of a central bank as a PFAS. The amount which a bank was entitled to borrow against prepositioned collateral, added to its existing central bank reserves, is a measure of the 'effective liquid assets' of a bank.

The second step is to look at the liabilities side of a bank's balance sheet – its total demand deposits and short-term unsecured debt (up to, say, one year) – which could run at short notice. That total is a measure of the bank's 'effective liquid liabilities'.[26] The regulatory requirement on banks and other financial intermediaries would be that their effective liquid assets should exceed their effective liquid liabilities. Almost all existing prudential capital and liquidity regulation, other than a limit on leverage, could be replaced by this one simple rule. The rule would act as a form of mandatory insurance so that in the event of a crisis a central bank would be free to lend on terms already agreed and without the necessity of a penalty rate on its loans. The penalty, or the price of the insurance, would be encapsulated by the haircuts required by the central bank on different forms of collateral. Just as motorists are compelled to take out third-party car insurance to protect other road-users, so banks should be made to take out a certain amount of liquidity insurance in normal times so that they can access central bank provision of their liquidity needs in times of crisis.

Consider a simple example of a bank with total assets and liabilities each equal to $100 million. Suppose that it has $10 million of assets in the form of reserves at the central bank, $40 million in holdings of relatively liquid securities and $50 million in the form of illiquid loans to businesses. If the central bank decided that the appropriate haircut on the liquid securities was 10 per cent and on the illiquid loans was 50 per cent, then it would be willing to lend $36 million against the former and $25 million against the latter, provided that the bank pre-positioned all its assets as available collateral. The bank's effective liquid assets would be $(10 + 36 + 25) million, a total of $71 million. It would have to finance itself with no more than $71 million of deposits and short-term debt.

Banks would be free to decide on the composition of their assets and liabilities, allowing variety and experimentation in the types of business they transacted, all subject to the constraint that alchemy in the private sector is eliminated. The PFAS adds a desirable degree of flexibility to the Chicago Plan.

It would be possible, and sensible, to implement the scheme gradually over a period of, say, ten to twenty years. The existing degree of alchemy can be calculated as the excess of effective liquid liabilities over effective liquid assets as a proportion of the total size of the balance sheet. Suppose that in the above example the bank today had liabilities of $50 million of deposits, $35 million of short-term unsecured debt (with a maturity of less than one year), $10 million of long-term debt and $5 million of equity. Its effective liquid liabilities would be $85 million, leaving a shortfall from its $71 million of effective liquid assets of $14 million and a current degree of alchemy of 14 per cent. With a twenty-year transition, the bank would be required to reduce that degree by 0.7 per cent each year so that by the end of the transition period it would completely satisfy the rule that its effective liquid assets exceeded its effective liquid liabilities, and there would be zero alchemy. During the transition it would probably be sensible to retain existing prudential regulation, and the ring-fencing restrictions imposed in recent legislation, partly to see how they worked and partly as an incentive for the financial sector to see the transition through. Because the PFAS builds on some of the extraordinary developments in central bank balance sheets, now is the ideal moment to begin reform. It may take something like twenty years to eliminate the alchemy in our system completely, but there is no reason to delay the start of that journey.

As with any reform of this kind, the scheme would apply to all financial intermediaries, banks and shadow banks, which issued unsecured debt with a maturity of less than one year above a *de minimis* proportion of the balance sheet. That is an arbitrary figure, and open to debate. A key challenge is to ensure that alchemy does not simply migrate outside the regulated sector, and end up benefiting from an implicit public subsidy.[27] No doubt there would be other practical issues to resolve, but the reason we employ high-quality public servants is to solve such problems and not allow lobbyists to use them as an excuse for resisting principled reform.

The idea of the pawnbroker for all seasons builds on both the tradition of the lender of last resort and the experience of the crisis of 2008. It has six main advantages.

First, the proposal recognises that in a real crisis the only source of liquidity is the central bank, supported by a solvent government, which can convert illiquid assets into liquid claims.

Second, the idea provides a natural transition to a state in which the alchemy of the present private sector system of money and banking is eliminated.

Third, it avoids the choice between either the status quo or the extreme radical solution of 100 per cent reserve banking with all lending financed by equity. It allows banks and other financial intermediaries to choose for themselves the structure of their balance sheet and how to relate particular types of assets to the structure of their liabilities. In so doing, it offers a way of promoting competition in the financial sector while restricting the degree of alchemy. Compared with the Chicago Plan, it lowers the cost of eliminating bank runs.

Fourth, it solves the moral hazard problem associated with the conventional lender of last resort. Banks will be required to take out insurance in the form of pre-positioned collateral with the central bank, so that, when required, liquidity can be provided quickly and cheaply on demand. There will be no need to apply a penalty rate on lending during a crisis because the disincentive to rely on the provision of central bank liquidity is provided by the haircuts on collateral. And the central bank can assess the collateral in normal times and not, as happened during the crisis, be forced to make snap judgements about collateral when the storm arrives. No doubt in normal times there will be pressure on the central bank to set haircuts to favour politically popular types of bank lending and intense lobbying by banks to lower the haircuts. But central banks are in a stronger position to resist such calls in normal times than after the crisis has hit. Moreover, a distortion of haircuts would not change the fact that with guaranteed access to central bank liquidity under PFAS, the incentive to run on a bank, or not to roll over short-term debt, would disappear. So the stigma of the use of LOLR assistance (see Chapter 5) would be much less.

Fifth, it exploits today's abnormal circumstances by incorporating two of them into a permanent feature of the PFAS. First, by creating money through quantitative easing, central banks have greatly expanded their balance sheets. The creation of this emergency money has raised the proportion of liquid assets on bank balance sheets. For example, the reserves of US banks held with the Federal Reserve rose from only 1 per cent of their total assets before the crisis to just over 20 per cent by September 2015.[28] This new higher level should be maintained, if necessary by central banks continuing to purchase government debt when existing holdings mature. Second, the infrastructure built up within central banks to assess and manage collateral during the crisis should be maintained as a permanent feature. This feature is already part of the regular operations of the Bank of England and the Reserve Bank of Australia.[29]

Sixth, regulation would be drastically simplified, comprising just two provisions: the PFAS rule that effective liquid assets must exceed effective liquid liabilities and a maximum value for the permitted leverage ratio. Most other capital and liquidity regulation could be abolished at the end of the transition. This would bring an enormous benefit in terms of simplicity and allow large amounts of extremely complex regulation to be discarded.

Each country could choose its own path to the end of alchemy, and there would be no need for international agreement on the details of banking regulation. The principle of the Basel regulations was to impose minimum standards on all countries, but the case against alchemy is a natural one, and countries should be allowed to adopt it at their own rate. The ability of a central bank to operate as either a LOLR or PFAS depends on the solvency of the state. A government that is insolvent, or cannot print its own currency, cannot easily support a banking system in a crisis. Regulation is gravitating naturally back to nation states because the provision of liquidity insurance inevitably involves fiscal risks. That is one reason why resolving the problems of the banks in the euro area is proving so fraught in the absence of fiscal and political union. It is likely that governments will increasingly feel that to be able to regulate banking activity appropriately, they must require all banks operating within their borders to be separate subsidiaries and not branches of foreign banks regulated overseas.

The essence of a successful pawnbroker is the willingness to lend to almost anyone against extremely valuable collateral. In 2008, banks had very few 'gold watches' and plenty of broken ones, and central banks were forced to lend against inadequate collateral in order to save the system. Before the next crisis it would be sensible to make sure that the banking system has sufficient pre-positioned collateral, including central bank reserves, to be able quickly to raise the funds to meet the demands of fleeing depositors or creditors who had decided not to roll over funding. Unlike a traditional high-street pawn-broker, central banks will want to take collateral that is more difficult and time-consuming to evaluate than gold watches. The PFAS rule is a strong incentive for banks to bring collateral to the central bank before a crisis.

The biggest problem in asking the central bank to act as a PFAS is the challenge of determining appropriate haircuts. If it is difficult to calculate risk weights for bank assets, why should it be easier to calculate haircuts? The answer is that the purpose of the two calculations is very different. For one, the aim is to compute the overall risk of a portfolio of different bank assets which requires knowledge of all the possible outcomes and the correlations of returns on different assets. For the other, the more limited aim is a rough and ready calculation of the dis-count at which an asset pledged as collateral could be sold when a bank could not repay the central bank, allowing for the fact that in a crisis the central bank would hold the collateral until more normal times had returned to financial markets. Once set, haircuts should remain unchanged for, say, three years and not be altered frequently. As with any pawnbroker, the central bank should be conservative when setting haircuts and, if in doubt, err on the high side. The size of the haircuts on different types of collateral are the equivalent of an insurance premium that banks are required to pay for access to liquidity on demand so that they are not exposed to runs and can cope with wholly unexpected shocks. They are the tax on alchemy. The size of that tax should reflect the cost to taxpayers of providing the implicit insurance in giving banks a call on liquidity on demand in return for pre-positioning collateral.

In a world of radical uncertainty there is no mathematical way of pricing such insurance. On most bank assets, other than reserves with the central bank, haircuts should be large. Under the Chicago Plan – a limiting case – they would be 100 per cent. With a PFAS, haircuts reflect the ability of the central bank to hold collateral while a crisis persists and dispose of it in more normal times. They will reflect the volatility and illiquidity of the assets, and once set, they cannot be altered during a crisis or they would not be a committed source of liquidity. So when setting haircuts on different assets, central banks need to be sure that they can absorb potential losses on collateral – although they would not need to liquidate quickly their holdings of assets brought to them in a general panic. Unlike the financial institutions requiring liquidity, a central bank could afford to wait until conditions returned to something closer to normal.

But that might still involve permanent changes in the relative prices of different assets, and haircuts need to take that risk into account. They are, therefore, likely to be much higher than in the normal commercial provision of short-term lending. And on some assets they may well be 100 per cent. In recent years, central banks have lent at haircuts ranging from only a few per cent to 60 per cent or more, depending on the type of asset in question. Setting large haircuts in normal times is the PFAS equivalent of taking the punchbowl away as the party is getting going. And it is important that central banks do not see their role as underpinning liquid markets in particular assets. It is not the role of central banks to subsidise the existence of markets that would not otherwise exist. For assets that are complex or obscure, a useful heuristic for setting haircuts would be to learn from Dennis Weatherstone of J.P. Morgan (see Chapter 4). If the central bank executive responsible for the management of collateral could not understand the nature of the asset in three fifteen-minute meetings, then the haircut would be 100 per cent.

From time to time banks will fail – indeed failure is part and parcel of a prosperous market economy. With a PFAS, banks at risk of failure would have a year in which to be reorganised. There would be no panic rescues over a weekend, no dramatic tales to retell in subsequent memoirs. Bank resolution – a special bankruptcy regime for banks – would be simpler than it is today because deposits (liabilities) and the collateral lodged with the central bank (assets) could be lifted out of the failed bank, and the deposits transferred to another bank together with the liquid reserves for which the collateral was pledged. That would enable the resolution authority to sort out the rest of the bank without serious disruption to its depositors.

In essence, when a bank fails it needs to be separated into its 'narrow' and 'wide' components. Sorting out the bankruptcy of a large, complex bank is a costly and messy business, as the failure of Lehman Brothers in 2008 showed only too clearly. People made careers out of overseeing the process, and it is still going on. It is important that regulators make banks recognise the true state of their balance sheet sooner rather than later. One lesson from the Finnish and Swedish banking crises of the early 1990s, and also from the decade-long problems in the Japanese banking system, is the importance of recognising losses early and promoting transparency about the true state of the balance sheet. A lack of transparency means that banks have the ability to drag their feet in recognising losses. That means that loans are tied up in businesses with few profitable investment opportunities, thus denying financing to companies with the ability to expand. It is a recipe for stagnation.

The debate about whether banks are 'too important to fail' boils down to a simple question. Are banks an extension of the state, as they are in centrally planned economies, or are they part of a market economy? If the latter, then to correct for the social costs they impose on society in a crisis, banks should be made to take out compulsory insurance through the PFAS and have sufficient 'loss-absorbing capacity', on the liability side of their balance sheets, to reduce the implicit taxpayer guarantee to bank creditors. Only equity finance guarantees that capacity.[30] The introduction of a PFAS would aid the gradual evolution of expectations towards the view that banks will not be bailed out. It is a question of creating a banking and financial system in which governments feel little incentive to step in and bail out failing firms.

Before the crisis, banks used too little equity and owned too few liquid assets. The right response is to require banks to use more equity finance and meet the PFAS rule. A minimum ratio of equity to total assets of 10 per cent would be a good start, compared with the 3–5 per cent common today. A century ago the ratio for many banks was 25 per cent![31] If the amount of equity finance is low, then any item of adverse news makes it more likely that short-term creditors will desert the bank, and shareholders have an incentive to take risks in order to 'gamble for resurrection', because large losses will fall on creditors or taxpayers.

The PFAS rule is not a pipe dream. Some central banks have already moved in that direction. For example, the Bank of England has for some while encouraged banks to pre-position collateral as way of obtaining liquidity insurance. In the spring of 2015, the value of collateral pre-positioned with the Bank was £469 billion and the average haircut was 33 per cent. Together with reserves at the Bank of £317 billion, the effective liquid assets of the banking system were £632 billion, compared with £1820 billion of total deposits.[32] There was still a substantial degree of alchemy, but around one-third of deposits were backed by 'effective' liquid assets and the idea of gradually eliminating alchemy through a PFAS is realistic. Alchemy can be squeezed out of the system by pressing from the two ends – by raising the required amount of equity and keeping central bank balance sheets, and hence bank reserves, at broadly their present level. That would allow the PFAS rule to complete the job. Far from being a radical and unrealistic objective, the elimination of alchemy could be achieved by building on actions that were taken during the crisis and the adoption of the PFAS rule. The idea is new; the means of implementation isn't. There is a natural path from today's 'extraordinary' measures to a permanent solution to alchemy.

The future of money

In a world of radical uncertainty, the demand for liquidity can change in an unpredictable and unexpected manner. Of the three roles for money described in Chapter 2, that of supplying liquidity is satisfied by the pawnbroker for all seasons. But do we really need money for the two other roles – to enable us to buy 'stuff' and to ensure a stable unit of account, or measuring rod, to value production? Could innovations in information technology make money redundant in respect of those two roles?

We no longer need cash to buy 'stuff' and even the use of cheques to make payments has been rapidly declining. We use electronic transfers instead. So should we stop issuing paper money? There would be some advantages. A large proportion of banknotes, especially those of large denominations, are used for illegal transactions, both to evade tax and for other criminal activities. In the United States, over $4000 in notes and coin circulate for every man, woman and child.[33] In Japan, the figure is almost double that. More than 75 per cent of those holdings are in the form of notes of the largest denomination, the $100 bill and the ¥10,000 note.

There is clearly a strong demand for anonymity when making payments. Much of that has been eroded in respect of electronic payments with counter-terrorism surveillance and the introduction of regulation to prevent money laundering that requires the disclosure of large amounts of information to governments. So the demand for paper money is unlikely to disappear quickly, and anonymity for illegal transactions is the opposite side of the coin of individual privacy.

Nevertheless, electronic payments are the way of the future. Even old-fashioned bank robberies are diminishing – they almost halved in the US between 2004 and 2014 – to be replaced by an explosion of cybercrime.[34] At present, electronic transfers simply move money from one bank account to another – convenient but not revolutionary – and banks then clear payments with each other through their own accounts at the central bank. In principle, two parties engaged in a transaction could instead settle directly by a transfer of money from one electronic account to another in 'real time'.

A step in that direction was the creation of bitcoin – a 'virtual' currency launched in 2009, allegedly by one or more individuals under the pseudonym of Satoshi Nakamoto. Ownership of bitcoins is transferred through bilateral transactions without the need for verification by a third party (necessary in all other current electronic payment systems). Transactions are verified by the use of a software accounting system accessible to all users.[35] The supply of bitcoins is governed by an algorithm embodied in the software that runs the system (with a maximum number of twenty-one million). If you can persuade someone to accept payment in bitcoins, then you can use them to buy 'stuff'. The price of bitcoins in terms of goods and services, or currencies such as the dollar, is determined in the market. Without any public body setting the standard for bitcoins as a unit of account, their price is highly volatile – less than $1 when launched, a peak of over $1100 in December 2013, and back to below $400 in late 2015.[36] With no one standing ready to redeem them in terms of any other commodity or currency, bitcoins are a highly speculative investment. They have no fundamental value: their price simply reflects the value that bitcoins are expected to have in the future.

The integrity of the algorithm determining the supply of bitcoins is vital. An indication of what can go wrong when confidence in that process is lost is the fate of a related venture, the auroracoin, a digital currency in Iceland. As an alternative to government-issued paper money, auroracoins were circulated in Iceland by a private entrepreneur in March 2014 through a 'helicopter' drop to every citizen listed on the national ID register. Within a few months they had lost over 96 per cent of their launch value.[37] Moreover, as described in Chapter 2, with any private fiat money new entry can undermine the value of existing currencies. What is to stop some new group of programmers from launching a digital currency under the name 'digidollars'? The aggregate supply of digital currency cannot be controlled by any one issuer, which is why governments have nationalised the production of paper currencies.

Digital currencies attract those who would like to make payments anonymously.[38] As an innovation in payments systems, and hence as a means of payment, bitcoins have generated genuine interest. But as money, they are more akin to a form of digital gold – appealing to those who distrust governments to control the supply of money but highly volatile in value.[39]

But why use money to make transactions when computers offer the possibility to exchange goods and services for wealth? With high-speed electronic transfers it is becoming feasible to transfer stocks and shares and other forms of marketable wealth from the buyer to the seller instead of money, so enabling buyers and sellers to avoid holding some of their wealth in a form that earns little or no interest. Pre-agreed instructions embedded in computer algorithms would determine the sequence in which financial assets belonging to the purchaser were sold and used to augment the financial assets of the vendor, also in a pre-agreed sequence. Assets used in this way could be any for which there were market-clearing prices in 'real time'. Someone buying a meal in a restaurant might use a card, as now, but the result would not be a transfer from their bank account to that of the restaurant; instead there would be a sale of shares from the diner's portfolio and the acquisition of different shares, or other assets, to the same value by the restaurant. The key to any such development is the ability of computers to communicate in 'real time' to permit instantaneous verification of the creditworthiness of the buyer and the seller, thereby enabling private sector settlement to occur with finality. There would be no unique role for something called money in order to buy 'stuff'.

Electronic transfers of wealth in 'real time' sound attractive because they economise on the use of money. But electronic messages that carry the instructions to make payments travel not instantaneously but at a rate bounded by the upper limit of the speed of light. Admittedly this is fast – around 186,000 miles (300,000 kilometres) a second – but not fast enough to avoid problems. Some professionals in financial markets, such as high-frequency traders, have invested heavily in microwave technology that is even faster than fibre-optic transmission to enable them to deploy the tactic known as front-running (see Chapter 4). Regulators are already concerned about this type of behaviour; imagine how much more serious front-running would be if all payments were made by selling and buying financial assets. Since transactions can never be literally instantaneous, I think it unlikely that we will move in the foreseeable future to a system of making payments that is entirely divorced from some form of money. Bank accounts, either to make anticipated payments or to hold a liquid reserve of generalised purchasing power, will be with us indefinitely, and so therefore will be the need for a pawnbroker for all seasons.

One way to reduce the demand for deposits, and to mitigate

the scale of operations of the pawnbroker for all seasons, would be for central banks to allow anyone at all to open an account with them for purposes of making payments to others and to hold liquidity. At present, central banks could not cope with a large influx of customers, although new technology would make the task of handling so many accounts easier to imagine. It is fair to say that anonymity would be unlikely to be a characteristic of such a system. Such a development would simplify and reduce risks in the system of money transmission. International transfers could then be cleared through central banks. But it is unclear why, when we can use the pawnbroker for all seasons to provide liquidity to a competitive banking system, such a benefit would outweigh the costs of foregoing the advantages of competition in the provision of customer services. Whatever arrangements come to dominate how we make and receive payments in future, it is already clear that it will be necessary to guard the computer systems used for settlement purposes as carefully as the gold at Fort Knox is guarded today.

If we ever moved to a world in which we bought and sold 'stuff' by transfers of wealth, then neither money nor central banks, in their present form, would be needed.[40] The need to control the supply of money would be replaced by a concern to ensure the integrity of the computer systems used for settlement purposes. Radical uncertainty means, however, that there will always be a demand for liquidity as a reserve of future purchasing power, and the ultimate source of liquidity is the central bank. Moreover, there is one additional role for a public body that it makes sense to give to the central bank – the regulation of the unit of account. Even if money disappears as a means of payment, we will always need a stable unit of account to price goods and services.[41]

There is an enormous advantage in all of us agreeing to use the same unit of account determined centrally rather than allowing a profusion of different monies. We rely on weights and measures inspectors to ensure that retailers who use yards (or metres) and pounds (or kilograms) as the units of length and weight define them in exactly the same way. It would be a great inconvenience if what was meant by a 'yard' was different in New York than in San Francisco or London. We can just about cope with the translation from yards to metres and from Fahrenheit to Celsius, but think how difficult it would be to order goods from different parts of the world if each locality had its own definition of the unit of length or weight. Converging on a common unit has enormous value, in the same way that a telephone is useful only if others can use the same network (if, in the jargon of economists, there are 'network externalities'). It is striking that Article 1, section 8 of the United States Constitution conflated the standards for physical weights and measures with regulation of the currency: 'The Congress shall have power ... To coin money, regulate the value thereof ... and fix the standard of weights and measures.' As George Washington said in the very first annual presidential message to Congress, 'Uniformity in the currency, weights, and measures of the United States is an object of great importance.' And as declared in Magna Carta eight hundred years ago, 'There shall be but one Measure throughout the Realm.'[42]

It may be that we could allow anyone to issue their own money, as advocated by the economist and Nobel Laureate Friedrich Hayek, trusting in competition to ensure that we would all decide to use the money of the 'best' issuer (the supplier most trusted not to abuse their ability to print money).[43] But competitive monies have arisen rarely, and usually only in situations where government money is either absent (as, for example, in the use of cigarettes as currency in prisoner-of-war camps) or badly managed (as in periods of hyperinflation). Despite the abolition of foreign exchange controls, competition among national currencies has not reduced the dominance, within each economy, of a single public currency. There are exceptions, but they are few and far between. The abandonment of their own currency by Panama and Ecuador, and their adoption of the dollar (see Chapter 7), is one example. In Germany, *Notgeld* (see Chapter 5) was an example of a thousand flowers blooming – but they faded when a viable national currency was re-established. Network externalities make it difficult for competing currencies to emerge.[44]

A single unit of account requires collective decisions as to the definition and management of that unit. Unlike measures of length and weight, where a physical definition is determined and monitored by inspectors of weights and measures, the value of money requires a degree of discretionary management to avoid the costs of excessive volatility in output and employment. It is pre-eminently a task for a central bank given a mandate to meet an inflation target over the long term, as explored in Chapter 5.

Whatever happens to money as a way of buying 'stuff', it will always have a future as the only true form of liquidity. There will always be a demand for the liabilities of the central bank and for a stable unit of account. And so central banks will retain their ability to set interest rates and the size of their balance sheet. It may be tempting to imagine that technological innovation will mean that the successors to Bill Gates (the founder of Microsoft) and Steve Jobs (the founder of Apple), although not issuing their own currencies but instead providing a way of exchanging stocks and shares for goods and services, will put the successors to Ben Bernanke and Janet Yellen out of business. But the management of our system of money and banking requires collective decisions.

I hope that by now the reader will have been persuaded that only a fundamental rethink of how we, as a society, organise our system of money and banking will prevent a repetition of the crisis that we experienced in 2008 and from which previous generations suffered in earlier episodes. A major failing before 2007 was that the monetary policy framework designed to deal with good times and the lender of last resort framework for bad times were not properly integrated. In the crisis, massive support was extended not to save the banks but in order to save the economy from the banks. The role of pawnbroker for all seasons demands a great deal of central banks but, as with monetary policy, they would be exercising discretion within a clear framework designed to cope with radical uncertainty.

Before the crisis, hubris – arrogance that inflicts suffering on the innocent – ran riot, and changed the culture in financial services to one of taking advantage of the opportunity to manage other people's money rather than acting as a steward on behalf of clients.[45] But 'the true steward never forgets that he is a steward only, acting for a principal'.[46] The maxim 'my word is my bond', which underpinned the traditions of the City of London for many years, means little if those words are incomprehensible. The sale of complex financial products by people who only half understand the risks involved to those who understand even less is not an attractive advertisement for the financial services industry. What kind of person takes pride in parting a fool from his money?

I have explained the principles on which a successful reform of the system should rest. It is a programme that will take many years, if not decades. There is time to put in place such a programme to protect future generations. But the reform of money and banking will not be easy. Most existing financial institutions, and the political interests they support, will resist strongly. At the end of 2014, Paul Volcker criticised the 'eternal lobbying' of Wall Street.[47] As Radical found when he left the City of Plunder in his quest for the City of Reform:

the party who had long enjoyed the privilege of putting their hands into their neighbour's pockets, were composed of two sects, one called the 'outs' and the other the 'ins'– the 'outs' maintained that there was no such city as that of 'Reform'; while the 'ins' thought there might be such a city as 'Reform', but it was at such a long distance, and the road was so intricate and beset with brambles and thorns, that it was dangerous for anyone to set out on such a journey just at *this peculiar time*.[48]

Keynes's optimism that 'the ideas of economists and political philosophers, both when they are right and when they are wrong, are more powerful than is commonly understood' has flattered academic scribblers ever since.[49] It might be more accurate to reverse Keynes's famous dictum about the influence held by economists over practical men to 'economists, who believe themselves to be quite exempt from any practical influences, are usually the slaves of some defunct banker'.[50] But there is nothing special about finance that requires us to abandon rational argument and leave our future in the hands of the gods of finance.

❧ ❧

8

HEALING AND HUBRIS:
THE WORLD ECONOMY TODAY

'Time present and time past
Are both perhaps present in time future
And time future contained in time past.'

T.S. Eliot, *Four Quartets*, 1935

'How is it possible to expect that Mankind will take
advice, when they will not so much as take warning?'

Jonathan Swift, 'Thoughts on Various Subjects', 1703

There is more to life than finance, and more to finance than the events of 2008. The world economy today seems incapable of restoring the prosperity we took for granted before the crisis. Many of the problems that seem to overwhelm us – poverty, rising inequality, crumbling infrastructure, ethnic tensions within and between countries – would all be eased by rates of growth that before the crisis seemed quite normal. But economic growth has fallen back across the developed world. Some blame this on a slowing of innovation and productivity as the information revolution proves less transformative than earlier technological revolutions. I see the issue differently – the struggle to revive the world economy is the result of the disequilibrium that led to the crisis itself.

As we saw in Chapter 1, both Britain and the United States have 'lost' around 15 per cent of national income relative to the pre-crisis growth path. Using actual growth rates between 2008 and 2014, along with IMF projections for the following three years, advanced economies more generally will, over the decade that started with the financial crisis, also have lost significant proportions of income and output. For the G7 economies as a whole the proportion of GDP 'lost' is also of the order of 15 per cent.[1] The lost decade is already upon us. Growth seems to depend upon continually falling interest rates. There is little sign that the lost output is being made up.

Not that this dismal performance has been achieved for want of trying by governments and central banks. Since 2008 we have seen the biggest monetary policy stimulus in the history of the world. Official interest rates across the industrialised world were cut to their lowest rates ever – first to zero and then in 2015 to negative levels in many European countries – and programmes of asset purchases by central banks expanded the monetary base several fold, an extraordinary and unprecedented increase.

Despite that massive policy stimulus to aggregate demand, economies have been limping along. Recoveries following financial crises have historically tended to be slower than downturns unaccompanied by such crises.[2] But there is no unique pattern across different episodes. Diagnoses using expressions such as 'balance sheet recession', 'headwinds' and 'secular stagnation', which have all entered the currency of popular debate, are descriptions of symptoms, not causes.[3] What are the underlying drivers of a prolonged period of low demand and weak growth? Why do 'crises' lead to a long period of stagnation? To answer those questions requires us to look more deeply into macroeconomics – the study of how the economy operates as a whole.

Keynesian and neoclassical macroeconomics

I applied to university in 1965. That was only twenty years after the end of the Second World War, but it felt a world apart. The harsh capitalist system of the inter-war period, with its depression, mass unemployment and poverty, had been banished. The secret was the intellectual revolution engineered by John Maynard Keynes in his magnum opus *The General Theory of Employment, Interest and Money*, published in 1936. We all felt that he had produced the answer to unemployment. Government intervention, through fiscal policy, could stabilise the economy at full employment. Keynesian economics formed a sharp intellectual dividing line between the pre-war capitalist economies and the new post-war confidence in state-led economic policy. We had avoided another Great Depression because of government intervention. So I decided to apply to study at King's College, Cambridge, where Keynes spent most of his life.

No sooner had I arrived at Cambridge than Keynesian economics started to become unfashionable. Government spending was leading to overheating of the economy and rising inflation. The major policy question was how to reduce inflation, not how to boost employment. Stabilising the economy was proving harder in practice than in theory. There were fierce intellectual battles. The disciples of Keynes, including some of his friends and colleagues, such as Richard Kahn and Joan

Robinson, tried to keep the faith and taught us the gospel. Others wanted the subject to develop, and, in particular, to exploit developments in mathematics and statistics that were in vogue in the United States. Their motivation was understandable. *The General Theory*, although it contains some beautiful and compelling prose, includes many arguments that are obscure and difficult, even at times almost incomprehensible.

Macroeconomics in this era became divided into two schools of thought: Keynesian and neoclassical.[4] The former focused on the role of the state in returning an economy from depression to full employment. The latter studied the conditions in which a market economy returns to full employment under its own steam after a temporary deviation from its normal equilibrium. Neoclassical economists often argue that the Keynesian analysis presents a special case in which employment is temporarily below its attainable level, often as a result of misguided government policies. But Keynes did not choose his title carelessly – he meant the book to refer to a general theory of how capitalist economies could run indefinitely at levels of demand and output well below potential. And these same arguments came back into focus when the downturn of 2008–9 turned into a prolonged period of weak growth, or even stagnation, with output in most advanced economies running well below its previous trend path.

The ferocity of the intellectual battle, one of not only ideas but personalities, obscured an important point that the Keynesian disciples made but were unable to translate into the language of modern economics. Expectations of what the future holds are central to the determination of current spending. Keynes attached a great deal of weight to the role of sentiment and expectations in determining investment spending, and hence the speed at which an economy would come out of recession:

a large proportion of our positive activities depend on spontaneous optimism rather than on a mathematical expectation,
whether moral or hedonistic or economic. Most, probably, of
our decisions to do something positive, the full consequences
of which will be drawn out over many days to come, can
only be taken as the result of animal spirits – a spontaneous
urge to action rather than inaction, and not as the outcome
of a weighted average of quantitative benefits multiplied by
quantitative probabilities.[5]

Keynes evidently believed in radical uncertainty. Booms
and slumps would come and go as animal spirits, inherently
volatile, rose and fell. But without any explanation of why and
when animal spirits would rise and fall, this did not amount to
a coherent theory of booms and depressions. As a consequence,
the Keynesian disciples were easily dismissed as backward-
looking intellectual renegades, guardians of a flame that had
already been extinguished, out of touch with the way the subject was developing. Neoclassical economists wanted to build
the foundations of economics on rational 'optimising' behaviour. By ignoring radical uncertainty, however, they failed to
capture the important insights of *The General Theory*.

Keynes's basic argument was that capitalism might fail to
deliver full employment because it could not coordinate the
spending plans of all the different participants in the economy.
This idea was contrary to the apparently common-sense view
that if every market equates supply and demand for its product,
then adding up across all markets means that aggregate demand
equals aggregate supply in the economy as a whole. How could
one explain this apparent paradox? Keynes was less than clear
on this point, and it was his misfortune to write *The General
Theory* some twenty years before economic theorists provided a
rigorous framework within which it was possible to understand

his intuition. As explained in Chapter 2, Kenneth Arrow and Gerard Debreu described how a grand auction could indeed equate supply and demand overall if, and only if, all of the markets for future goods and services were incorporated into the auction process. Self-evidently, that world is fictional – radical uncertainty means that many of the markets for future goods and services are simply missing. The concept of the grand auction is of value, however, precisely because it shows why Keynes's intuition was correct. In the absence of markets for many of the goods and services that businesses are planning to produce and consumers to purchase in the future, there is no mechanism to guarantee that spending plans for the future will be coordinated among all economic agents.

The oil market provides a good example. World oil production is around 90 million barrels a day.[6] At a price of $50 a barrel, annual turnover is over $1.6 trillion – a lot of money. Higher oil prices should in theory stimulate more investment in production and extraction of oil. But the supply response to higher oil prices is dampened because potential producers cannot be confident of the prices they will receive in future. With long time lags between investment and subsequent production, only the signals from prices set in oil futures markets can provide adequate incentives to encourage exploration and development. Although there is some trading in oil futures in London and New York, contracts are for delivery on dates no more than five or six years ahead, whereas an oilfield might take thirty years or more to develop and exploit.[7] There is one very good economic reason why a liquid futures market for oil to be delivered at dates many years into the future has not developed. It would be attractive to many potential oil producers, such as those developing the Canadian tar sands, to be able to sell oil today for delivery in the future. That would remove the uncertainty about price and make the investment decision a matter of mere calculation rather than entrepreneurial judgement. Equally, those considering investing in alternative sources of energy would have more confidence about the future because they would know the price they would have to match.

But a futures market cannot develop unless there is demand as well as supply. At first sight, it might seem that heavy users of oil, such as airlines, would wish to buy in a futures market. That would reduce the uncertainty surrounding their future fuel costs. But the problem for any airline contemplating doing this is that they cannot sell forward their own outputs, namely airline tickets. So by buying oil forward at the price in today's market, they would be leaving themselves open to competitors who could enter the market if the future price of oil turned out to be well below today's future price. Only by selling forward both their inputs and outputs would airlines and other energy users find it attractive to use a futures market. And the reason there is no futures market in airline tickets is because travellers do not know today where they will want to fly in the distant future, and how much they are willing to pay for the trip. The crucial factor determining the demand for new planes will be the expectations of airline companies about the demand for flights over a particular horizon in the future. Despite the best efforts of airline analysts, those expectations will inevitably be subjective. If they could today sell tickets for the relevant future dates then the market would coordinate supply and demand for flights, and in turn for oil. But in the absence of those futures markets, such coordination is impossible.

The coordination problem is replicated right across the economy. So if families and businesses for some reason become cautious today, and reduce their spending, there are no market signals to tell producers whether this reduction corresponds to a plan to increase spending in the future and, if so, on what goods and services. The inability of households and businesses to coordinate their future spending plans through markets means that aggregate demand may fall below its full-employment potential. If confidence falls, people are likely to spend more only if they are confident that others will do likewise.[8] A failure to coordinate may also generate excess demand if people are too optimistic about future spending, leading to unnecessary investment and an unsustainable boom. The existence of coordination problems tells us little about whether we should expect a boom or a depression, and under what conditions one might lead to the other. In the circumstances of the 1930s, that did not seem important – mass unemployment was evident for all to see – but as a theory it left a gap.

An implication of the Keynesian argument is that it is misleading to think of the economy as a whole as if it were simply a single household. If one household saves more today with a view to spending more tomorrow, its income is unaffected. But if many households try to save more today, total spending falls and so do total incomes and actual saving – the so-called 'paradox of thrift'. Only if households' intention to save today and spend tomorrow can be communicated to producers might investment rise to offset the fall in consumption. But in the absence of a complete set of markets, no producer will receive a signal that the demand for her production in the future has increased. The coordination problem is an instance of the prisoner's dilemma. Collective action is needed to stabilise the economy – for example, by expanding government spending in a downturn or reining in private spending in a boom.

The challenge to Keynes came in the form of two questions. First, why could unemployment not be cured by cutting wages in order to stimulate the demand for labour? Keynes was vehement that – contrary to the beliefs of most of his predecessors and contemporaries – a cut in wages was not the answer to a slump in demand. It took the rigour of the auction model to show why his intuition was correct. In the grand auction, a cut in the price of a good for which supply exceeds demand can restore balance between the two because that price cut takes place only in the context of a complete resetting of all prices to ensure balance between demand and supply in each and every market. In the world, Keynes argued, a cut in wages might, as incomes fell, lead to a fall in consumer spending, which in turn would change the expectations of businesses and households about future demand. That could lead to a self-reinforcing fall in overall spending – a 'multiplier' effect. Wage and price flexibility does help to coordinate plans when all the markets relevant to future spending decisions exist. But in practice they do not, and in those circumstances cuts in wages and prices may lower incomes without stimulating current demand.

The second, and related, question was why would an increase in money supply not stimulate spending, returning the economy to full employment? Keynes's reply was that in a slump the demand for liquidity – emergency money – was so high that further injections of money would simply be absorbed in idle cash balances as a claim on generalised future purchasing power without any impact on current spending. The economy would be stuck in a 'liquidity trap'. The argument was set out in Chapters 13 and 14 of *The General Theory*. They are among the more difficult and obscure parts of the book. It was left to Britain's first Nobel Laureate in Economic Science, Sir John Hicks, to explain them in a famous article published in 1937 entitled 'Mr Keynes and the Classics'. Even almost eighty years on, the article remains a tour de force and a brilliant exposition of the Keynesian framework translated into more modern language. It homed in on the fact that interest rates cannot fall below a certain level (the 'lower bound'), and so monetary policy might be unable to reduce interest rates to the level necessary to stimulate demand and attain full employment.

The lower bound on short-term interest rates was thought to be zero – attempts to impose negative interest rates would lead households and financial institutions to switch from deposits or Treasury bills offering a negative rate to cash offering a zero rate. But by 2015 several central banks had actually instituted negative interest rates on accounts held with them by commercial banks. It remains to be seen for how long it will be possible to maintain such low levels, and whether, as seems unlikely, they will result in negative interest rates on deposits held by ordinary depositors. So the lower bound on short-term interest rates is somewhat below zero but not much below.

The lower bound on long-term interest rates arose from a somewhat different reason. Government bonds pay their holders a regular fixed sum, the coupon payment, the equivalent of the dividend on a stock. But unlike dividends, coupons are fixed in money terms when the bond is first issued. When the long-term interest rate (the rate at which future coupons are discounted back to the present) moves up and down, the price of government bonds moves in the opposite direction. So when long-term rates are close to zero, bond prices are not likely to rise much further but could easily fall sharply. Investment in bonds is almost a one-way bet, with all the risk on the downside. Since most investors have some aversion to risk, there is a ceiling on the price of bonds, which translates into a lower bound to long-term rates. Precisely where above zero that bound is located depends on the risk aversion of investors.

Keynes argued that when short-term and long-term interest rates had reached their respective lower bounds, further increases in the money supply would just be absorbed by the hoarding of money and would not lead to lower interest rates and higher spending. Once caught in this liquidity trap, the economy could persist in a depressed state indefinitely. Since economies were likely to find themselves in such conditions only infrequently, Hicks described Keynes's theory as special rather than general, and relevant only to depression conditions. And this has remained the textbook interpretation of Keynes ever since. Its main implication is that in a liquidity trap monetary policy is impotent, whereas fiscal policy is powerful because additional government expenditure is quickly translated into higher output.

This 'modern' view of Keynes does not, however, do full justice to the fundamental nature of the coordination problems in a capitalist economy. Even when the economy is not in a liquidity trap, the inability to coordinate spending plans may inhibit the response of total demand to monetary and fiscal stimulus. It all depends on expectations. And they will reflect the particular historical circumstances in which the stimulus is applied.

It is, I think, surprising that the Keynesian argument that a cut in wages might not reduce unemployment has not been extended to the corresponding proposition for interest rates. In the past few years it has been taken for granted by economists that if only real interest rates were sufficiently negative then investment and consumption spending would be stimulated, with output returning to its normal level. The zero lower bound on official interest rates is to blame, it is argued, for the inability of central banks to stimulate the economy. But in a world where many key markets are simply missing, coordination problems make this far from obvious.

If wage cuts don't restore employment, then why should interest rate cuts restore spending? Other things being equal, a fall in real interest rates would be expected to stimulate both consumption and investment spending. But other things are not equal. For example, the imposition of a negative real interest rate – effectively a wealth tax – on all forms of financial wealth expropriates the incomes of savers and might alter expectations of future effective rates of wealth taxes. If you are told, for example, that all your assets held in accounts fixed in money terms will be subject to a 5-percentage-point wealth tax, you might, it is true, decide to spend today, but you might well, fearful of what the government could do next year, batten down the hatches and cut spending. Households and businesses might simply conserve their resources to cope with an unpredictable and unknowable future. The outcome will depend on expectations.

The analysis of the 'liquidity trap' that has underpinned much recent analysis of the reason for slow growth is based on the model of the economics of 'stuff' rather than the economics of 'stuff happens'. The common failing of Keynesian and neoclassical models of fluctuations in the economy as a whole is that they are concerned with the economics of 'stuff'. By this I mean that they focus on total spending – aggregate demand – rather than take seriously the fact that it is the very multiplicity of things which households could buy that creates problems in coordinating spending plans in the economy. If the only choice for households and businesses was to buy 'stuff', then it would be easier to coordinate plans because only one price – the real interest rate (the price of 'stuff' today in terms of 'stuff' tomorrow) – would need to move to coordinate total desired saving with desired investment. But the purpose of a market economy is to provide households and businesses with opportunities to spend their money on a wide variety of goods and services, as well as holding some back for unimaginable events or opportunities. Radical uncertainty ('stuff happens') means that many of the markets in which prices might move to produce an equilibrium simply cannot and do not exist. The market economy cannot, therefore, coordinate spending plans. There are too many missing markets. As a result, a market economy is not self-stabilising, leading to occasional sharp ups and downs in total spending. Traditional macroeconomics is the economics of 'stuff'. We need instead the economics of 'stuff happens'.

Even if monetary policy could lower the real interest rate into negative territory, there is no guarantee that demand would pick up. In the world of the economics of 'stuff' it might work by bringing spending forward. But in a world where 'stuff happens', the missing markets for future goods and services provide no price signals to encourage investment to meet future demand. Indeed, digging a hole in expected future demand may actually cause investment to fall. There is a good case to be made for saying that the importance of the zero lower bound on interest rates has been overstated as the source of our macro-economic problems.

In his otherwise first-rate exposition of the Keynesian model, Paul Krugman (another Nobel Laureate) divides the admirers of Keynes into two types: those who think his most important message is the importance of uncertainty, and those who believe it is the possibility of a general shortfall in aggregate demand.[9] Krugman places himself in the latter camp. But the division is a false one, because the two issues are inextricably linked – the consequence of radical uncertainty is the coordination problem that creates the possibility of boom and slump. Unfortunately, the failure to understand this led to a growing divergence between Keynesian and neoclassical theories. The Keynesian disciples in Cambridge rejected Hicks's formalisation of the master's ideas because the dry though elegant diagrams had sucked the essence of the coordination problems from the analysis. Keynes's key insight was that radical uncertainty means that a capitalist economy needs money and credit and as a result is a different creature from the general equilibrium of the auction economy. The prisoner's dilemma of coordinating individual spending plans and maintaining full employment is ever present. Neoclassical economists thought the Keynesian story lacked a rigorous basis, and they proceeded to develop theories on the assumption that uncertainty about the future could be represented as a known probability distribution defined over an exhaustive list of future outcomes. In other words, radical uncertainty was ruled out.

To be sure, many important aspects of economic behaviour can be understood within a framework of probability. In particular, the role of expectations turned out to be highly significant in trying to understand why rising inflation coincided with high unemployment during the 1970s. Central to the resolution of this puzzle was the idea of 'rational' expectations, that is, expectations consistent with the underlying reality, an idea originated by John Muth at Carnegie Mellon and developed by the Nobel Laureate and Chicago economist, Robert Lucas.[10] Rational expectations are an economist's version of 'you can fool all the people some of the time, and some of the people all the time, but you cannot fool all the people all the time'. And the idea helped to explain why allowing inflation to rise did not lead to a permanently lower unemployment rate. Imagine an economy where unemployment is at its 'natural' rate, with the labour market in balance, and inflation is constant. If the government boosts spending to bring unemployment below its natural rate, then the increased demand for labour will push wages up. But to restore firms' profits, prices will also rise, and real wages will fall back to their original level. If people expect that the government will keep trying to push unemployment down, then wages and prices will chase each other up in an escalating spiral. In the end, unemployment will return to its natural rate, and accelerating inflation will have achieved nothing by way of a permanent reduction in unemployment. That was the fate of the British government which, after the experience of rising inflation and unemployment in the 1960s and 1970s, eventually came to understand that there was no permanent trade-off between the two.

The important idea here was that private-sector expectations reflect systematic patterns of behaviour by governments and central banks as people learn about how the authorities behave. It was central to the development of monetary policy and the case for independent central banks. The impact of changes in interest rates depends upon whether they are unexpected or the predictable result of a systematic 'policy rule'. As we saw in Chapter 5, this way of thinking had a major influence on the way central banks conducted monetary policy. Rational expectations, therefore, became central to modern macroeconomics.

Despite its importance in analysing policy interventions, the concept of rational expectations does not have universal validity. In a world of radical uncertainty there is no way of identifying the probabilities of future events and no set of equations that describes people's attempt to cope with, rather than optimise against, that uncertainty. A common saying among economists is that 'it takes a model to beat a model'. But this overlooks the fact that whereas a world of risk can be described by equations representing optimising behaviour, a world of radical uncertainty cannot be so described. In the latter world, the economic relationships between money, income, saving and interest rates are unpredictable, although they are the outcome of attempts by rational people to cope with an uncertain world.[11] There is no unique 'optimising' behaviour to pin down the equations in the models used by central banks and other economists to make forecasts. It is not that either people or markets are irrational; it is just that we do not understand how rational businesses and households cope with radical uncertainty, and so we cannot predict sharp movements in the economy. As a consequence, many of the statistical estimates of economic relationships turn out to be unstable, and break down during periods of crisis.

By the time the crisis hit with full force in 2008, however, the neoclassical way of thinking had come to dominate the less rigorous Keynesian approach. Some concessions had been made to the idea that markets did not always work smoothly. So-called 'New Keynesian' models (more new than Keynesian) assumed that prices and wages, although not rigid, moved less quickly in response to news than did interest rates or other financial market prices.[12] Changes in money supply and interest rates were not, therefore, immediately reflected in prices but led to temporary changes in real interest rates. Since spending decisions are influenced by real interest rates, central banks could influence the short-term path of output by raising or lowering official interest rates. During the Great Stability such models proved useful in forecasting the relatively small fluctuations in output and inflation that characterised the period before the crisis. But during the crisis they performed poorly.

Most of the large-scale econometric models used by governments and central banks to make forecasts are based on sophisticated versions of 'New Keynesian' models.[13] They afford little role for money or banks, a property that has been a source of embarrassment, both intellectual and practical. They also have one other unfortunate feature – inflation is, in the long run, determined not by the amount of money in circulation but by the expectations of the private sector. Moreover, the inflation target is assumed to be completely and perfectly credible, meaning that people are assumed to set wages and prices in a way that leads the target to become self-fulfilling. As a result, forecasts of inflation made by central banks always tend to revert to the target in the medium term.[14] Because they assume rather than explain inflation in the long run, the models are reminiscent of the old joke about the physicist, the chemist and the economist stranded on a desert island with a single can of food. How are they to open it? The economist's answer is, 'Assume we have a can opener.'

It is not surprising, therefore, that the crisis created a serious challenge to conventional economic thinking. Many of the large shifts in macroeconomic variables, such as productivity and real wages, output and inflation, migration and population size, are determined ultimately by unobservable and unpredictable events: the political changes that led to the oil price shocks of the 1970s; the Vietnam War that led to the political decision to accept high levels of inflation in the United States and elsewhere; the political decision to go ahead with monetary union in Europe in 1999; the political reforms in China that led to its rapid growth and integration in the world economy. None of those would have found a place in the economic forecasting models used by central banks. They are 'political economy' variables. Yet these big surprises were in fact the driving force of major developments in the world economy. They represent not the random shocks of the forecasters' models but the realisation of radical uncertainty.[15] The intellectual framework of the neoclassical model, as implemented empirically in New Keynesian models, appeared the best on offer, but it was inadequate to explain the build-up of a disequilibrium that resulted in the crisis.[16]

To sum up, neither Keynesian nor neoclassical theories provide an adequate explanation of booms and depressions. After the recent crisis there was a resurgence of interest in theories that purported to explain the transition from periods of boom to periods of slump. Foremost among these was the theory of Hyman Minsky, an American economist who tried to reinterpret Keynes, that market economies inevitably exhibit financial instability.[17] Long periods of stability would, he argued, create excessive confidence in the future, leading to the underpricing of risk and overpricing of assets, a boom in spending and activity, and excessive accumulation of debt, ending in a financial crash which, because of high debt burdens, would lead to a deep recession. Inevitably, in the wake of a crisis such ideas appear common sense and highly plausible; up to a point, they are. But they suffer from two problems.

The first is that Minsky believed there would always be a boom before the bust. But in the recent crisis there was no boom beforehand – growth in the major economies in the five years leading up to the start of the crisis was close to its long-term average – although there was certainly a post-crisis bust. There was a rapid rise in asset prices, debt and leverage of the banking system, but output growth, unemployment and inflation were all rather stable. Each crisis has its own distinctive pattern. No two are the same. Their causes differ, although most are accompanied by sharp changes in levels of money and debt and entail problems in the banking sector. Sometimes a crisis is a reaction to a dramatic and wholly unexpected event, as in 1914, when the shock was the realisation of the inevitability of the First World War. Sometimes it is the consequence of the gradual build-up of an unsustainable position where one more apparently modest addition to the pile of credits and debts is the straw that breaks the camel's back, as in 2008. Other times, bad policy judgements by governments or central banks, whether about monetary and fiscal policy or decisions to interfere with well-functioning markets, can cause trouble – as happened in the 1970s, when governments in several countries resorted to direct controls of wages and prices to deal with inflation, and in the 2000s, when the US government distorted the supply of finance to the housing market.

The second problem with Minsky's theory is that it depends on the irrationality of households and businesses. Periods of stability are characterised by excessive optimism, inevitably followed by excessive pessimism. The idea that people have a psychological propensity to underestimate the probability of events that have not occurred for some time – and so under-estimate the chances of a crisis – underlies recent work on the psychology of financial crises.[18] A similar story is used in the study of the link between debt and crises by Reinhart and Rogoff, whose thesis is captured by the ironic title of their book *This Time Is Different*. The problem with such explanations is that they share the weaknesses of all behavioural economics, as discussed in Chapter 4: they add complexity in order to explain observed 'anomalies' without improving our ability to predict. It is no accident that interest in Minsky surged *after* the crisis. Exactly the same critique applies to the attempt since the crisis to incorporate features of the banking and financial system into conventional models.[19]

Rather than relying on particular instances of irrational behaviour, I believe it is more fruitful to see 'mistakes' or 'misperceptions' as the result of attempts by economic agents to behave rationally in a world of radical uncertainty. In this way, it may be possible to understand why there was a bust without a prior boom, as I discuss below. To do this we need to look more closely at how families and businesses allocate their spending between the present and the future. The Keynesian analysis of saving is simple – rather too simple. Keynes argued that 'the fundamental psychological law, upon which we are entitled to depend with great confidence both *a priori* from our knowledge of human nature and from the detailed facts of experience, is that men are disposed, as a rule and on the average, to increase their consumption as their income increases, but not by as much as the increase in their income'.[20] The proposition that this is a fundamental psychological law, as opposed to an alleged empirical observation, would have seemed faintly ridiculous had not the circumstances of the times in which Keynes wrote made the theoretical framework less important than the urgent need to deal with mass unemployment.

Keynes could fall back on his earlier quip that 'in the long run we are all dead'.[21] A brilliant debating ploy, but a good example of a witty saying that obscures the real argument. Not only is it untrue – future generations will replace those alive today and we all care to a greater or lesser extent about the welfare of our successors – but it seriously underplays the impact of expectations of the future on the present. Perhaps Keynes was in a hurry to influence economic policy; as Hicks rather unkindly wrote, 'the things against which he [Keynes] protested had usually already happened, so that it was only to a slight degree that he changed the course of events'.[22]

The neoclassical 'optimising' model does a better job of explaining saving and investment decisions. It recognises that when a household can borrow and save, the constraint on its spending is its income over its lifetime, not its current income. In other words, it faces a 'lifetime budget constraint'. Of course, some families may be unable to borrow and are constrained by their inability to access credit. But most consumption is enjoyed by households that can borrow via mortgages and save through pension schemes. For such families, spending today is at the expense of spending tomorrow. Most people do not want to experience sharp falls in their standard of living from one year to the next, so they try to smooth their consumption spending. As a result, permanent changes in a family's income lead to broadly equivalent increases in spending, whereas temporary changes have a much smaller effect on current spending. The problem with the neoclassical approach is that it assumes that the unexpected surprises confronting households take the form of a stable and known statistical distribution of temporary 'shocks'. This characterisation of uncertainty cannot explain crises, except as very exceptional events visited upon us like a biblical plague of locusts.

A different story: fuzzy budget constraints, narratives and disequilibrium

The crisis raised deep questions about the foundations of the economic models used by central banks around the world. Those models ignore radical uncertainty and assume that everyone has rational expectations. In so doing, they assume away the coordination problems that are the consequence of radical uncertainty. Yet the concept of 'rational' expectations has no clear meaning in a world of radical uncertainty. Many economists will be reluctant to abandon the assumption of rational expectations because to do so appears to undermine the subject as a science and opens the door to a line of reasoning where expectations have a life of their own – the indiscipline of behavioural economics. I am sympathetic to those concerns. Great damage was done in the past by drawing policy conclusions from economic models with arbitrary assumptions about expectations. But ideas that by their nature cannot be expressed in a formal mathematical model should not be dismissed out of hand. I do not suggest that we abandon the assumption that people try to behave in a rational manner. But as explained in Chapter 4, the question facing households and businesses is what it means to be rational in the face of radical uncertainty. I suggested that saving and investment decisions might be better understood by referring to them as the result of 'coping' than 'optimising' behaviour.

Faced with an unknowable future, businesses and households create a narrative that guides their decisions on spending and saving. That narrative is embodied in a coping strategy which generates a heuristic to help them respond to information about prices and incomes. The choices of narrative and heuristic do not constitute a general theory of behaviour – they are highly specific to particular historical circumstances.

Central to the choice of a coping strategy is the impact of radical uncertainty on lifetime budget constraints. Ask anyone what they think their lifetime income will be, and the answer will reveal that it is shrouded in uncertainty. Older readers might like to cast their mind back to when they were starting work. How much of what has happened to you since was imaginable, and would you have been able to form then a good estimate of your subsequent lifetime income? No one can honestly be clear about the precise constraint that will be imposed by their lifetime income. Radical uncertainty creates a degree of 'fuzziness' in lifetime budget constraints. This is not to suggest that households behave as if they face no budget constraint at all, but that the precise location of such a path is inevitably vague and cannot be described by a probability distribution.

The problem is not just complexity but also the pretence of knowledge. Since it is impossible to be confident of knowing the future chances of particular income levels, the risk of losing one's job, the correlations between different investment opportunities and countless other relevant factors, the danger in trying to 'optimise', even if one has a large computer, is that the pretence of knowledge leads you to select an optimal solution based on assumptions that are almost certainly false – the right answer to the wrong question. Optimising over a false model is in many instances worse than the use of a coping strategy that works in your particular environment. Rather than attempt complex statistical calculations, it is better to make investment decisions using a choice of heuristic that reflects a sensible narrative.

Fuzzy constraints matter because, if households can borrow and lend, the degree of restriction implied by a lifetime budget constraint is extremely weak in the short term. It is possible for spending to deviate from a sustainable level for a long time.

The feedback from a fuzzy constraint may take several years to impact on spending decisions, creating the possibility of a slow build-up of a big misperception or 'mistake' about the constraint implied by future incomes. The result is a disequilibrium in spending and saving.

The narrative people use to estimate their lifetime income will relate both to individual factors, such as current earnings, job prospects and health, and to a view about the economy as a whole, its likely evolution and stability. That suggests a two-part heuristic for spending decisions. First, if the path for total spending in the economy as a whole appears sustainable, then one should hold expected lifetime income constant. In other words, people infer estimates of changes in 'fuzzy' lifetime incomes from perceptions of the sustainability of current spending rather than, as in conventional economic models, the other way round. Second, one should revise the estimate of lifetime income only in response to individual news (for example, a marked change in personal circumstances such as sickness, sudden promotion, or marriage and divorce) or in the event of a major change in beliefs about the economy that changes the plausibility of the view that the current path is sustainable.

Those estimates of lifetime income would be divided between current and future spending along the lines suggested by neoclassical theory – defer spending if interest rates are high and bring it forward if rates are low. In normal circumstances, with positive real interest rates at their average historical level, planned spending will rise steadily over time because the benefits from deferring consumption to the future – earning interest on the implied saving – will more than offset our natural impatience to spend today rather than tomorrow. In today's conditions, with real interest rates close to zero, the profile of planned spending will be rather flat or, possibly, declining.

The implications of this two-part heuristic – the stability

heuristic – for aggregate consumer spending are twofold. First, in the absence of a major shock to perceptions about the sustainability of the path of the economy, consumption is likely to be rather stable. Changes to personal circumstances may cause a sharp change in the spending of individual families but are unlikely to have a significant impact overall – shifts in beliefs about lifetime budget constraints are idiosyncratic and wash out in the aggregate. The numbers of sicknesses, births and deaths, marriages and divorces, promotions and career disappointments do not change radically from one year to the next, even if their realisation is dramatic for the person concerned. So they will not have a noticeable impact on overall spending. Only a large shock to perceptions of sustainability will prompt households to revise their estimates of lifetime income and hence their current spending. During the Great Stability the heuristic meant that aggregate lifetime income was expected to be remarkably stable.

The second implication is that households and businesses are likely to make 'mistakes' about the consistency of their current estimates of lifetime income with the underlying reality. An apparently stable, but ultimately unsustainable, path of total spending, as was seen in the Great Stability, can lead households to infer that their own spending is consistent with their lifetime budget constraints. Since all households are using aggregate spending to make those inferences, their mistakes will all be in the same direction. The mistakes do not cancel out for the economy as a whole, and lead to a disequilibrium in which current spending plans slowly but steadily drift away from the path implied by the underlying reality. That disequilibrium may appear stable, but it is not sustainable indefinitely. It will persist until something happens to make people revise the narrative of their lifetime income, at which point past mistakes will need to be corrected. That is precisely, I think, what happened in the crisis when it became apparent that expectations about future spending in countries such as the US and the UK had been too optimistic.

The existence of fuzzy budget constraints means that misperceptions and mistakes are almost inevitable, as are their subsequent correction. During the decade before the crisis – one I christened the NICE (non-inflationary consistently expansionary) decade – the rhetoric of economists, central bankers and politicians was largely, if not entirely, directed to the belief that the Great Stability would continue.[23] But the purpose of the NICE label was precisely to point out that it could not continue and that future decades would not be so nice. The longer the disequilibrium persists, the greater the correction will be. And once the narrative has been revised, it is rational to move to the new path of spending quickly.

The concept of rational expectations played an important role in alerting economists to the fact that policy interventions might prove less effective than Keynesians had assumed, but it overlooked the fact that in a highly uncertain world, businesses and households might make persistent over- or underestimates of their true potential spending or wealth. Those mistakes can generate misperceptions of wealth and affect asset prices. Indeed, the existence of financial markets can make matters worse.

Take a very simple, if extreme, example. Two friends meet and talk about the prospects for the stock market over the next year. One is convinced that the market will rise; the other that it will fall. They agree to differ and are about to go home when a bookmaker on an adjoining table offers to arrange a bet of $1 million on the level of the market a year ahead. The first person is so convinced that the market will rise that he bets $1 million that it will be higher a year from now. Sure that he will be much richer in a year's time, he starts to spend now. The second person bets that the market will fall over the coming year and, extremely confident of being much richer, he also starts to spend now. The bookmaker covers his bets.

Financial markets thrive on differences of opinion – they make the horse race. They also create 'mistakes' in perceptions of wealth or spending power. After the bet has been placed, perceived expected wealth is $2 million higher than before – both people think they will be $1 million better off. At the end of the year one person will have won $1 million, as expected, and the other will have lost $1 million and be $2 million worse off than he had expected. The ability to place bets or make transactions on financial markets creates swings in perceptions of spending power and actual current spending. In the world of the grand auction of Chapter 2, markets make people better off. In a world of radical uncertainty, they may lead to big mistakes. This is one of the ways in which financial markets affect the workings of the real economy and generate volatility in asset prices, which in turn affects the stability of the banking system.

A major question for central banks is whether they should try to correct mistakes in beliefs that are leading to an unsustainable path for the economy. In my view, this is the most important challenge for monetary policy, and especially to inflation targeting, in the future. For such an approach to be feasible, a central bank must not only be confident of identifying the mistakes that have led others astray, but also find a way to change the incorrect perceptions of businesses and households without making the state of the economy worse. That is a difficult task, as we will see below when analysing an alternative to the monetary policies adopted during the Great Stability.

The Keynesian story of a recession is one in which the inability to coordinate future spending plans means that a loss of confidence in the willingness of others to spend leads businesses to cut back on investment and production, resulting in a cumulative contraction in total demand – 'the only thing we have to fear is fear itself', in the words of President Franklin Roosevelt in 1933.[24] When we view the problem facing households and businesses in the light of coping strategies, we can see that there is an alternative reason for episodes of weak aggregate demand. There can be lengthy periods during which the information used to construct estimates of lifetime income (here, the stability of the path of total spending) is providing no signal to households that their own current spending is unsustainable. At some point a new signal arrives that leads all households to make corrections in their spending. When the narrative for lifetime income changes, then a major adjustment to spending plans occurs. That new level of demand is not a temporary deficiency of aggregate demand in a Keynesian sense, but a rational response to the realisation that past spending was based on a misperception of lifetime income.

Both explanations of a downturn derive from radical uncertainty, and they are by no means incompatible. But the crucial difference between the two stories lies in the appropriate policy response to weak demand. In a Keynesian downturn, policies to boost aggregate demand in the short term, by monetary or fiscal stimulus, can help to dispel fear and restore both confidence and spending to their previous paths. In a narrative revision downturn, however, it is a mistake to try to return to the earlier path of spending. Policies to boost demand in the short term may appear to help but do not alter the need for a correction of the disequilibrium.

Financial crises are often seen as the materialisation of a low-probability event that was simply not expected. People were caught by surprise. But as Chapter 1 showed, financial crises are fairly frequent. So it seems odd to see them as the consequence of very infrequent events. Another explanation is that people underestimate the likely frequency of extreme outcomes which, in fact, are drawn from probability distributions with 'fat tails', that is, the likelihood of extreme outcomes is much greater than normally assumed. As Alan Greenspan remarked, 'the tails must be not merely fat but morbidly obese to explain what has happened over the years'.[25] The problem with all such interpretations is that they see crises as the result of a throw of the dice by the economic gods, randomness that fools mere mortals. What is missing is the possibility that the evolution of the economy itself creates a build-up of misperceptions and mistakes. Sharp swings in sentiment are not irrational, the product of random changes in 'animal spirits' independent of economic circumstances, but the result of rational attempts to cope with radical uncertainty. And when judgements about lifetime incomes are revised, as reality eventually dawns, they produce the sudden and large changes in asset values associated with a crisis.

Causes and consequences of the 2008 crisis

The economic record of advanced economies between 1950 and 1970 was one of success. Recovery from the devastation of war led to rapid economic growth and rising standards of living in all the major industrialised economies, including those who suffered most from the conflict of the Second World War. A key explanation for the success and stability of the immediate post-war decades was a degree of confidence that Keynesian economics could guarantee stability. While businesses believed in the heuristic that governments could and would ensure steady economic expansion, investment seemed less risky than during the instability of the inter-war period. So investment continued to rise at a steady rate, producing stable growth. Expectations of continued steady growth were self-reinforcing.[26]

Unfortunately, the belief that governments could eliminate the business cycle proved illusory. After the success of the immediate post-war period, problems emerged that could not be concealed by a belief in the effectiveness of Keynesian policy stimulus. The oil price shocks of 1973 and 1979 raised inflation and reduced potential output in the industrialised world. Unemployment could be maintained at previous low levels only by accepting cuts in real wages. But attempts to ignore those shocks by continuing to run economies at low rates of unemployment without reductions in real wages led to rising, indeed accelerating, inflation. It soon became clear that the fall in real wages implied by the rise in oil prices could not be avoided, and that attempts to do so would create unemployment which, if it persisted, would erode skills and lead more people to drop out of the labour force altogether. The only way to reduce the growing level of unemployment, especially in Europe, with its inflexible labour markets, was to lower the 'natural' rate of unemployment as determined by the supply and demand for labour by introducing major reforms. They included legislation to rein in union power, reductions in unemployment benefits relative to average wages, and measures to reduce job protection by introducing temporary labour contracts.[27] Stability-oriented macroeconomic policies could then ensure low and stable inflation. So successful was this approach that inflation fell across the industrialised world, which then experienced an unprecedented period of stable growth and low inflation – the Great Stability.

The conquering of inflation was an important achievement. It was possible to manage paper money in a democracy. But the flaw with the Great Stability was that many people confused stability with sustainability. In the major economies, output during the Great Stability rose at rates close to their previous historical averages. From the perspective of the economics of 'stuff', and conventional macroeconomics, the situation looked sustainable. But the composition of demand was not. The origins of this growing disequilibrium were explained in Chapter 1. Countries such as China and Germany, for different reasons, pursued policies to encourage exports, ensured their exchange rates were undervalued, and as a result ran large trade surpluses.[28] The arithmetic consequence of those trade surpluses was significant lending to the rest of the world. From the early 1990s, more and more savings were invested in the world capital market. Long-term real interest rates – which move to match savings and investment – started to fall. By 2008 they had fallen from over 4 per cent to below 2 per cent a year. An immediate consequence of such a sharp fall in the rate at which future profits and dividends were discounted was that asset prices – of stocks, bonds, houses and most other assets – rose during the intervening period. Households and businesses were encouraged by the fall in real interest rates to bring forward both consumption and investment spending from the future to the present. Countries such as the United States and United Kingdom, facing structural trade deficits, cut their official short-term interest rates in order to boost domestic demand.

The narrative that took hold was one of stability. After all, GDP as a whole was evolving on a sustainable path, with growth around historical average rates and low and stable inflation. Trade deficits and savings ratios were stable relative to GDP. So, using the stability heuristic described above, households inferred that lifetime income was moving along a stable path. Stability at the aggregate level metamorphosed into a belief in its sustainability. Nothing seemed to happen to challenge the narrative. So households and businesses came to believe that levels of domestic demand were also sustainable.

How could households be so misled for so long? Why did they not understand the argument that demand was unsustainably high? Few families have the following conversation over dinner at home: 'Darling, I'm worried that domestic spending in the economy is too high, and that at some point real interest rates will have to rise and the trade deficit come down. At that point, domestic spending will fall and we'll be part of that adjustment. Perhaps we should adjust our own spending now to a new and more sustainable path.' Moreover, at any time when that conversation could have taken place, financial markets and professional investors appeared equally complacent about the growing disequilibrium. Markets set prices in a widespread belief that real interest rates would stay low for a long time. Households were in good company.

The interesting question is why businesses and households, investors in financial markets and policy-makers all believed that for long-term real interest rates to stay so low for so long was compatible with a growing market economy. The explanation is that the intellectual framework that has come to dominate economic thinking, including that of almost all central banks, rules out by assumption the disequilibrium described above.

There was, nevertheless, plenty of room to disagree about the likely effect of rising asset prices. Before the crisis hit, there was a debate between the Federal Reserve and the Bank of England about the impact of house prices on consumer spending. The Federal Reserve argued that an increase in household wealth would boost consumption. Since housing makes up a substantial proportion of total personal wealth, an increase in house prices should increase consumer spending. Statistical evidence for the post-war period seemed to back up this proposition. In contrast, the Bank of England argued that an increase in house prices would in itself not increase household spending. After all, if you are told that the value of your house has gone up by 25 per cent during the past week, you may feel wealthier but you have no more income to spend. The only way in which you could generate funds would be to move into a smaller home or borrow against the higher value of the house (and for most families housing is the best form of collateral which they can pledge).[29] A homeowner is both landlord and tenant in her own property. A rise in house prices increases the wealth of the homeowner as landlord but increases the implicit rent paid by the owner-occupier as tenant. That is an economist's way of expressing the common-sense observation that a rise in the price of the home that you own does not mean that you will now be able to afford a new car or expensive holiday.[30]

The stability heuristic seemed to apply to households and policy-makers alike, and for a time reinforced the stability of spending. The level of spending continued at unsustainably high levels in the United States, United Kingdom and some other countries in Europe, and at unsustainably low levels in Germany and China. That created an imbalance within those countries, with spending either too high or too low relative to current and prospective incomes. And the imbalance between countries – large trade surpluses and deficits – grew. These developments were not irrational, but were the consequence of people struggling to behave rationally in a world of radical uncertainty, part and parcel of a market economy.

All this added up to a disequilibrium within and between major economies. There was neither internal nor external balance. From the mid-1990s, international meetings settled into a pattern in which European officials would berate the United States for saving so little, American officials would lambast Europeans for failing to understand the need for a change in trade balances, and Japanese officials would remain knowingly silent. Chinese officials would report the latest historically high growth rate. But there seemed little understanding of how all these factors fitted together.

The disequilibrium in the world economy became

increasingly serious. Real interest rates were distorted well below the likely expected return on capital investment in an economy growing at its normal rate, encouraging investment in areas where demand was subsequently revealed to be unsustainably high. Real exchange rates were distorted, so creating unsustainable trade deficits and surpluses, along with a flow of capital from countries where returns on investment were high to countries where they were low. Bad investments were made – in housing in the US and some countries in Europe, in commercial property, such as shopping centres, in the UK, in construction in China and in the export sector in Germany. In order to encourage a shift of resources into the export sectors of the countries with trade deficits, it was necessary to raise the price of tradeable goods and services relative to the price of non-tradeable goods and services. But the rigidity of exchange rates and the pursuit of low inflation combined to make it difficult to achieve the rise required.

A good example of the tensions lying below the surface of the Great Stability is the experience of the UK. Only after the crisis hit was it possible, through a sharp fall in the sterling exchange rate and a willingness to let inflation rise above the 2 per cent inflation target for several years while the higher prices of imports and other tradeable products were being absorbed, to start the process of rebalancing the economy. And that process was interrupted in 2014–15 by the understandable desire of the European Central Bank to weaken the value of the euro in order to stimulate the economies of France and Italy, in particular, which reversed the earlier sterling depreciation. Across the world, government policies have, whether by design or accident, impeded movements in exchange rates and pushed long-term interest rates down to unsustainably low levels.

In the long run, these key prices – real interest rates, real exchange rates and the price of tradeable versus non-tradeable goods – must adjust to a new and sustainable equilibrium. If governments do not allow that to happen, then the debts and credits that have built up during the interim period of disequilibrium will eventually have to be cancelled. Capital flows will be transformed from loans to gifts or 'transfers'. Such a development is likely to provoke conflict between creditor and debtor nations. The stability heuristic explains why the horizon over which a disequilibrium persists can be long. And the longer this horizon, the weaker will be demand once expectations of future incomes are brought back into line with the underlying reality.

Something has to give. Stability does not necessarily contain the seeds of its own destruction – in that sense Minsky was wrong. But stability accompanied by unsustainability offers only the appearance of true stability and must at some point come to an end. As in so many crises, the point of greatest vulnerability was in the banking sector. It had become so highly leveraged that, as described in Chapter 1, relatively small items of news from the housing market in the United States in 2006 and the position of some European banks in 2007 led to nervousness about the state of the sector. After the collapse of Lehman Brothers in September 2008, there was both a full-blown banking crisis and an enormous shock to confidence around the world. The stability heuristic was no longer appropriate. The narrative changed. It was now far from obvious how to estimate lifetime income. All that was clear was that spending patterns would have to change. Caution prevailed, borrowers were reluctant to borrow and lenders to lend. There was a synchronised de-leveraging of balance sheets, and a large downward correction in spending and output, in countries where demand had been unsustainably high. That had a substantial consequential effect on countries that had relied on trade to support growth. China, for example, suffered a sharp fall in exports, especially to Europe. From 2000 to 2008, the average annual growth rate of China's exports of goods exceeded 20 per cent. In 2009, exports fell by 11 per cent, and although growth rebounded in 2010 in subsequent years, it has been only at single-digit rates.[31] Around the world, the realisation that a lower path of spending was likely to be appropriate, and the uncertainty surrounding the location of that path, combined to create a period of sustained weakness in both consumption and investment spending.

After 2008 it became commonplace to argue that the crisis originated in the financial sector, or possibly, in the United States, in the housing market. This is to confuse symptoms and causes. Undoubtedly, the fragile nature of our banking system made the crisis acute and fast-moving. But across the world there was a massive macroeconomic disequilibrium both within and between most major economies. The failure to appreciate the nature of this imbalance contributed not only to the build-up of a highly unstable pattern of credits and debts, but also to a faulty diagnosis of the slow and faltering recovery in the advanced economies after the banking crisis came to an end in 2009.

In 2014, Jaime Caruana, the General Manager of the Bank for International Settlements, said, 'there is simply too much debt in the world today'.[32] And Adair Turner, former Chairman of the Financial Services Authority, asserted that 'The most fundamental reason why the 2008 financial crisis has been followed by such a deep and long-lasting recession is the growth of real economy leverage across advanced economies over the previous half-century.'[33] The problem with such statements is that, although they correctly point to the greater fragility resulting from high debt levels, debt was a consequence, not a cause of the problems that led to the crisis. Debt did not descend like manna from heaven but was a conscious response by borrowers to the situation they faced. Most bank lending to households and companies in recent years was to finance property.[34] But banks did not set out to create a bubble in house prices. Rather they were responding to the demand for borrowing that resulted from the need to finance higher values of the stock of property. In turn, those higher values were a rational reflection of the lower level of long-term real interest rates documented in Chapter 1. The real causes of the rise in debt were the 'savings glut' and the response to it by western central banks that led to and sustained the fall in real interest rates.

The danger with the 'economics of stuff', whether Keynesian or neoclassical, is that it leads to the complacent view that a chronic deficiency in demand is always of a Keynesian type and is the sole explanation of slow growth in the world today. Once we recognise that demand is divided between consumption today and consumption tomorrow, and also between consumption of goods made exclusively at home and goods that can be traded overseas (either exports or imports), and that total spending can be either consumption or investment, then it is clear that 'aggregate demand' is an incomplete concept for understanding the current situation. The problem with limiting the diagnosis to a shortage of aggregate demand is that it has led economists to infer that the remedy is to boost current spending through whatever means is to hand – easier monetary policy, fiscal expansion or words of encouragement by governments that the worst is over.

These Keynesian remedies have their place in dealing with a shock to confidence, such as we saw in 2008–9. But beneath the surface was a much deeper disequilibrium between spending and saving, as the choice between spending today and spending tomorrow had been distorted for many years by falling real interest rates. As a result, we experienced, first, the calmness of the Great Stability, then the turbulence of the crisis, followed by the Great Recession. Policy-makers allowed the disequilibrium to build up, then correctly adopted a Keynesian response to the downturn in 2008–9 but failed to tackle the underlying disequilibrium. Understandably concerned with the paradox of thrift, they adopted policies that led to the paradox of policy – where policy measures that are desirable in the short term are diametrically opposite to those needed in the long term.[35]

Short-term Keynesian stimulus boosts consumption, reduces saving, and encourages households to borrow more. But in the long term, policy in the US and UK needs to bring about a shift away from domestic spending and towards exports, to reduce the trade deficit, to lower the leverage on household and bank balance sheets, and to raise the rate of national saving and investment. The irony is that those countries most in need of this long-term adjustment, the US and UK, have been the most active in pursuing the short-term stimulus.

Looking back, an example of a downturn in which policy-makers did not impede adjustment to a new equilibrium, and so did not create a paradox of policy, was the episode in 1920–1. In 1919 the Federal Reserve started to raise interest rates to combat inflation. In 1920, the American economy entered a deep recession. Commodity prices around the world started to fall that spring. During the downturn, producer prices fell by 41 per cent and industrial production by over 30 per cent. Stock prices fell by almost one-half.[36] Farmers and other producers defaulted on their debts. No official body in those days calculated measures of GDP, but subsequent researchers have estimated that total output fell by between 3 and 7 per cent.[37] Unemployment rose to not far short of 20 per cent. Many employees accepted substantial cuts in wages and by the autumn of 1921, activity had started to recover. The depression came to an end and activity and prices were stabilised. The striking fact is that throughout the episode there was no active stabilisation policy by the government or central bank, and prices moved in a violent fashion. It was, in the words of James Grant, the Wall Street financial journalist and writer, 'the depression that cured itself'.[38]

The 'mistake' made in this case by consumers, businesses and banks was to assume that the rise in commodity prices after the First World War, from cotton and sugar to automobiles and steel, was permanent. It led to overinvestment in inventories and stocks of raw materials and finished goods, and generated a natural fall in prices when that excess supply became evident. The excess stock levels were disposed of and the fall in prices stimulated a recovery in demand and employment. Grant argues that it was the wage and price flexibility of the period that enabled a speedy recovery to follow an initial deep downturn. It is certainly possible that the greater flexibility of wages and prices in the early 1920s, at least compared with the later experience in the 1930s and early post-war period, was helpful in stimulating a more rapid recovery. But part of the reason for that was a rise in the real stock of money as prices fell – a sort of passive stabilising monetary policy.

The key lesson from the experience of 1920–1 is that it is a mistake to think of all recessions as having similar causes and requiring similar remedies. Sharp swings in inventory prices and stocks may be self-correcting. A Keynesian downturn resulting from a lack of confidence can be overcome by policies that restore confidence in the future path of total spending. A recession created by central banks trying to bring down inflation can be undone by restoring monetary policy to its normal setting once inflation expectations have been reduced to a desired level. And a narrative revision downturn can be resolved only by moving the economy to a new equilibrium in which spending comes into line with realistic perceptions of lifetime budget constraints.

The appropriate policy response, therefore, depends upon the nature of the downturn. Sometimes a recession reflects more than one cause. In 2008, the shock to confidence following the banking collapse led to a Keynesian downturn around the world on top of which was superimposed the adjustment to businesses and households' earlier 'mistake' in assessing the sustainable level of spending. As explained above, that complicated the required policy response and led to the paradox of policy. The Great Depression in the 1930s saw violent swings of output and employment. In their classic study of the monetary history of the United States, Friedman and Schwartz argued that this was the fault of the Federal Reserve for remaining passive in the face of a sharp decline in the amount of money as banks failed and reduced lending. Out of this experience was born the view that an activist monetary and fiscal policy was essential. Stabilisation policy was a phrase that entered the textbooks. But policy also had to tackle the underlying solvency issues in the banking sector, leading to the creation of the Federal Deposit Insurance Corporation. No single model will capture all the relevant features of a crisis, and that is one of the dangers of the mindset instilled by the 'economics of stuff'.

An alternative history of the pre-crisis period

Could and should policy-makers have reacted sooner to the disequilibrium that was building up prior to the crisis? What strategies might have been deployed by the G7 countries before the crisis? With the benefit of hindsight, should interest rates have been higher during the period of the so-called Great Stability? We can explore these questions by going back to the pre-crisis period and asking whether there was an alternative policy that might have produced a different result.

As a medium-sized, open economy, the United Kingdom

offers a good example of how to think about an alternative monetary policy prior to the crisis. In the build-up to the crisis of 2007–9, the average growth rate of GDP was only a fraction above the previous fifty-year annual average of 2.75 per cent. There was no 'boom' in output growth that heralded an inevitable 'bust'. Inflation was steady and close to the 2 per cent target; unemployment was close to estimates of its natural rate. In terms of the economy as a whole, the appearance was not just of stability but of sustainability. But although the growth rate of output was sustainable, its composition was not. Since the late 1990s, the UK, like the US, had run a large trade deficit, reflecting the structural surpluses of countries like China and a substantial appreciation of the sterling exchange rate of around 25 per cent against most other currencies. Consumer demand had risen at the expense of exports. Investment had been directed to the sectors producing to meet consumer demand – including commercial property (although not residential housing, which was subject to strong planning restrictions on development). To meet the inflation target it was necessary to stimulate domestic demand, at the cost of exacerbating the internal and external imbalances, in order to compensate for weak external demand.

As early as the late 1990s, there was an intense debate within the Monetary Policy Committee (MPC) of the Bank of England about whether we should try to offset this unsustainable imbalance in the pattern of demand.[39] The problem was that if domestic demand grew too rapidly for too long, then the longer the correction was deferred, the sharper the ultimate adjustment would be, as turned out to be the case when the adjustment finally started in 2008–9.[40] The committee faced an unpalatable choice between continuing with steady growth and low inflation, knowing that this would exacerbate the imbalances and risk a sharp downturn later, and deliberately creating a slowdown in order to return to a more sustainable path for domestic demand at the cost of rising unemployment and inflation below the mandated target in the short run. Not surprisingly, perhaps, the committee opted for the former.[41] The position was summed up by my predecessor as Governor, Eddie George, in 2002 when he said, 'So in effect we have taken the view that unbalanced growth in our present situation is better than no growth – or as some commentators have put it, a two-speed economy is better than a no-speed economy.'[42]

In choosing the 'two-speed growth is better than no growth' strategy, the Monetary Policy Committee endorsed the build-up of imbalances and the likelihood of a subsequent sharp downward adjustment in domestic demand. Should policy have erred on the side of slower growth and undershooting of the inflation target in order to reduce the risk of a destabilising correction later? The alternative policy would have been to keep interest rates higher in the hope that a slowing of domestic demand would change the narrative driving spending decisions. Asset prices, debt and bank leverage might have risen by somewhat less. Any such alternative path for the economy would have implied recession and unemployment, as well as inflation below the target. But it is possible that accepting a smaller recession then would have dampened the Great Recession a decade later.

So what would have happened had the MPC adopted the alternative policy of higher interest rates prior to 2008? It is impossible to be sure, and much depends on what sort of coping strategy households and investors might have employed. On the committee, two views were discussed. One was that by setting interest rates at a much higher level, so dampening domestic demand and output growth, expectations of a sustainable path for domestic demand might be 'jolted' down to a lower, more realistic path. That would, under the stability heuristic, have led to expectations of a fall in the long-term exchange rate, consistent with a sustainable path of domestic demand, lower real wages and lower domestic spending. The narrative underpinning the high level of domestic demand would have changed to one based on lower, and more realistic, expectations of potential consumer spending. The exchange rate would have fallen, allowing higher external demand (exports less imports) to offset weaker domestic demand. After a time, we might have attained 'one-speed' growth, so avoiding the unpalatable choice between 'two-speed' growth and no growth.

The other view was that UK monetary policy alone, by raising interest rates to a level higher than those in other countries, would not have had much impact on beliefs about the long-term sustainability of the economy or on the expected long-term equilibrium value of sterling. In other words, the stability heuristic would have led to unchanged beliefs about the long-term exchange rate. In that case, higher interest rates would instead have caused an immediate upwards jump in the exchange rate in the short term as investors could earn more on sterling than on other currencies. Far from rebalancing the economy, the higher exchange rate would have meant even weaker external demand, and some slowing of growth.[43]

The dilemma was an inevitable consequence of the disequilibrium that had built up in the world economy. The stability heuristic suggests that shaking the confidence of consumers in the sustainability of their path of spending was a necessary precondition of rebalancing the UK economy, but the proposition was never put to the test. Not until years later, when the crisis hit, did people make adjustments to their expectations of real incomes.

The United Kingdom was not the only country facing this dilemma. If all countries had set higher interest rates, then it is possible that the resulting slowdown would have changed the narrative guiding expectations and spending both in countries with deficits and those with surpluses. But no single country seemed able to achieve that. Each central bank acting on its own was faced with the invidious choice between raising interest rates sufficiently to dampen the level of domestic demand, knowing that the likely result would be a recession at home, and continuing on a path that would in the end prove unsustainable and lead to an even bigger recession. And even the former path would not have prevented the global financial crisis. The excessive risk-taking and expansion of bank leverage was the result of low long-term interest rates around the world, not simply short-term official rates in one country. Since the crisis, the twin challenges of healing our economies and overcoming hubris have been exacerbated by the fact that central banks, along with most other players in the story, are facing a prisoner's dilemma.

In a Keynesian downturn the inability of economic agents to coordinate today on their future spending plans creates the possibility that demand may be well below its full employment potential. With radical uncertainty, however, there are other possible explanations of downturns in the economy. In a downturn brought about by a narrative revision, the evolution of the economy is less the result of external shocks to confidence and more the playing out of the build-up and correction of misperceptions about the future. Long periods during which people are liable to misperceive their wealth and future income – supported by the stability heuristic – can lead to a disequilibrium that distorts the balance between spending and saving and the level of asset prices. When the narrative changes, the correction in both spending and asset prices can be violent – the economics of 'stuff happens' rather than the economics of 'stuff'. Both before and during the correction, financial markets are only the messenger and not the cause of these misperceptions.

The failure to allow for such 'mistakes' can, and in the

context of the crisis did, lead to a misdiagnosis of the state of the economy and hence of the appropriate policy response. Relying solely on traditional Keynesian monetary and fiscal stimulus risks recreating the disequilibrium of the previous spending path when a move to a new equilibrium is what is required. Such stimulus may smooth the adjustment for the move to a new equilibrium, but is not a substitute for it. At some point, the 'paradox of policy' must be confronted.

The problems of diagnosing the disequilibrium in the build-up to the crisis were compounded by the fact that no country on its own could easily have found a way to a new equilibrium in the absence of similar adjustments by other countries. All the major economies faced a prisoner's dilemma. After the crisis, the burden of restoring the world economy to health has been laid fairly and squarely at the door of central banks. They continue to struggle with the responsibility of generating a recovery in the world economy. Were there other policy instruments, unavailable to central banks, which might have resolved those coordination problems, and would they contribute to the healing process today? Or are we headed for another crisis?

9

⤞⤝

THE AUDACITY OF PESSIMISM:
THE PRISONER'S DILEMMA AND
THE COMING CRISIS

'Hope in the face of difficulty, hope in the face of
uncertainty, the audacity of hope.'

Barack Obama, Speech to the Democratic
National Convention, Boston, 27 July 2004

'What experience and history teaches us is that people
and governments have never learned anything from
history, or acted on principles deduced from it.'

Georg Wilhelm Friedrich Hegel,
Lectures on the Philosophy of History (1832)

In earlier chapters I dwelled on past crises. But what about
the next crisis? Without reform of the financial system, as
proposed in Chapter 7, another crisis is certain, and the failure

to tackle the disequilibrium in the world economy makes it likely that it will come sooner rather than later. Rather than give in to pessimism, however, we have the opportunity to do something about it.

The most obvious symptom of the current disequilibrium is the extraordinarily low level of interest rates which, since the crisis, have fallen further. The consequences have been further rises in asset prices and a desperate search for yield as investors, from individuals to insurance companies, realise that the current return on their investments is inadequate to support their spending needs. Central banks are trapped into a policy of low interest rates because of the continuing belief that the solution to weak demand is further monetary stimulus. They are in a prisoner's dilemma: if any one of them were to raise interest rates, they would risk a slowing of growth and possibly another downturn.

When interest rates were cut almost to zero at the height of the crisis, no one expected that they would still be at those emergency levels more than six years later. A long period of zero interest rates is unprecedented. For much of the post-war period the worry was that interest rates might be too high. Now the concern is that low rates are eroding savings. It is reminiscent of Walter Bagehot's maxim about the archetypal Englishman: 'John Bull can stand many things, but he cannot stand 2 per cent.'[1] For more than six years now, he has had to stand rates well below that.

From its foundation in 1694 until 315 years later in 2009, the Bank of England never set bank rate below 2 per cent. By 2015, the major central banks had all lowered official policy rates to as close to zero as made no difference, and a number of European economies, including the euro area, Denmark, Sweden and Switzerland, had embraced negative interest rates. Some mortgage borrowers on floating rates were actually being paid to borrow. Over the long sweep of history, the long-term annual real rate of interest has averaged between 3 and 4 per cent. The world real interest rate on ten-year inflation-protected government bonds has been close to zero for several years and by 2015 was little more than 0.5 per cent. In part that reflects the belief that short-term official interest rates will remain low for a few years more.

What does the market think will happen in the future? Suppose it takes ten years to get back to somewhere close to normal, a pessimistic view according to most central banks. What is the market expectation today of where the ten-year real interest rate will be ten years from now? An estimate of that can be made by noting that the interest rate today on a twenty-year security is the average of the rate over the first ten years (the rate today on a ten-year security) and the rate over the second ten years (the ten-year rate that is expected today to prevail ten years from now). So we can infer the latter from observations on market interest rates on ten- and twenty-year index-linked government bonds. Such a calculation reveals that the ten-year real rate expected in ten years' time has averaged little more than 1 per cent in recent years and by late 2015 was still below 1.5 per cent, well below any level that could be considered remotely 'normal'. Markets do not expect interest rates to return to normal for many years.

If real interest rates remain close to zero, the disequilibrium in spending and saving will continue and the ultimate adjustment to a new equilibrium will be all the more painful. If real interest rates start to move back to more normal levels, markets will reassess their view of the future and asset prices could fall sharply. Neither prospect suggests a smooth and gradual return to a stable path for the economy. Further turbulence in the world economy, and quite possibly another crisis, are to be expected. The epicentre of the next financial earthquake is as hard to predict as a geological earthquake. It is unlikely to be among banks in New York or London, where the aftershocks of 2008 have led to efforts to improve the resilience of the financial system. But there are many places where the underlying forces of the disequilibrium in their economies could lead to cracks in the surface – emerging markets that have increased indebtedness, the euro area with its fault lines, China with a financial sector facing large losses, and the middle and near east with a rise in political tensions.

Since the end of the immediate banking crisis in 2009, recovery has been anaemic at best. By late 2015, the world recovery had been slower than predicted by policy-makers, and central banks had postponed the inevitable rise in interest rates for longer than had seemed either possible or likely. There was a continuing shortfall of demand and output from their pre-crisis trend path of close to 15 per cent. Stagnation – in the sense of output remaining persistently below its previously anticipated path – had once again become synonymous with the word capitalism. Lost output and employment of such magnitude has revealed the true cost of the crisis and shaken confidence in our understanding of how economies behave. How might we restore growth, and what could happen if we don't?

The coming crisis: sovereign debt forgiveness – necessary but not sufficient

Maintaining interest rates at extraordinarily low levels for years on end has contributed to the rise in asset prices and the increase in debt. Debt has now reached a level where it is a drag on the willingness to spend and likely to be the trigger for a future crisis. The main risks come from the prospect of a fall in asset prices, as interest rates return to normal levels, and the writing down of the value of investments as banks and companies start to reflect economic reality in their balance sheets. In both cases, a wave of defaults might lead to corporate failures and household bankruptcies. By 2015, corporate debt defaults in the industrial and emerging market economies were rising.[2] Disruptive though a wave of defaults would be in the short run, it might enable a 'reboot' of the economy so that it could grow in a more sustainable and balanced way. More difficult is external debt – debt owed by residents of one country to residents of another country – especially when that debt is denominated in a foreign currency.

When exchange rates are free to move, they reflect the underlying circumstances of different economies. Some governments, such as China in relation to the US dollar and Germany in relation to its European neighbours, have limited that freedom so that economies have had to adapt to exchange rates rather than the other way round. As a result, trade surpluses and deficits have also contributed to the build-up of debts and credits that now threaten countries' ability to maintain full employment at current exchange rates. Nowhere is this more evident than in the euro area, although emerging market economies could also run into trouble. Sovereign debts are likely to be a major headache for the world in the years to come, both in emerging markets and in the euro area. Should these debts be forgiven?

The situation in Greece encapsulates the problems of external indebtedness in a monetary union. GDP in Greece has collapsed by more than in the United States during the Great Depression. Despite an enormous fiscal contraction bringing the budget deficit down from around 12 per cent of GDP in 2010 to below 3 per cent in 2014, the ratio of government debt to GDP has continued to rise, and is now almost 200 per cent.[3] All of this debt is denominated in a currency that is likely to rise in value relative to Greek incomes. Market interest rates are extremely high and Greece has little access to international capital markets. When debt was restructured in 2012, private sector creditors were bailed out. Most Greek debt is now owed to public sector institutions such as the European Central Bank, other member countries of the euro area, and the IMF. Fiscal austerity has proved self-defeating because the exchange rate could not fall to stimulate trade. In their 1980s debt crisis, Latin American countries found a route to economic growth only when they were able to move out from under the shadow of an extraordinary burden of debt owed to foreigners. To put it another way, there is very little chance now that Greece will be able to repay its sovereign debt. And the longer the austerity programme continues, the worse becomes the ability of Greece to repay.

Much of what happened in Greece is reminiscent of an earlier episode in Argentina. In 1991, Argentina fixed the exchange rate of its currency, the peso, to the US dollar. It had implemented a raft of reforms in the 1990s, and was often cited as a model economy. At the end of the 1990s, there was a sharp drop in commodity prices and Argentina went into recession. Locked into a fixed-rate regime, the real exchange rate had become too high, and the only way to improve competitiveness was through a depression that reduced domestic wages and prices. Argentina's debt position was akin to that of Greece, and it had a similarly high unemployment rate. So in the face of a deep depression, the exchange rate regime was abandoned and capital controls were introduced. Bank accounts were redenominated in new pesos, imposing substantial losses on account holders. Initially, the chaos led to a 10 per cent drop in GDP during 2002. But after the initial turmoil, Argentina was able to return to a period of economic growth. Commodity prices rose steadily for a decade and Argentina was able to enjoy rapid growth of GDP – almost 10 per cent a year for five years.

It is evident, as it has been for a very long while, that the only way forward for Greece is to default on (or be forgiven) a substantial proportion of its debt burden and to devalue its currency so that exports and the substitution of domestic products for imports can compensate for the depressing effects of the fiscal contraction imposed to date. Structural reforms would help ease the transition, but such reforms will be effective only if they are adopted by decisions of the Greek people rather than being imposed as external conditions by the IMF or the European Commission. The lack of trust between Greece and its creditors means that public recognition of the underlying reality is some way off.

The inevitability of restructuring Greek debt means that taxpayers in Germany and elsewhere will have to absorb substantial losses. It was more than a little depressing to see the countries of the euro area haggling over how much to lend to Greece so that it would be able to pay them back some of the earlier loans. Such a circular flow of payments made little difference to the health, or lack of it, of the Greek economy. It is particularly unfortunate that Germany seemed to have forgotten its own history.

At the end of the First World War, the Treaty of Versailles imposed reparations on the defeated nations – primarily Germany, but also Austria, Hungary, Bulgaria and Turkey.[4] Some of the required payments were made in kind (for example, coal and livestock), but in the case of Germany most payments were to be in the form of gold or foreign currency. The Reparations Commission set an initial figure of 132 billion gold marks. Frustrated by Germany's foot-dragging in making payments, France and Belgium occupied the Ruhr in January 1923, allegedly to enforce payment. That led to an agreement among the Allies – the Dawes Plan of 1924 – that restructured and reduced the burden of reparations. But even those payments were being financed by borrowing from overseas, an unsustainable position. So a new conference met in the spring of 1929 and after four months of wrangling produced the Young Plan, signed in Paris in June at the Hotel George V, which further lowered the total payment to 112 billion marks and extended the period of repayment to expire in 1988. But the economic reality was that, unless Germany could obtain an export surplus, its only method of financing payments of reparations was borrowing from overseas. In May 1931, the failure of the Austrian bank Creditanstalt led to a crisis of the Austrian and German banking systems, and a month later the Hoover Moratorium suspended reparations. They were largely cancelled altogether at the Lausanne conference in 1932. In all, Germany paid less than 21 billion marks, much of which was financed by overseas borrowing on which Germany subsequently defaulted.

After the Versailles Treaty was agreed, Keynes and others argued that to demand substantial reparations from Germany would be counterproductive, leading to a collapse of the mark and of the German economy, damaging the wider European economy in the process.[5] But the most compelling statement of Germany's predicament came from its central bank governor, Hjalmar Schacht.[6] In 1934, writing in that most respectable and most American of publications, *Foreign Affairs*, Schacht explained that 'a debtor country can pay only when it has earned a surplus on its balance of trade, and ... the attack on German exports by means of tariffs, quotas, boycotts, etc., achieves the opposite result'.[7] Not a man to question his own judgements (the English version of his autobiography was titled *My First Seventy-six Years*, although sadly a second volume never appeared), on this occasion Schacht was unquestionably correct. As he wrote in his memoirs about a visit to Paris in January 1924:

It took another eight years before the Allied politicians realised that the whole policy of reparations was an economic
evil which was bound to inflict the utmost injury not only
upon Germany but upon the Allied nations as well. Of the
120 milliards which Germany was supposed to pay, between
10 and 12 milliards were actually paid during the years 1924
to 1932. And they were not paid out of surplus exports as they
should have been. During those eight years Germany never
achieved any surplus exports. Rather they were paid out of
the proceeds of loans which other countries, acting under a
complete misapprehension as to Germany's resources, pressed
upon her to such an extent that in 1931 it transpired that she
could no longer meet even the interest on them. Finally, in
1932, there followed the Lausanne Conference at which the
reparations commitments were practically written off.[8]

After the Second World War, and with Germany divided,
the problem of German debt reared its ugly head again. In
1953, the London Agreement on German External Debts
rescheduled and restructured the debts of the new Federal
Republic of Germany. Repayment of some of the debts
incurred by the whole of Germany was made conditional
on the country's reunification. In 1990 the condition was
triggered and on 3 October 2010 a final payment of German
war debts of €69.9 million was made. More interesting from
today's perspective is the statement in the Agreement that West
Germany would have to make repayments only when it was
running a trade surplus, and the repayments were limited to
3 per cent of export earnings. The euro area could learn from
this experience.[9] One way of easing the financing problems of
the periphery countries would be to postpone repayment of
external debts to other member countries of the euro area until
the debtor country had achieved an export surplus, creating an

incentive for creditors and debtors to work together to reduce trade imbalances.

It is deeply ironic that today it is Germany that is insisting on repayments of debt from countries that are unable to earn an export surplus, out of which their external debts could be serviced, because of the constraints of monetary union. Schacht must be turning in his grave. As the periphery countries of southern Europe embark on the long and slow journey back to full employment, their external deficits will start to widen again, and it is far from clear how existing external debt, let alone any new borrowing from abroad, can be repaid. Inflows of private-sector capital helped the euro area survive after 2012, but they are most unlikely to continue for ever. It is instructive to quote Keynes's analysis in the inter-war period, replacing Germany in 1922 with Greece in 2015, and France then with Germany today: 'The idea that the rest of the world is going to lend to Greece, for her to hand over to Germany, about 100 per cent of their liquid savings – for that is what it amounts to – is utterly preposterous. And the sooner we get that into our heads the better.'[10]

Much of the euro area has either created or gone along with the illusion that creditor countries will always be repaid. When a debtor country has difficulties in repaying, the answer is to 'extend and pretend' by lengthening the repayment period and valuing the assets represented by the loans at face value. It is a familiar tactic of banks unwilling to face up to losses on bad loans, and it has crept into sovereign lending. To misquote Samuel Taylor Coleridge (in his poem *The Rime of the Ancient Mariner*), 'Debtors, debtors everywhere, and not a loss in sight.'[11]

Debt forgiveness is more natural within a political union. But with different political histories and traditions, a move to political union is unlikely to be achieved quickly through popular support. Put bluntly, monetary union has created a conflict between a centralised elite on the one hand, and the forces of democracy at the national level on the other. This is extraordinarily dangerous. In 2015, the Presidents of the European Commission, the Euro Summit, the Eurogroup, the European Central Bank and the European Parliament (the existence of five presidents is testimony to the bureaucratic skills of the elite) published a report arguing for fiscal union in which 'decisions will increasingly need to be made collectively' and implicitly supporting the idea of a single finance minister for the euro area.[12] This approach of creeping transfer of sovereignty to an unelected centre is deeply flawed and will meet popular resistance. As Otmar Issing, the first Chief Economist of the European Central Bank and the intellectual force behind the ECB in its early years, argued, 'Political union . . . cannot be achieved through the back door, by eroding members' fiscal-policy sovereignty. Attempting to compel transfer payments would generate moral hazard on the part of the recipients and resistance from the donors.'[13] In pursuit of peace, the elites in Europe, the United States and international organisations such as the IMF, have, by pushing bailouts and a move to a transfer union as the solution to crises, simply sowed the seeds of divisions in Europe and created support for what were previously seen as extreme political parties and candidates. It will lead to not only an economic but a political crisis.

In 2012, when concern about sovereign debt in several periphery countries was at its height, it would have been possible to divide the euro area into two divisions, some members being temporarily relegated to a second division with the clear expectation that after a period – perhaps ten or fifteen years – of real convergence, those members would be promoted back to the first division. It may be too late for that now. The underlying differences among countries and the political costs of accepting defeat have become too great. That is unfortunate both for the countries concerned – because sometimes premature promotion can be a misfortune and relegation the opportunity for a new start – and for the world as a whole because the euro area today is a drag on world growth.

Germany faces a terrible choice. Should it support the weaker brethren in the euro area at great and unending cost to its taxpayers, or should it call a halt to the project of monetary union across the whole of Europe? The attempt to find a middle course is not working. One day German voters may rebel against the losses imposed on them by the need to support their weaker brethren, and undoubtedly the easiest way to divide the euro area would be for Germany itself to exit. But the more likely cause of a break-up of the euro area is that voters in the south will tire of the grinding and relentless burden of mass unemployment and the emigration of talented young people. The counter-argument – that exit from the euro area would lead to chaos, falls in living standards and continuing uncertainty about the survival of the currency union – has real weight. But if the alternative is crushing austerity, continuing mass unemployment, and no end in sight to the burden of debt, then leaving the euro area may be the only way to plot a route back to economic growth and full employment. The long-term benefits outweigh the short-term costs. Outsiders cannot make that choice, but they can encourage Germany, and the rest of the euro area, to face up to it.

If the members of the euro decide to hang together, the burden of servicing external debts may become too great to remain consistent with political stability. As John Maynard Keynes wrote in 1922, 'It is foolish ... to suppose that any means exist by which one modern nation can exact from another an annual tribute continuing over many years.'[14] It would be desirable, therefore, to create a mechanism by which international sovereign debts could be restructured within a framework supported by the expertise and neutrality of the IMF, so avoiding, at least in part, the animosity and humiliation that accompanied the latest agreement on debt between Greece and the rest of the euro area in 2015. It was, I regret to say, an Englishman, the First Lord of the Admiralty, Sir Eric Campbell-Geddes, who set the tone for the harsh treatment of debtors when he said in a speech before the Versailles Peace Conference that 'we shall squeeze the German lemon until the pips squeak!'

As early as 2003, the IMF debated the creation of a 'sovereign debt restructuring mechanism'. The idea was to ensure a timely resolution of debt problems to help both debtors and creditors, and to recognise the prisoner's dilemma in which an individual creditor had an incentive to hold out for full repayment, even though, collectively, creditors would be better off by negotiating with the debtor. Progress on the creation of such a mechanism was defeated by opposition from the United States, which favoured bailouts over defaults, and Germany, which did not want to encourage the belief that sovereigns might be allowed to default. Neither objection made sense. By failing to impose losses on the private-sector creditors of periphery countries in the euro area in 2012, the IMF and the European institutions took on obligations on which they were subsequently forced to accept losses. It is all too easy to pretend that throwing yet more money at a highly indebted country will solve the immediate crisis. It is only too likely that a sovereign debt restructuring mechanism will be needed in the foreseeable future. Without one, an ad hoc international debt conference to sort out the external sovereign debts that have built up may be needed.

But debt forgiveness, inevitable though it may be, is not a sufficient answer to all our problems. In the short run, it could even have the perverse effect of slowing growth. Sovereign borrowers have already had their repayment periods extended, easing the pressure on their finances. There would be little change in their immediate position following explicit debt forgiveness. Creditors, by contrast, may be under a misapprehension that they will be repaid in full, and when reality dawns they could reduce their spending. The underlying challenge is to move to a new equilibrium in which new debts are no longer being created on the same scale as before.

Escaping the prisoner's dilemma: wider international reforms

A major impediment to the resolution of the disequilibrium facing so many economies is the prisoner's dilemma they face – if they and they alone take action, they could be worse off (see Chapter 8). The task now is how to reconcile the prisoner's dilemma with people's overwhelming desire to control their own destiny. The prisoner's dilemma prevented countries from rebalancing their economies. A coordinated move to a new equilibrium would be the best outcome for all. By this I do not mean attempts to coordinate monetary and fiscal policy. Such efforts have a poor track record, ranging from the policies of the Federal Reserve in the 1920s, which held down interest rates in order to help other countries rejoin the gold standard, so creating a boom that led to the stock market crash in 1929 and the Great Depression, to the attempts in the mid-1980s to stabilise exchange rates among the major economies, which led to the stock market crash in 1987. Moreover, monetary and fiscal policies are not the route to a new equilibrium.

Many countries can now see that they have taken monetary policy as far as it can go. The weakness of demand across the world means that many, if not most, countries can credibly say that if only the rest of the world were growing normally then they would be in reasonable shape. But since it isn't, they aren't. So with interest rates close to zero, and fiscal policy constrained by high government debt, the objective of economic policy in a growing number of countries is to lower the exchange rate.[15] In countries as far apart as New Zealand, Australia, Japan, France and Italy, central banks and governments are becoming more and more strident in their determination to talk the exchange rate down. Competitive depreciation is a zero-sum game as countries try to 'steal' demand from each other. In the 1930s, the abandonment of the gold standard, and hence of fixed exchange rates between countries, allowed central banks across the globe to adopt easier monetary policies. Although the benefits of the reduction in exchange rates cancelled each other out, the easier monetary policies helped to bring about a recovery from the Great Depression. Today, however, monetary policy is already about as loose as it could be. There is a real risk of an implicit or explicit 'currency war'.

These questions are symptomatic of a wider problem in the world economy – a problem that Dani Rodrik of Harvard University has christened the 'political trilemma of the global economy'.[16] It is the mutual incompatibility of democracy, national sovereignty and economic integration. Which one do we surrender? If national sovereignty is eroded without clear public support, democracy will come under strain, as we are seeing in Europe, where democracy and national sovereignty are closely intertwined. Political union, in the sense of a genuinely federal Europe, has stalled. To reconcile democracy and monetary union would require clearly defined procedures for exit from monetary union. There are none. The degree of political integration necessary for survival of monetary union is vastly greater than, and wholly different from, the political cooperation necessary to create a path towards a sustainable economic recovery in Europe. Even if the former could be imposed by the central authorities on countries in the euro area – and there are few signs that this would be a popular development – to extend the same degree of integration to countries outside the euro area would surely shatter the wider union. For the foreseeable future, the European Union will comprise two categories of member: those in and those not in the euro area. Arrangements for the evolution of the European Union need to reflect that fact.

Such issues are a microcosm of broader challenges to the global order. The Asian financial crisis of the 1990s, when Thailand, South Korea and Indonesia borrowed tens of billions of dollars from western countries through the IMF to support their banks and currencies, showed how difficult it is to cope with sudden capital reversals resulting from a change in sentiment about the degree of currency or maturity mismatch in a nation's balance sheet, and especially in that of its banking system. The IMF cannot easily act as a lender of last resort because it does not own or manage a currency. In the Asian crisis, therefore, it was almost inevitable that conditionality was set by the US because the need of those countries was for dollars. The result was the adoption by a number of Asian countries of do-it-yourself lender of last resort policies, which involved their building up huge reserves of US dollars out of large trade surpluses. That, together with their export-led growth strategy, led directly to the fall in real interest rates across the globe after the fall of the Berlin Wall. Resentment towards the conditions imposed by the IMF (or the US) in return for financial support has also led to the creation of new institutions in Asia, ranging from the Chiang Mai Initiative, a network of bilateral swap arrangements between China, Japan, Korea and the ASEAN countries to serve as a regional safety-net mechanism now amounting to $240 billion, to the new Chinese-led Asian Infrastructure Investment Bank that was created in 2015. It is likely that Asia will develop its own informal arrangements that will, in essence, create an Asian IMF, an idea that was floated in 1997 at the IMF Annual Meetings in Hong Kong and killed off by the United States. Twenty years on, the power of the United States to prevent a mutual insurance arrangement among Asian countries is limited.

The governance of the global monetary order is in danger of fragmentation. In the evolving multi-polar world, there are few remnants of the idealism of Bretton Woods. The combination of free trade and American power was a stabilising force. As the financier and historian James Macdonald puts it, 'The unspoken bargain was that the United States would exercise a near monopoly of military force. However, it would use its force not to gain exclusive economic advantages, but as an impartial protector of Western interests. Under the American umbrella, the non-Communist world flourished.'[17]

The world of Bretton Woods passed away a long while ago, and with it the effectiveness of the post-war institutions that defined it – the International Monetary Fund, the World Bank and the Organisation for Economic Cooperation and Development (OECD). The veto power of the United States in the IMF, and the distribution of voting rights more generally, undermines the legitimacy of the Bretton Woods institutions in a world where economic and political power is moving in new directions. It is not easy for any multilateral institution to adapt to major changes in the assumptions that underlay its creation. The continuing refusal of the US Congress to agree to relatively minor changes to the governance of the IMF threatens to condemn the latter to a declining role. The stance of the IMF in the Asian crisis, its role as part of the so-called troika in the European crisis, and its reputation in Latin America mean that it is in danger of becoming ineffective. A key role of the IMF is to speak truth to power, not the other way round as it came close to doing in Asia in the 1990s and in Europe more recently. The United States is still the largest player in the world economy, and the dollar the dominant currency. But little else has remained the same. In Asia and in Europe, new players have emerged. China is now, with output measured in comparable prices, the largest economy in the world, returning to the position it occupied by virtue of its population size in the nineteenth century.[18] China and the United States will have an uneasy coexistence as the two major powers in Asia and, until a new more equal relationship emerges, uncertainty about the most vibrant region of the world will cast a shadow over economic prospects for the continent.[19] A multi-polar world is inherently more unstable than the post-war stability provided by the umbrella of the *Pax Americana*.[20]

Misguided attempts to suppress national sovereignty in the management of an integrated world economy will threaten democracy and the legitimacy of the world order. Yet, acting alone, countries may not be able to achieve a desirable return to full employment. There are too many countries in the world today for an attempt to renew the visionary ideals of the Bretton Woods conference to be feasible. For a short time in 2008–9, countries did work together, culminating in the G20 summit in London in the spring of 2009. But since then, leadership from major countries, the international financial institutions and bodies such as the G7 and G20 has been sorely lacking. They provide more employment for security staff and journalists than they add value to our understanding of the world economy, as a glance at their regular communiqués reveals. Talking shops can be useful, but only if the talk is good.

As time goes by, parallels between the inter-war period and the present become disturbingly more apparent. The decade before 2007, when the financial crisis began, seems in retrospect to have more in common with the 1920s than we realised. Both were periods when growth was satisfactory, but not exceptional, when the financial sector expanded, and when commentators were beginning to talk about 'a new paradigm'. After 2008, the parallels with the 1930s also began to grow. The collapse of the gold standard mirrors more recent problems with fixed exchange rates. The attempt to keep the euro together produced austerity on a scale not seen since the Great Depression, and led to the rise of extreme political parties across Europe.

A prisoner's dilemma is still holding back the speed of recovery. A sensible coping strategy to deal with this problem is not artificially to coordinate policies that naturally belong to national governments, but to seek agreement on an orderly recovery and rebalancing of the global economy. The way in which each country will choose to rebalance is a matter for itself, but it is in the interests of all countries to find a common timetable for that rebalancing. The natural broker for an agreement is the IMF. Our best chance of solving the prisoner's dilemma, while retaining national sovereignty, is to use the price mechanism, not suppress it. Arrangements to fix or limit movements of exchange rates tend to backfire as unexpected events require changes in rates to avoid economic suffering. At the heart of the problem is the question that so troubled the negotiators at Bretton Woods. How can one create symmetric obligations on countries with trade surpluses and trade deficits? The international monetary order set up after the Second World War failed to do so, and the result is that fixed exchange rates have proved deflationary. For a long time the conventional wisdom among central banks has been that if each country pursues a stable domestic monetary and fiscal policy then they will come close to achieving a cooperative outcome.[21] There is certainly much truth in this view. But when the world becomes stuck in a disequilibrium, the prisoner's dilemma bites. Cooperation then becomes essential. Placing obligations on surplus countries has not and will not work. There is no credible means of enforcing any such obligations. Enlightened self-interest to find a way back to the path of strong growth is the only hope. The aim should be fourfold: to reinvigorate the IMF and reinforce its legitimacy by reforms to its voting system, including an end to a veto by any one country; to put in place a permanent system of swap agreements among central banks, under which they can quickly lend to each other in whichever currencies are needed to meet short-term shortages of liquidity; to accept floating exchange rates; and to agree on a timetable for rebalancing of major economies, and a return to normal real interest rates, with the IMF as the custodian of the process. The leadership of the IMF must raise its game.

The two main threats to the world economy today are the continuing disequilibrium between spending and saving, both within and between major economies, and a return to a multipolar world with similarities to the unstable position before the First World War. Whether the next crisis will be another collapse of our economic and financial system, or whether it will take the form of political or even military conflict, is impossible to say. Neither is inevitable. But only a new world order could prevent such an outcome. We must hope that the pressure of events will drive statesmen, even those of 'inconceivable stupidity', to act.

The audacity of pessimism

The experience of stubbornly weak growth around the world since the crisis has led to a new pessimism about the ability of market economies today to generate prosperity. One increasingly common view is that the long-term potential rate of economic growth has fallen.[22] In the United States, there is no shortage of plausible explanations for such a change – the marked fall since the crisis in the proportion of the population who are available to work, slower growth of the population itself, and heavier regulatory burdens on employers. It is important not to be carried away by changes over short periods of time. The US Bureau of Labor Statistics (BLS) estimates the contribution to growth of increases in labour supply (hours worked), the amount of capital with which people work, and the efficiency of the labour and capital employed. Ultimately, the benefits of economic growth stem from this last factor, which reflects scientific and technical progress – 'multifactor productivity', in the phrase of the BLS statisticians. From the mid-1980s until the onset of the crisis in 2007, multifactor productivity rose at about 1 per cent a year.[23] Between 2007 and 2014, it rose by 0.5 per cent a year.[24] As a result, the annual rate of growth of output per hour worked – reflecting both technical progress and the amount of capital with which each person works – fell from just over 2 per cent between the mid-1980s and 2007 to around 1.5 per cent between 2007 and 2014.[25] If that reduction persisted it would affect living standards in the long run. But growth rates of productivity are quite volatile over short periods of time and it is far from clear that they represent a significant change to the future potential of the economy.

Is there good cause for pessimism about the rate at which economies can grow in future? There are three reasons for caution about adopting this new-found pessimism. First, the proposition that the era of great discoveries has come to an end because the major inventions, such as electricity and aeroplanes, have been made and humankind has plucked the low-hanging fruit is not convincing. In areas such as information technology and biological research on genetics and stem cells we are living in a golden age of scientific discovery. By definition, ideas that provide breakthroughs are impossible to predict, so it is too easy to fall into the trap of thinking that the future will generate fewer innovations than those we saw emerge in the past. When Alvin Hansen proposed the idea of 'secular stagnation' in the 1930s, he fell into just this trap. In fact the 1930s witnessed significant innovation, which was obscured by the dramatic macroeconomic consequences of the Great Depression. Alexander Field, an American economist, has documented large technological improvements in industries such as chemicals, transport and power generation.[26] By 1950 real GDP in the US had regained its pre-Depression trend path, and rose by 90 per cent in a decade after the end of the Great Depression.

Second, although the recovery from the downturn of 2008–9 has been unusually slow in most countries, the factors contributing to the growth of labour supply have behaved quite differently across countries. For example, in contrast to the US, the UK has experienced buoyant population growth and rising participation in the labour force. And even some of the periphery countries in the euro area, such as Spain, have recently seen rises in measured average productivity growth. The factors determining long-term growth seem to be more varied across countries than the shared experience of a slow recovery since the crisis, suggesting that the cause of the latter is rooted in macroeconomic behaviour rather than a deterioration in the pace of innovation.

Third, economists have a poor track record in predicting demographic changes. Books on the theme of the economic consequences of a declining population were common in the 1930s. A decade and a world war later, there was a baby boom.[27] Agnosticism about future potential growth is a reasonable position; pessimism is not. History suggests that changes to underlying productivity growth occur only slowly. Many economists in the past have mistakenly called jumps in trend growth on the basis of short-term movements that proved short-lived.

The case for pessimism concerns prospective demand growth. In the wake of a powerful shock to confidence, monetary and fiscal stimulus in 2008 and 2009 was the right answer. But it exhibits diminishing returns. In recent years, extraordinary monetary stimulus has brought forward consumption from the future, digging a hole in future demand. With a prospect of weak demand in the future, the expected return on investment becomes depressed. Even with unprecedentedly low interest rates and the printing of money, it becomes harder and harder to stimulate domestic consumption and investment. What began as an imbalance between countries has over time become a major internal disequilibrium between saving and spending within economies. Spending is weak today, not because of irrational caution on the part of households and businesses following the shock of the crisis, but because of a rational narrative that in countries like the US and UK, consumer spending was unsustainably high before the crisis and must now follow a path below the pre-crisis trend. In countries like China and Germany, exports were unsustainably high, and they too are now experiencing weak growth as demand in overseas markets slows. Neither individually nor collectively have those countries been able to move to a new equilibrium, and until they do, recovery will be held back. In circumstances characterised by a paradox of policy – in which short-term stimulus to spending takes us further away from the long-term equilibrium – Keynesian stimulus can boost demand in the short run, but its effects fade as the paradox of policy kicks in. Only a move to a new equilibrium consistent with the revised narrative will end stagnation. Low growth in the global economy reflects less a lack of 'animal spirits' and more the inability of the market, constrained by governments, to move to a new set of real interest rates and real exchange rates in order to find a new equilibrium.

Plotting a route to a new equilibrium is the challenge we now face. The paradox of policy applies to all countries, both those that previously consumed and borrowed too much and those that spent too little. Short-term stimulus reinforces the misallocation of investment between sectors of the economy, and its impact on spending peters out when households and businesses come to realise that the pattern of spending is unsustainable. China and Germany need investment to produce goods and services to meet domestic consumer demand, rather than to support the export sector. The opposite is the case in the United States, United Kingdom and parts of Europe.

Most discussion of this demand pessimism fall into one of two camps. On the one hand, there are those who argue that our economies are facing unusually strong but temporary 'headwinds' which will, in due course, die down, allowing central banks to raise interest rates to more normal levels without undermining growth. We simply need to be patient, and a natural recovery will then follow. As explained earlier, this view is in my judgement an incomplete and misleading interpretation of the factors that have produced persistently weak growth. A change in the narrative used by households to judge future incomes is not a 'headwind' that will gradually abate, but a permanent change in the desired level of spending. We cannot expect the United States to continue as the 'consumer of last resort' and China to maintain its growth rate by investing in unprofitable construction projects. Central banks, like the cyclist climbing an ever-steeper hill, will become exhausted. And if recovery does not come, they will be seen to have failed, eroding the support for the independence of central banks that was vital to the earlier achievement in conquering inflation.

On the other hand, there are those who advocate even more monetary and fiscal stimulus to trigger a recovery. To be sure, it is hard to argue against a well-designed programme of public infrastructure spending, financed by government borrowing, especially when you are travelling through New York's airports. But the difficulty of organising quickly a coherent plan for expanding public investment, while maintaining confidence in long-term fiscal sustainability, makes this option one for the future rather than today, albeit one worthy of careful preparation. Further monetary stimulus, however, is likely to achieve little more than taking us further down the dead-end road of the paradox of policy. More extreme versions of monetary and fiscal expansion include proposals for an increase in government spending that would be financed by printing money, and 'helicopter drops' of money into the pockets of all citizens. Radical though they sound, neither is in fact different in essence from the policies that have so far failed to generate a return to pre-crisis paths of output. Financing more government spending by printing money is equivalent, in economic terms, to a combination of (a) additional government spending financed by issuing more government debt and (b) the creation of money by the central bank to buy government debt (the process known as quantitative easing). Equally, helicopter drops of money are equivalent to a combination of debt-financed tax cuts and quantitative easing – the only difference being that the size of spending or tax cuts is decided by government and the amount of money created is decided by the central bank. Since both elements of the combination have been tried on a large scale and have run into diminishing returns, it is hard to see how even more of both, producing a short-run boost to demand that will soon peter out, will resolve the paradox of policy. Dealing with the underlying disequilibrium is paramount.

The narrative revision downturn, triggered by the crisis,

has left a hole in total spending. Central banks have, largely successfully, filled that hole by cutting interest rates and printing electronic money to encourage households and businesses to bring forward spending from the future. But because the underlying disequilibrium pattern of demand has not been corrected, it is rational to be pessimistic about future demand. That is a significant deterrent to investment today, reinforced by uncertainty about the composition of future spending. Since traditional macroeconomic policies will not lead us to a new equilibrium, and there are no easy alternatives, policy-makers have little choice but to be audacious. What should they do to escape the trap of rational pessimism? In broad terms, the aim must be twofold – to boost expected incomes through a bold programme to raise future productivity, and to encourage relative prices, especially exchange rates, to move in a direction that will support a more sustainable pattern of demand and production. Those aims are easy to state and hard to achieve, but there is little alternative, other than waiting for a crash in asset values and the resulting defaults to reset the economy. With the audacity of pessimism, we can do better. A reform programme might comprise three elements.

First, the development and gradual implementation of measures to boost productivity. Since the crisis, productivity growth has been barely noticeable, and well below pre-crisis rates. A major reason for this disappointing performance is that there has been a sharp fall in the growth rate, and perhaps even in the level, of the effective capital stock in the economy. Part of this reflects the fact that past investment was in some cases a mistake, directed to sectors in which there was little prospect of future growth, and is now much less productive than had been hoped. Some of the capital stock is worth less than is estimated in either company accounts or official statistics, or even in economists' models. Part reflects pessimism about future demand and uncertainty about its composition which has led to a fall in business investment spending around the world. Current demand is being met by expanding employment. Companies do not wish to repeat the mistake of investing in capital for which there is little future profitable use. If future demand turns out to be weak then it will be cheaper to adjust production by laying off employees. A higher ratio of labour to effective capital explains weaker productivity growth. Reforms to improve the efficiency of the economy, and so the rate of return on new investment, would stimulate investment and allow real interest rates to return to a level consistent with a new equilibrium. Over time, as investment rebuilt the effective capital stock, productivity growth would return to rates reflecting the underlying innovation in a dynamic capitalist economy.

Reforms to boost productivity are not a 'get out of jail free' card – they are easier to conceive than implement, and hit political obstacles from potential losers who express their concerns more vocally than the potential winners. But changing the narrative about expected future incomes is the only alternative to large and costly shifts in relative prices. And there certainly exist opportunities to boost productivity – in the product market to reduce monopolies and increase competition; in the tax system to reduce distortions between saving and spending, eliminate complex deductions and lower marginal tax rates; in the public sector to reduce the cost of providing public services; in the field of regulation to lower the burden imposed on the private sector; and more generally to improve public infrastructure to support the rest of the economy. The specific nature of the microeconomic policies required will vary from country to country. In the past, when economies were already close to full employment, politicians were reluctant to use up political capital to make structural reforms when the benefits were to be seen only in the distant future. Today, however, the attraction of reform is that the anticipation of higher productivity will boost current spending, helping economies to emerge from the present relative stagnation.

Second, the promotion of trade. Throughout the post-war period, the expansion of trade has been one of the most successful routes to faster productivity growth, allowing countries to specialise and exchange ideas about new products and processes. In the latest attempt to reach an agreement on further reductions in tariffs and other trade barriers, the so-called Doha Round (which started in 2001) of the World Trade Organisation has run into the sand. One of the impediments was the attempt by the larger emerging market economies to protect their domestic sectors. The best way forward now would be for the advanced economies to push further liberalisation in trade of services – the dominant part of our economies and a growing proportion of overall trade – not only to benefit from increased trade and its effects on productivity but also to demonstrate to the emerging markets that they cannot block all progress in this area. The US government, if not Congress, has been supportive of such initiatives, both among the Pacific region and with Europe. In October 2015, the US, Japan and ten other Pacific Rim countries signed the Trans-Pacific Partnership (TPP) which lowered trade barriers. It is now up to legislators to implement the agreement. A companion agreement between the United States and Europe – the Transatlantic Trade and Investment Partnership (TTIP) – is being negotiated. Those two agreements are an important part of any attempt to raise real incomes.

Third, the restoration of floating exchange rates. The experiment with fixing exchange rates has not been successful and it is important that exchange rates are free to play their stabilising role in order to correct the current disequilibrium.

The principle behind such a programme is to raise expected

future incomes, not by recreating the false beliefs held before the crisis, but by boosting productivity. Consider first those countries that have become reliant on exports to maintain full employment. Export-led growth is no longer a viable strategy for a large emerging market because Europe and North America cannot sustain the domestic demand required to import so much. China is committed to a gradual transition to domestic demand-led growth, as revealed by the Third Plenum in Beijing in November 2013. For this to occur, the high saving ratio in China must fall, despite a rapidly ageing population. Steps to provide more social insurance against future loss of income would raise current consumption, consistent with the required rebalancing of the Chinese economy. Its growth rate has fallen markedly from a peak of around 12 per cent in 2010 to below 7 per cent today, on the official figures, and the likelihood is that actual growth is much lower. China ceased to be self-sufficient in energy after 1993, and is now the largest oil importer in the world. Similarly, it imports massive quantities of iron ore, copper and indeed food. After the crisis, demand for Chinese exports fell away, especially from Europe, and so the Chinese authorities allowed credit to expand in order to boost construction spending. But before the crisis there was already excessive investment in commercial property. As a result, empty blocks of apartments and offices are a commonplace sight in new Chinese cities. House prices have now fallen. Rates of return on new investment in many parts of the economy are low.

A major challenge to Chinese policy-makers is to lower the high savings of state-owned enterprises. Falling profitability will reduce their surpluses, and so China's saving rate, but the reallocation of investment from exports and construction to enterprises geared to meet consumer demand will not be an easy transition. After substantial overinvestment in property, the necessary slowdown in Chinese construction activity will threaten not only demand and output, but also the health of the financial sector, which financed most of its expansion. Regional governments in China set up wholly owned financing vehicles to borrow from state banks in order to overcome restrictions on their spending imposed by the centre. Many of these are in poor health. China now faces serious risks from its financial sector. A policy of investing one-half of its national income at low rates of return financed by debt is leading to an upward spiral of debt in relation to national income. Sharp falls in stock prices in 2015 and a further slowing in growth showed how difficult it will be to achieve a smooth rebalancing, which is as important for China as for western economies. Even China, long associated with a policy of limiting upward market pressure on its currency, will find that its exchange rate comes under downward pressure.

Japan too has long exhibited 'excess' saving. After gradually restructuring its financial sector following a crash in the late 1980s, Japan has been recovering slowly but steadily from its 'lost decade'. Then in 2012, Prime Minister Abe launched his 'three arrows' of monetary easing, fiscal expansion and structural reforms to boost economic growth. Unfortunately, only one arrow seemed to hit the target – monetary easing – and Japan is now engaging in large amounts of money creation to purchase increasing quantities of government debt. In the absence of any serious structural reforms, Japan is on a path to inflation as the only means of reducing the burden of its growing national debt.

The change in policy required in Germany is rather different. By dint of wage restraint and the reform of labour markets, Germany has become extremely competitive within the euro area. It has an undervalued real exchange rate and a large trade surplus. Conversely, periphery countries such as Cyprus, Greece, Portugal and Spain – and to a lesser extent also France and Italy – have overvalued real exchange rates. If Germany were outside the euro area, its exchange rate would appreciate markedly, helping to rebalance its economy and boost consumption. Unless it finds a way to allow its real exchange rate to appreciate – by leaving the euro area or somehow engineering a much higher rate of wage inflation than in other parts of the euro area – Germany will find that continuing trade surpluses mean that it is accumulating more and more claims on other countries, with the risk that those claims turn out to be little more than worthless paper. That is already true of some of the claims of the euro area as a whole on Greece. Both China and Germany are discovering that being a country in surplus is a mixed blessing in a world that is on an unsustainable trajectory.

In those countries where the composition of demand needs to be rebalanced in favour of exports, finding a solution has been made more complicated by the weakness of the world economy. Following the crisis, households in those countries revised downwards their beliefs about future lifetime incomes. Consumer spending has moved to a lower trajectory. To compensate, exchange rates should fall to stimulate exports and encourage a switch to domestic substitutes for imports. But a slow recovery in the rest of the world, especially the euro area, has led to movements in exchange rates that are perverse in the light of the need for rebalancing. In 2015, the US dollar and sterling both rose. So policies to raise productivity will be even more important if the United States and the United Kingdom are to find a new equilibrium path on which it is possible to grow as real interest rates return to more normal levels.

Over time, and with sufficient investment to support it, a move to a new equilibrium will enable economies to regain their pre-crisis path of productivity.[28] Given the magnitude of the shock to the world economy after the financial crisis in 2007–9, that would be a significant achievement. In the nineteenth century, Karl Marx and Friedrich Engels saw the collapse of capitalism as inevitable – 'what the bourgeoisie produces, above all, are its own gravediggers'.[29] In their view, either the rate of return on capital would continually fall, leading to the end of capital accumulation and economic growth, or the share of capital in national income would continually increase, provoking the workers to revolution. There was no possibility of an equilibrium in which capitalists and workers would receive stable shares of national income. Such a pessimistic analysis fell into disrepute not only because its predictions were not borne out in reality, but also because after the Second World War economists devised theories to explain how stable growth was indeed compatible with a rate of return on capital sufficient to bring forth new investment and steadily rising real wages.[30] Moreover, those theories did conform to experience. The key to squaring the circle was technical progress: ideas for new products or new ways of improving existing processes. It remains key to our economic future because capitalism is about growth and change. It is a dynamic system. It is not a timeless board game in which, as in the textbooks, all we have to do is throw the dice and discover our economic fate.

Equally, there is nothing predetermined about the inevitable triumph of capitalism. Improbable as it seemed after the fall of the Berlin Wall, faith in capitalism has been badly shaken by subsequent events. To restore that belief is both necessary and possible. Capitalism is far from perfect – it is not an answer to problems that require collective solutions, nor does it lead to an equal distribution of income or wealth. But it is the best way to create wealth. It provides incentives for the innovation that drives productivity growth. Only when people are free to pursue, develop and market new ideas will they translate those ideas into increased output.

To restore faith in capitalism will require bold action – to raise productivity, rebalance our economies, and reform our system of money and banking. At present, the world's finance ministers and central bank governors, well intentioned and hard working, meet regularly and issue communiqués rededicating themselves to achieving the objective of 'strong, sustainable and balanced growth'.[31] Whatever can be said about the world recovery since the crisis, it has been neither strong, nor sustainable, nor balanced. There seems little political willingness to be bold, and so perhaps we should fear that the size of the ultimate adjustment will just go on getting bigger. But as Winston Churchill remarked in 1932, 'there is still time ... to bring back again the sunshine which has been darkened by clouds of human folly'.[32] We can roll back the black cloud of uncertainty and allow the rays of supply-side sunshine to peer through in order to return to a more balanced and sustainable path of economic growth.

Few of the above solutions to the current disequilibrium of the world economy are new, but the ideas that lie behind them are. Over the past half-century, mainstream macroeconomics has developed an impressive toolkit to analyse swings in aggregate demand and output. But by embracing so closely the idea of optimising behaviour, and by deeming any other form of analysis as illegitimate, it has failed to illuminate key parts of the economic landscape. Optimising behaviour is a special case of a more general theory of behaviour under uncertainty. And in situations of radical uncertainty, where it is impossible to optimise, a new approach is required. I have suggested a possible starting point with the idea of coping strategies; others will be able to take forward the study of macroeconomics under radical uncertainty – the economics of 'stuff happens' rather than the economics of 'stuff'.

Four concepts have run through this book in order to

explain the nature of financial alchemy and the reasons for the present disequilibrium of the world economy: disequilibrium, radical uncertainty, the prisoner's dilemma and trust. It is hard to think about money and banking, and their role in the economy, except in those terms.

In a capitalist economy, money and banks play a critical role because they are the link between the present and the future. Nevertheless, they are manmade institutions that reflect the technology of their time. Although they have provided the wherewithal to accumulate capital – vital to economic growth – they have done so through financial alchemy by turning illiquid real assets into liquid financial assets. Over time, the alchemy has been exposed. Unlike aeroplane crashes, financial crises have become more, not less frequent. Precisely because money and banks are manmade institutions, they can be reshaped and redesigned to support a successful and more stable form of capitalism.

Dealing with the immediate symptoms of crises by taking short-term measures to maintain market confidence – usually by throwing large amounts of money at it – will only perpetuate the underlying disequilibrium. Almost every financial crisis starts with the belief that the provision of more liquidity is the answer, only for time to reveal that beneath the surface are genuine problems of solvency. A reluctance to admit that the issue is solvency rather than liquidity – even if the provision of liquidity is part of a bridge to the right solution – lay at the heart of Japan's slow response to its problems after the asset price bubble burst in the late 1980s, different countries' responses to the banking collapse in 2008, and the continuing woes of the euro area. Over the past two decades, successive American administrations dealt with the many financial crises around the world by acting on the assumption that the best way to restore market confidence was to provide liquidity – and lots of it.

In appreciating the speed and violence of the market response to a collapse of confidence, they were following in the footsteps of earlier leaders. As Lloyd George wrote in his memoirs about the financial crisis at the outset of the First World War: 'I saw Money before the war, I saw it immediately after the outbreak of war. I lived with it for days and days and did my best to steady its nerve, for I knew how much depended on restoring its confidence and I can say that Money was a frightened and trembling thing.'[33] Political pressures will always favour the provision of liquidity; lasting solutions require a willingness to tackle the solvency issues. The same holds true when contemplating the lessons of the crisis for reform of money and banking. Banks need to finance themselves with more equity so that they can absorb likely losses without the prospect of default and taxpayer support. And I have suggested that to prevent runs on banks we should replace the traditional lender of last resort by a pawnbroker for all seasons. It is time to end the alchemy.

The prisoner's dilemma means that it will not be easy for any one country to solve the economic problem or reform its system of money and banking on its own. Changes in the way the world is governed take place more often after periods of war than in times of peace. Only in the former are the fissures that lie dormant in peacetime exposed as the economic and political tectonic plates shift. The experience of designing the post-war settlement was described by one of its progenitors, US Secretary of State Dean Acheson, in his memoirs as being 'present at the creation'.[34] To those of us involved in handling the financial crisis of 2007–9, it was more a case of being 'present at the destruction', as the financial system collapsed. After the longest period of steady economic expansion in living memory, the crisis destroyed the credibility of economic policy and the reputation of the banking system of the advanced economies.

The economic and financial crisis of the past decade has

cast a long shadow. As the eighteenth-century man of letters, Horace Walpole, said, 'the world is a comedy to those that think, a tragedy to those that feel'. The triumph of capitalism is that it has raised the pleasure of the here and now immeasurably for most of us, and we have a responsibility to share that around. Inequality is one of the most important challenges to our economic system, but it was a symptom not a cause of the crisis.

Fifty years from now, will our grandchildren ask why we lacked the courage to put in place reforms to stop a crisis happening again? I hope not. Events drive ideas, and the experience of crisis is driving economists to develop new ideas about how our economies work. They will be needed to overcome the power of vested interests and lobby groups.

Only a recognition of the severity of the disequilibrium into which so many of the biggest economies of the world have fallen, and of the nature of the alchemy of our system of money and banking, will provide the courage to undertake bold reforms – the audacity of pessimism.

Why has almost every industrialised country found it difficult to overcome the challenges of the stagnation that followed the financial crisis in 2007–9? Is this a failure of individuals, institutions or ideas? That is the fundamental question posed in this book. As a society, we rely on all three to drive prosperity. But the greatest of these is ideas. In the preface I referred to the wisdom of my Chinese friend who remarked about the western world's management of money and banking that 'I don't think you've quite got the hang of it yet.' I have tried to explain how we can get the hang of it.

For many centuries, money and banking were financial alchemy, seen as a source of strength when in fact they were the weak link of a capitalist economy. A long-term programme for the reform of money and banking and the institutions of the global economy will be driven only by an intellectual revolution. Much of that will have to be the task of the next generation. But we must not use that as an excuse to postpone reform. It is the young of today who will suffer from the next crisis – and without reform the economic and human costs of that crisis will be bigger than last time. That is why, more than ever, we need the audacity of pessimism. It is our best hope.

NOTES

INTRODUCTION

1 There was no need for him to add that neither has China.
2 Too many simple-minded critics of economics are scathing about its use of mathematics. But as the great British economist Alfred Marshall once wrote: '(1) Use mathematics as a shorthand language, rather than an engine of inquiry. (2) Keep them till you have done. (3) Translate into English. (4) Then illustrate by examples that are important in real life. (5) Burn the mathematics. (6) If you can't succeed in (4), burn (3)' (Marshall, 1906).
3 In a commentary on Goethe's great play *Faust*, Hans Binswanger wrote, in a conscious reference to Clausewitz, that 'The modern economy is a continuation of alchemy by other means.' (Binswanger, 1994, p. 33). Clausewitz's famous dictum was that 'war is a continuation of policy by other means'.
4 This is simpler than the classic prisoner's dilemma in which there are four pay-offs: acquittal, light, medium and harsh sentences. In that form of the 'game' the strategy of incriminating the other is the dominating one, whereas in my example there is some probability that silence will yield the best outcome.
5 Waley (1938), xii, 7, p. 164.
6 James Carville, reported in the *Wall Street Journal* (25 February 1993, p. A1).

1 THE GOOD, THE BAD AND THE UGLY

1 The expression was coined by Carlyle in an essay on the slave trade written in 1849.
2 Temin (2014) describes capitalism as a subset of the full range of market economies as they evolved over the centuries.
3 See Neal and Williamson (2014).
4 Smith (1776), pp. 4–5. British £20 banknotes issued after 2007 have on one side a picture of the pin factory.

5   Maddison (2004).

6   A history of UK exchange controls can be found in the Bank of England archives on http://www.bankofengland.co.uk/archive/Documents/historicpubs/qb/1967/qb67q3245260.pdf

7   In October 1973, in response to western help to Israel during the Yom Kippur War, the Arab members of the Organisation of Petroleum Exporting Countries (OPEC) plus Egypt, Syria and Tunisia proclaimed an oil embargo. By the end of the embargo in March 1974, the price of oil had risen from $3 per barrel to nearly $12. In 1979 decreased oil output in the wake of the Iranian Revolution caused oil prices to rise from around $16 to almost $40.

8   King (2007).

9   Federal Reserve Bank of St Louis and Bank of England, http://www.bankofengland.co.uk/publications/Documents/quarterlybulletin/2013/qb130406.pdf.

10 The Big Bang on 27 October had started as an anti-trust case by the Office of Fair Trading against the London Stock Exchange under the Restrictive Practices Act of 1956. The aim was to end the separation between brokers acting as agents for their clients and jobbers who made the markets, and to allow both foreign and domestic firms combining the two roles to become members of the Stock Exchange.

11 Those new financial products, such as derivatives, are explained in Chapter 4.

12 In the pre-crisis period banks also funded themselves in the short term by putting some of their assets in off-balance-sheet vehicles to which they offered a guarantee. Such contingent liabilities are a form of funding.

13 D'Hulster (2009), Table 2; Kalemli-Ozcan, Sorensen and Yesiltas (2012).

14 In the former camp is Gorton (2012), and in the latter are Admati and Hellwig (2013) and Taylor (2015). The latter states that 'The Global Financial Crisis of 2008 was fundamentally a credit crisis on a massive, international scale.'

15 Notable exceptions are Dumas (2010) and Wolf (2014).

16 In 1989 Francis Fukuyama published a famous essay 'The End of History?' in the international affairs journal *The National Interest*. He later wrote, 'What we may be witnessing is not just the end of the Cold War, or the passing of a particular period of post-war history, but the end of history as such: that is, the end point of mankind's ideological evolution and the universalisation of Western liberal democracy as the final form of human government.' (Fukuyama, 1992).

17 US Bureau of Labor Statistics website: Workforce Statistics on manufacturing employment; Eurostat website: employment and unemployment database, tables on employment by sex, age and economic activity.

18 World Trade Organisation website: Statistics Database.

19 The policy was relaxed at the end of 2013, and became a two-child policy in October 2015.

20 Bernanke (2005).

21   The fundamental drivers of high saving and weak investment that led to falling real interest rates are a matter for continuing research – see Rachel and Smith (2015).

22   Since the 1980s, it has been possible to measure real interest rates quite accurately by looking at how much governments have to pay to borrow in the form of securities (bonds) on which the returns are indexed to inflation. Such bonds have been issued by a number of industrialised countries over the past thirty years (King and Low, 2014).

23   Germany, with its own objective of promoting its export sector, was a notable exception.

24   Charles Dumas (2004, 2006 (with Chovleva)) provided an early analysis of this problem.

25   Its reversal was a striking feature of what came to be known as the Bretton Woods II international monetary system. Although some foreign direct investment did move from advanced to emerging economies, it was more than offset by financial flows in the opposite direction. This analysis of the Bretton Woods II system was first put forward by Dooley, Folkerts-Landau and Garber (2003). Those authors refined and extended the analysis in a series of papers over the following decade. A key part of their argument is that China wanted to lend large sums to advanced economies so that, in the event of a major economic or political disturbance, these claims would act as 'collateral' against the foreign direct investment made by the same economies in China. This made it possible for China to obtain the direct investment it needed to support development, and required China to run a large and continuing trade surplus. In any event, export-led growth meant that China had to invest overseas the proceeds of its trade surplus.

     Some economists have placed more emphasis on the gross flows of capital among countries, and especially within the advanced world, than on the net flows from emerging to advanced economies. The most compelling arguments were set out by Borio and Disyatat (2011) and Shin (2012). It is true that European banks invested more money in the United States than did China. But they also borrowed far more from American money market and hedge funds. Those gross flows of capital were recycling money that could have been channelled through the US banking system but were instead intermediated through European banks, which were eager to grow by granting new loans and acquiring assets, so expanding the size of their balance sheets. When the crisis hit, banks belatedly reduced their leverage and, as a result, gross capital flows between Europe and the United States fell sharply – by almost 75 per cent. But the driver of the fall in real interest rates, and hence in the rise of the prices of bonds, shares and houses, was the additional net saving injected into the world capital market by economies with high propensities to save and large trade surpluses, and the decision by central banks in the West to keep official interest rates low in order to maintain steady growth and an inflation rate close to target.

26   Shin (2012).

27 King (2006).

28 Other Asian countries had experienced the 'Asian crisis' in the late 1990s when borrowing by their banks in US dollars at low interest rates to lend at higher rates in domestic currency led to a currency mismatch in their banking system and so the need to turn to the West to borrow dollars, often with harsh conditions attached. They wanted to build up large dollar reserves as an insurance policy against the need to lend to their own banking system in a crisis.

29 I learned this from the late Rudiger Dornbusch of MIT.

30 BNP press release, 9 August 2007.

31 Lender of last resort support was extended to HBoS on 1 October 2008 and to RBS on 7 October 2008. The former facility was fully repaid by 16 January 2009 and the latter by 16 December 2008. The peak intraday lending by the Bank of England to the two institutions was £61.5 billion on 17 October 2008 (Review of the Bank of England's provision of emergency liquidity assistance in 2008–9, Report by Ian Plenderleith, Bank of England, October 2012).

32 Paulson (2010), p. 349.

33 The so-called Basel capital and liquidity requirements for banks are determined by a group of central banks and regulators drawn from the G20 countries. Much of this work is discussed in the international body encompassing the same group of countries and known as the Financial Stability Board.

34 World Bank Tables and author's own calculations.

35 IMF World Economic Outlook Database, April 2015.

36 The discussion of secular stagnation was revived in an important contribution by Summers (2014).

37 King (2009).

2 GOOD AND EVIL: IN MONEY WE TRUST

1 Created as one element of Britain's national memorial to President John F. Kennedy, the scholarships enable young British graduates to study at either Harvard or MIT. The other element was the gift of an acre of land at Runnymede, which is now US territory.

2 Maddison (2004).

3 One of the best descriptions of the corrosive effects on civil society of hyper-inflation in Central Europe in the 1920s is the autobiography of the Austrian writer Stefan Zweig, *The World of Yesterday.*

4 Keynes (1930). Goodhart (2015) provides an excellent discussion of the process of money creation.

5 Domesday was the Old English term for the day of judgement. Its contents are available on the National Archives website, www.nationalarchives.gov.uk

6 Smith (1766).

7   Smith (1776), p. 20.

8   Ibid., pp. 20–1.

9   Rae (1895), p. 49.

10 Ricardo (1816), p. 24.

11 MacGregor (2010), Ch. 72. There is a wonderful example of a later Ming dynasty banknote from the fourteenth century in the remarkable Citi Money Gallery of the British Museum in London.

12 Chinese banknotes of the early Ming dynasty carried the warning: 'Whosoever forges notes or circulates counterfeit notes shall be beheaded' (Kranister, 1989).

13 Following the application of the 1720 Bubble Act to the colonies in 1741, joint-stock corporations (which permitted many people to share in the ownership of a company operating on a much larger scale than any of the owners could individually afford) became illegal, which made banking operations virtually impossible. So no money was created by banks.

14 Johnson (1997), p.75.

15 In 1764 the British Parliament passed the Currency Act, which outlawed the use of all such paper money in the colonies as legal tender. But, as noted in the text, legal tender is far less important than the general acceptability of a currency, and the new bills circulated successfully in the colonies for a number of years. On that episode see Grubb (2015), Celia and Grubb (2014) and Priest (2001).

16 Franklin (1767) in Labaree, Vol. 14, pp. 34–5.

17 Massachusetts was, perhaps, an exception (Priest, 2001).

18 Harris (2008).

19 The proportion had been reversed by the end of the free banking era.

20 There were two episodes, in 1839 and 1859, in which convertibility into gold was suspended. But there were still discounts of the value of banknotes at a distance from head office from the par value that would be offered at head office.

21 Gorton (1989).

22 Data for 2014 from the respective central banks.

23 Goodhart is persuasive on this point (2015). There are also too many examples of the irresponsible encouragement of people on low incomes to borrow for one to be sanguine about the behaviour of the financial services industry.

24 Gibbon (1776), Vol. 1, p. 282.

25 Although when the British bank Northern Rock started to fail in September 2007, a surprising proportion of depositors who withdrew their money were prepared to leave a branch of the bank clutching a cheque drawn on Northern Rock itself.

26 Between the spring of 2007 and the spring of 2009 the demand for £50 notes rose by 28 per cent, double the increase for other denominations. See Bank of England statistics: http://www.bankofengland.co.uk/banknotes/Pages/about/stats.aspx#1

27 Bernanke and James (1991).

28   In 2013 the Freedom From Religion Foundation, a group of atheists, took legal action against the United States Treasury Department claiming that the inclusion of this traditional motto was unconstitutional on the grounds that whenever they used money they were being 'forced to proselytise' for a god in whom they didn't believe. The suit was rejected by US District Judge Harold Bauer Jr because the motto had a long-standing secular purpose, and didn't constitute a 'substantial burden' on atheists.

29   In 2009 the North Korean People's won collapsed in external value and its citizens were given a week to exchange old won for new notes that had two zeroes knocked off their value.

30   Roberts (2014), p. 771.

31   For a detailed study of the impact of the hyperinflation on the society and politics of Germany see Feldman (1993).

32   Using the modern definition of one trillion as 1,000,000,000,000.

33   For a magisterial history of inflation over many centuries see Fischer (1996).

34   For example, Holzer (1981) and Cato Institute (2014).

35   There were periods, especially in the nineteenth century, when some countries, including the United States, used a bimetallic standard linked to gold and silver. Fluctuations in the market price of one metal against the other made the system unstable, as the metal with the higher price tended to disappear from circulation. In the US, bimetallism ended during the Civil War.

36   Data on the gold price may be found on the Bank of England website and on www.kitco.com

37   Data supplied by Diggers and Dealers, Kalgoorlie, Western Australia.

38   Some of the gold in New York is held on behalf of overseas owners; other official US holdings are stored in Fort Knox.

39   In a delicious irony, it was exactly 200 years later, to the month, that the then Chancellor, Gordon Brown, restored the monetary independence of the Bank that had been taken away by Pitt.

40   Speech to the Democratic National Convention in Chicago, 9 July 1896.

41   Keynes (1923a), p. 172.

42   See, for example, Greenspan (1966).

43   Figures on gold reserves can be found on the World Gold Council website.

44   Friedman and Schwartz (1963), Friedman (1960).

45   Sims (2013).

46   Hahn (1982), p. 1.

47   Arrow (1951), Arrow and Debreu (1954), Debreu (1951).

48   If people are expected to renege on their contracts then the auction process will disallow bids that cannot be enforced. That will greatly reduce the benefits from trade. Ultimately it may mean that there is no possibility of trade between individuals. An efficient outcome requires that contracts are enforced.

49   O'Neill (2002), Reith Lectures, No. 1.

50   The idea of an economy comprising 'overlapping generations' was analysed by the great economist Paul Samuelson (1958).

51 The view that money can help to overcome the constraint of the double coincidence of wants and the implied restriction to exchange by barter was set out in detail by Carl Menger (1892), and was modelled explicitly by Nobuhiro Kiyotaki and Randall Wright (1989).

52 Kiyotaki and Moore (2002). Which came first – money or evil? To judge by the book of Genesis, evil appeared in the Garden of Eden before money. But it was not long, in the book of Deuteronomy, before the Lord commanded Moses, 'Ye shall buy meat of them for money, that ye may eat; and ye shall also buy water of them for money, that ye may drink' (Deuteronomy 2:6, King James Bible).

53 Hammond (1975) pointed out that the best outcome in such an overlapping generations model was a cooperative equilibrium of the intergenerational game. For the cognoscenti, in modern game-theoretic terminology, where each generation is represented by a single player, the equilibrium is sub-game perfect and renegotiation proof.

54 Willetts (2010).

55 Binswanger (1994).

56 In the debate over the Re-charter of the Bank Bill (1809).

3 INNOCENCE LOST: ALCHEMY AND BANKING

1 Hastings (2013), p. xvi.

2 *New York Times*, 10 July 2007.

3 When I became Governor of the Bank of England I decided to formalise a long-standing interest in such matters, and so, in conjunction with Charles Aldington (then of Deutsche Bank), I started a dining group to meet regularly and discuss key episodes in financial history. A short account of the Financial History Dining Club was published in 2015 (Aldington et al., 2015).

4 The bank holiday was announced on 6 March. On 9 March Congress passed the Emergency Banking Act. On 13 March, only four days after the emergency legislation came into effect, member banks in Federal Reserve cities received permission to reopen. By 15 March, banks controlling 90 per cent of the country's banking resources had resumed operations. But around 4000 insolvent banks never reopened.

5 Source: https://www.fdic.gov/about/history/3-12-33transcript.html

6 Figures are from the Banker Database: www.thebankerdatabase.com. Data are for end 2014.

7 Worldwide bank assets are the total assets of the largest 1000 banks in the world, as listed in the Banker Database.

8 The Banker Database, www.thebankerdatabase.com

9 The description 'socially useless' was used by Adair Turner, chairman of the Financial Services Authority in the UK from 2008 to 2013, in his Turner Report on the financial crisis in United Kingdom; The phrase 'doing God's work' was used by the CEO of Goldman Sachs, Lloyd Blankfein, in an interview published in the *Sunday Times*, 8 November 2009.

10   Figures from the Banker Database, www.thebankerdatabase.com, as of end 2014.

11   Because for any bank total assets must equal total liabilities, leverage can be measured by the ratio of either assets or liabilities to equity capital.

12   Brennan, Haldane and Madouros (2010).

13   I prefer 'too important to fail' (TITF) to 'too big to fail' (TBTF) as a description of the problem, because a small bank can be significant if it is highly interconnected with other banks or if its failure would be a signal leading to contagion to other banks.

14   Wolf (2010).

15   Bank of England (2009).

16   Bank for International Settlements (BIS), Derivative Statistics 2015.

17   Abbey National demutualised in 1989 and has survived as part of Santander UK.

18   That attitude was brilliantly captured in the book *Liar's Poker* by Michael Lewis (1989).

19   CCP Research Foundation estimates of conduct costs 2010–14, http://conductcosts.ccpresearchfoundation.com/conduct-costs-results. The estimate includes provisions made by banks of around $70 billion for future settlements of conduct cases relating to past behaviour.

20   Moggridge (1992), p. 95.

21   Keynes in a 1934 letter quoted by Chambers et al. (2014).

22   Bernie Madoff, former chairman of the NASDAQ stock exchange, for many years managed funds for private investors in which the money paid out was financed by new money coming in – what is known as a Ponzi scheme. He is estimated to have defrauded his investors of around $18 billion and in 2009 was sentenced to the maximum term in prison of 150 years.

23   Quoted in Alan Harrington, 'The Tyranny of Forms', *Life in the Crystal Palace* (Knopf, 1959).

24   This is not to say that accounting standards guarantee a fair and accurate description of the health of a bank (Dowd, 2015, Kerr, 2011).

25   The success of an investment in Berkshire Hathaway is in part the judgement of Warren Buffett and in part the fact that he does not operate his company as a hedge fund, which would typically charge an annual fee of 2 per cent of capital and 20 per cent of profits. Charges of that size drastically reduce the returns to the ultimate investors.

26   Bank of America Annual Report 2014, Table 6. Financial and other assets comprise holdings of equity, debt, securities purchased through agreements to resell (collateralised repos – where one party contracts to sell and then buy back an asset at an agreed price on a specified date) and other assets. Other borrowing includes short- and long-term borrowing as well as borrowing through collateralised repo transactions.

27   The standard analysis of a bank run when banks engage in maturity transformation was explained in a famous article by Douglas Diamond and Philip Dybvig (1983).

28 Macey, Jonathan R. and Miller, Geoffrey P. (1992).

29 An excellent account of the failure of the City of Glasgow Bank, and the subsequent legislation to remove unlimited liability, is contained in the Masters thesis of Thomas Ward at the University of Edinburgh: 'The Regulatory Response to the Collapse of the City of Glasgow Bank, 1878 to 79', Masters thesis, 21 August 2009.

30 *The Economist*, 25 October 1879.

31 This point was first made forcefully by Hellwig (1995).

32 The fate of money market funds and the response by the Federal Reserve is vividly described in Bernanke (2015).

33 The vehicles were also known as conduits or structured investment vehicles (SIVs). Their liabilities were known as asset-backed commercial paper (ABCP).

34 Bagehot (1873), p. 49.

35 Calomiris and Haber (2014).

36 The five banks are Royal Bank of Canada, Toronto Dominion Bank, Bank of Nova Scotia, Bank of Montreal, and the Canadian Imperial Bank of Commerce.

37 Although deposit insurance schemes are nominally supported by the banking system as a whole, in times of crisis, as in 2008, the government provides the finance to ensure that depositors can be paid.

38 See the account of the rise and fall of Enron in McLean and Elkind (2004).

4 RADICAL UNCERTAINTY: THE PURPOSE OF FINANCIAL MARKETS

1 Paul Lambert lost his job in February 2015, an event which, despite his own advice, took him by surprise.

2 Gigerenzer (2002, 2015), Gigerenzer and Gray (2011).

3 *Financial Times*, 13 August 2007; in other words, the moves in prices that he observed were twenty-five times larger than the standard deviation, a measure of dispersion, of the past experience of changes in prices.

4 Syed (2011).

5 Smith (2012).

6 This example as discussed in Gigerenzer (2014).

7 This is an example of the 'turkey illusion', originated by Bertrand Russell (1912) and popularised by Taleb and Blyth (2011), in which the turkey mistakes the pattern of being fed each day for a process that will continue for ever, and is caught unawares when, the day before Thanksgiving, the farmer kills rather than feeds the turkey. The failure to understand the context, or the model, of the process leads to a big surprise for the turkey, similar to the surprise many homeowners got when house prices stopped rising.

8 Letter to Frederick William, Prince of Prussia, 28 November 1770, in Tallentyre, S.G., (1919), p. 232.

9   Knight (1921).

10 Malthus (1798), Chapter IX. 7.

11 The Actuarial Profession, a body of life assurance companies and annuity providers, forecast in 1980 that a man who was 60 in that year could expect to live another 20 years. At that time, it was thought that someone who reached 60 in 1999 would live a further 21 years. But by 1999 the forecast was that a man of 60 would live another 26 years. Over a twenty-year period, expected length of life was revised up by 5 years.

12 Other sources of inefficiencies in a market economy arise from monopoly, 'externalities' (unpriced outputs, such as pollution) or public goods, which create a prisoner's dilemma in terms of how to fund them.

13 Samuelson (1937) and Houthakker (1950) showed that the assumption that rational agents would maximise expected utility could be derived from one basic axiom – the Generalised Axiom of Revealed Preference – that agents who choose among alternative outcomes A, B and C, and prefer B to C and A to B, would never choose C over A.

14 A good example is the bestseller by Levitt and Dubner, *Freakonomics* (2005).

15 Friedman (1953).

16 Gigerenzer (2002).

17 In the literature, this is known as the 'gaze heuristic' (Gigerenzer, 2014).

18 Keynes (1937a).

19 Although there is also no need to retain them in a world of radical uncertainty where coping strategies are about adapting to new environments, which may naturally result in decisions that appear inconsistent over time.

20 Kahneman (2011), Kahneman and Tversky (1979), Tversky and Kahneman (1974), Thaler (1991), Thaler and Sunstein (2008).

21 An early alternative to optimising theories was the idea of 'satisficing'. It is the rule of thumb of searching through a set of alternatives until one of them meets some threshold of acceptability rather than searching for the optimum among the entire set (a sensible approach to dealing with an extensive menu in a restaurant when one would prefer to speak to a companion), and was proposed by Herbert Simon (1956). Satisficing is one possible rule of thumb for a class of problems where it is relatively easy from past experience to define an acceptability threshold. An interesting application of the concept of satisficing to monetary policy, using the rigorous tool of viability theory, is Krawczyk and Kim (2009). For other problems, where past experience offers little guide, it is of less use.

22 Kahneman (2011).

23 Gigerenzer and Brighton (2009).

24 Tuckett (2011), p.13.

25 For an example of the latest research into heuristics applied to inter-temporal decisions – that is, decisions that have consequences at different points in time – see Ericson, White, Laibson and Cohen (2015).

26 Knight (1921), p. 227.

27 Gigerenzer and Brighton (2009); Gigerenzer (2014).

28   In his remarkably original (and long) book *Antifragile*, Nassim Taleb proposes a general approach to embracing the unexpected. The opposite of fragile, he argues, is not robust but antifragile, a system that learns from shocks. As Taleb puts it, 'A complex system, contrary to what people believe, does not require complicated systems and regulations and intricate policies. On the contrary, the simpler, the better. Complications lead to multiplicative chains of unanticipated effects.'

29   The standards are set by the so-called Basel Committee, comprising central bank governors and regulators of the group of G20 countries.

30   Aikman et al. (2014). 'Failure' is defined to include cases where it is judged that a bank would have defaulted without substantial government intervention of a kind not given to the generality of banks.

31   Shin (2009).

32   Tuckman (2015).

33   I am indebted, in a straightforward way, to Michael Pescod for this example.

34   Warren Buffett in his annual letter to Berkshire Hathaway shareholders of 2002.

35   For example, my own speech at the Mansion House, 20 June 2007: http://www.bankofengland.co.uk/archive/Documents/historicpubs/speeches/2007/speech313.pdf

36   See Tuckman (2013).

37   Knight (1921), p. 232. Arrow and Debreu themselves were well aware that, beautiful though their theoretical construction was, their achievement was to show that the conditions under which a competitive market economy was efficient were so restrictive as to be wholly implausible.

38   Grossman and Miller (1988).

39   The panel comprises between eight and sixteen banks, depending on the maturity and currency of the interest rate, and LIBOR is the average of the quoted rates after discarding extreme observations on either side.

40   Wheatley (2012), p. 30.

41   Similar improper and illegal behaviour was discovered in the foreign exchange market, and in 2015 a number of global banks were fined billions of dollars for their manipulation of the market.

42   The only sensible solution is to abandon LIBOR as a continuous benchmark rate and replace it with a rate on an instrument, such as an overnight official interest rate, not likely to suffer from the occasional disappearance of liquidity. Since such a large proportion of the existing stock of financial instruments uses LIBOR as the reference rate, a switch to an alternative would raise yet another prisoner's dilemma: no one firm on its own could change the benchmark for derivative contracts. A much-needed change will take coordinated action among market participants, prodded by regulators and central banks.

43   The three were Eugene Fama, Robert Merton and Robert Shiller.

44   Schumpeter (1942).

45   Keynes (1936), p. 156.

46   See Tuckett (2012), who argues, 'given that the prices of financial assets

cannot be set by fundamentals – which are unknowable – they are set by stories about fundamentals – specifically the stories which market consensus at any one moment judges true. And because which stories are most popular and judged true can change very much quicker than fundamentals, asset valuations can change very rapidly indeed.'

47 A microsecond is one millionth of a second. The story of high frequency trading is told by Lewis (2014).

48 At present, high-frequency traders can learn about the order flow for a stock by placing a bid, receiving a quotation for the price, and then almost immediately (in microseconds) reversing or withdrawing the bid. With an auction system, they would receive no feedback on the bid until the auction had taken place.

49 This dimension of the structure of trading on stock markets was analysed long ago by Admati and Pfleiderer (1988).

5 HEROES AND VILLAINS: THE ROLE OF CENTRAL BANKS

1 Jarvie (1934).

2 Keynes (1931).

3 Goodhart (1988), pp. 122–3.

4 The Federal Reserve Act was passed by Congress and signed into law by President Woodrow Wilson on 23 December 1913.

5 The former was the description of Sir Joseph Banks, the English botanist who was President of the Royal Society for over forty years; the latter is from the magazine *The Black Dwarf* of 31 March 1819.

6 Veto Message Regarding the Bank of the United States, 10 July 1832 (emphasis added).

7 Goodhart (1988), chapter 5.

8 The slogan is also the title of a 2009 book by Congressman Ron Paul.

9 In his opinion (Ruling 11-779C, 15 June 2015), Judge Wheeler found that the Fed's action 'constituted an illegal exaction under the Fifth Amendment' and that it 'did not have the legal right to become the owner of AIG'. But, he also ruled, 'the inescapable conclusion is that AIG would have filed for bankruptcy' without the bailout and 'the value of the shareholders' common stock would have been zero.' He declined to award any damages. The ruling could be appealed.

10 The concerns relate to Outright Monetary Transactions designed to bring down interest rates on periphery countries' sovereign debt. In 2015 the European Court of Justice (ECJ) ruled them legal, but the German Federal Constitutional Court (FCC) has yet to respond. Whatever the outcome, the respective powers of the FCC and the ECJ are far from clear, creating some uncertainty about the legal powers of the ECB.

11 Hume (1752). See also Smith (1776).

12 In 1992 the UK adopted an inflation target for the Treasury and Bank of

England together to achieve; independence in respect of monetary policy was granted to the Bank only in 1997.

13 Greenspan (2002).

14 Blinder (1995).

15 Gibbon (1776) Vol. 1, p. 346.

16 For a broader investigation of the independence movement among central banks see Crowe and Meade (2007).

17 'Just do it' is the phrase from the well-known Nike advertisement.

18 In a deep sense, only a complete understanding of the nature of the frictions makes it possible to decide on the objectives of monetary policy. Woodford (2003) and others discuss the link between that fundamental analysis and the proposition that monetary policy should aim to stabilise inflation and output.

19 The dual mandate was set out in the Federal Reserve Reform Act of 1977.

20 An excellent example is *Interest and Prices* by Michael Woodford (2003), which builds on the ideas of the Swedish economist Knut Wicksell one hundred years ago that the key to price stability lies in thinking about the appropriate path for future nominal interest rates.

21 The bill was introduced into the House on 8 July 2014.

22 For a discussion of the achievements of inflation targeting in reducing the level and volatility of inflation see King (2012).

23 The general confession in the Book of Common Prayer is 'We have left undone those things which we ought to have done; and we have done those things which we ought not to have done; and there is no health in us.'

24 Paul Volcker was Chairman of the Federal Reserve from 1979 to 1987, and was the architect of the reduction in inflation in the United States during that period.

25 Albeit that the appointments of Mark Carney and Janet Yellen in 2013 added a certain glamour that was missing from their predecessors.

26 In October 1993 Chairman Greenspan disclosed in evidence before Congress that transcripts of committee meetings were kept. Publication of transcripts began in 1994 with a delay of five years.

27 Friedman (1956). Some of the most important and imaginative analysis of a monetary economy is contained in Patinkin (1956).

28 By 'private sector' I mean any private sector person or institution other than a bank. If a bank sells bonds to the central bank, there is no increase in the deposits of the non-bank private sector that corresponds to something that one can call money.

29 The nomenclature reflected the fact that creating money to purchase government bonds effectively meant that the government did not have to sell as much debt to the private sector and so was 'underfunding itself', whereas the opposite was the case when extra bonds were sold to limit the growth of money.

30 An injection of money into the economy will lead those people who sold bonds to the central bank to spend some of the money they received on other financial instruments, pushing up their price and lowering their yields relative to yields on government bonds. The difference between the yields on

government bonds and yields on other financial instruments is called the risk premium or credit spread. Some economists, as a result, call QE credit easing.

31 Bernanke (2014).

32 Woodford (2013).

33 In tribute to the successful French Montignac diet, I like to call inflation targeting the monetary equivalent – Montignac monetarism.

34 Evidence by Sir Ernest Harvey to the Macmillan Committee in 1930.

35 Bernanke (2014).

36 Thornton (1802), p. 145 in the 1807 US edition published in Philadelphia by James Humphreys.

37 Cowen, Sylla and Wright (2009).

38 Evidence by Jeremiah Harman to the Committee of Secrecy on the Bank of England Charter in 1832, Minutes of Evidence, p. 154, response to Question 2217. Harman was Governor from 1816 to 1818 but gave evidence on behalf of the Bank.

39 *The Bankers' Magazine*, June 1866, p. 646.

40 Bagehot (1873), p. 51.

41 See also Mehrling (2011).

42 Hankey (1867), p. 24 of 1887 edn.

43 Ibid, p. 29.

44 Friedman and Schwartz (1963).

45 I expressed my concerns about the parallels with 1914 in a breakfast meeting with Niall Ferguson on 15 December 2006. As he later wrote in a circular for Drobny Associates in 2007, 'In his [the Governor's] view, it was perfectly possible to imagine a liquidity crisis too big for the monetary authorities to handle alone. As in 1914, governments would need to step in.' The two best accounts of the financial crisis of 1914 are Roberts (2013) for the story in London and Silber (2007) for events in New York.

46 Clark (1974).

47 Keynes (1914a), p.4.

48 Quoted in Fildes (2013).

49 Keynes (1914b), p. 473.

50 Grant (2014) and Silber (2007) differ as to the role of McAdoo in the closing of the exchange.

51 Quoted in Roberts (2013), p. 109.

52 Lloyd George (1933), p. 62.

53 Ibid, p. 62.

54 Keynes (1914a), p. 484.

55 Hargrave (1939).

56 Lloyd George (1933), p. 66.

57 The need to recapitalise the banks was at the heart of the policy discussions between the Bank of England and the British government throughout 2008. It culminated in the announcement on Wednesday 8 October 2008 of a major recapitalisation of UK banks (and a coordinated interest rate cut by the principal central banks).

And the turning point of the crisis was when the Americans followed the UK's example and announced that they would use the money reluctantly appropriated by Congress for the so-called Troubled Asset Relief Program (TARP) to recapitalise their banks instead. When that duly happened in the spring of 2009, following the stress tests of US banks, the banking crisis effectively ended.

58 MacGregor (2014).
59 Roberts (2013), p. 165.
60 Comptroller of the Currency, *Annual Report 1907*, p. 74, quoted in Silber (2007), p. 77.
61 Silber (2007), p. 81.
62 *Daily Gazetteer*, 7 April 1737.

6 MARRIAGE AND DIVORCE: MONEY AND NATIONS

1 Mundell (1961).
2 There is much more to an optimum currency area than considerations of trade and changes in competitiveness. Agreement on the objectives of monetary policy, and in particular on the importance of price stability, is essential to a happy union. Chari et al. (2013) have extended the economic calculus of monetary unions to include the benefits of associating with like-minded countries to insure each other against idiosyncratic shocks to market 'credibility'.
3 Colley (2014), pp. 9–10.
4 Mill, John Stuart (1848), p. 153.
5 http://www.nytimes.com/2014/11/15/world/middleeast/islamic-state-says-it-plans-to-issue-its-own-currency-.html
6 The International Organisation for Standardisation (ISO) lists 152 currency codes for official currencies; the IMF membership, adjusting for monetary unions, accounts for (with the addition of Cuba) 146 currencies – Table 2 of the 2014 IMF Annual Report on Exchange Arrangements and Exchange Restrictions.
7 Wales was formally annexed to England in 1542. The Acts of Union of 1707 created the Kingdom of Great Britain. The Acts of Union of 1800 incorporated Ireland into the United Kingdom of Great Britain and Ireland. Following the creation of the Irish Free State in 1921, and the resulting partition of Ireland, the United Kingdom of Great Britain and Northern Ireland came into being in 1927.
8 In the many discussions I had with colleagues in Europe, I was struck that more than one of them saw in European Monetary Union the opportunity to recreate the Holy Roman Empire.
9 The seven were Bosnia, Croatia, Kosovo, Macedonia, Montenegro, Serbia and Slovenia.
10 In practice the LMU ended in 1914, although some elements of its formal structure limped on until 1927; see Flandreau (2000).

11 Only after its nationalisation in 1946 was the Bank of England able to print notes depicting the sovereign. The first such banknote containing the Queen's head appeared in 1960. Coins were produced not by the Bank of England but by the Royal Mint, under the UK Treasury, and had depicted the sovereign for many centuries.

12 Mohr (2014).

13 Austria, Belgium, Finland, France, Germany, Ireland, Italy, Luxembourg, the Netherlands, Portugal and Spain were founder members in 1999. Subsequent joiners were Greece in 2001, Slovenia in 2007, Cyprus and Malta in 2008, Slovakia in 2009, Estonia in 2011, Latvia in 2014 and Lithuania in 2015.

14 Bagehot (1869), p. 9.

15 Jackson (2001).

16 This view was especially associated with Tommaso Padoa-Schioppa, a key adviser to Jacques Delors, President of the European Commission, and later a leading Italian central bank and government official. He was briefly finance minister of Italy.

17 Quoted in Alexander Woollcott, 'The First Mrs. Tanqueray', *While Rome Burns* (1934).

18 An excellent account of the birth of the euro is Issing (2008).

19 World Bank database.

20 Translation of letter from Archbishop Hieronymos to Prime Minister Papademos by staff at the Bank of England; the letter was posted on the website of the Archdiocese of Athens on 2 February 2012.

21 https://www.ecb.europa.eu/press/key/date/2012/html/sp120726.en.html

22 In January 2015, the Advocate General of the European Court of Justice stated that the programme was in principle compatible with the Treaty on the Functioning of the European Union, provided that it was for the purpose of monetary policy. It is not easy to see how purchases of the debt of some countries but not others can be construed as solely an act of monetary policy. The Advocate General also raised questions about the potential conflict between the ECB's roles in setting conditions for the eligibility of a country to join the programme and in deciding to buy sovereign debt.

23 Figures from Eurostat.

24 http://www.theguardian.com/news/datablog/2014/oct/02/crowdsourcing-youth-migration-from-southern-europe-to-the-uk. See also data from the respective national statistical organisations.

25 http://www.bbc.co.uk/news/world-europe-33535205

26 IMF Country Report No. 15/186, International Monetary Fund, Washington DC, 14 July 2015.

27 Connolly (1997).

28 If full-employment current account deficits (the trade deficit plus the net costs of servicing external debt) as a share of GDP returned to their 2007 levels then the external financing requirements of Greece, Portugal and Spain alone (ignoring Italy and France) would amount to 4.2 per cent of the GDP of Germany and the Netherlands (IMF WEO database, April 2015).

29 John Maynard Keynes, *New Statesman and Nation*, 10 July 1937.

30 Bergsten (2014).

31 Issing (2015).

32 'The German export success of German business also helps others in Europe ... The eurozone as a whole has a level external balance. Without our contribution, we would, in relation to the rest of the world, have a rather serious situation.' Wolfgang Schäuble, German Finance Minister, *Financial Times*, 30 June 2014.

33 The essay by Brendan Simms (http://www.newstatesman.com/politics/2015/07/why-we-need-british-europe-not-european-britain), which argues that political unions are events, not gradual processes, is persuasive in that, having moved to monetary union, the option of a gradual convergence and eventual political union in the euro area has been removed.

34 At no stage did the Kurdish groups lay claim to the Swiss dinar as their currency. They had no control over it, as shown by the interview given to Gulf News on 30 January 2003 by the Kurdistan Regional Government Prime Minister Barzani, who said, 'We don't have our own currency.'

35 Sources for this data include the United Nations (from the oil-for-food programme) and the Central Bank of Iraq.

36 Compiled by the Central Bank of Iraq, based on data collected by the United Nations World Food Program.

37 See Bank of England Museum (2010).

38 Although banknotes issued by Scottish banks are already in existence, by law they have to be fully backed by English banknotes – special million-pound notes printed by the Bank of England for this very purpose.

39 The experience of dollarisation is discussed extensively by Bogetic (2000). In the absence of its own currency, a dollarised country cannot print money to finance government expenditure. A spendthrift government may be tempted to abandon dollarisation and print its own money. In 2014, President Correa of Ecuador announced that it would start to issue its own digital currency. Panama minted its own coins – the balboa – in 2011 – and it is unclear whether these are fully backed by a combination of US dollars and the metallic value of the coins themselves. Several countries have adopted the euro, including Montenegro, which is not a member of the European Union.

40 There would also be no loss of tax revenues to a Scottish government. At present Scotland does not receive tax revenues on the profits of the large banks resident there, because as part of the United Kingdom it has no separate corporation tax.

7 INNOCENCE REGAINED:
REFORMING MONEY AND BANKING

1 Bagehot (1873), p. 158–9.

2 Blakey (1839), p. 4.

3   The book is attributed variously to Robert Blakey (by the British Library and the Bodleian), Thomas Doubleday (by Goldsmiths Catalogue, and Ashton, Fryson & Roberts, 1999) and Thomas Ainge Devyr (in a handwritten entry in the first edition in my possession). Robert Blakey was a radical politician in the North-East of England in the nineteenth century. He was the owner of the *Northern Liberator*, a radical Newcastle paper. Thomas Doubleday was a close friend of Blakey and was one of the main contributors to the paper. Devyr, an Irishman, was the paper's sub-editor. He later emigrated to New York to escape prosecution for conspiring to promote violent Chartist activities. Devyr's career was described by an American friend: 'he was a Nationalist in Ireland, a Chartist in England, a kind of revolutionist even in America. Anyway, he had only scorn and contempt for the politicians of America' (Adams, 1903). Blakey was prosecuted for seditious libel, eventually pleading guilty, and was bound over to keep the peace for three years. He closed the *Northern Liberator* in 1840.

4   Blakey (1839), pp. 58–9.

5   In today's money roughly equivalent to £5000.

6   In the UK, ring-fencing followed the recommendations of the Independent Commission on Banking chaired by Sir John Vickers, which reported in 2011, and in the US the Dodd-Frank Wall Street Reform and Consumer Protection Act of 2010 included the so-called Volcker rule, which outlawed proprietary trading for their own account by banks.

7   Basel Committee on Banking Supervision, *Regulatory Consistency Assessment Program Analysis of Risk-weighted Assets for Credit Risk in the Banking Book*, July 2013.

8   Bingham (2010) relates the story of a case in Britain in which neither the lawyers nor the judges realised that the relevant regulations applying to the case at hand had changed between the date of the alleged offence and the date of the hearing because there was no easy way of finding out.

9   Mansfield (1761).

10 Haldane (2013).

11 Information supplied by the Bank of England.

12 A comprehensive survey of proposals to end fractional reserve banking is Lainà (2015).

13 A six-page memorandum describing the plan was circulated confidentially by Henry Simons to about forty individuals in 1933.

14 Fisher (1936a, 1936b), Friedman (1960), Minsky (1994), Tobin (1985).

15 Keynes was nevertheless scathing about bankers. In his memoir of Keynes published by King's College, Cambridge, in 1949, G. Wansborough wrote: 'many of us will remember with what unholy joy we used to read in the *Nation* his annual review of the speeches of the Bank Chairmen, which he greeted, if I remember his words, as "the twittering of swallows to presage the end of winter".' He went on, 'his very brilliance of exposition probably frustrated to some extent the contribution he had to make to the formation of policy; and if he had been more tender of the susceptibilities of those in

high places, his wisdom would probably have brought practical advantage to this country many years earlier than it did.'

16 Cochrane (2014), Benes and Kumhof (2012), Jackson and Dyson (2013), Kay (2009, 2015), Kotlikoff (2010), Wolf (2014).

17 As proposed by Kareken (1986) and Litan (1987).

18 Although the Chicago Plan did not envisage the separation of a bank into two parts, the implication of 100 per cent reserves is that banks could not create deposits by extending loans. In economic terms, therefore, a bank would be in effect a combination of a narrow bank and a wide bank, with no ability to mix the financing of safe and risky assets.

19 The advantage claimed by Benes and Kumhof (2012) that government debt and interest would be sharply reduced relies heavily on the assumption that seigniorage income (the profit derived from printing money) would rise because the central bank would not pay interest on reserves. That is unlikely to be sustainable if public money is to survive on the same scale as private money at present, and paying interest on reserves is a feature of a growing number of central banks for purposes of monetary management.

20 Fisher (1936b), p. 15.

21 See the discussion in Holmstrom (2015).

22 Geithner (2014), p. 508.

23 Sedgwick (1840), pp. 104–5.

24 Bulow and Klemperer (2013, 2015) have been thinking about the use of collateral in the context of reforming the capital regulation of banks and the allocation of losses when banks fail.

25 Such assets could not also be used as collateral with other creditors.

26 A more sophisticated, albeit more complicated, measure of effective liquid liabilities would be to weight liabilities by their remaining duration. Short-term secured borrowing, such as in the repo markets, is excluded because if the lender doesn't roll over the loan the bank receives back the collateral which can be either sold to provide liquid funds, used to borrow from another lender, or taken to the central bank.

27 Institutions that appear to offer to redeem holdings of illiquid assets at fixed prices, money market funds and certain other fund managers, for example, should either make clear that redemptions will be at actual transaction prices or subject to the regulation of the PFAS – see Cochrane (2014).

28 Federal Reserve Board, Banking Statistics Table 5, return H.4.1.

29 Reserve Bank of Australia, Domestic Market Operations August 2015, http://www.rba.gov.au/mkt-operations/dom-mkt-oper.html#tiotb3ls

30 See the persuasive arguments in Admati and Hellwig (2013). In recent years, there has been much interest in the idea of creating new forms of debt that are 'bail-inable' – that is, convertible into equity – in the event that the bank crosses a threshold determined either by a regulator or a particular level of its capital ratio. The most interesting of these new instruments is the proposal for equity recourse notes by Jeremy Bulow and Paul Klemperer (2015), which is designed to provide incentives for banks to issue equity. Once markets

understand that such forms of debt really are bail-inable, and that the authorities will not hesitate to enforce that option, then it is hard to see, other than its potential to reduce a bank's tax liability, why the market would price such debt differently from equity. The decision in November 2015 by the Financial Stability Board to count bail-inable debt issued by other banks as part of the effective loss-absorbing capacity of banks is a backward step and weakens the system. Equity has the attraction that it absorbs losses without the intervention of a regulator to trigger the bail-in. Bank resolution would naturally go hand-in-hand with a greater reliance on instruments such as bail-inable debt or contingent capital. Problems will arise if such debt is held by other leveraged firms, because a bail-in to protect firm A could lead to problems in firm B and so on. Equity held by final investors is the only safe buffer to absorb losses. Moreover, all resolution regimes, being legal instruments, are inherently national in character. Banks are global in life and national in death. There would be enormous challenges in resolving global banks that spanned countries with different legal jurisdictions. The prospective failure of a large cross-border bank would, I fear, prompt telephone calls between political leaders to override regulators and prevent the closure of a well-known institution. The only satisfactory defence against failure is to finance with equity.

31 Admati and Hellwig (2013) recommend a ratio of 20 per cent or more. That could be a long-term objective.

32 Bank of England, http://www.bankofengland.co.uk/markets/Documents/smf/annualreport15.pdf

33 Rogoff (2014).

34 In the US bank robberies fell from 7556 in 2004 to 3961 in 2014 (Federal Bureau of Investigation Bank Crime Statistics, 2004 and 2014). The increase of cybercrime is analysed in the 2014 US State of Cybercrime Survey, www.pwc.com/cybersecurity

35 This system, effectively a public ledger of all current and past transactions, is known as the block chain technology.

36 Similar huge swings in prices can be seen in related digital currencies, for example Scotcoins in Scotland.

37 http://auroracoin.org

38 Although, unlike cash, transactions with bitcoins leave a permanent record in the software accounting system, leading commentators such as Brito and Castillo (2013) to describe them not as anonymous but pseudonymous. Money stored as bitcoins can also be stolen by hackers or lost through carelessness, just as cash is vulnerable to theft or loss.

39 Yermack (2013) provides data on the relative volatilities of the prices of bitcoins, gold and the major currencies. The volatility of bitcoins is an order of magnitude higher than the other currencies.

40 Economies of this kind have been discussed by Fama (1980), Hall (1983) and Issing (1999).

41 On money as a unit of account see Doepke and Schneider (2013).

42 Magna Carta, chapter 35, translation of the original Latin of 1215.

43 Hayek (1976). A theoretical discussion can be found in King (1983) and the response by Summers (1983).

44 The second possible problem with a free market in paper money is that, even with a common unit of account, new entrants can undermine confidence in existing monies. Suppose that we start with one paper money, which is called a dollar. The cost of printing a dollar banknote is at most a few cents. So the right to print money is very profitable, provided the issue does not have to be backed by real assets of equivalent value. Now suppose that other issuers are allowed to enter. If they can print currency with a face value of a dollar, they might be tempted to issue new notes backed by fewer real assets (whether gold or loans). If the market can correctly value these new notes they will sell at a discount, as in the world of free banking discussed in Chapter 2. But if consumers have difficulty in valuing the notes of different banks, or if by law they must exchange at par, then the new notes will be used to make payments and the older ones hoarded. The new entrants will earn large profits. In the limit, the supply of currency might expand until its value was equal to the cost of printing the notes. Bad money would have driven out good. This phenomenon is known as Gresham's Law, after Sir Thomas Gresham, a sixteenth-century British crown agent, who explained why debased coins issued by Henry VIII were circulating widely and the older coins had disappeared from circulation. That, of course, is exactly the aim of counterfeiters of official banknotes today, and it is why Mr Van Court's Banknote Reporter included information to aid the detection of counterfeits.

45 See the excellent recent book by Kay (2015).

46 A sermon preached to the annual service of Barclays Bank in May 1955 by the Reverend J. d'E. Firth who, as a pupil in 1918, took all ten wickets for Winchester against Eton (reprinted in *The Trusty Servant*, Winchester College, May 2010).

47 *Financial Times*, 19 December 2014.

48 Blakey (1839), p. 6.

49 Keynes (1936), p. 383.

50 Ibid, p. 383: 'Practical men who believe themselves to be quite exempt from any intellectual influence are usually the slaves of some defunct economist.'

8 HEALING AND HUBRIS: THE WORLD ECONOMY TODAY

1 IMF World Economic Outlook Database, Spring 2015.

2 Reinhart and Rogoff (2009).

3 Central banks have been referring to 'headwinds' regularly since 2008; for a number of years the Bank for International Settlements promoted the idea that the risks from rising levels of debt were a threat to stability and that the resulting crisis was a 'balance sheet recession' (see various of their annual

reports). Lawrence Summers, the Harvard economist and former Treasury Secretary, argued at an International Monetary Fund conference on 16 November 2013 that an age of secular stagnation, in which the equilibrium interest rate was negative, might explain the lack of inflationary pressure before the crisis of 2008 and the lack of growth after it.

4 Keynes himself described his work as a contrast to the 'classical' theory of economics. The counter-revolution is described as 'neoclassical' economics, but is in the same tradition as the 'classical' approach of Walras, Ricardo, Marshall and Pigou. More recently, there has been an attempt to integrate the two in a so-called New Keynesian model, which I discuss later in Chapter 8.

5 Keynes (1936), chapter 12, p. 161.

6 US Energy Information Administration.

7 There are many grades of crude oil, but two benchmarks have emerged, Brent and West Texas Intermediate, traded on ICE Futures Europe (formerly the International Petroleum Exchange) in London and the New York Mercantile Exchange (NYMEX) respectively. In addition, there is an active over-the-counter market in bilateral transactions.

8 Several theoretical papers have tried to express coordination failures in terms of an abstract game-theoretic description of an economy; for example, Cooper and John (1988) and, more recently, Angeletos et al. (2014). Such abstraction is not necessary to understand the coordination problem, even if its consequences are fundamental.

9 Krugman (2011).

10 Other path-breaking contributions were made by, among others, the American economists Tom Sargent and Neil Wallace.

11 Random shifts in the distributions generating shocks in a neoclassical model, termed 'extrinsic uncertainty' by Hendry and Mizon (2014), are similar to radical uncertainty.

12 Such models were described as 'New Keynesian' despite the fact that Keynes's view of recessions did not depend on the slow adjustment of wages and prices to external shocks and that the essence of Keynes, namely radical uncertainty and the resulting prisoner's dilemma, was absent from them.

13 They are sometimes described as 'dynamic stochastic general equilibrium' (DSGE) models, and have become the basis for much modern macroeconomics. In particular, the forecasting models used by central banks around the world to analyse monetary policy are New Keynesian DSGE models.

14 In practice, central banks also look carefully at survey estimates of inflation expectations and the behaviour of yields on index-linked government securities when making forecasts, but those forecasts revert to target for the reasons explained in the text.

15 There is room for debate over how many of the political events mentioned here could have been foreseen, and incorporated into model forecasts, and how many represented radical uncertainty. But the general point stands.

16 One view that most economists do not find compelling is that there are times in which people want to spend less and take more leisure, and periods

in which they want to do the opposite. The former are periods in which employment is low and the latter in which it is high. Business cycles are rational phenomena. Such models are called 'real business cycle' models.

17 Minsky (1975, 1986). He died in 1996, some twelve years or so before there was a resurgence of interest in his ideas.

18 See Gennaioli, Shleifer and Vishny (2015), and Eggertsson and Krugman (2012).

19 Such features are sometimes described as 'financial frictions', which gives the game away because they are seen as tweaks to a basically true model rather than posing a challenge to the model itself.

20 Keynes (1936), p. 96.

21 Keynes (1923a), p. 80.

22 Hicks (1974), p. 1.

23 The phrase the 'NICE decade' was used first in King (2003).

24 Inaugural Address of President Franklin D. Roosevelt, Saturday 4 March 1933. More modern discussions of the effect of lack of confidence on aggregate economic activity can be found in the work of George-Marios Angeletos (Angeletos et al., 2014) and Roger Farmer (Farmer, 2012).

25 Greenspan (2014), p. 44.

26 A perceptive discussion of why the post-war period experienced more stable investment growth than in earlier periods is Matthews (1960).

27 Davidsson (2011). In the UK reforms were instituted in the 1980s, and elsewhere in Europe introduced much later. For example, the so-called Hartz plan to make new job creation easier was implemented in Germany by Chancellor Schröder in 2003.

28 After re-unification of Germany in 1990, for a period Germany ran a trade deficit but over time this became a substantial trade surplus.

29 Borrowing against the increase in the value of your home, and using the proceeds to finance consumption, is described as 'equity withdrawal'.

30 One explanation of the Federal Reserve's statistical evidence was that it was drawn from a period in which many of the movements in house prices coincided with upswings and downswings in the economy. Those swings would be likely to have generated corresponding changes in consumer spending, which would be correlated with, but not caused by, changes in house prices.

31 IMF World Economic Outlook Database, April 2015.

32 Caruana (2014).

33 Turner (2014).

34 Taylor (2015).

35 King (2009).

36 Grant (2014).

37 Ibid.

38 Ibid.

39 See the minutes of the Monetary Policy Committee, especially during 2001. All MPC minutes are available at www.bankofengland.co.uk/publications/minutes/Pages/mpc/

40 As anticipated in King (2000).
41 See in particular the minutes of the MPC for January 2002.
42 http://www.bankofengland.co.uk/publications/Documents/speeches/2002/speech156.pdf
43 Consistent with this, those on the MPC most worried about the high level of the exchange rate advocated lower, not higher, interest rates in order to bring about a depreciation, at the risk of making the imbalances more acute.

9 THE AUDACITY OF PESSIMISM:
THE PRISONER'S DILEMMA AND THE COMING CRISIS

1 Bagehot (1873), pp. 138–9.
2 Standard and Poor's and *Financial Times*, 23 November 2015.
3 IMF World Economic Database, October 2015.
4 Reparations imposed on countries other than Germany were dropped rather quickly, given the state of their economies.
5 Keynes (1919).
6 Schacht (1877–1970) was not a man to hide his light under a bushel. He was President of the Reichsbank from 1923 to 1930 and again from 1933 to 1939, and later Hitler's Economic Affairs Minister. He was imprisoned for a number of years, and subsequently acquitted by a denazification court in 1950. Schacht was later immortalised by Liaquat Ahamed in his book *Lords of Finance*, about the four central bank governors (Schacht, Montagu Norman, Benjamin Strong and Emile Moreau) who worked together in the 1920s and dominated international finance during that period.
7 Schacht (1934).
8 Schacht (1955), p. 211. As he wrote, 'my opponents in this struggle [against foreign indebtedness] were as short-sighted as they were numerous' (Ibid., p. 217).
9 Benjamin Friedman (2014) has made this point forcefully.
10 John Maynard Keynes (1923b), *Collected Writings*, Vol. 18, p. 14.
11 Samuel Taylor Coleridge's poem *The Rime of the Ancient Mariner*, published in 1798, contained the line 'Water, water, everywhere, nor any drop to drink'.
12 The Five Presidents' Report, 'Completing Europe's Economic and Monetary Union', European Commission, 22 June 2015, Brussels.
13 Issing (2015).
14 Keynes (1923b), p. 41.
15 In economists' language, the equilibrium full-employment exchange rate for a country is, at least temporarily, below its long-term equilibrium level.
16 Rodrik (2011).
17 Macdonald (2015), p. 217.
18 If GDP is measured at purchasing power parity rather than market exchange rates, then China became the largest economy in the world in 2014.
19 A perceptive analysis was outlined by Paul Keating (2014).

20 Macdonald (2015).

21 Taylor (2014).

22 See, for example, Gordon (2016).

23 http://www.bls.gov/news.release/pdf/prod3.pdf

24 Weale (2015) reports similar data for OECD countries as a whole. Experimental data for the UK from the Office for National Statistics (http://www.ons.gov.uk/ons/publications/re-reference-tables.html? edition=tcm%3A77-386314) suggests that over the same period annual multifactor productivity growth fell from around 0.75 per cent to a negative rate. Estimates of negative growth rates suggest measurement error rather than technical progress.

25 http://www.bls.gov/news.release/pdf/prod3.pdf

26 Field (2012).

27 For example, Keynes (1937b) and Reddaway (1939).

28 Whether the pre-crisis path of total output (GDP) will be reached depends on the growth of population and participation in the labour force, both of which are notoriously difficult to predict (Goodhart et al. 2015).

29 Marx and Engels (1848).

30 See, for example, Solow (1956).

31 For example, the communiqué of the G20 finance ministers and central bank governors meeting on 9–10 February 2015 in Istanbul.

32 Winston Churchill, Speech to the Economic Club of New York, 9 February 1932.

33 Lloyd George (1933), Vol. I, p. 74.

34 Acheson (1969).

BIBLIOGRAPHY

Acheson, Dean (1969), *Present at the Creation: My Years in the State Department*, W. W. Norton, New York.

Adams, W.E. (1903), *Memoirs of a Social Atom*, Dodo Press, London.

Admati, Anat and Martin Hellwig (2013), *The Bankers' New Clothes: What's Wrong with Banking and What to Do About It*, Princeton University Press, Princeton, New Jersey.

Admati, Anat and Paul Pfleiderer (1988), 'A Theory of Intraday Patterns: Volume and Price Variability', *The Review of Financial Studies*, Vol. 1, No. 1, pp. 3–40.

Ahamed, Liaquat (2009), *Lords of Finance: The Bankers Who Broke the World*, Penguin, New York.

Aikman, David, Mirta Galesic, Gerd Gigerenzer, Sujit Kapadia, Konstantinos Katsikopoulos, Amit Kothiyal, Emma Murphy and Tobias Neumann (2014), 'Taking Uncertainty Seriously: Simplicity Versus Complexity in Financial Regulation', Financial Stability Paper No. 28, Bank of England, London.

Aldington, Charles, Peter Garber, James Macdonald and Richard Roberts (2014), *Financial History Dinners 2003–2013: A Memoir*, Printed by Blissetts, London.

Angeletos, George-Marios, Fabrice Collard and Harris Dellas

(2014) 'Quantifying Confidence', mimeo, Massachusetts Institute of Technology, Cambridge, Massachusetts.

Arrow, K.J. (1951), 'An Extension of the Basic Theorems of Classical Welfare Economics', in *Proceedings of the Second Berkeley Symposium on Mathematical Statistics and Probability*, J. Neyman (ed.), Berkeley: University of California Press, pp. 507–32.

Arrow, K.J. and Debreu, G. (1954) 'Existence of an Equilibrium for a Competitive Economy', *Econometrica*, Vol. 22, pp. 265–90.

Ashton, Owen, Robert Fyson and Stephen Roberts (1999), *The Chartist Legacy*, Merlin Press, Suffolk.

Bagehot, Walter (1869), *A Universal Money*, reprinted in 'The Collected Works of Walter Bagehot', *The Economist*, 1965.

—— (1873), *Lombard Street: A Description of the Money Market*, Henry S. King and Co., London.

Bank of England (2009), 'Financial Stability Report', June 2009, available at http://www.bankofengland.co.uk/publications/fsr/2009/fsrfull0906.pdf

Bank of England Museum (2010), *La Caisse Centrale de la France Libre: De Gaulle's Bank in London*, Governor and Company of the Bank of England, London.

Benes, Jaromir and Michael Kumhof (2012), 'The Chicago Plan Revisited', IMF Working Paper 12/202, mimeo, Washington.

Bergsten, C. Fred (2014) 'Germany and the Euro: The Revenge of Helmut Schmidt', Kurt Viermetz Lecture, American Academy of Berlin, 5 June 2014.

Bernanke, Ben (2005), 'The Global Savings Glut and the US Current Account Deficit', Sandbridge Lecture, Virginia Association of Economists, 10 March.

—— (2014), 'Central Banking After the Great Recession:

Lessons Learned and Challenges Ahead', Discussion at the Brookings Institution, 16 January 2014.

—— (2015), *The Courage to Act: A Memoir of a Crisis and Its Aftermath*, W.W. Norton, New York.

Bernanke, Ben and Harold James (1991), 'The Gold Standard, Deflation, and Financial Crisis in the Great Depression: An International Comparison', pp. 33–68 in R. Glenn Hubbard (ed.), *Financial Markets and Financial Crises*, University of Chicago Press, Chicago.

Bingham, Tom (2010), *The Rule of Law*, Penguin, London.

Binswanger, Hans (1994), *Money and Magic*, University of Chicago Press, Chicago.

Blakey, Robert (1839), *The Political Pilgrim's Progress*, John Bell, Newcastle-upon-Tyne.

Blinder, Alan (1995), 'The Strategy of Monetary Policy', *The Region*, Federal Reserve Bank of Minneapolis, 1 September 1995.

—— (1998), *Central Banking in Theory and Practice*, MIT Press, Cambridge, Massachusetts.

Bogetic, Zeljko (2000), 'Official Dollarization: Current Experiences and Issues', *Cato Journal,* Vol. 20, No. 2, pp. 179–213.

Borio, Claudio and Piti Disyatat (2011), 'Global Imbalances and the Financial Crisis: Link or No Link?', BIS Working Paper No. 346, Basel, Switzerland.

Brennan, Simon, Andrew Haldane and Vasileios Madouros (2010), 'The Contribution of the Financial Sector Miracle or Mirage?', London School of Economics Report on the Future of Finance, London.

Brito, Jerry and Andrea Castillo (2013), 'Bitcoin: A Primer for Policymakers', Mercatus Center, George Mason University, Arlington, Virginia.

Bulow, Jeremy and Paul Klemperer (2013), 'Market-Based

Bank Capital Regulation', mimeo, University of Oxford, Oxford.

—— (2015), 'Equity Recourse Notes: Creating Counter-cyclical Bank Capital', mimeo, University of Oxford, Oxford.

Calomiris, Charles and Stephen Haber (2014), *Fragile By Design: The Political Origins of Banking Crises and Scarce Credit*, Princeton University Press, Princeton, New Jersey.

Carlyle, Thomas (1849), 'Occasional Discourse on the Negro Question', *Fraser's Magazine for Town and Country*, Vol. X, p. 672.

Caruana, Jaime (2014), 'Debt: The View from Basel', *BIS Papers* No. 80, Bank for International Settlements, Basel.

Cato Institute (2014), http://object.cato.org/sites/cato.org/files/serials/files/cato-journal/2014/5/cato-journal-v34n2-14.pdf

Celia, Jim and Farley Grubb (2014), 'Non-Legal-Tender Paper Money: The Structure and Performance of Maryland's Bills of Credit, 1767–1775', National Bureau of Economic Research Working Paper 20524, mimeo, Cambridge, Massachusetts.

Chambers, David, Elroy Dimson and Justin Foo (2014), 'Keynes, King's and Endowment Asset Management', National Bureau of Economic Research Working Paper 20421, mimeo, Cambridge, Massachussetts.

Chari, V.V., Alessandro Dovis and Patrick J. Kehoe (2013), 'Rethinking Optimal Currency Areas', Federal Reserve Bank of Minneapolis Research Department Staff Report, mimeo.

Clark, Kenneth (1974), *Another Part of the Wood: A Self Portrait*, Harper and Row, London and New York.

Cobbett, William (1828), *Paper Against Gold*, W. Cobbett, London.

Cochrane, John H. (2014), 'Toward a Run-Free Financial System', in (eds.) Baily, Martin and John Taylor, *Across the Great Divide: New Perspectives on the Financial Crisis*, Hoover Press, Stanford.

Colley, Linda (2014), *Acts of Union and Disunion*, Profile Books, London.

Connolly, Bernard (1997), 'Kohl's Compromise Won't Satisfy French Demands', *Wall Street Journal*, 5 June.

Cooper, Russell and Andrew John (1988), 'Coordinating Coordination Failures in Keynesian Models', *Quarterly Journal of Economics*, Vol. 103, No. 3, pp. 441–63.

Cowen, David, Richard Sylla and Robert Wright (2006), 'Alexander Hamilton, Central Banker: Crisis Management During the U.S. Financial Panic of 1972', *Business History Review*, Vol. 83, No. 1, pp. 61–86.

Cowen, Tyler (2011), 'The Great Stagnation: How America Ate All the Low-Hanging Fruit of Modern History, Got Sick, and Will (Eventually) Feel Better', Penguin eSpecial.

Crowe, Christopher and Ellen Meade (2007), 'The Evolution of Central Bank Governance around the World', *Journal of Economic Perspectives*, Vol. 21, No. 4, pp. 69–90.

Davidsson, Johan Bo (2011), 'An Analytical Overview of Labour Market Reforms Across the EU: Making Sense of the Variation', European University Institute, mimeo.

Debreu, G. (1951), 'The Coefficient of Resource Utilization', *Econometrica*, Vol. 19, pp. 273–92.

D'Hulster, Katia (2009), 'The Leverage Ratio', Crisis Report Note: number 11, World Bank, Washington DC.

Diamond, D.W. and P.H. Dybvig (1983), 'Bank Runs, Deposit Insurance, and Liquidity', *The Journal of Political Economy*, Vol. 91, No. 3, pp. 401–19.

Doepke, Matthias and Martin Schneider (2013), 'Money as a Unit

of Account', mimeo, http://faculty.wcas.northwestern
.edu/~mdo738/research/Doepke_Schneider_1013.pdf

Dooley, Michael, David Folkerts-Landau and Peter Garber
(2003), 'An Essay on the Revived Bretton-Woods System',
National Bureau of Economic Research Working Paper
9971, Cambridge, Massachusetts.

Dowd, Kevin (2015), 'Central Bank Stress Tests: Mad, Bad,
and Dangerous', *Cato Journal*, Vol. 35, No. 3, pp. 507–24.

—— (2015), *No Stress: The Flaws in the Bank of England's Stress
Testing Programme*, Adam Smith Research Trust, London.

Dumas, Charles (2004), 'US Balance Sheets Serially Trashed
by Eurasian Surplus', Lombard Street Research *Monthly
International Review*, No. 143, London.

—— (2010), *Globalization Fractures: How Major Nations' Interests
Are Now In Conflict*, Profile Books, London.

Dumas, Charles and Diana Choyleva (2006), *The Bill from the
China Shop*, Profile Books, London.

Eggertsson, Gauti and Paul Krugman (2012), 'Debt,
Deleveraging, and the Liquidity Trap: A Fisher-Minsky-
Koo Approach', *Quarterly Journal of Economics*, Vol. 127,
No. 3, pp. 1469–1513.

Ericson, Keith, John White, David Laibson and Jonathan Cohen
(2015), 'Money Early or Later? Simple Heuristics Explain
Intertemporal Choices Better Than Delay Discounting',
National Bureau of Economic Research Working Paper
20948, mimeo, Cambridge, Massachusetts.

Fama, Eugene (1980), 'Banking in the Theory of Finance',
Journal of Monetary Economics, Vol. 6, No. 2, pp. 39–57.

Farmer, Roger (2012), 'Confidence Crashes and Animal
Spirits', *Economic Journal*, Vol. 122, pp. 155–172.

Feldman, Gerald (1993), *The Great Disorder: Politics, Economics,
and Society in the German Inflation 1914–1924*, Oxford
Books, New York.

Field, Alexander J. (2012), *A Great Leap Forward: 1930s Depression and U.S. Economic Growth*, Yale University Press, New Haven.

Fildes, Christopher (2013), 'Review of *Saving the City* by Richard Roberts', mimeo.

Fischer, David H. (1996), *The Great Wave: Price Revolution and the Rhythm of History*, Oxford University Press, New York.

Fischer, Stanley (2014), 'The Great Recession: Moving Ahead', speech in Stockholm, Board of Governors of the Federal Reserve System, 11 August 2014.

—— (2014), 'The Federal Reserve and the Global Economy', Per Jacobsson Foundation Lecture, Annual Meetings of the International Monetary Fund and the World Bank Group, 11 October 2014.

Fisher, Irving (1936a), *100% Money*, second edition, Adelphi Company, New York.

—— (1936b), '100% Money and the Public Debt', *Economic Forum*, April-June, pp. 406–20.

Flandreau, Marc (2000), 'The Economics and Politics of Monetary Unions: A Reassessment of the Latin Monetary Union, 1865–1871', *Financial History Review*, Vol. 7, No. 1, pp. 25–44.

Franklin, Benjamin (1767), *The Papers of Benjamin Franklin, Volume 14*, ed. Leonard Labaree, Yale University Press, New Haven, 1970.

Friedman, Benjamin (2014), 'A Predictable Pathology', Keynote Address at the BIS Annual Conference, Lucerne, Switzerland, 27 June 2014.

Friedman, Milton (1953), *Essays in Positive Economics, I – The Methodology of Positive Economics,* University of Chicago Press, Chicago.

—— (1956), 'The Quantity Theory of Money – A Restatement', in M. Friedman (ed.), *Studies in the Quantity*

Theory of Money, University of Chicago Press, Chicago, pp. 3–21.

——— (1960), *A Program for Monetary Stability*, Fordham University Press, New York.

Friedman, Milton and Anna Schwartz (1963), *A Monetary History of the United States, 1867–1960*, Princeton University Press, Princeton, New Jersey.

Fukuyama, Francis (1992), *The End of History and the Last Man*, Free Press, New York.

Geithner, Timothy (2014), *Stress Tests: Reflections on Financial Crises*, Crown Publishers, New York.

Gennaioli, Nicola, Andrei Shleifer and Robert Vishny (2015), 'Neglected Risks: The Psychology of Financial Crises', National Bureau of Economic Research Working Paper 20875, mimeo, Cambridge, Massachusetts.

Gibbon, Edward (1776), *The History of the Decline and Fall of the Roman Empire*, page number references to the Everyman edition of 1993, Random House, London.

Gigerenzer, Gerd (2002), *Calculated Risks: How to Know When Numbers Deceive You,* Simon and Schuster, New York.

——— (2007), *Gut Feelings: The Intelligence of the Unconscious*, Viking Books, New York.

——— (2014), *Risk Savvy: How to Make Good Decisions*, Allen Lane, London.

——— (2015), *Simply Rational*, Oxford University Press, Oxford.

Gigerenzer, Gerd and Henry Brighton (2009), 'Homo Heuristicus: Why Biased Minds Make Better Inferences', *Topics in Cognative Science*, Vol. 1, pp. 107–143.

Gigerenzer, Gerd and Muir Gray eds. (2011), *Better Doctors, Better Patients, Better Decisions*, MIT Press, Cambridge, Massachusetts.

Goodhart, Charles (1988), *The Evolution of Central Banks*, MIT Press, Cambridge, Massachusetts.

—— (2015), 'The Determination of the Quantity of Bank Deposits', London School of Economics, mimeo.

Goodhart, Charles, Manoj Pradhan and Pratyancha Pardeshi (2015), 'Could Demographics Reverse Three Multi-Decade Trends?', Morgan Stanley Research Global Economics, mimeo.

Gordon, Robert J. (2012), 'Is US Economic Growth Over? Faltering Innovation Confronts the Six Headwinds', National Bureau of Economic Research Working Paper 18315, Cambridge, Massachusetts.

—— (2016) *The Rise and Fall of American Growth: The U.S. Standard of Living since the Civil War*, Princeton University Press, Princeton, New Jersey.

Gorton, Gary B. (1989), 'Public Policy and the Evolution of Banking Markets', in *Bank System Risk: Charting a New Course*, Proceedings of a Conference on Bank Structure and Competition, Federal Reserve Bank of Chicago, pp. 233–52.

—— (2012), *Misunderstanding Financial Crises*, Oxford University Press, Oxford.

Grant, James (2014), *The Forgotten Depression: 1921: The Crash That Cured Itself*, Simon and Schuster, New York.

Greenspan, Alan (1966), 'Gold and Economic Freedom', *The Objectivist*.

—— (2002), 'Transparency in Monetary Policy,' *Federal Reserve of St Louis Review*, Vol. 84, No. 4, July/August, pp. 5–6.

—— (2014), *The Map and the Territory 2.0: Risk, Human Nature and the Future of Forecasting*, Penguin Press, New York.

Grossman, Sanford and Merton Miller (1988), 'Liquidity and Market Structure', *Journal of Finance*, Vol. 43, No. 3, pp. 617–33.

Grubb, Farley (2015), 'Is Paper Money Just Paper Money? Experimentation and Local Variation in the Fiat Paper Monies Issued by the Colonial Governments of British North America, 1690–1775: Part I', Working Paper Series 2015-07, Department of Economics, University of Delaware, mimeo.

Hahn, Frank (1982), *Money and Inflation*, MIT Press, Cambridge, Massachusetts.

Haldane, Andrew G. (2013), 'Turning the Red Tape Tide', Speech at the International Financial Law Review Dinner, Bank of England, London.

Hall, Robert (1983), 'Optimal Fiduciary Monetary Systems', *Journal of Monetary Economics*, Vol. 12, No. 1, pp. 33–50.

Hammond, Peter J. (1975), 'Charity: Altruism or Cooperative Egoism?' in E.S. Phelps (ed.), *Altruism, Morality, and Economic Theory*, Russell Sage Foundation, New York, pp. 115–131.

Hankey, Thomson (1867), *The Principles of Banking*, Effingham Wilson, London (page references to the 1887 fourth edition reprinted in 2006 by Elibron Classics).

Hargrave, John (1939), *Professor Skinner alias Montagu Norman*, Wells Gardner, Darton & Co Ltd, London.

Harris, William (ed.) (2008), *Monetary Systems of the Greeks and Romans*, Oxford University Press, New York.

Hastings, Max (2013), *Catastrophe*, William Collins, London.

Hayek, Friedrich (1976), *The Denationalization of Money*, Institute of Economic Affairs, London.

Hayward, Ian (ed.) (1999), *Chartist Fiction: Thomas Doubleday, 'The Pilgrim's Progress' and Thomas Martin Wheeler, 'Sunshine And Shadow'*, Ashgate Publishing, London.

Hellwig, Martin (1995), 'Systemic Aspects of Risk Management in Banking and Finance', *Swiss Journal of Economics and Statistics*, Vol. 131, Issue IV, pp. 723–37.

Hendry, David and Grayham Mizon (2014a), 'Unpredictability in Economic Analysis, Econometric Modeling and Forecasting', *Journal of Econometrics*, Vol. 182, No. 1, pp. 186–95.

—— (2014b), 'Why DSGEs Crash During Crises', http://www. voxeu.org/article/why-standard-macro-models-fail-crises

Hicks, John R. (1937), 'Mr. Keynes and the "Classics": A Suggested Interpretation', *Econometrica*, Vol. 5, No.2, pp. 147–59.

—— (1974), *The Crisis in Keynesian Economics*, Basil Blackwell, Oxford.

Holmstrom, Bengt (2015), 'Understanding the Role of Debt in the Financial System', BIS Working Paper No. 479, mimeo, Basel, Switzerland.

Holzer, Henry (1981), *Government's Money Monopoly*, Books in Focus, New York.

Houthakker, Hendrik (1950), 'Revealed Preference and the Utility Function', *Economica*, New Series, Vol. 17, No. 66, pp. 159–74.

Hume, David (1752), 'Of Money' in *Political Discourses*, A. Kincaid, Edinburgh.

Hunter, William W. (1868), *The Annals of Rural Bengal*, second edition, Smith, Elder and Co., London.

Issing, Otmar (1999), 'Hayek – Currency Competition and European Monetary Union', Speech at the Annual Memorial Lecture hosted by the Institute of Economics Affairs, London, 27 May 1999.

—— (2008), *The Birth of the Euro,* Cambridge University Press, Cambridge.

—— (2015), 'Completing the Unfinished House: Towards a Genuine Economic and Monetary Union?', Center for Financial Studies Working Paper 521, Frankfurt, forthcoming in *International Finance*.

Jackson, Andrew and Ben Dyson (2013), *Modernizing Money: Why Our Monetary System is Broken and How it Can be Fixed*, Positive Money, London.

Jackson, Julian (2001), *France: The Dark Years 1940–44*, Oxford University Press.

Jarvie, J.R. (1934), *The Old Lady Unveiled: A Criticism and Explanation of the Bank of England*, Wishart & Company, London.

Johnson, Paul (1997), *A History of the American People*, Weidenfeld and Nicolson, London.

Kahneman, Daniel (2011), *Thinking, Fast and Slow*, Farrar, Straus and Giroux, New York.

Kahneman, Daniel and Amos Tversky (1979), 'Prospect Theory: An Analysis of Decision under Risk', *Econometrica*, Vol. 47, pp. 263–91.

Kalemli-Ozcan, Sebnem, Bent E. Sorensen and Sevcan Yesiltas (2012), 'Leverage Across Firms, Banks and Countries', Federal Reserve Bank of Dallas Conference on Financial Frictions and Monetary Policy in an Open Economy, mimeo.

Kareken, John (1986), 'Federal Bank Regulatory Policy: A Description and Some Observations', *Journal of Business*, 59, pp. 3–48.

Kay, John (2009), 'Narrow Banking: The Reform of Banking Regulation', Center for the Study of Financial Innovation Report, 15 September 2009.

—— (2015), *Other People's Money: The Real Business of Finance*, PublicAffairs, New York.

Keating, Paul (2014), 'Avoiding the Thucydides Trap in Asia', mimeo, Sydney.

Kerr, Gordon (2011), *The Law of Opposites: Illusory Profits in the Financial Sector*, Adam Smith Research Trust, London.

Keynes (1914a), *The Collected Writings of John Maynard Keynes,*

Volume 18, Activities: 1914–1919, Macmillan, London, 1971, p. 4.

—— (1914b), 'War and the Financial System', *Economic Journal*, 24, 1971, p. 473.

—— (1919), *The Economic Consequences of the Peace*, Macmillan & Co., London.

—— (1922), *The Collected Writings of John Maynard Keynes, Volume 17, Activities: 1920–1922: Treaty Revision and Reconstruction*, ed. Elizabeth Johnson, Macmillan, London, 1977.

—— (1923a), *A Tract on Monetary Reform*, Macmillan, London.

—— (1923b), *The Collected Writings of John Maynard Keynes, Volume 18, Activities: 1922–1932: The End of Reparations*, ed. Elizabeth Johnson, Macmillan, London, 1978.

—— (1930), *A Treatise on Money*, Macmillan, London.

—— (1931), 'Economic Possibilities for our Grandchildren', in *Essays in Persuasion*, Macmillan, London.

—— (1936), *The General Theory of Employment, Interest and Money*, Macmillan, London.

—— (1937a), 'The General Theory of Employment', *Quarterly Journal of Economics*, Vol. 51, pp. 209–23.

—— (1937b), 'Some Economic Consequences of a Declining Population', The Galton Lecture published in *Eugenics Review*, XXIX, pp. 13–17.

King, Mervyn (2000), 'Balancing the Economic See-Saw', Speech at the Plymouth Chamber of Commerce and Industry 187th Anniversary Banquet, 14 April 2000, Bank of England website.

—— (2003), Speech in Leicester, 14 October, Bank of England website.

—— (2006), Speech in Ashford, Kent, 16 January, Bank of England website.

—— (2007), 'The MPC Ten Years On', Lecture to the Society of Business Economists, 2 May, Bank of England website.

—— (2009), Speech to the CBI Dinner, Nottingham, at the East Midlands Conference Centre, 20 January, Bank of England website.

—— (2012), 'Twenty Years of Inflation Targeting', Stamp Memorial Lecture, London School of Economics, 9 October, Bank of England website.

King, Mervyn and David Low (2014), 'Measuring the "World" Real Interest Rate', National Bureau of Economic Research Working Paper 19887, Cambridge, Massachusetts.

King, Robert (1983), 'On the Economics of Private Money', *Journal of Monetary Economics*, Vol. 12, No. 1, pp. 127–58.

Kiyotaki, Nobuhiro and John Moore (2002), 'Evil is the Root of All Money', *American Economic Review*, Vol. 92, No. 2, pp. 62–6.

Kiyotaki, Nobuhiro and Randall Wright (1989), 'On Money as a Medium of Exchange', *Journal of Political Economy*, Vol. 97, pp. 927–54.

Knight, Frank (1921), *Risk, Uncertainty and Profit*, Houghton Mifflin, Boston and New York.

Kotlikoff, Laurence J. (2010), *Jimmy Stewart is Dead: Ending the World's Ongoing Financial Plague with Limited Purpose Banking*, John Wiley and Sons, Hoboken, New Jersey.

Kranister, W. (1989), *The Moneymakers International*, Black Bear Publishing, Cambridge.

Krawczyk, Jacek and Kunhong Kim (2009), 'Satisficing Solutions to a Monetary Policy Problem', *Macroeconomic Dynamics*, Vol. 13, pp. 46–80.

Krugman, Paul (2011), 'Mr. Keynes and the Moderns', *Vox*, 21 June 2011.

Kynaston, David (1994), *The City of London: Vol 1: A World of Its Own, 1815–90*, Chatto and Windus, London.

Lainà, Patrizio (2015), 'Proposals for Full-Reserve Banking: A Historical Survey from David Ricardo to Martin Wolf', University of Helsinki, mimeo.

Levitt, Steven and Stephen Dubner (2005), *Freakonomics: A Rogue Economist Explores the Hidden Side of Everything*, William Morrow/Harper Collins, New York.

Lewis, Michael (1989), *Liar's Poker*, W. W. Norton, New York.

—— (2014), *Flash Boys: A Wall Street Revolt*, W. W. Norton, New York.

Litan, Robert (1987), *What Should Banks Do?* Brookings Institution, Washington, DC.

Lloyd George, David (1933) *War Memoirs of David Lloyd George, Volume I*, Odhams Press Limited, London.

Lowenstein, Roger (2015), *America's Bank: The Epic Struggle to Create the Federal Reserve*, Penguin Press, New York.

Macdonald, James (2015), *When Globalization Fails: The Rise and Fall of Pax Americana*, Farrar, Strauss and Giroux, New York.

Macey, Jonathan and Geoffrey Miller (1992), 'Double Liability of Bank Shareholders: History and Implications', *Wake Forest Law Review*, Vol. 27, pp. 31–62.

MacGregor, Neil (2010), *A History of the World in 100 Objects*, Allen Lane, London.

—— (2014), *Germany: Memories of a Nation*, Allen Lane, London.

McLean, Bethany and Peter Elkind (2003), *The Smartest Guys in the Room: The Amazing Rise and Scandalous Fall of Enron*, Portfolio, New York.

Maddison, Angus (2004), *The World Economy: Historical Statistics*, OECD, Paris.

Malthus, Thomas (1798), *An Essay on the Principle of Population*, J. Johnson in St Paul's Church-yard, London.

Mansfield, William (1761), *Hamilton v. Mendes*, 2 Burr 1198.

Marshall, Alfred (1906), Letter to A.L. Bowley in A.C. Pigou (ed.) (1925) *Memorials of Alfred Marshall*, Macmillan, London.

Marx, Karl (1867), *Das Kapital*, Otto Meissner, Hamburg.

Marx, Karl and Friedrich Engels (1848), *The Communist Manifesto*, Section 1, para 53, lines 11–13.

Matthews, Robin (1960), *The Trade Cycle*, Cambridge University Press, Cambridge.

Mehrling, Perry (2011), *The New Lombard Street: How the Fed Became the Dealer of Last Resort*, Princeton University Press, Princeton, New Jersey.

Menger, Carl (1892), 'On the Origins of Money', *Economic Journal*, Vol. 2, pp. 239–55.

Mill, John Stuart (1848), *Principles of Political Economy*, John W. Parker, London.

Minsky, Hyman (1975), *John Maynard Keynes*, Columbia University Press, New York.

—— (1986), *Stabilizing an Unstable Economy*, Yale University Press, New Haven.

—— (1994), 'Financial Instability and the Decline (?) of Banking: Public Policy Implications', *Hyman P. Minsky Archive*, Paper 88. http://digitalcommons.bard.edu/hm_archive/88.

Moggridge, Donald E. (1992), *Maynard Keynes: An Economist's Biography*, Routledge, London.

Mohr, Thomas (2014), 'The Political Significant of the Coinage of the Irish Free State', University College of Dublin Working Papers in Law, Criminology and Socio-Legal Studies Research Paper No. 11, 25 September 2014.

Mundell, Robert (1961), 'Theory of Optimum Currency Areas', *American Economic Review*, Vol. 51, No. 4, pp. 657–65.

Neal, Larry and Geoffrey G. Williamson (eds.) (2014), *The Cambridge History of Capitalism*, Cambridge University Press, Cambridge.

O'Neill, Onora (2002), 'A Question of Trust', *BBC Reith Lectures 2000*, Cambridge University Press, Cambridge.

Patinkin, Don (1956), *Money, Interest, and Prices: An Integration of Monetary and Value Theory*, Row, Peterson and Co., Evanston, Illinois.

Paulson, Hank (2010), *On the Brink: Inside the Race to Stop the Collapse of the Global Financial System*, Business Plus, New York.

Priest, Claire (2001), 'Currency Policies and Legal Development in Colonial New England', 110 *Yale Law Journal*, 1303.

Rachel, Lukasz and Thomas Smith (2015), 'Drivers of Long-Term Global Interest Rates – Can Weaker Growth Explain the Fall?' Bank Underground, Bank of England website.

Rae, John (1895), *The Life of Adam Smith*, Macmillan and Co., London.

Reddaway, W. Brian (1939), *The Economic Consequences of a Declining Population*, Allen and Unwin, London.

Reinhart, Carmen M. and Kenneth S. Rogoff (2009), *This Time is Different: Eight Centuries of Financial Folly*, Princeton University Press, Princeton, New Jersey.

Reinhart, Carmen, Vincent Reinhart and Kenneth Rogoff (2015), 'Dealing with Debt', *Journal of International Economics*, forthcoming.

Ricardo, David (1816), *Proposals for an Economical and Secure Currency*, T. Davison, London.

Roberts, Andrew (2014), *Napoleon the Great*, Allen Lane, London.

Roberts, Richard (2013), *Saving the City*, Oxford University Press, Oxford.

Robertson, James (2012), *Future Money: Breakdown or Breakthrough?* Green Books, Totnes, Devon.

Rodrik, Dani (2011), *The Globalization Paradox*, second edition, Oxford University Press, Oxford.

Rogoff, Kenneth (2014), 'The Costs and Benefits of Phasing Out Paper Currency', National Bureau of Economic Research Macroeconomics Annual, Vol. 29.

Russell, Bertrand (1912), *The Problems of Philosophy*, Williams and Norgate, London.

Samuelson, Paul (1937), 'Some Aspects of the Pure Theory of Capital', *Quarterly Journal of Economics*, Vol. 51, pp. 469–96.

—— (1958), 'An Exact Consumption-Loan Model of Interest With or Without the Social Contrivance of Money', *Journal of Political Economy*, Vol. 68, pp. 467–82.

Schacht, Hjalmar (1934), 'German Trade and German Debt', *Foreign Affairs*, October 1934.

—— (1955), *My First Seventy-Six Years*, Allan Wingate, London.

Schumpeter, Joseph (1942), *Capitalism, Socialism and Democracy*, Harper and Row, New York.

Sedgwick, Theodore Jr. (ed.), (1840), *A Collection of the Political Writings of William Leggett*, Vol. I, Taylor and Dodd, New York.

Shin, Hyun Song, (2009), 'Reflections on Northern Rock: The Bank Run that Heralded the Global Financial Crisis', *Journal of Economic Perspectives*, Vol. 23, No. 1, pp. 101–19.

—— (2012), 'Global Banking Glut and Loan Risk Premium', *IMF Economic Review*, Vol. 60, No. 2, pp. 152–92.

Silber, William (2007), *When Washington Shut Down Wall Street*, Princeton University Press, Princeton, New Jersey.

Simon, Herbert (1956), 'Rational Choice and the Structure of the Environment', *Psychological Review*, Vol. 63, No. 2, pp. 129–38.

Sims, Christopher (2013), 'Paper Money', *American Economic Review*, Vol. 103, No. 2, pp. 563–84.

Smith, Adam (1759), *Theory of Moral Sentiments*, A. Millar, London.

—— (1766), *Lectures on Jurisprudence*, B, Report dated 1766, p. 493.

—— (1776), *Wealth of Nations*, W. Strahan and T. Cadell, London.

Smith, Ed (2012), *Luck: What it Means and Why it Matters*, Bloomsbury Publishing, London.

Solow, Robert M. (1956), 'A Contribution to the Theory of Economic Growth', *Quarterly Journal of Economics*, 70(1), pp. 65–94.

Stiglitz, Joseph (2014), 'Reconstructing Macroeconomic Theory to Manage Economic Policy', National Bureau of Economic Research Working Paper 20517, mimeo, Cambridge, Massachusetts.

Summers, Lawrence H. (1983), '"On the Economics of Private Money" by Robert G. King', *Journal of Monetary Economics*, Vol. 12, No. 1, pp. 159–62.

—— (2014), 'U.S. Economic Prospects: Secular Stagnation, Hysteresis, and the Zero Lower Bound', *Business Economics*, Vol. 49, pp. 65–73.

—— (2015), 'Reflections on Secular Stagnation', Speech at the Julius-Rabinowitz Center, Princeton University, 19 February 2015.

Syed, Matthew (2011), *Bounce: The Myth of Talent and the Power of Practice*, Fourth Estate, London.

Taleb, Nassim (2012), *Antifragile: How to Live in a World We Don't Understand*, Allen Lane, London.

Taleb, Nassim and M. Blyth (2011), 'The Black Swan of Cairo', *Foreign Affairs*, Vol. 90, No. 3.

Tallentyre, S.G. (ed.) (1919), *Voltaire in His Letters*, G.P. Putnam's Sons, New York.

Taylor, Alan (2015), 'Credit, Financial Stability, and the

Macroeconomy', *Annual Review of Economics*, Vol. 7, pp. 309–39.

Taylor, John B. (2014), 'The Federal Reserve in a Globalized World Economy', Federal Reserve Bank of Dallas Conference, September 2014, mimeo.

Temin, Peter (2014), 'The Cambridge History of "Capitalism"', National Bureau of Economic Research Working Paper 20658, Cambridge, Massachusetts.

Thaler, Richard (1991), *Quasi Rational Economics*, Russell Sage Foundation, New York.

Thaler, Richard and Cass Sunstein (2008), *Nudge: Improving Decisions about Health, Wealth and Happiness*, Yale University Press, New Haven.

Thornton, Henry (1802), *An Enquiry into the Nature and Effects of the Paper Credit of Great Britain*, J. Hatchard, London.

Tobin, James (1985), 'Financial Innovation and Deregulation in Perspective', *Bank of Japan Monetary and Economic Studies*, Vol. 3, No. 2, pp. 19–29.

Tuckett, David (2011), *Minding the Markets: An Emotional Finance View of Financial Instability*, Palgrave Macmillan, London.

—— (2012), 'The Role of Emotions in Financial Decisions', The Barbon Lecture, 24 May 2012.

Tuckman, Bruce (2013), 'Embedded Financing: The Unsung Virtue of Derivatives', *The Journal of Derivatives*, Vol. 21, No. 1, pp. 73–82.

—— (2015), 'In Defense of Derivatives: From Beer to the Financial Crisis', *Policy Analysis*, Number 781, Cato Institute.

Turner, Adair (2014), 'Central Banking and Monetary Policy after the Crisis', City Lecture at the Official Monetary and Financial Institutions Forum (OMFIF), London, 9 December 2014.

—— (2015), *Between Debt and the Devil,* Princeton University Press, Princeton, New Jersey.

Tversky, Amos and Daniel Kahneman (1974), 'Judgment under Uncertainty: Heuristics and Biases', *Science*, Vol. 185, No. 4157, pp. 1124–31.

Waley, Arthur (1938), *The Analects of Confucius*, Allen and Unwin, London.

Weale, Martin (2015), 'Prospects for Supply Growth in Western Europe', Speech at the Rijksuniversiteit, Groningen, 12 October, Bank of England website.

Wheatley, Martin (2012), *The Wheatley Review of LIBOR – Final Report*, HM Treasury, London.

Willetts, David (2010), *The Pinch: How the Baby Boomers Took Their Children's Future – And How They Can Give it Back*, Atlantic Books, London.

Wolf, Martin (2010), 'The Challenge of Halting the Financial Doomsday Machine', *Financial Times*, 20 April 2010.

—— (2014), *The Shifts and the Shocks*, Penguin, London.

Woodford, Michael (2003), *Interest and Prices*, Princeton University Press, Princeton, New Jersey.

—— (2013), 'Forward Guidance by Inflation-Targeting Central Banks', mimeo, Columbia University.

Woollcott, Alexander (1934), *While Rome Burns*, Viking Press, New York.

Yermack, David (2013), 'Is Bitcoin a Real Currency?', National Bureau of Economic Research Working Paper 19747, Cambridge, Massachusetts.

Zweig, Stefan (1943) *The World of Yesterday*, Viking Press, New York.

INDEX

ABOUT THE AUTHOR

Mervyn King was Governor of the Bank of England from 2003 to 2013, and is currently Professor of Economics and Law at New York University and School Professor of Economics at the London School of Economics. Lord King was made a life peer in 2013, and appointed by the Queen a Knight of the Garter in 2014.